The History of the Thirty Years War

MW01154598

By
Friedrich Schiller

ANODOS
BOOKS

Friedrich Schiller (1759-1805)
Originally published in 1897 translated by Alexander James William Morrison

Copyright © 2019 Anodos Books. All rights reserved.

Anodos Books
1c Kings Road
Whithorn
Newton Stewart
Dumfries & Galloway
DG8 8PP

Contents

Book I.

From the beginning of the religious wars in Germany, to the peace of Munster, scarcely any thing great or remarkable occurred in the political world of Europe in which the Reformation had not an important share. All the events of this period, if they did not originate in, soon became mixed up with, the question of religion, and no state was either too great or too little to feel directly or indirectly more or less of its influence.

Against the reformed doctrine and its adherents, the House of Austria directed, almost exclusively, the whole of its immense political power. In France, the Reformation had enkindled a civil war which, under four stormy reigns, shook the kingdom to its foundations, brought foreign armies into the heart of the country, and for half a century rendered it the scene of the most mournful disorders. It was the Reformation, too, that rendered the Spanish yoke intolerable to the Flemings, and awakened in them both the desire and the courage to throw off its fetters, while it also principally furnished them with the means of their emancipation. And as to England, all the evils with which Philip the Second threatened Elizabeth, were mainly intended in revenge for her having taken his Protestant subjects under her protection, and placing herself at the head of a religious party which it was his aim and endeavour to extirpate. In Germany, the schisms in the church produced also a lasting political schism, which made that country for more than a century the theatre of confusion, but at the same time threw up a firm barrier against political oppression. It was, too, the Reformation principally that first drew the northern powers, Denmark and Sweden, into the political system of Europe; and while on the one hand the Protestant League was strengthened by their adhesion, it on the other was indispensable to their interests. States which hitherto scarcely concerned themselves with one another's existence, acquired through the Reformation an attractive centre of interest, and began to be united by new political sympathies. And as through its influence new relations sprang up between citizen and citizen, and between rulers and subjects, so also entire states were forced by it into new relative positions. Thus, by a strange course of events, religious disputes were the means of cementing a closer union among the nations of Europe.

Fearful indeed, and destructive, was the first movement in which this general political sympathy announced itself; a desolating war of thirty years, which, from the interior of Bohemia to the mouth of the Scheldt, and from the banks of the Po to the coasts of the Baltic, devastated whole countries, destroyed harvests, and reduced towns and villages to ashes; which opened a grave for many thousand combatants, and for half a century smothered the glimmering sparks of civilization in Germany, and threw back the improving manners of the country into their pristine barbarity and wildness. Yet out of this fearful war Europe came forth free and independent. In it she first learned to recognize herself as a community of nations; and this intercommunion of states, which originated in the thirty years' war, may alone be sufficient to reconcile the philosopher to its horrors. The hand of industry has slowly but gradually effaced the traces of its ravages, while its beneficent influence still survives; and this general sympathy among the states of Europe, which grew out of the troubles in Bohemia, is our guarantee for the continuance of that peace which was the result of the war. As the sparks of destruction found their way from the interior of Bohemia, Moravia, and Austria, to kindle Germany, France, and the half of Europe, so also will the torch of civilization make a path for itself from the latter to enlighten the former countries.

All this was effected by religion. Religion alone could have rendered possible all that was accomplished, but it was far from being the *sole* motive of the war. Had not private advantages and state interests been closely connected with it, vain and powerless would have been the arguments of theologians; and the cry of the people would never have met with princes so willing to espouse their cause, nor the new doctrines have found such numerous, brave, and persevering champions. The Reformation is undoubtedly owing in a great measure to the invincible power of truth, or of opinions which were held as such. The abuses in the old church, the absurdity of many of its dogmas, the extravagance of its requisitions, necessarily revolted the tempers of men, already half-won with the promise of a better light, and favourably disposed them towards the new doctrines. The charm of independence, the rich plunder of monastic institutions, made the Reformation attractive in the eyes of princes, and tended not a little to strengthen their inward convictions. Nothing, however, but political considerations could have driven them to espouse it. Had not Charles the Fifth, in the intoxication of success, made an attempt on the independence of the German States, a Protestant league would scarcely have rushed to arms in defence of freedom of belief; but for the ambition of the Guises, the Calvinists in France would never have beheld a Conde or a Coligny at their head. Without the exaction of the tenth and the twentieth penny, the See of Rome had never lost the United Netherlands. Princes fought in self-defence or for aggrandizement, while religious enthusiasm recruited their armies, and opened to them the treasures of their subjects. Of the multitude who flocked to their standards, such as were not lured by the hope of plunder imagined they were fighting for the truth, while in fact they were shedding their blood for the personal objects of their princes.

And well was it for the people that, on this occasion, their interests coincided with those of their princes. To this coincidence alone were they indebted for their deliverance from popery. Well was it also for the rulers, that the subject contended too for his own cause, while he was fighting their battles. Fortunately at this date no European sovereign was so absolute as to be able, in the pursuit of his political designs, to dispense with the goodwill of his subjects. Yet how difficult was it to gain and to set to work this goodwill! The most impressive arguments drawn from reasons of state fall powerless on the ear of the subject, who seldom understands, and still more rarely is interested in them. In such circumstances, the only course open to a prudent prince is to connect the interests of the cabinet with some one that sits nearer to the people's heart, if such exists, or if not, to create it.

In such a position stood the greater part of those princes who embraced the cause of the Reformation. By a strange concatenation of events, the divisions of the Church were associated with two circumstances, without which, in all probability, they would have had a very different conclusion. These were, the increasing power of the House of Austria, which threatened the liberties of Europe, and its active zeal for the old religion. The first aroused the princes, while the second armed the people.

The abolition of a foreign jurisdiction within their own territories, the supremacy in ecclesiastical matters, the stopping of the treasure which had so long flowed to Rome, the rich plunder of religious foundations, were tempting advantages to every sovereign. Why, then, it may be asked, did they not operate with equal force upon the princes of the House of Austria? What prevented this house, particularly in its German branch, from yielding to the pressing demands of so many of its subjects, and, after the example of other princes, enriching itself at the expense of a defenceless clergy? It is difficult to credit that a belief in the infallibility of the Romish Church had any greater influence on the pious adherence of this house, than the opposite conviction had on the revolt of the Protestant princes. In fact, several circumstances combined to make the Austrian princes zealous supporters of popery. Spain and Italy, from which Austria derived its principal strength, were still devoted to the See of Rome with that blind obedience which, ever since the days of the Gothic dynasty, had been the peculiar characteristic of the Spaniard. The slightest approximation, in a Spanish prince, to the obnoxious tenets of Luther and Calvin, would have alienated for ever the affections of his subjects, and a defection from the Pope would have cost him the kingdom. A Spanish prince had no alternative but orthodoxy or abdication. The same restraint was imposed upon Austria by her Italian dominions, which she was obliged to treat, if possible, with even greater indulgence; impatient as they naturally were of a foreign yoke, and possessing also ready means of shaking it off. In regard to the latter provinces, moreover, the rival pretensions of France, and the neighbourhood of the Pope, were motives sufficient to prevent the Emperor from declaring in favour of a party which strove to annihilate the papal see, and also to induce him to show the most active zeal in behalf of the old religion. These general considerations, which must have been equally weighty with every Spanish monarch, were, in the particular case of Charles V., still further enforced by peculiar and personal motives. In Italy this monarch had a formidable rival in the King of France, under whose protection that country might throw itself the instant that Charles should incur the slightest suspicion of heresy. Distrust on the part of the Roman Catholics, and a rupture with the church, would have been fatal also to many of his most cherished designs. Moreover, when Charles was first called upon to make his election between the two parties, the new doctrine had not yet attained to a full and commanding influence, and there still subsisted a prospect of its reconciliation with the old. In his son and successor, Philip the Second, a monastic education combined with a gloomy and despotic disposition to generate an unmitigated hostility to all innovations in religion; a feeling which the thought that his most formidable political opponents were also the enemies of his faith was not calculated to weaken. As his European possessions, scattered as they were over so many countries, were on all sides exposed to the seductions of foreign opinions, the progress of the Reformation in other quarters could not well be a matter of indifference to him. His immediate interests, therefore, urged him to attach himself devotedly to the old church, in order to close up the sources of the heretical contagion. Thus, circumstances naturally placed this prince at the head of the league which the Roman Catholics formed against the Reformers. The principles which had actuated the long and active reigns of Charles V. and Philip the Second, remained a law for their successors; and the more the breach in the church widened, the firmer became the attachment of the Spaniards to Roman Catholicism.

The German line of the House of Austria was apparently more unfettered; but, in reality, though free from many of these restraints, it was yet confined by others. The possession of the imperial throne — a dignity it was impossible for a Protestant to hold, (for with what consistency could an apostate from the Romish Church wear the crown of a Roman emperor?) bound the successors of Ferdinand I. to the See of Rome. Ferdinand himself was, from conscientious motives, heartily attached to it. Besides, the German princes of the House of Austria were not powerful enough to dispense with the support of Spain, which, however, they would have forfeited by the least show of leaning towards the new doctrines. The imperial dignity, also, required them to preserve the existing political system of Germany, with which the maintenance of their own authority was closely bound up, but which it was the aim of the Protestant League to destroy. If to these grounds we add the indifference of the Protestants to the Emperor's necessities and to the common dangers of the empire, their encroachments on the temporalities of the church, and their aggressive violence when they became conscious of their own power, we can easily conceive how so many concurring motives must have determined the emperors to the side of popery, and how their own interests came to be intimately interwoven with those of the Roman Church. As its fate seemed to depend altogether on the part taken by Austria, the princes of this house came to be regarded by all Europe as the pillars of popery. The hatred, therefore, which the Protestants bore against the latter, was turned exclusively upon Austria; and the cause became gradually confounded with its protector.

But this irreconcileable enemy of the Reformation — the House of Austria — by its ambitious projects and the overwhelming force which it could bring to their support, endangered, in no small degree, the freedom of Europe, and more especially of the German States. This circumstance could not fail to rouse the latter from their security, and to render them vigilant in self-defence. Their ordinary resources were quite insufficient to resist so formidable a power. Extraordinary exertions were required from their subjects; and when even these proved far from adequate, they had recourse to foreign assistance; and, by means of a common league, they endeavoured to oppose a power which, singly, they were unable to withstand.

But the strong political inducements which the German princes had to resist the pretensions of the House of Austria, naturally did not extend to their subjects. It is only immediate advantages or immediate evils that set the people in action, and for these a sound policy cannot wait. Ill then would it have fared with these princes, if by good fortune another effectual motive had not offered itself, which roused the passions of the people, and kindled in them an enthusiasm which might be directed against the political danger, as having with it a common cause of alarm.

This motive was their avowed hatred of the religion which Austria protected, and their enthusiastic attachment to a doctrine which that House was endeavouring to extirpate by fire and sword. Their attachment was ardent, their hatred invincible. Religious fanaticism anticipates even the remotest dangers. Enthusiasm never calculates its sacrifices. What the most pressing danger of the state could not gain from the citizens, was effected by religious zeal. For the state, or for the prince, few would have drawn the sword; but for religion, the merchant, the artist, the peasant, all cheerfully flew to arms. For the state, or for the prince, even the smallest additional impost would have been avoided; but for religion the people readily staked at once life, fortune, and all earthly hopes. It trebled the contributions which flowed into the exchequer of the princes, and the armies which marched to the field; and, in the ardent excitement produced in all minds by the peril to which their faith was exposed, the subject felt not the pressure of those burdens and privations under which, in cooler moments, he would have sunk exhausted. The terrors of the Spanish Inquisition, and the massacre of St. Bartholomew's, procured for the Prince of Orange, the Admiral Coligny, the British Queen Elizabeth, and the Protestant princes of Germany, supplies of men and money from their subjects, to a degree which at present is inconceivable.

But, with all their exertions, they would have effected little against a power which was an overmatch for any single adversary, however powerful. At this period of imperfect policy, accidental circumstances alone could determine distant states to afford one another a mutual support. The differences of government, of laws, of language, of manners, and of character, which hitherto had kept whole nations and countries as it were insulated, and raised a lasting barrier between them, rendered one state insensible to the distresses of another, save where national jealousy could indulge a malicious joy at the reverses of a rival. This barrier the Reformation destroyed. An interest more intense and more immediate than national aggrandizement or patriotism, and entirely independent of private utility, began to animate whole states and individual citizens; an interest capable of uniting numerous and distant nations, even while it frequently lost its force among the subjects of the same government. With the inhabitants of Geneva, for instance, of England, of Germany, or of Holland, the French Calvinist possessed a common point of union which he had not with his own countrymen. Thus, in one important particular, he ceased to be the citizen of a single state, and to confine his views and sympathies to his own country alone. The sphere of his views became enlarged. He began to calculate his own fate from that of other nations of the same religious profession, and to make their cause his own. Now for the first time did princes venture to bring the affairs of other countries before their own councils; for the first time could they hope for a willing ear to their own necessities, and prompt assistance from others. Foreign affairs had now become a matter of domestic policy, and that aid was readily granted to the religious confederate which would have been denied to the mere neighbour, and still more to the distant stranger. The inhabitant of the Palatinate leaves his native fields to fight side by side with his religious associate of France, against the common enemy of their faith. The Huguenot draws his sword against the country which persecutes him, and sheds his blood in defence of the liberties of Holland. Swiss is arrayed against Swiss; German against German, to determine, on the banks of the Loire and the Seine, the succession of the French crown. The Dane crosses the Eider, and the Swede the Baltic, to break the chains which are forged for Germany.

It is difficult to say what would have been the fate of the Reformation, and the liberties of the Empire, had not the formidable power of Austria declared against them. This, however, appears certain, that nothing so completely damped the Austrian hopes of universal monarchy, as the obstinate war which they had to wage against the new religious opinions. Under no other circumstances could the weaker princes have roused their subjects to such extraordinary exertions against the ambition of Austria, or the States themselves have united so closely against the common enemy.

The power of Austria never stood higher than after the victory which Charles V. gained over the Germans at Muehlberg. With the treaty of Smalcalde the freedom of Germany lay, as it seemed, prostrate for ever; but it revived under Maurice of Saxony, once its most formidable enemy. All the fruits of the victory of Muehlberg were lost again in the congress of Passau, and the diet of Augsburg; and every scheme for civil and religious oppression terminated in the concessions of an equitable peace.

The diet of Augsburg divided Germany into two religious and two political parties, by recognizing the independent rights and existence of both. Hitherto the Protestants had been looked on as rebels; they were henceforth to be regarded as brethren — not indeed through affection, but necessity. By the Interim[1], the Confession of Augsburg was allowed temporarily to take a sisterly place alongside of the olden religion, though only as a tolerated neighbour. To every secular state was conceded the right of establishing the religion it acknowledged as supreme and exclusive within its own territories, and of forbidding the open profession of its rival. Subjects were to be free to quit a country where their own religion was not tolerated. The doctrines of Luther for the first time received a positive sanction; and if they were trampled under foot in Bavaria and Austria, they predominated in Saxony and Thuringia. But the sovereigns alone were to determine what form of religion should prevail within their territories; the feelings of subjects who had no representatives in the diet were little attended to in the pacification. In the ecclesiastical territories, indeed, where the unreformed religion enjoyed an undisputed supremacy, the free exercise of their religion was obtained for all who had previously embraced the Protestant doctrines; but this indulgence rested only on the personal guarantee of Ferdinand, King of the Romans, by whose endeavours chiefly this peace was effected; a guarantee, which, being rejected by the Roman Catholic members of the Diet, and only inserted in the treaty under their protest, could not of course have the force of law.

If it had been opinions only that thus divided the minds of men, with what indifference would all have regarded the division! But on these opinions depended riches, dignities, and rights; and it was this which so deeply aggravated the evils of division. Of two brothers, as it were, who had hitherto enjoyed a paternal inheritance in common, one now remained, while the other was compelled to leave his father's house, and hence arose the necessity of dividing the patrimony. For this separation, which he could not have foreseen, the father had made no provision. By the beneficent donations of pious ancestors the riches of the church had been accumulating through a thousand years, and these benefactors were as much the progenitors of the departing brother as of him who remained. Was the right of inheritance then to be limited to the paternal house, or to be extended to blood? The gifts had been made to the

---

[1]A system of Theology so called, prepared by order of the Emperor Charles V. for the use of Germany, to reconcile the differences between the Roman Catholics and the Lutherans, which, however, was rejected by both parties — Ed.

church in communion with Rome, because at that time no other existed, — to the first-born, as it were, because he was as yet the only son. Was then a right of primogeniture to be admitted in the church, as in noble families? Were the pretensions of one party to be favoured by a prescription from times when the claims of the other could not have come into existence? Could the Lutherans be justly excluded from these possessions, to which the benevolence of their forefathers had contributed, merely on the ground that, at the date of their foundation, the differences between Lutheranism and Romanism were unknown? Both parties have disputed, and still dispute, with equal plausibility, on these points. Both alike ʰ   ound it difficult to prove their right. Law can be applied only to conceivable cases, and pe·'   ual foundations are not among the number of these, and still less where the conditions of   enerally extended to a system of doctrines; for how is it conceivable that a permanent   uld be made of opinions left open to change?

                    r decide, is usually determined by might, and such was the case here. The one party
                    · could no longer be wrested from it — the other defended what it still possessed. All
                    abbeys which had been secularized *before* the peace, remained with the Protestants;
                    use, the unreformed Catholics provided that none should thereafter be secularized.
                    f an ecclesiastical foundation, who held immediately of the Empire, whether
ε   ot, forfeited his benefice and dignity the moment he embraced the Protestant
be.   n that event instantly to resign its emoluments, and the chapter was to proceed
to a   tly as if his place had been vacated by death. By this sacred anchor of the
Eccles   n, (`Reservatum Ecclesiasticum',) which makes the temporal existence of a
spiritua.   'ependent on his fidelity to the olden religion, the Roman Catholic Church in
Germany   and precarious, indeed, would be its situation were this anchor to give way.
The princiƥ   iastical Reservation was strongly opposed by the Protestants; and though it
was at last ac   treaty of peace, its insertion was qualified with the declaration, that parties
had come to ι   ination on the point. Could it then be more binding on the Protestants
than Ferdinand ,   ι favour of Protestant subjects of ecclesiastical states was upon the Roman
Catholics? Thus ν   ο important subjects of dispute left unsettled in the treaty of peace, and by
them the war was re ιndled.

Such was the position of things with regard to religious toleration and ecclesiastical property: it was the same with regard to rights and dignities. The existing German system provided only for one church, because one only was in existence when that system was framed. The church had now divided; the Diet had broken into two religious parties; was the whole system of the Empire still exclusively to follow the one? The emperors had hitherto been members of the Romish Church, because till now that religion had no rival. But was it his connexion with Rome which constituted a German emperor, or was it not rather Germany which was to be represented in its head? The Protestants were now spread over the whole Empire, and how could they justly still be represented by an unbroken line of Roman Catholic emperors? In the Imperial Chamber the German States judge themselves, for they elect the judges; it was the very end of its institution that they should do so, in order that equal justice should be dispensed to all; but would this be still possible, if the representatives of both professions were not equally admissible to a seat in the Chamber? That one religion only existed in Germany at the time of its establishment, was accidental; that no one estate should have the means of legally oppressing another, was the essential purpose of the institution. Now this object would be entirely frustrated if one religious party were to have the exclusive power of deciding for the other. Must, then, the design be sacrificed, because that which was merely accidental had changed? With great difficulty the Protestants, at last, obtained for the representatives of their religion a place in the Supreme Council, but still there was far from being a perfect equality of voices. To this day no Protestant prince has been raised to the imperial throne.

Whatever may be said of the equality which the peace of Augsburg was to have established between the two German churches, the Roman Catholic had unquestionably still the advantage. All that the Lutheran Church gained by it was toleration; all that the Romish Church conceded, was a sacrifice to necessity, not an offering to justice. Very far was it from being a peace between two equal powers, but a truce between a sovereign and unconquered rebels. From this principle all the proceedings of the Roman Catholics against the Protestants seemed to flow, and still continue to do so. To join the reformed faith was still a crime, since it was to be visited with so severe a penalty as that which the Ecclesiastical Reservation held suspended over the apostacy of the spiritual princes. Even to the last, the Romish Church preferred to risk to loss of every thing by force, than voluntarily to yield the smallest matter to justice. The loss was accidental and might be repaired; but the abandonment of its pretensions, the concession of a single point to the Protestants, would shake the foundations of the church itself. Even in the treaty of peace this principle was not lost sight of. Whatever in this peace was yielded to the Protestants was always under condition. It was expressly declared, that affairs were to remain on the stipulated footing only till the next general council, which was to be called with the view of effecting an union between the two confessions. Then only, when this last attempt should have failed, was the religious treaty to become valid and conclusive. However little hope there might be of such a reconciliation, however little perhaps the Romanists themselves were in earnest with it, still it was something to have clogged the peace with these stipulations.

Thus this religious treaty, which was to extinguish for ever the flames of civil war, was, in fact, but a temporary truce, extorted by force and necessity; not dictated by justice, nor emanating from just notions either of religion or toleration. A religious treaty of this kind the Roman Catholics were as incapable of granting, to be candid, as in truth the Lutherans were unqualified to receive. Far from evincing a tolerant spirit towards the Roman Catholics, when it was in their power, they even oppressed the Calvinists; who indeed just as little deserved toleration, since they were unwilling to practise it. For such a peace the times were not yet ripe — the minds of men not yet sufficiently enlightened. How could one party expect from another what itself was incapable of performing? What each side saved or gained by the treaty of Augsburg, it owed to the imposing attitude of strength which it maintained at the time of its negociation. What was won by force was to be maintained also by force; if the peace was to be permanent, the two parties to it must preserve the same relative positions. The boundaries of the two churches had been marked out with the sword; with the sword they must be preserved, or woe to that party which should be first disarmed! A sad and fearful prospect for the tranquillity of Germany, when peace itself bore so threatening an aspect.

A momentary lull now pervaded the empire; a transitory bond of concord appeared to unite its scattered limbs into one body, so that for a time a feeling also for the common weal returned. But the division had penetrated its inmost being, and to restore its original harmony was impossible. Carefully as the treaty of peace appeared to have defined the rights of both parties, its interpretation was nevertheless the subject of many disputes. In the heat of conflict it had produced a cessation of hostilities; it covered, not extinguished, the fire, and unsatisfied claims remained on either side. The Romanists imagined they had lost too much, the Protestants that they had gained too little; and the treaty which neither party could venture to violate, was interpreted by each in its own favour.

The seizure of the ecclesiastical benefices, the motive which had so strongly tempted the majority of the Protestant princes to embrace the doctrines of Luther, was not less powerful after than before the peace; of those whose founders had not held their fiefs immediately of the empire, such as were not already in their possession would it was evident soon be so. The whole of Lower Germany was already secularized; and if it were otherwise in Upper Germany, it was owing to the vehement resistance of the Catholics, who had there the preponderance. Each party, where it was the most powerful, oppressed the adherents of the other; the ecclesiastical princes in particular, as the most defenceless members of the empire, were incessantly tormented by the ambition of their Protestant neighbours. Those who were too weak to repel force by force, took refuge under the wings of justice; and the complaints of spoliation were heaped up against the Protestants in the Imperial Chamber, which was ready enough to pursue the accused with judgments, but found too little support to carry them into effect. The peace which stipulated for complete religious toleration for the dignitaries of the Empire, had provided also for the subject, by enabling him, without interruption, to leave the country in which the exercise of his religion was prohibited. But from the wrongs which the violence of a sovereign might inflict on an obnoxious subject; from the nameless oppressions by which he might harass and annoy the emigrant; from the artful snares in which subtilty combined with power might enmesh him — from these, the dead letter of the treaty could afford him no protection. The Catholic subject of Protestant princes complained loudly of violations of the religious peace — the Lutherans still more loudly of the oppression they experienced under their Romanist suzerains. The rancour and animosities of theologians infused a poison into every occurrence, however inconsiderable, and inflamed the minds of the people. Happy would it have been had this theological hatred exhausted its zeal upon the common enemy, instead of venting its virus on the adherents of a kindred faith!

Unanimity amongst the Protestants might, by preserving the balance between the contending parties, have prolonged the peace; but as if to complete the confusion, all concord was quickly broken. The doctrines which had been propagated by Zuingli in Zurich, and by Calvin in Geneva, soon spread to Germany, and divided the Protestants among themselves, with little in unison save their common hatred to popery. The Protestants of this date bore but slight resemblance to those who, fifty years before, drew up the Confession of Augsburg; and the cause of the change is to be sought in that Confession itself. It had prescribed a positive boundary to the Protestant faith, before the newly awakened spirit of inquiry had satisfied itself as to the limits it ought to set; and the Protestants seemed unwittingly to have thrown away much of the advantage acquired by their rejection of popery. Common complaints of the Romish hierarchy, and of ecclesiastical abuses, and a common disapprobation of its dogmas, formed a sufficient centre of union for the Protestants; but not content with this, they sought a rallying point in the promulgation of a new and positive creed, in which they sought to embody the distinctions, the privileges, and the essence of the church, and to this they referred the convention entered into with their opponents. It was as professors of this creed that they had acceded to the treaty; and in the benefits of this peace the advocates of the confession were alone entitled to participate. In any case, therefore, the situation of its adherents was embarrassing. If a blind obedience were yielded to the dicta of the Confession, a lasting bound would be set to the spirit of inquiry; if, on the other hand, they dissented from the formulae agreed upon, the point of union would be lost. Unfortunately both incidents occurred, and the evil results of both were quickly felt. One party rigorously adhered to the original symbol of faith, and the other abandoned it, only to adopt another with equal exclusiveness.

Nothing could have furnished the common enemy a more plausible defence of his cause than this dissension; no spectacle could have been more gratifying to him than the rancour with which the Protestants alternately persecuted each other. Who could condemn the Roman Catholics, if they laughed at the audacity with which the Reformers had presumed to announce the only true belief? — if from Protestants they borrowed the weapons against Protestants? — if, in the midst of this clashing of opinions, they held fast to the authority of their own church, for which, in part, there spoke an honourable antiquity, and a yet more honourable plurality of voices. But this division placed the Protestants in still more serious embarrassments. As the covenants of the treaty applied only to the partisans of the Confession, their opponents, with some reason, called upon them to explain who were to be recognized as the adherents of that creed. The Lutherans could not, without offending conscience, include the Calvinists in their communion, except at the risk of converting a useful friend into a dangerous enemy, could they exclude them. This unfortunate difference opened a way for the machinations of the Jesuits to sow distrust between both parties, and to destroy the unity of their measures. Fettered by the double fear of their direct adversaries, and of their opponents among themselves, the Protestants lost for ever the opportunity of placing their church on a perfect equality with the Catholic. All these difficulties would have been avoided, and the defection of the Calvinists would not have prejudiced the common cause, if the point of union had been placed simply in the abandonment of Romanism, instead of in the Confession of Augsburg.

But however divided on other points, they concurred in this — that the security which had resulted from equality of power could only be maintained by the preservation of that balance. In the meanwhile, the continual reforms of one party, and the opposing measures of the other, kept both upon the watch, while the interpretation of the religious treaty was a never-ending subject of dispute. Each party maintained that every step taken by its opponent was an infraction of the peace, while of every movement of its own it was asserted that it was essential to its maintenance. Yet all the measures of the Catholics did not, as their opponents alleged, proceed from a spirit of encroachment — many of them were the necessary precautions of self-defence. The Protestants had shown unequivocally enough what the Romanists might expect if they were unfortunate enough to become the weaker party. The greediness of the former for the property of the church, gave no reason to expect indulgence; — their bitter hatred left no hope of magnanimity or forbearance.

But the Protestants, likewise, were excusable if they too placed little confidence in the sincerity of the Roman Catholics. By the treacherous and inhuman treatment which their brethren in Spain, France, and the Netherlands, had suffered; by the disgraceful subterfuge of the Romish princes, who held that the Pope had power to relieve them from the obligation of the most solemn oaths; and above all, by the detestable maxim, that faith was not to be kept with heretics, the Roman Church, in the eyes of all honest men, had lost its honour. No engagement, no oath, however sacred, from a Roman Catholic, could satisfy a Protestant. What security then could the religious peace afford, when, throughout Germany, the Jesuits represented it as a measure of mere temporary convenience, and in Rome itself it was solemnly repudiated.

The General Council, to which reference had been made in the treaty, had already been held in the city of Trent; but, as might have been foreseen, without accommodating the religious differences, or taking a single step to effect such accommodation, and even without being attended by the Protestants. The latter, indeed, were now solemnly excommunicated by it in the name of the church, whose representative the Council gave itself out to be. Could, then, a secular treaty, extorted moreover by force of arms, afford them adequate protection against the ban of the church; a treaty, too, based on a condition which the decision of the Council seemed entirely to abolish? There was then a show of right for violating the peace, if only the Romanists possessed the power; and henceforward the Protestants were protected by nothing but the respect for their formidable array.

Other circumstances combined to augment this distrust. Spain, on whose support the Romanists in Germany chiefly relied, was engaged in a bloody conflict with the Flemings. By it, the flower of the Spanish troops were drawn to the confines of Germany. With what ease might they be introduced within the empire, if a decisive stroke should render their presence necessary? Germany was at that time a magazine of war for nearly all the powers of Europe. The religious war had crowded it with soldiers, whom the peace left destitute; its many independent princes found it easy to assemble armies, and afterwards, for the sake of gain, or the interests of party, hire them out to other powers. With German troops, Philip the Second waged war against the Netherlands, and with German troops they defended themselves. Every such levy in Germany was a subject of alarm to the one party or the other, since it might be intended for their oppression. The arrival of an ambassador, an extraordinary legate of the Pope, a conference of princes, every unusual incident, must, it was thought, be pregnant with destruction to some party. Thus, for nearly half a century, stood Germany, her hand upon the sword; every rustle of a leaf alarmed her.

Ferdinand the First, King of Hungary, and his excellent son, Maximilian the Second, held at this memorable epoch the reins of government. With a heart full of sincerity, with a truly heroic patience, had Ferdinand brought about the religious peace of Augsburg, and afterwards, in the Council of Trent, laboured assiduously, though vainly, at the ungrateful task of reconciling the two religions. Abandoned by his nephew, Philip of Spain, and hard pressed both in Hungary and Transylvania by the victorious armies of the Turks, it was not likely that this emperor would entertain the idea of violating the religious peace, and thereby destroying his own painful work. The heavy expenses of the perpetually recurring war with Turkey could not be defrayed by the meagre contributions of his exhausted hereditary dominions. He stood, therefore, in need of the assistance of the whole empire; and the religious peace alone preserved in one body the otherwise divided empire. Financial necessities made the Protestant as needful to him as the Romanist, and imposed upon him the obligation of treating both parties with equal justice, which, amidst so many contradictory claims, was truly a colossal task. Very far, however, was the result from answering his expectations. His indulgence of the Protestants served only to bring upon his successors a war, which death saved himself the mortification of witnessing. Scarcely more fortunate was his son Maximilian, with whom perhaps the pressure of circumstances was the only obstacle, and a longer life perhaps the only want, to his establishing the new religion upon the imperial throne. Necessity had taught the father forbearance towards the Protestants — necessity and justice dictated the same course to the son. The grandson had reason to repent that he neither listened to justice, nor yielded to necessity.

Maximilian left six sons, of whom the eldest, the Archduke Rodolph, inherited his dominions, and ascended the imperial throne. The other brothers were put off with petty appanages. A few mesne fiefs were held by a collateral branch, which had their uncle, Charles of Styria, at its head; and even these were afterwards, under his son, Ferdinand the Second, incorporated with the rest of the family dominions. With this exception, the whole of the imposing power of Austria was now wielded by a single, but unfortunately weak hand.

Rodolph the Second was not devoid of those virtues which might have gained him the esteem of mankind, had the lot of a private station fallen to him. His character was mild, he loved peace and the sciences, particularly astronomy, natural history, chemistry, and the study of antiquities. To these he applied with a passionate zeal, which, at the very time when the critical posture of affairs demanded all his attention, and his exhausted finances the most rigid economy, diverted his attention from state affairs, and involved him in pernicious expenses. His taste for astronomy soon lost itself in those astrological reveries to which timid and melancholy temperaments like his are but too disposed. This, together with a youth passed in Spain, opened his ears to the evil counsels of the Jesuits, and the influence of the Spanish court, by which at last he was wholly governed. Ruled by tastes so little in accordance with the dignity of his station, and alarmed by ridiculous prophecies, he withdrew, after the

Spanish custom, from the eyes of his subjects, to bury himself amidst his gems and antiques, or to make experiments in his laboratory, while the most fatal discords loosened all the bands of the empire, and the flames of rebellion began to burst out at the very footsteps of his throne. All access to his person was denied, the most urgent matters were neglected. The prospect of the rich inheritance of Spain was closed against him, while he was trying to make up his mind to offer his hand to the Infanta Isabella. A fearful anarchy threatened the Empire, for though without an heir of his own body, he could not be persuaded to allow the election of a King of the Romans. The Austrian States renounced their allegiance, Hungary and Transylvania threw off his supremacy, and Bohemia was not slow in following their example. The descendant of the once so formidable Charles the Fifth was in perpetual danger, either of losing one part of his possessions to the Turks, or another to the Protestants, and of sinking, beyond redemption, under the formidable coalition which a great monarch of Europe had formed against him. The events which now took place in the interior of Germany were such as usually happened when either the throne was without an emperor, or the Emperor without a sense of his imperial dignity. Outraged or abandoned by their head, the States of the Empire were left to help themselves; and alliances among themselves must supply the defective authority of the Emperor. Germany was divided into two leagues, which stood in arms arrayed against each other: between both, Rodolph, the despised opponent of the one, and the impotent protector of the other, remained irresolute and useless, equally unable to destroy the former or to command the latter. What had the Empire to look for from a prince incapable even of defending his hereditary dominions against its domestic enemies? To prevent the utter ruin of the House of Austria, his own family combined against him; and a powerful party threw itself into the arms of his brother. Driven from his hereditary dominions, nothing was now left him to lose but the imperial dignity; and he was only spared this last disgrace by a timely death.

At this critical moment, when only a supple policy, united with a vigorous arm, could have maintained the tranquillity of the Empire, its evil genius gave it a Rodolph for Emperor. At a more peaceful period the Germanic Union would have managed its own interests, and Rodolph, like so many others of his rank, might have hidden his deficiencies in a mysterious obscurity. But the urgent demand for the qualities in which he was most deficient revealed his incapacity. The position of Germany called for an emperor who, by his known energies, could give weight to his resolves; and the hereditary dominions of Rodolph, considerable as they were, were at present in a situation to occasion the greatest embarrassment to the governors.

The Austrian princes, it is true were Roman Catholics, and in addition to that, the supporters of Popery, but their countries were far from being so. The reformed opinions had penetrated even these, and favoured by Ferdinand's necessities and Maximilian's mildness, had met with a rapid success. The Austrian provinces exhibited in miniature what Germany did on a larger scale. The great nobles and the ritter class or knights were chiefly evangelical, and in the cities the Protestants had a decided preponderance. If they succeeded in bringing a few of their party into the country, they contrived imperceptibly to fill all places of trust and the magistracy with their own adherents, and to exclude the Catholics. Against the numerous order of the nobles and knights, and the deputies from the towns, the voice of a few prelates was powerless; and the unseemly ridicule and offensive contempt of the former soon drove them entirely from the provincial diets. Thus the whole of the Austrian Diet had imperceptibly become Protestant, and the Reformation was making rapid strides towards its public recognition. The prince was dependent on the Estates, who had it in their power to grant or refuse supplies. Accordingly, they availed themselves of the financial necessities of Ferdinand and his son to extort one religious concession after another. To the nobles and knights, Maximilian at last conceded the free exercise of their religion, but only within their own territories and castles. The intemperate enthusiasm of the Protestant preachers overstepped the boundaries which prudence had prescribed. In defiance of the express prohibition, several of them ventured to preach publicly, not only in the towns, but in Vienna itself, and the people flocked in crowds to this new doctrine, the best seasoning of which was personality and abuse. Thus continued food was supplied to fanaticism, and the hatred of two churches, that were such near neighbours, was farther envenomed by the sting of an impure zeal.

Among the hereditary dominions of the House of Austria, Hungary and Transylvania were the most unstable, and the most difficult to retain. The impossibility of holding these two countries against the neighbouring and overwhelming power of the Turks, had already driven Ferdinand to the inglorious expedient of recognizing, by an annual tribute, the Porte's supremacy over Transylvania; a shameful confession of weakness, and a still more dangerous temptation to the turbulent nobility, when they fancied they had any reason to complain of their master. Not without conditions had the Hungarians submitted to the House of Austria. They asserted the elective freedom of their crown, and boldly contended for all those prerogatives of their order which are inseparable from this freedom of election. The near neighbourhood of Turkey, the facility of changing masters with impunity, encouraged the magnates still more in their presumption; discontented with the Austrian government they threw themselves into the arms of the Turks; dissatisfied with these, they returned again to their German sovereigns. The frequency and rapidity of these transitions from one government to another, had communicated its influences also to their mode of thinking; and as their country wavered between the Turkish and Austrian rule, so their minds vacillated between revolt and submission. The more unfortunate each nation felt itself in being degraded into a province of a foreign kingdom, the stronger desire did they feel to obey a monarch chosen from amongst themselves, and thus it was always easy for an enterprising noble to obtain their support. The nearest Turkish pasha was always ready to bestow the Hungarian sceptre and crown on a rebel against Austria; just as ready was Austria to confirm to any adventurer the possession of provinces which he had wrested from the Porte, satisfied with preserving thereby the shadow of authority, and with erecting at the same time a barrier against the Turks. In this way several of these magnates, Batbori, Boschkai, Ragoczi, and Bethlen succeeded in establishing themselves, one after another, as tributary sovereigns in Transylvania and Hungary; and they maintained their ground by no deeper policy than that of occasionally joining the enemy, in order to render themselves more formidable to their own prince.

Ferdinand, Maximilian, and Rodolph, who were all sovereigns of Hungary and Transylvania, exhausted their other territories in endeavouring to defend these from the hostile inroads of the Turks, and to put down intestine rebellion. In this quarter destructive wars were succeeded but by brief truces, which were scarcely less hurtful: far and wide the land lay waste, while the injured serf had to complain equally of his enemy and his protector. Into these countries also the Reformation had penetrated; and protected by the freedom of the States, and under the cover of the internal disorders, had made a noticeable progress. Here too it was incautiously attacked, and party spirit thus became yet more dangerous from religious enthusiasm. Headed by a bold rebel, Boschkai, the nobles of Hungary and Transylvania raised the standard of rebellion. The Hungarian insurgents were upon the point of making common cause with the discontented Protestants in Austria, Moravia, and Bohemia, and uniting all those countries in one fearful revolt. The downfall of popery in these lands would then have been inevitable.

Long had the Austrian archdukes, the brothers of the Emperor, beheld with silent indignation the impending ruin of their house; this last event hastened their decision. The Archduke Matthias, Maximilian's second son, Viceroy in Hungary, and Rodolph's presumptive heir, now came forward as the stay of the falling house of Hapsburg. In his youth, misled by a false ambition, this prince, disregarding the interests of his family, had listened to the overtures of the Flemish insurgents, who invited him into the Netherlands to conduct the defence of their liberties against the oppression of his own relative, Philip the Second. Mistaking the voice of an insulated faction for that of the entire nation, Matthias obeyed the call. But the event answered the expectations of the men of Brabant as little as his own, and from this imprudent enterprise he retired with little credit.

Far more honourable was his second appearance in the political world. Perceiving that his repeated remonstrances with the Emperor were unavailing, he assembled the archdukes, his brothers and cousins, at Presburg, and consulted with them on the growing perils of their house, when they unanimously assigned to him, as the oldest, the duty of defending that patrimony which a feeble brother was endangering. In his hands they placed all their powers and rights, and vested him with sovereign authority, to act at his discretion for the common good. Matthias immediately opened a communication with the Porte and the Hungarian rebels, and through his skilful management succeeded in saving, by a peace with the Turks, the remainder of Hungary, and by a treaty with the rebels, preserved the claims of Austria to the lost provinces. But Rodolph, as jealous as he had hitherto been careless of his sovereign authority, refused to ratify this treaty, which he regarded as a criminal encroachment on his sovereign rights. He accused the Archduke of keeping up a secret understanding with the enemy, and of cherishing treasonable designs on the crown of Hungary.

The activity of Matthias was, in truth, anything but disinterested; the conduct of the Emperor only accelerated the execution of his ambitious views. Secure, from motives of gratitude, of the devotion of the Hungarians, for whom he had so lately obtained the blessings of peace; assured by his agents of the favourable disposition of the nobles, and certain of the support of a large party, even in Austria, he now ventured to assume a bolder attitude, and, sword in hand, to discuss his grievances with the Emperor. The Protestants in Austria and Moravia, long ripe for revolt, and now won over to the Archduke by his promises of toleration, loudly and openly espoused his cause, and their long-menaced alliance with the Hungarian rebels was actually effected. Almost at once a formidable conspiracy was planned and matured against the Emperor. Too late did he resolve to amend his past errors; in vain did he attempt to break up this fatal alliance. Already the whole empire was in arms; Hungary, Austria, and Moravia had done homage to Matthias, who was already on his march to Bohemia to seize the Emperor in his palace, and to cut at once the sinews of his power.

Bohemia was not a more peaceable possession for Austria than Hungary; with this difference only, that, in the latter, political considerations, in the former, religious dissensions, fomented disorders. In Bohemia, a century before the days of Luther, the first spark of the religious war had been kindled; a century after Luther, the first flames of the thirty years' war burst out in Bohemia. The sect which owed its rise to John Huss, still existed in that country; — it agreed with the Romish Church in ceremonies and doctrines, with the single exception of the administration of the Communion, in which the Hussites communicated in both kinds. This privilege had been conceded to the followers of Huss by the Council of Basle, in an express treaty, (the Bohemian Compact); and though it was afterwards disavowed by the popes, they nevertheless continued to profit by it under the sanction of the government. As the use of the cup formed the only important distinction of their body, they were usually designated by the name of Utraquists; and they readily adopted an appellation which reminded them of their dearly valued privilege. But under this title lurked also the far stricter sects of the Bohemian and Moravian Brethren, who differed from the predominant church in more important particulars, and bore, in fact, a great resemblance to the German Protestants. Among them both, the German and Swiss opinions on religion made rapid progress; while the name of Utraquists, under which they managed to disguise the change of their principles, shielded them from persecution.

In truth, they had nothing in common with the Utraquists but the name; essentially, they were altogether Protestant. Confident in the strength of their party, and the Emperor's toleration under Maximilian, they had openly avowed their tenets. After the example of the Germans, they drew up a Confession of their own, in which Lutherans as well as Calvinists recognized their own doctrines, and they sought to transfer to the new Confession the privileges of the original Utraquists. In this they were opposed by their Roman Catholic countrymen, and forced to rest content with the Emperor's verbal assurance of protection.

As long as Maximilian lived, they enjoyed complete toleration, even under the new form they had taken. Under his successor the scene changed. An imperial edict appeared, which deprived the Bohemian Brethren of their religious freedom. Now these differed in nothing from the other Utraquists. The sentence, therefore, of their condemnation, obviously included all the partisans of the Bohemian Confession. Accordingly, they all combined to oppose the imperial mandate in the Diet, but without being able to procure its revocation. The Emperor and the Roman Catholic Estates took their ground on the Compact and the Bohemian Constitution; in which nothing appeared in favour of a religion which had not then obtained the voice of the country. Since that time, how completely had affairs changed! What then formed but an inconsiderable opinion, had now become the predominant religion of the country. And what was it then, but a subterfuge to limit a newly spreading religion by the terms of obsolete treaties? The Bohemian Protestants appealed to the verbal guarantee of Maximilian, and the religious freedom of the Germans, with whom they argued they ought to be on a footing of equality. It was in vain — their appeal was dismissed.

Such was the posture of affairs in Bohemia, when Matthias, already master of Hungary, Austria, and Moravia, appeared in Kolin, to raise the Bohemian Estates also against the Emperor. The embarrassment of the latter was now at its height. Abandoned by all his other subjects, he placed his last hopes on the Bohemians, who, it might be foreseen, would take advantage of his necessities to enforce their own demands. After an interval of many years, he once more appeared publicly in the Diet at Prague; and to convince the people that he was really still in existence, orders were given that all the windows should be opened in the streets through which he was to pass — proof enough how far things had gone with him. The event justified his fears. The Estates, conscious of their own power, refused to take a single step until their privileges were confirmed, and religious toleration fully assured to them. It was in vain to have recourse now to the old system of evasion. The Emperor's fate was in their hands, and he must yield to necessity. At present, however, he only granted their other demands — religious matters he reserved for consideration at the next Diet.

The Bohemians now took up arms in defence of the Emperor, and a bloody war between the two brothers was on the point of breaking out. But Rodolph, who feared nothing so much as remaining in this slavish dependence on the Estates, waited not for a warlike issue, but hastened to effect a reconciliation with his brother by more peaceable means. By a formal act of abdication he resigned to Matthias, what indeed he had no chance of wresting from him, Austria and the kingdom of Hungary, and acknowledged him as his successor to the crown of Bohemia.

Dearly enough had the Emperor extricated himself from one difficulty, only to get immediately involved in another. The settlement of the religious affairs of Bohemia had been referred to the next Diet, which was held in 1609. The reformed Bohemians demanded the free exercise of their faith, as under the former emperors; a Consistory of their own; the cession of the University of Prague; and the right of electing 'Defenders', or 'Protectors' of 'Liberty', from their own body. The answer was the same as before; for the timid Emperor was now entirely fettered by the unreformed party. However often, and in however threatening language the Estates renewed their remonstrances, the Emperor persisted in his first declaration of granting nothing beyond the old compact. The Diet broke up without coming to a decision; and the Estates, exasperated against the Emperor, arranged a general meeting at Prague, upon their own authority, to right themselves.

They appeared at Prague in great force. In defiance of the imperial prohibition, they carried on their deliberations almost under the very eyes of the Emperor. The yielding compliance which he began to show, only proved how much they were feared, and increased their audacity. Yet on the main point he remained inflexible. They fulfilled their threats, and at last resolved to establish, by their own power, the free and universal exercise of their religion, and to abandon the Emperor to his necessities until he should confirm this resolution. They even went farther, and elected for themselves the *defenders* which the Emperor had refused them. Ten were nominated by each of the three Estates; they also determined to raise, as soon as possible, an armed force, at the head of which Count Thurn, the chief organizer of the revolt, should be placed as general defender of the liberties of Bohemia. Their determination brought the Emperor to submission, to which he was now counselled even by the Spaniards. Apprehensive lest the exasperated Estates should throw themselves into the arms of the King of Hungary, he signed the memorable Letter of Majesty for Bohemia, by which, under the successors of the Emperor, that people justified their rebellion.

The Bohemian Confession, which the States had laid before the Emperor Maximilian, was, by the Letter of Majesty, placed on a footing of equality with the olden profession. The Utraquists, for by this title the Bohemian Protestants continued to designate themselves, were put in possession of the University of Prague, and allowed a Consistory of their own, entirely independent of the archiepiscopal see of that city. All the churches in the cities, villages, and market towns, which they held at the date of the letter, were secured to them; and if in addition they wished to erect others, it was permitted to the nobles, and knights, and the free cities to do so. This last clause in the Letter of Majesty gave rise to the unfortunate disputes which subsequently rekindled the flames of war in Europe.

The Letter of Majesty erected the Protestant part of Bohemia into a kind of republic. The Estates had learned to feel the power which they gained by perseverance, unity, and harmony in their measures. The Emperor now retained little more than the shadow of his sovereign authority; while by the new dignity of the so-called defenders of liberty, a dangerous stimulus was given to the spirit of revolt. The example and success of Bohemia afforded a tempting seduction to the other hereditary dominions of Austria, and all attempted by similar means to extort similar privileges. The spirit of liberty spread from one province to another; and as it was chiefly the disunion among the Austrian princes that had enabled the Protestants so materially to improve their advantages, they now hastened to effect a reconciliation between the Emperor and the King of Hungary.

But the reconciliation could not be sincere. The wrong was too great to be forgiven, and Rodolph continued to nourish at heart an unextinguishable hatred of Matthias. With grief and indignation he brooded over the thought, that the Bohemian sceptre was finally to descend into the hands of his enemy; and the prospect was not more consoling, even if Matthias should die without issue. In that case, Ferdinand, Archduke of Graetz, whom he equally disliked, was the head of the family. To exclude the latter as well as Matthias from the succession to the throne of Bohemia, he fell upon the project of diverting that inheritance to Ferdinand's brother, the Archduke Leopold, Bishop of Passau, who among all his relatives had ever been the dearest and most deserving. The prejudices of the Bohemians in favour of the elective freedom of their crown, and their attachment to Leopold's person, seemed to favour this scheme, in which Rodolph consulted rather his own partiality and vindictiveness than the good of his house. But to carry out this project, a military force was requisite, and Rodolph actually assembled an army in the bishopric of Passau. The object of this force was hidden from all. An inroad, however,

12

which, for want of pay it made suddenly and without the Emperor's knowledge into Bohemia, and the outrages which it there committed, stirred up the whole kingdom against him. In vain he asserted his innocence to the Bohemian Estates; they would not believe his protestations; vainly did he attempt to restrain the violence of his soldiery; they disregarded his orders. Persuaded that the Emperor's object was to annul the Letter of Majesty, the Protectors of Liberty armed the whole of Protestant Bohemia, and invited Matthias into the country. After the dispersion of the force he had collected at Passau, the Emperor remained helpless at Prague, where he was kept shut up like a prisoner in his palace, and separated from all his councillors. In the meantime, Matthias entered Prague amidst universal rejoicings, where Rodolph was soon afterwards weak enough to acknowledge him King of Bohemia. So hard a fate befell this Emperor; he was compelled, during his life, to abdicate in favour of his enemy that very throne, of which he had been endeavouring to deprive him after his own death. To complete his degradation, he was obliged, by a personal act of renunciation, to release his subjects in Bohemia, Silesia, and Lusatia from their allegiance, and he did it with a broken heart. All, even those he thought he had most attached to his person, had abandoned him. When he had signed the instrument, he threw his hat upon the ground, and gnawed the pen which had rendered so shameful a service.

While Rodolph thus lost one hereditary dominion after another, the imperial dignity was not much better maintained by him. Each of the religious parties into which Germany was divided, continued its efforts to advance itself at the expense of the other, or to guard against its attacks. The weaker the hand that held the sceptre, and the more the Protestants and Roman Catholics felt they were left to themselves, the more vigilant necessarily became their watchfulness, and the greater their distrust of each other. It was enough that the Emperor was ruled by Jesuits, and was guided by Spanish counsels, to excite the apprehension of the Protestants, and to afford a pretext for hostility. The rash zeal of the Jesuits, which in the pulpit and by the press disputed the validity of the religious peace, increased this distrust, and caused their adversaries to see a dangerous design in the most indifferent measures of the Roman Catholics. Every step taken in the hereditary dominions of the Emperor, for the repression of the reformed religion, was sure to draw the attention of all the Protestants of Germany; and this powerful support which the reformed subjects of Austria met, or expected to meet with from their religious confederates in the rest of Germany, was no small cause of their confidence, and of the rapid success of Matthias. It was the general belief of the Empire, that they owed the long enjoyment of the religious peace merely to the difficulties in which the Emperor was placed by the internal troubles in his dominions, and consequently they were in no haste to relieve him from them.

Almost all the affairs of the Diet were neglected, either through the procrastination of the Emperor, or through the fault of the Protestant Estates, who had determined to make no provision for the common wants of the Empire till their own grievances were removed. These grievances related principally to the misgovernment of the Emperor; the violation of the religious treaty, and the presumptuous usurpations of the Aulic Council, which in the present reign had begun to extend its jurisdiction at the expense of the Imperial Chamber. Formerly, in all disputes between the Estates, which could not be settled by club law, the Emperors had in the last resort decided of themselves, if the case were trifling, and in conjunction with the princes, if it were important; or they determined them by the advice of imperial judges who followed the court. This superior jurisdiction they had, in the end of the fifteenth century, assigned to a regular and permanent tribunal, the Imperial Chamber of Spires, in which the Estates of the Empire, that they might not be oppressed by the arbitrary appointment of the Emperor, had reserved to themselves the right of electing the assessors, and of periodically reviewing its decrees. By the religious peace, these rights of the Estates, (called the rights of presentation and visitation,) were extended also to the Lutherans, so that Protestant judges had a voice in Protestant causes, and a seeming equality obtained for both religions in this supreme tribunal.

But the enemies of the Reformation and of the freedom of the Estates, vigilant to take advantage of every incident that favoured their views, soon found means to neutralize the beneficial effects of this institution. A supreme jurisdiction over the Imperial States was gradually and skilfully usurped by a private imperial tribunal, the Aulic Council in Vienna, a court at first intended merely to advise the Emperor in the exercise of his undoubted, imperial, and personal prerogatives; a court, whose members being appointed and paid by him, had no law but the interest of their master, and no standard of equity but the advancement of the unreformed religion of which they were partisans. Before the Aulic Council were now brought several suits originating between Estates differing in religion, and which, therefore, properly belonged to the Imperial Chamber. It was not surprising if the decrees of this tribunal bore traces of their origin; if the interests of the Roman Church and of the Emperor were preferred to justice by Roman Catholic judges, and the creatures of the Emperor. Although all the Estates of Germany seemed to have equal cause for resisting so perilous an abuse, the Protestants alone, who most sensibly felt it, and even these not all at once and in a body, came forward as the defenders of German liberty, which the establishment of so arbitrary a tribunal had outraged in its most sacred point, the administration of justice. In fact, Germany would have had little cause to congratulate itself upon the abolition of club-law, and in the institution of the Imperial Chamber, if an arbitrary tribunal of the Emperor was allowed to interfere with the latter. The Estates of the German Empire would indeed have improved little upon the days of barbarism, if the Chamber of Justice in which they sat along with the Emperor as judges, and for which they had abandoned their original princely prerogative, should cease to be a court of the last resort. But the strangest contradictions were at this date to be found in the minds of men. The name of Emperor, a remnant of Roman despotism, was still associated with an idea of autocracy, which, though it formed a ridiculous inconsistency with the privileges of the Estates, was nevertheless argued for by jurists, diffused by the partisans of despotism, and believed by the ignorant.

To these general grievances was gradually added a chain of singular incidents, which at length converted the anxiety of the Protestants into utter distrust. During the Spanish persecutions in the Netherlands, several Protestant families had taken refuge in Aix-la-Chapelle, an imperial city, and attached to the Roman Catholic faith, where they settled and insensibly extended their adherents. Having succeeded by stratagem in introducing some of their members into the municipal council, they demanded a church and the public exercise of their worship, and the demand being unfavourably received, they succeeded by violence in enforcing it, and also in usurping the entire government of the city. To see so important a city in Protestant hands was too heavy a blow for the Emperor and the Roman Catholics. After all the Emperor's requests and commands for the restoration of the olden government had proved ineffectual, the Aulic Council proclaimed the city under the ban of the Empire, which, however, was not put in force till the following reign.

Of yet greater importance were two other attempts of the Protestants to extend their influence and their power. The Elector Gebhard, of Cologne, (born Truchsess[2] of Waldburg,) conceived for the young Countess Agnes, of Mansfield, Canoness of Gerresheim, a passion which was not unreturned. As the eyes of all Germany were directed to this intercourse, the brothers of the Countess, two zealous Calvinists, demanded satisfaction for the injured honour of their house, which, as long as the elector remained a Roman Catholic prelate, could not be repaired by marriage. They threatened the elector they would wash out this stain in his blood and their sister's, unless he either abandoned all further connexion with the countess, or consented to re-establish her reputation at the altar. The elector, indifferent to all the consequences of this step, listened to nothing but the voice of love. Whether it was in consequence of his previous inclination to the reformed doctrines, or that the charms of his mistress alone effected this wonder, he renounced the Roman Catholic faith, and led the beautiful Agnes to the altar.

This event was of the greatest importance. By the letter of the clause reserving the ecclesiastical states from the general operation of the religious peace, the elector had, by his apostacy, forfeited all right to the temporalities of his bishopric; and if, in any case, it was important for the Catholics to enforce the clause, it was so especially in the case of electorates. On the other hand, the relinquishment of so high a dignity was a severe sacrifice, and peculiarly so in the case of a tender husband, who had wished to enhance the value of his heart and hand by the gift of a principality. Moreover, the Reservatum Ecclesiasticum was a disputed article of the treaty of Augsburg; and all the German Protestants were aware of the extreme importance of wresting this fourth[3] electorate from the opponents of their faith. The example had already been set in several of the ecclesiastical benefices of Lower Germany, and attended with success. Several canons of Cologne had also already embraced the Protestant confession, and were on the elector's side, while, in the city itself, he could depend upon the support of a numerous Protestant party. All these considerations, greatly strengthened by the persuasions of his friends and relations, and the promises of several German courts, determined the elector to retain his dominions, while he changed his religion.

But it was soon apparent that he had entered upon a contest which he could not carry through. Even the free toleration of the Protestant service within the territories of Cologne, had already occasioned a violent opposition on the part of the canons and Roman Catholic 'Estates' of that province. The intervention of the Emperor, and a papal ban from Rome, which anathematized the elector as an apostate, and deprived him of all his dignities, temporal and spiritual, armed his own subjects and

[2]Grand-master of the kitchen.

[3]Saxony, Brandenburg, and the Palatinate were already Protestant.

chapter against him. The Elector assembled a military force; the chapter did the same. To ensure also the aid of a strong arm, they proceeded forthwith to a new election, and chose the Bishop of Liege, a prince of Bavaria.

A civil war now commenced, which, from the strong interest which both religious parties in Germany necessarily felt in the conjuncture, was likely to terminate in a general breaking up of the religious peace. What most made the Protestants indignant, was that the Pope should have presumed, by a pretended apostolic power, to deprive a prince of the empire of his imperial dignities. Even in the golden days of their spiritual domination, this prerogative of the Pope had been disputed; how much more likely was it to be questioned at a period when his authority was entirely disowned by one party, while even with the other it rested on a tottering foundation. All the Protestant princes took up the affair warmly against the Emperor; and Henry IV. of France, then King of Navarre, left no means of negotiation untried to urge the German princes to the vigorous assertion of their rights. The issue would decide for ever the liberties of Germany. Four Protestant against three Roman Catholic voices in the Electoral College must at once have given the preponderance to the former, and for ever excluded the House of Austria from the imperial throne.

But the Elector Gebhard had embraced the Calvinist, not the Lutheran religion; and this circumstance alone was his ruin. The mutual rancour of these two churches would not permit the Lutheran Estates to regard the Elector as one of their party, and as such to lend him their effectual support. All indeed had encouraged, and promised him assistance; but only one appanaged prince of the Palatine House, the Palsgrave John Casimir, a zealous Calvinist, kept his word. Despite of the imperial prohibition, he hastened with his little army into the territories of Cologne; but without being able to effect any thing, because the Elector, who was destitute even of the first necessaries, left him totally without help. So much the more rapid was the progress of the newly-chosen elector, whom his Bavarian relations and the Spaniards from the Netherlands supported with the utmost vigour. The troops of Gebhard, left by their master without pay, abandoned one place after another to the enemy; by whom others were compelled to surrender. In his Westphalian territories, Gebhard held out for some time longer, till here, too, he was at last obliged to yield to superior force. After several vain attempts in Holland and England to obtain means for his restoration, he retired into the Chapter of Strasburg, and died dean of that cathedral; the first sacrifice to the Ecclesiastical Reservation, or rather to the want of harmony among the German Protestants.

To this dispute in Cologne was soon added another in Strasburg. Several Protestant canons of Cologne, who had been included in the same papal ban with the elector, had taken refuge within this bishopric, where they likewise held prebends. As the Roman Catholic canons of Strasburg hesitated to allow them, as being under the ban, the enjoyment of their prebends, they took violent possession of their benefices, and the support of a powerful Protestant party among the citizens soon gave them the preponderance in the chapter. The other canons thereupon retired to Alsace-Saverne, where, under the protection of the bishop, they established themselves as the only lawful chapter, and denounced that which remained in Strasburg as illegal. The latter, in the meantime, had so strengthened themselves by the reception of several Protestant colleagues of high rank, that they could venture, upon the death of the bishop, to nominate a new Protestant bishop in the person of John George of Brandenburg. The Roman Catholic canons, far from allowing this election, nominated the Bishop of Metz, a prince of Lorraine, to that dignity, who announced his promotion by immediately commencing hostilities against the territories of Strasburg.

That city now took up arms in defence of its Protestant chapter and the Prince of Brandenburg, while the other party, with the assistance of the troops of Lorraine, endeavoured to possess themselves of the temporalities of the chapter. A tedious war was the consequence, which, according to the spirit of the times, was attended with barbarous devastations. In vain did the Emperor interpose with his supreme authority to terminate the dispute; the ecclesiastical property remained for a long time divided between the two parties, till at last the Protestant prince, for a moderate pecuniary equivalent, renounced his claims; and thus, in this dispute also, the Roman Church came off victorious.

An occurrence which, soon after the adjustment of this dispute, took place in Donauwerth, a free city of Suabia, was still more critical for the whole of Protestant Germany. In this once Roman Catholic city, the Protestants, during the reigns of Ferdinand and his son, had, in the usual way, become so completely predominant, that the Roman Catholics were obliged to content themselves with a church in the Monastery of the Holy Cross, and for fear of offending the Protestants, were even forced to suppress the greater part of their religious rites. At length a fanatical abbot of this monastery ventured to defy the popular prejudices, and to arrange a public procession, preceded by the cross and banners flying; but he was soon compelled to desist from the attempt. When, a year afterwards, encouraged by a favourable imperial proclamation, the same abbot attempted to renew this procession, the citizens proceeded to open violence. The inhabitants shut the gates against the monks on their return, trampled their colours under foot, and followed them home with clamour and abuse. An imperial citation was the consequence of this act of violence; and as the exasperated populace even threatened to assault the imperial commissaries, and all attempts at an amicable adjustment were frustrated by the fanaticism of the multitude, the city was at last formally placed under the ban of the Empire, the execution of which was intrusted to Maximilian, Duke of Bavaria. The citizens, formerly so insolent, were seized with terror at the approach of the Bavarian army; pusillanimity now possessed them, though once so full of defiance, and they laid down their arms without striking a blow. The total abolition of the Protestant religion within the walls of the city was the punishment of their rebellion; it was deprived of its privileges, and, from a free city of Suabia, converted into a municipal town of Bavaria.

Two circumstances connected with this proceeding must have strongly excited the attention of the Protestants, even if the interests of religion had been less powerful on their minds. First of all, the sentence had been pronounced by the Aulic Council, an arbitrary and exclusively Roman Catholic tribunal, whose jurisdiction besides had been so warmly disputed by them; and secondly, its execution had been intrusted to the Duke of Bavaria, the head of another circle. These unconstitutional steps seemed to be the harbingers of further violent measures on the Roman Catholic side, the result, probably, of secret conferences and dangerous designs, which might perhaps end in the entire subversion of their religious liberty.

In circumstances where the law of force prevails, and security depends upon power alone, the weakest party is naturally the most busy to place itself in a posture of defence. This was now the case in Germany. If the Roman Catholics really meditated any evil against the Protestants in Germany, the probability was that the blow would fall on the south rather than the north, because, in Lower Germany, the Protestants were connected together through a long unbroken tract of country, and could therefore easily combine for their mutual support; while those in the south, detached from each other, and surrounded on all sides by Roman Catholic states, were exposed to every inroad. If, moreover, as was to be expected, the Catholics availed themselves of the divisions amongst the Protestants, and levelled their attack against one of the religious parties, it was the Calvinists who, as the weaker, and as being besides excluded from the religious treaty, were apparently in the greatest danger, and upon them would probably fall the first attack.

Both these circumstances took place in the dominions of the Elector Palatine, which possessed, in the Duke of Bavaria, a formidable neighbour, and which, by reason of their defection to Calvinism, received no protection from the Religious Peace, and had little hope of succour from the Lutheran states. No country in Germany had experienced so many revolutions in religion in so short a time as the Palatinate. In the space of sixty years this country, an unfortunate toy in the hands of its rulers, had twice adopted the doctrines of Luther, and twice relinquished them for Calvinism. The Elector Frederick III. first abandoned the confession of Augsburg, which his eldest son and successor, Lewis, immediately re-established. The Calvinists throughout the whole country were deprived of their churches, their preachers and even their teachers banished beyond the frontiers; while the prince, in his Lutheran zeal, persecuted them even in his will, by appointing none but strict and orthodox Lutherans as the guardians of his son, a minor. But this illegal testament was disregarded by his brother the Count Palatine, John Casimir, who, by the regulations of the Golden Bull, assumed the guardianship and administration of the state. Calvinistic teachers were given to the Elector Frederick IV., then only nine years of age, who were ordered, if necessary, to drive the Lutheran heresy out of the soul of their pupil with blows. If such was the treatment of the sovereign, that of the subjects may be easily conceived.

It was under this Frederick that the Palatine Court exerted itself so vigorously to unite the Protestant states of Germany in joint measures against the House of Austria, and, if possible, bring about the formation of a general confederacy. Besides that this court had always been guided by the counsels of France, with whom hatred of the House of Austria was the ruling principle, a regard for his own safety urged him to secure in time the doubtful assistance of the Lutherans against a near and overwhelming enemy. Great difficulties, however, opposed this union, because the Lutherans' dislike of the Reformed was scarcely less than the common aversion of both to the Romanists. An attempt was first made to reconcile the two professions, in order to facilitate a political union; but all these attempts failed, and generally ended in both parties adhering the more strongly to their respective opinions. Nothing then remained but to increase the fear and the distrust of the Evangelicals, and in this way to impress upon them the necessity of this alliance. The power of the Roman Catholics and the magnitude of the danger were exaggerated, accidental incidents were ascribed to deliberate plans, innocent actions misrepresented by invidious constructions, and the whole conduct of the professors of the olden religion was interpreted as the result of a well-weighed and systematic plan, which, in all probability, they were very far from having concerted.

The Diet of Ratisbon, to which the Protestants had looked forward with the hope of obtaining a renewal of the Religious Peace, had broken up without coming to a decision, and to the former grievances of the Protestant party was now added the late oppression of Donauwerth. With incredible speed, the union, so long attempted, was now brought to bear. A conference took place at Anhausen, in Franconia, at which were present the Elector Frederick IV., from the Palatinate, the Palsgrave of Neuburg, two Margraves of Brandenburg, the Margrave of Baden, and the Duke John Frederick of Wirtemburg, — Lutherans as well as Calvinists, — who for themselves and their heirs entered into a close confederacy under the title of the Evangelical Union. The purport of this union was, that the allied princes should, in all matters relating to religion and their civil rights, support each other with arms and counsel against every aggressor, and should all stand as one man; that in case any member of the alliance should be attacked, he should be assisted by the rest with an armed force; that, if necessary, the territories, towns, and castles of the allied states should be open to his troops; and that, whatever conquests were made, should be divided among all the confederates, in proportion to the contingent furnished by each.

The direction of the whole confederacy in time of peace was conferred upon the Elector Palatine, but with a limited power. To meet the necessary expenses, subsidies were demanded, and a common fund established. Differences of religion (betwixt the Lutherans and the Calvinists) were to have no effect on this alliance, which was to subsist for ten years, every member of the union engaged at the same time to procure new members to it. The Electorate of Brandenburg adopted the alliance, that of Saxony rejected it. Hesse-Cashel could not be prevailed upon to declare itself, the Dukes of Brunswick and Luneburg also hesitated. But the three cities of the Empire, Strasburg, Nuremburg, and Ulm, were no unimportant acquisition for the league, which was in great want of their money, while their example, besides, might be followed by other imperial cities.

After the formation of this alliance, the confederate states, dispirited, and singly, little feared, adopted a bolder language. Through Prince Christian of Anhalt, they laid their common grievances and demands before the Emperor; among which the principal were the restoration of Donauwerth, the abolition of the Imperial Court, the reformation of the Emperor's own administration and that of his counsellors. For these remonstrances, they chose the moment when the Emperor had scarcely recovered breath from the troubles in his hereditary dominions, — when he had lost Hungary and Austria to Matthias, and had barely preserved his Bohemian throne by the concession of the Letter of Majesty, and finally, when through the succession of Juliers he was already threatened with the distant prospect of a new war. No wonder, then, that this dilatory prince was more irresolute than ever in his decision, and that the confederates took up arms before he could bethink himself.

The Roman Catholics regarded this confederacy with a jealous eye; the Union viewed them and the Emperor with the like distrust; the Emperor was equally suspicious of both; and thus, on all sides, alarm and animosity had reached their climax. And, as if to crown the whole, at this critical conjuncture by the death of the Duke John William of Juliers, a highly disputable succession became vacant in the territories of Juliers and Cleves.

Eight competitors laid claim to this territory, the indivisibility of which had been guaranteed by solemn treaties; and the Emperor, who seemed disposed to enter upon it as a vacant fief, might be considered as the ninth. Four of these, the Elector of Brandenburg, the Count Palatine of Neuburg, the Count Palatine of Deux Ponts, and the Margrave of Burgau, an Austrian prince, claimed it as a female fief in name of four princesses, sisters of the late duke. Two others, the Elector of Saxony, of the line of Albert, and the Duke of Saxony, of the line of Ernest, laid claim to it under a prior right of reversion granted to them by the Emperor Frederick III., and confirmed to both Saxon houses by Maximilian I. The pretensions of some foreign princes were little regarded. The best right was perhaps on the side of Brandenburg and Neuburg, and between the claims of these two it was not easy to decide. Both courts, as soon as the succession was vacant, proceeded to take possession; Brandenburg beginning, and Neuburg following the example. Both commenced their dispute with the pen, and would probably have ended it with the sword; but the interference of the Emperor, by proceeding to bring the cause before his own cognizance, and, during the progress of the suit, sequestrating the disputed countries, soon brought the contending parties to an agreement, in order to avert the common danger. They agreed to govern the duchy conjointly. In vain did the Emperor prohibit the Estates from doing homage to their new masters; in vain did he send his own relation, the Archduke Leopold, Bishop of Passau and Strasburg, into the territory of Juliers, in order, by his presence, to strengthen the imperial party. The whole country, with the exception of Juliers itself, had submitted to the Protestant princes, and in that capital the imperialists were besieged.

The dispute about the succession of Juliers was an important one to the whole German empire, and also attracted the attention of several European courts. It was not so much the question, who was or was not to possess the Duchy of Juliers; — the real question was, which of the two religious parties in Germany, the Roman Catholic or the Protestant, was to be strengthened by so important an accession — for which of the two *religions* this territory was to be lost or won. The question in short was, whether Austria was to be allowed to persevere in her usurpations, and to gratify her lust of dominion by another robbery; or whether the liberties of Germany, and the balance of power, were to be maintained against her encroachments. The disputed succession of Juliers, therefore, was matter which interested all who were favourable to liberty, and hostile to Austria. The Evangelical Union, Holland, England, and particularly Henry IV. of France, were drawn into the strife.

This monarch, the flower of whose life had been spent in opposing the House of Austria and Spain, and by persevering heroism alone had surmounted the obstacles which this house had thrown between him and the French throne, had been no idle spectator of the troubles in Germany. This contest of the Estates with the Emperor was the means of giving and securing peace to France. The Protestants and the Turks were the two salutary weights which kept down the Austrian power in the East and West; but it would rise again in all its terrors, if once it were allowed to remove this pressure. Henry the Fourth had before his eyes for half a lifetime, the uninterrupted spectacle of Austrian ambition and Austrian lust of dominion, which neither adversity nor poverty of talents, though generally they check all human passions, could extinguish in a bosom wherein flowed one drop of the blood of Ferdinand of Arragon. Austrian ambition had destroyed for a century the peace of Europe, and effected the most violent changes in the heart of its most considerable states. It had deprived the fields of husbandmen, the workshops of artisans, to fill the land with enormous armies, and to cover the commercial sea with hostile fleets. It had imposed upon the princes of Europe the necessity of fettering the industry of their subjects by unheard-of imposts; and of wasting in self-defence the best strength of their states, which was thus lost to the prosperity of their inhabitants. For Europe there was no peace, for its states no welfare, for the people's happiness no security or permanence, so long as this dangerous house was permitted to disturb at pleasure the repose of the world.

Such considerations clouded the mind of Henry at the close of his glorious career. What had it not cost him to reduce to order the troubled chaos into which France had been plunged by the tumult of civil war, fomented and supported by this very Austria! Every great mind labours for eternity; and what security had Henry for the endurance of that prosperity which he had gained for France, so long as Austria and Spain formed a single power, which did indeed lie exhausted for the present, but which required only one lucky chance to be speedily re-united, and to spring up again as formidable as ever. If he would bequeath to his successors a firmly established throne, and a durable prosperity to his subjects, this dangerous power must be for ever disarmed. This was the source of that irreconcileable enmity which Henry had sworn to the House of Austria, a hatred unextinguishable, ardent, and well-founded as that of Hannibal against the people of Romulus, but ennobled by a purer origin.

The other European powers had the same inducements to action as Henry, but all of them had not that enlightened policy, nor that disinterested courage to act upon the impulse. All men, without distinction, are allured by immediate advantages; great minds alone are excited by distant good. So long as wisdom in its projects calculates upon wisdom, or relies upon its own strength, it forms none but chimerical schemes, and runs a risk of making itself the laughter of the world; but it is certain of success, and may reckon upon aid and admiration when it finds a place in its intellectual plans for barbarism, rapacity, and superstition, and can render the selfish passions of mankind the executors of its purposes.

In the first point of view, Henry's well-known project of expelling the House of Austria from all its possessions, and dividing the spoil among the European powers, deserves the title of a chimera, which men have so liberally bestowed upon it; but did it merit that appellation in the second? It had never entered into the head of that excellent monarch, in the choice of those who must be the instruments of his designs, to reckon on the sufficiency of such motives as animated himself and Sully to the enterprise. All the states whose co-operation was necessary, were to be persuaded to the work by the strongest motives that can set a political power in action. From the Protestants in Germany nothing more was required than that which, on other grounds, had been long their object, — their throwing off the Austrian yoke; from the Flemings, a similar revolt from the Spaniards. To the Pope and all the Italian republics no inducement could be more powerful than the hope of driving the Spaniards for ever from their peninsula; for England, nothing more desirable than a revolution which should free it from its bitterest enemy. By this division of the Austrian conquests, every power gained either land or freedom, new possessions or security for the old; and as all gained, the balance of power remained undisturbed. France might magnanimously decline a share in the spoil, because by the ruin of Austria it doubly profited, and was most powerful if it did not become more powerful. Finally, upon condition of ridding Europe of their presence, the posterity of Hapsburg were to be allowed the liberty of augmenting her territories in all the other known or yet undiscovered portions of the globe. But the dagger of Ravaillac delivered Austria from her danger, to postpone for some centuries longer the tranquillity of Europe.

With his view directed to this project, Henry felt the necessity of taking a prompt and active part in the important events of the Evangelical Union, and the disputed succession of Juliers. His emissaries were busy in all the courts of Germany, and the little which they published or allowed to escape of the great political secrets of their master, was sufficient to win over minds inflamed by so ardent a hatred to Austria, and by so strong a desire of aggrandizement. The prudent policy of Henry cemented the Union still more closely, and the powerful aid which he bound himself to furnish, raised the courage of the confederates into the firmest confidence. A numerous French army, led by the king in person, was to meet the troops of the Union on the banks of the Rhine, and to assist in effecting the conquest of Juliers and Cleves; then, in conjunction with the Germans, it was to march into Italy, (where Savoy, Venice, and the Pope were even now ready with a powerful reinforcement,) and to overthrow the Spanish dominion in that quarter. This victorious army was then to penetrate by Lombardy into the hereditary dominions of Hapsburg; and there, favoured by a general insurrection of the Protestants, destroy the power of Austria in all its German territories, in Bohemia, Hungary, and Transylvania. The Brabanters and Hollanders, supported by French auxiliaries, would in the meantime shake off the Spanish tyranny in the Netherlands; and thus the mighty stream which, only a short time before, had so fearfully overflowed its banks, threatening to overwhelm in its troubled waters the liberties of Europe, would then roll silent and forgotten behind the Pyrenean mountains.

At other times, the French had boasted of their rapidity of action, but upon this occasion they were outstripped by the Germans. An army of the confederates entered Alsace before Henry made his appearance there, and an Austrian army, which the Bishop of Strasburg and Passau had assembled in that quarter for an expedition against Juliers, was dispersed. Henry IV. had formed his plan as a statesman and a king, but he had intrusted its execution to plunderers. According to his design, no Roman Catholic state was to have cause to think this preparation aimed against itself, or to make the quarrel of Austria its own. Religion was in nowise to be mixed up with the matter. But how could the German princes forget their own purposes in furthering the plans of Henry? Actuated as they were by the desire of aggrandizement and by religious hatred, was it to be supposed that they would not gratify, in every passing opportunity, their ruling passions to the utmost? Like vultures, they stooped upon the territories of the ecclesiastical princes, and always chose those rich countries for their quarters, though to reach them they must make ever so wide a detour from their direct route. They levied contributions as in an enemy's country, seized upon the revenues, and exacted, by violence, what they could not obtain of free-will. Not to leave the Roman Catholics in doubt as to the true objects of their expedition, they announced, openly and intelligibly enough, the fate that awaited the property of the church. So little had Henry IV. and the German princes understood each other in their plan of operations, so much had the excellent king been mistaken in his instruments. It is an unfailing maxim, that, if policy enjoins an act of violence, its execution ought never to be entrusted to the violent; and that he only ought to be trusted with the violation of order by whom order is held sacred.

Both the past conduct of the Union, which was condemned even by several of the evangelical states, and the apprehension of even worse treatment, aroused the Roman Catholics to something beyond mere inactive indignation. As to the Emperor, his authority had sunk too low to afford them any security against such an enemy. It was their Union that rendered the confederates so formidable and so insolent; and another union must now be opposed to them.

The Bishop of Wurtzburg formed the plan of the Catholic union, which was distinguished from the evangelical by the title of the League. The objects agreed upon were nearly the same as those which constituted the groundwork of the Union. Bishops formed its principal members, and at its head was placed Maximilian, Duke of Bavaria. As the only influential secular member of the confederacy, he was entrusted with far more extensive powers than the Protestants had committed to their chief. In addition to the duke's being the sole head of the League's military power, whereby their operations acquired a speed and weight unattainable by the Union, they had also the advantage that supplies flowed in much more regularly from the rich prelates, than the latter could obtain them from the poor evangelical states. Without offering to the Emperor, as the sovereign of a Roman Catholic state, any share in their confederacy, without even communicating its existence to him as emperor, the League arose at once formidable and threatening; with strength sufficient to crush the Protestant Union and to maintain itself under three emperors. It contended, indeed, for Austria, in so far as it fought against the Protestant princes; but Austria herself had soon cause to tremble before it.

The arms of the Union had, in the meantime, been tolerably successful in Juliers and in Alsace; Juliers was closely blockaded, and the whole bishopric of Strasburg was in their power. But here their splendid achievements came to an end. No French army appeared upon the Rhine; for he who was to be its leader, he who was the animating soul of the whole enterprize, Henry IV., was no more! Their supplies were on the wane; the Estates refused to grant new subsidies; and the confederate free cities were offended that their money should be liberally, but their advice so sparingly called for. Especially were they displeased at being put to expense for the expedition against Juliers, which had been expressly excluded from the affairs of the Union — at the united princes appropriating to themselves large pensions out of the common treasure — and, above all, at their refusing to give any account of its expenditure.

The Union was thus verging to its fall, at the moment when the League started to oppose it in the vigour of its strength. Want of supplies disabled the confederates from any longer keeping the field. And yet it was dangerous to lay down their weapons in the sight of an armed enemy. To secure themselves at least on one side, they hastened to conclude a peace with their old enemy, the Archduke Leopold; and both parties agreed to withdraw their troops from Alsace, to exchange prisoners, and to bury all that had been done in oblivion. Thus ended in nothing all these promising preparations.

The same imperious tone with which the Union, in the confidence of its strength, had menaced the Roman Catholics of Germany, was now retorted by the League upon themselves and their troops. The traces of their march were pointed out to them, and plainly branded with the hard epithets they had deserved. The chapters of Wurtzburg, Bamberg, Strasburg, Mentz, Treves, Cologne, and several others, had experienced their destructive presence; to all these the damage done was to be made good, the free passage by land and by water restored, (for the Protestants had even seized on the navigation of the Rhine,) and everything replaced on its former footing. Above all, the parties to the Union were called on to declare expressly and unequivocally its intentions. It was now their turn to yield to superior strength. They had not calculated on so formidable an opponent; but they themselves had taught the Roman Catholics the secret of their strength. It was humiliating to their pride to sue for peace, but they might think themselves fortunate in obtaining it. The one party promised restitution, the other forgiveness. All laid down their arms. The storm of war once more rolled by, and a temporary calm succeeded. The insurrection in Bohemia then broke out, which deprived the Emperor of the last of his hereditary dominions, but in this dispute neither the Union nor the League took any share.

At length the Emperor died in 1612, as little regretted in his coffin as noticed on the throne. Long afterwards, when the miseries of succeeding reigns had made the misfortunes of his reign forgotten, a halo spread about his memory, and so fearful a night set in upon Germany, that, with tears of blood, people prayed for the return of such an emperor.

Rodolph never could be prevailed upon to choose a successor in the empire, and all awaited with anxiety the approaching vacancy of the throne; but, beyond all hope, Matthias at once ascended it, and without opposition. The Roman Catholics gave him their voices, because they hoped the best from his vigour and activity; the Protestants gave him theirs, because they hoped every thing from his weakness. It is not difficult to reconcile this contradiction. The one relied on what he had once appeared; the other judged him by what he seemed at present.

The moment of a new accession is always a day of hope; and the first Diet of a king in elective monarchies is usually his severest trial. Every old grievance is brought forward, and new ones are sought out, that they may be included in the expected reform; quite a new world is expected to commence with the new reign. The important services which, in his insurrection, their religious confederates in Austria had rendered to Matthias, were still fresh in the minds of the Protestant free cities, and, above all, the price which they had exacted for their services seemed now to serve them also as a model.

It was by the favour of the Protestant Estates in Austria and Moravia that Matthias had sought and really found the way to his brother's throne; but, hurried on by his ambitious views, he never reflected that a way was thus opened for the States to give laws to their sovereign. This discovery soon awoke him from the intoxication of success. Scarcely had he shown himself in triumph to his Austrian subjects, after his victorious expedition to Bohemia, when a humble petition awaited him which was quite sufficient to poison his whole triumph. They required, before doing homage, unlimited religious toleration in the cities and market towns, perfect equality of rights between Roman Catholics and Protestants, and a full and equal admissibility of the latter to all offices of state. In several places, they of themselves assumed these privileges, and, reckoning on a change of administration, restored the Protestant religion where the late Emperor had suppressed it. Matthias, it is true, had not scrupled to make use of the grievances of the Protestants for his own ends against the Emperor; but it was far from being his intention to relieve them. By a firm and resolute tone he hoped to check, at once, these presumptuous demands. He spoke of his hereditary title to these territories, and would hear of no stipulations before the act of homage. A like unconditional submission had been rendered by their neighbours, the inhabitants of Styria, to the Archduke Ferdinand, who, however, had soon reason to repent of it. Warned by this example, the Austrian States persisted in their refusal; and, to avoid being compelled by force to do homage, their deputies (after urging their Roman Catholic colleagues to a similar resistance) immediately left the capital, and began to levy troops.

They took steps to renew their old alliance with Hungary, drew the Protestant princes into their interests, and set themselves seriously to work to accomplish their object by force of arms.

With the more exorbitant demands of the Hungarians Matthias had not hesitated to comply. For Hungary was an elective monarchy, and the republican constitution of the country justified to himself their demands, and to the Roman Catholic world his concessions. In Austria, on the contrary, his predecessors had exercised far higher prerogatives, which he could not relinquish at the demand of the Estates without incurring the scorn of Roman Catholic Europe, the enmity of Spain and Rome, and the contempt of his own Roman Catholic subjects. His exclusively Romish council, among which the Bishop of Vienna, Melchio Kiesel, had the chief influence, exhorted him to see all the churches extorted from him by the Protestants, rather than to concede one to them as a matter of right.

But by ill luck this difficulty occurred at a time when the Emperor Rodolph was yet alive, and a spectator of this scene, and who might easily have been tempted to employ against his brother the same weapons which the latter had successfully directed against him — namely, an understanding with his rebellious subjects. To avoid this blow, Matthias willingly availed himself of the offer made by Moravia, to act as mediator between him and the Estates of Austria. Representatives of both parties met in Vienna, when the Austrian deputies held language which would have excited surprise even in the English Parliament. "The Protestants," they said, "are determined to be not worse treated in their native country than the handful of Romanists. By the help of his Protestant nobles had Matthias reduced the Emperor to submission; where 80 Papists were to be found, 300 Protestant barons might be counted. The example of Rodolph should be a warning to Matthias. He should take care that he did not lose the terrestrial, in attempting to make conquests for the celestial." As the Moravian States, instead of using their powers as mediators for the Emperor's advantage, finally adopted the cause of their co-religionists of Austria; as the Union in Germany came forward to afford them its most active support, and as Matthias dreaded reprisals on the part of the Emperor, he was at length compelled to make the desired declaration in favour of the Evangelical Church.

This behaviour of the Austrian Estates towards their Archduke was now imitated by the Protestant Estates of the Empire towards their Emperor, and they promised themselves the same favourable results. At his first Diet at Ratisbon in 1613, when the most pressing affairs were waiting for decision — when a general contribution was indispensable for a war against Turkey, and against Bethlem Gabor in Transylvania, who by Turkish aid had forcibly usurped the sovereignty of that land, and even threatened Hungary — they surprised him with an entirely new demand. The Roman Catholic votes were still the most numerous in the Diet; and as every thing was decided by a plurality of voices, the Protestant party, however closely united, were entirely without consideration. The advantage of this majority the Roman Catholics were now called on to relinquish; henceforward no one religious party was to be permitted to dictate to the other by means of its invariable superiority. And in truth, if the evangelical religion was really to be represented in the Diet, it was self-evident that it must not be shut out from the possibility of making use of that privilege, merely from the constitution of the Diet itself. Complaints of the judicial usurpations of the Aulic Council, and of the oppression of the Protestants, accompanied this demand, and the deputies of the Estates were instructed to take no part in any general deliberations till a favourable answer should be given on this preliminary point.

The Diet was torn asunder by this dangerous division, which threatened to destroy for ever the unity of its deliberations. Sincerely as the Emperor might have wished, after the example of his father Maximilian, to preserve a prudent balance between the two religions, the present conduct of the Protestants seemed to leave him nothing but a critical choice between the two. In his present necessities a general contribution from the Estates was indispensable to him; and yet he could not conciliate the one party without sacrificing the support of the other. Insecure as he felt his situation to be in his own hereditary dominions, he could not but tremble at the idea, however remote, of an open war with the Protestants. But the eyes of the whole Roman Catholic world, which were attentively regarding his conduct, the remonstrances of the Roman Catholic Estates, and of the Courts of Rome and Spain, as little permitted him to favour the Protestant at the expense of the Romish religion.

So critical a situation would have paralysed a greater mind than Matthias; and his own prudence would scarcely have extricated him from his dilemma. But the interests of the Roman Catholics were closely interwoven with the imperial authority; if they suffered this to fall, the ecclesiastical princes in particular would be without a bulwark against the attacks of the Protestants. Now, then, that they saw the Emperor wavering, they thought it high time to reassure his sinking courage. They imparted to him the secret of their League, and acquainted him with its whole constitution, resources and power. Little comforting as such a revelation must have been to the Emperor, the prospect of so powerful a support gave him greater boldness to oppose the Protestants. Their demands were rejected, and the Diet broke up without coming to a decision. But Matthias was the victim of this dispute. The Protestants refused him their supplies, and made him alone suffer for the inflexibility of the Roman Catholics.

The Turks, however, appeared willing to prolong the cessation of hostilities, and Bethlem Gabor was left in peaceable possession of Transylvania. The empire was now free from foreign enemies; and even at home, in the midst of all these fearful disputes, peace still reigned. An unexpected accident had given a singular turn to the dispute as to the succession of Juliers. This duchy was still ruled conjointly by the Electoral House of Brandenburg and the Palatine of Neuburg; and a marriage between the Prince of Neuburg and a Princess of Brandenburg was to have inseparably united the interests of the two houses. But the whole scheme was upset by a box on the ear, which, in a drunken brawl, the Elector of Brandenburg unfortunately inflicted upon his intended son-in-law. From this moment the good understanding between the two houses was at an end. The Prince of Neuburg embraced popery. The hand of a princess of Bavaria rewarded his apostacy, and the strong support of Bavaria and Spain was the natural result of both. To secure to the Palatine the exclusive possession of Juliers, the Spanish troops from the Netherlands were marched into the Palatinate. To rid himself of these guests, the Elector of Brandenburg called the Flemings to his assistance, whom he sought to propitiate by embracing the Calvinist religion. Both Spanish and Dutch armies appeared, but, as it seemed, only to make conquests for themselves.

The neighbouring war of the Netherlands seemed now about to be decided on German ground; and what an inexhaustible mine of combustibles lay here ready for it! The Protestants saw with consternation the Spaniards establishing themselves upon the Lower Rhine; with still greater anxiety did the Roman Catholics see the Hollanders bursting through the frontiers of the empire. It was in the west that the mine was expected to explode which had long been dug under the whole of Germany. To the west, apprehension and anxiety turned; but the spark which kindled the flame came unexpectedly from the east.

The tranquillity which Rodolph II.'s 'Letter of Majesty' had established in Bohemia lasted for some time, under the administration of Matthias, till the nomination of a new heir to this kingdom in the person of Ferdinand of Gratz.

This prince, whom we shall afterwards become better acquainted with under the title of Ferdinand II., Emperor of Germany, had, by the violent extirpation of the Protestant religion within his hereditary dominions, announced himself as an inexorable zealot for popery, and was consequently looked upon by the Roman Catholic part of Bohemia as the future pillar of their church. The declining health of the Emperor brought on this hour rapidly; and, relying on so powerful a supporter, the Bohemian Papists began to treat the Protestants with little moderation. The Protestant vassals of Roman Catholic nobles, in particular, experienced the harshest treatment. At length several of the former were incautious enough to speak somewhat loudly of their hopes, and by threatening hints to awaken among the Protestants a suspicion of their future sovereign. But this mistrust would never have broken out into actual violence, had the Roman Catholics confined themselves to general expressions, and not by attacks on individuals furnished the discontent of the people with enterprising leaders.

Henry Matthias, Count Thurn, not a native of Bohemia, but proprietor of some estates in that kingdom, had, by his zeal for the Protestant cause, and an enthusiastic attachment to his newly adopted country, gained the entire confidence of the Utraquists, which opened him the way to the most important posts. He had fought with great glory against the Turks, and won by a flattering address the hearts of the multitude. Of a hot and impetuous disposition, which loved tumult because his talents shone in it — rash and thoughtless enough to undertake things which cold prudence and a calmer temper would not have ventured upon — unscrupulous enough, where the gratification of his passions was concerned, to sport with the fate of thousands, and at the same time politic enough to hold in leading-strings such a people as the Bohemians then were. He had already taken an active part in the troubles under Rodolph's administration; and the Letter of Majesty which the States had extorted from that Emperor, was chiefly to be laid to his merit. The court had intrusted to him, as burgrave or castellan of Calstein, the custody of the Bohemian crown, and of the national charter. But the nation had placed in his hands something far more important — *itself* — with the office of defender or protector of the faith. The aristocracy by which the Emperor was ruled, imprudently deprived him of this harmless guardianship of the dead, to leave him his full influence over the living. They took from him his office of burgrave, or constable of the castle, which had rendered him dependent on the court, thereby opening his eyes to the importance of the other which remained, and wounded his vanity, which yet was the thing that made his ambition harmless. From this moment he was actuated solely by a desire of revenge; and the opportunity of gratifying it was not long wanting.

In the Royal Letter which the Bohemians had extorted from Rodolph II., as well as in the German religious treaty, one material article remained undetermined. All the privileges granted by the latter to the Protestants, were conceived in favour of the Estates or governing bodies, not of the subjects; for only to those of the ecclesiastical states had a toleration, and that precarious, been conceded. The Bohemian Letter of Majesty, in the same manner, spoke only of the Estates and imperial towns, the magistrates of which had contrived to obtain equal privileges with the former. These alone were free to erect churches and schools, and openly to celebrate their Protestant worship; in all other towns, it was left entirely to the government to which they belonged, to determine the religion of the inhabitants. The Estates of the Empire had availed themselves of this privilege in its fullest extent; the secular indeed without opposition; while the ecclesiastical, in whose case the declaration of Ferdinand had limited this privilege, disputed, not without reason, the validity of that limitation. What was a disputed point in the religious treaty, was left still more doubtful in the Letter of Majesty; in the former, the construction was not doubtful, but it was a question how far obedience might be compulsory; in the latter, the interpretation was left to the states. The subjects of the ecclesiastical Estates in Bohemia thought themselves entitled to the same rights which the declaration of Ferdinand secured to the subjects of German bishops, they considered themselves on an equality with the subjects of imperial towns, because they looked upon the ecclesiastical property as part of the royal demesnes. In the little town of Klostergrab, subject to the Archbishop of Prague; and in Braunau, which belonged to the abbot of that monastery, churches were founded by the Protestants, and completed notwithstanding the opposition of their superiors, and the disapprobation of the Emperor.

In the meantime, the vigilance of the defenders had somewhat relaxed, and the court thought it might venture on a decisive step. By the Emperor's orders, the church at Klostergrab was pulled down; that at Braunau forcibly shut up, and the most turbulent of the citizens thrown into prison. A general commotion among the Protestants was the consequence of this measure; a loud outcry was everywhere raised at this violation of the Letter of Majesty; and Count Thurn, animated by revenge, and particularly called upon by his office of defender, showed himself not a little busy in inflaming the minds of the people. At his instigation deputies were summoned to Prague from every circle in the empire, to concert the necessary measures against the common danger. It was resolved to petition the Emperor to press for the liberation of the prisoners. The answer of the Emperor, already offensive to the states, from its being addressed, not to them, but to his viceroy, denounced their conduct as illegal and rebellious, justified what had been done at Klostergrab and Braunau as the result of an imperial mandate, and contained some passages that might be construed into threats.

Count Thurn did not fail to augment the unfavourable impression which this imperial edict made upon the assembled Estates. He pointed out to them the danger in which all who had signed the petition were involved, and sought by working on their resentment and fears to hurry them into violent resolutions. To have caused their immediate revolt against the Emperor, would have been, as yet, too bold a measure. It was only step by step that he would lead them on to this unavoidable result. He held it, therefore, advisable first to direct their indignation against the Emperor's counsellors; and for that purpose circulated a report, that the imperial proclamation had been drawn up by the government at Prague, and only signed in Vienna. Among the imperial delegates, the chief objects of the popular hatred, were the President of the Chamber, Slawata, and Baron Martinitz, who had been elected in place of Count Thurn, Burgrave of Calstein. Both had long before evinced pretty openly their hostile feelings towards the Protestants, by alone refusing to be present at the sitting at which the Letter of Majesty had been inserted in the Bohemian constitution. A threat was made at the time to make them responsible for every violation of the Letter of Majesty; and from this moment, whatever evil befell the Protestants was set down, and not without reason, to their account. Of all the Roman Catholic nobles, these two had treated their Protestant vassals with the greatest harshness. They were accused of hunting them with dogs to the mass, and of endeavouring to drive them to popery by a denial of the rites of baptism, marriage, and burial. Against two characters so unpopular the public indignation was easily excited, and they were marked out for a sacrifice to the general indignation.

On the 23rd of May, 1618, the deputies appeared armed, and in great numbers, at the royal palace, and forced their way into the hall where the Commissioners Sternberg, Martinitz, Lobkowitz, and Slawata were assembled. In a threatening tone they demanded to know from each of them, whether he had taken any part, or had consented to, the imperial proclamation. Sternberg received them with composure, Martinitz and Slawata with defiance. This decided their fate; Sternberg and Lobkowitz, less hated, and more feared, were led by the arm out of the room; Martinitz and Slawata were seized, dragged to a window, and precipitated from a height of eighty feet, into the castle trench. Their creature, the secretary Fabricius, was thrown after them. This singular mode of execution naturally excited the surprise of civilized nations. The Bohemians justified it as a national custom, and saw nothing remarkable in the whole affair, excepting that any one should have got up again safe and sound after such a fall. A dunghill, on which the imperial commissioners chanced to be deposited, had saved them from injury.

It was not to be expected that this summary mode of proceeding would much increase the favour of the parties with the Emperor, but this was the very position to which Count Thurn wished to bring them. If, from the fear of uncertain danger, they had permitted themselves such an act of violence, the certain expectation of punishment, and the now urgent necessity of making themselves secure, would plunge them still deeper into guilt. By this brutal act of self-redress, no room was left for irresolution or repentance, and it seemed as if a single crime could be absolved only by a series of violences. As the deed itself could not be undone, nothing was left but to disarm the hand of punishment. Thirty directors were appointed to organise a regular insurrection. They seized upon all the offices of state, and all the imperial revenues, took into their own service the royal functionaries and the soldiers, and summoned the whole Bohemian nation to avenge the common cause. The Jesuits, whom the common hatred accused as the instigators of every previous oppression, were banished the kingdom, and this harsh measure the Estates found it necessary to justify in a formal manifesto. These various steps were taken for the preservation of the royal authority and the laws — the language of all rebels till fortune has decided in their favour.

The emotion which the news of the Bohemian insurrection excited at the imperial court, was much less lively than such intelligence deserved. The Emperor Matthias was no longer the resolute spirit that formerly sought out his king and master in the very bosom of his people, and hurled him from three thrones. The confidence and courage which had animated him in an usurpation, deserted him in a legitimate self-defence. The Bohemian rebels had first taken up arms, and the nature of circumstances drove him to join them. But he could not hope to confine such a war to Bohemia. In all the territories under his dominion, the Protestants were united by a dangerous sympathy — the common danger of their religion might suddenly combine them all into a formidable republic. What could he oppose to such an enemy, if the Protestant portion of his subjects deserted him? And would not both parties exhaust themselves in so ruinous a civil war? How much was at stake if he lost; and if he won, whom else would he destroy but his own subjects?

Considerations such as these inclined the Emperor and his council to concessions and pacific measures, but it was in this very spirit of concession that, as others would have it, lay the origin of the evil. The Archduke Ferdinand of Gratz congratulated the Emperor upon an event, which would justify in the eyes of all Europe the severest measures against the Bohemian Protestants. "Disobedience, lawlessness, and insurrection," he said, "went always hand-in-hand with Protestantism. Every privilege which had been conceded to the Estates by himself and his predecessor, had had no other effect than to raise their demands. All the measures of the heretics were aimed against the imperial authority. Step by step had they advanced from defiance to defiance up to this last aggression; in a short time they would assail all that remained to be assailed, in the person of the Emperor. In arms alone was there any safety against such an enemy — peace and subordination could be only established upon the ruins of their dangerous privileges; security for the Catholic belief was to be found only in the total destruction of this sect. Uncertain, it was true, might be the event of the war, but inevitable was the ruin if it were pretermitted. The confiscation of the lands of the rebels would richly indemnify them for its expenses, while the terror of punishment would teach the other states the wisdom of a prompt obedience in future." Were the Bohemian Protestants to blame, if they armed themselves in time against the enforcement of such maxims? The insurrection in Bohemia, besides, was directed only against the successor of the Emperor, not against himself, who had done nothing to justify the alarm of the Protestants. To exclude this prince from the Bohemian throne, arms had before been taken up under Matthias, though as long as this Emperor lived, his subjects had kept within the bounds of an apparent submission.

But Bohemia was in arms, and unarmed, the Emperor dared not even offer them peace. For this purpose, Spain supplied gold, and promised to send troops from Italy and the Netherlands. Count Bucquoi, a native of the Netherlands, was named generalissimo, because no native could be trusted, and Count Dampierre, another foreigner, commanded under him. Before the army took the field, the Emperor endeavoured to bring about an amicable arrangement, by the publication of a manifesto. In this he assured the Bohemians, "that he held sacred the Letter of Majesty — that he had not formed any resolutions inimical to their religion or their privileges, and that his present preparations were forced upon him by their own. As soon as the nation laid down their arms, he also would disband his army." But this gracious letter failed of its effect, because the leaders of the insurrection contrived to hide from the people the Emperor's good intentions. Instead of this, they circulated the most alarming reports from the pulpit, and by pamphlets, and terrified the deluded populace with threatened horrors of another Saint Bartholomew's that existed only in their own imagination. All Bohemia, with the exception of three towns, Budweiss, Krummau, and Pilsen, took part in this insurrection. These three towns, inhabited principally by Roman Catholics, alone had the courage, in this general revolt, to hold out for the Emperor, who promised them assistance. But it could not escape Count Thurn, how dangerous it was to leave in hostile hands three places of such importance, which would at all times keep open for the imperial troops an entrance into the kingdom. With prompt determination he appeared before Budweiss and Krummau, in the hope of terrifying them into a surrender. Krummau surrendered, but all his attacks were steadfastly repulsed by Budweiss.

And now, too, the Emperor began to show more earnestness and energy. Bucquoi and Dampierre, with two armies, fell upon the Bohemian territories, which they treated as a hostile country. But the imperial generals found the march to Prague more difficult than they had expected. Every pass, every position that was the least tenable, must be opened by the sword, and resistance increased at each fresh step they took, for the outrages of their troops, chiefly consisting of Hungarians and Walloons, drove their friends to revolt and their enemies to despair. But even now that his troops had penetrated into Bohemia, the Emperor continued to offer the Estates peace, and to show himself ready for an amicable adjustment. But the new prospects which opened upon them, raised the courage of the revolters. Moravia espoused their party; and from Germany appeared to them a defender equally intrepid and unexpected, in the person of Count Mansfeld.

The heads of the Evangelic Union had been silent but not inactive spectators of the movements in Bohemia. Both were contending for the same cause, and against the same enemy. In the fate of the Bohemians, their confederates in the faith might read their own; and the cause of this people was represented as of solemn concern to the whole German union. True to these principles, the Unionists supported the courage of the insurgents by promises of assistance; and a fortunate accident now enabled them, beyond their hopes, to fulfil them.

The instrument by which the House of Austria was humbled in Germany, was Peter Ernest, Count Mansfeld, the son of a distinguished Austrian officer, Ernest von Mansfeld, who for some time had commanded with repute the Spanish army in the Netherlands. His first campaigns in Juliers and Alsace had been made in the service of this house, and under the banner of the Archduke Leopold, against the Protestant religion and the liberties of Germany. But insensibly won by the principles of this religion, he abandoned a leader whose selfishness denied him the reimbursement of the monies expended in his cause, and he transferred his zeal and a victorious sword to the Evangelic Union. It happened just then that the Duke of Savoy, an ally of the Union, demanded assistance in a war against Spain. They assigned to him their newly acquired servant, and Mansfeld received instructions to raise an army of 4000 men in Germany, in the cause and in the pay of the duke. The army was ready to march at the very moment when the flames of war burst out in Bohemia, and the duke, who at the time did not stand in need of its services, placed it at the disposal of the Union. Nothing could be more welcome to these troops than the prospect of aiding their confederates in Bohemia, at the cost of a third party. Mansfeld received orders forthwith to march with these 4000 men into that kingdom; and a pretended Bohemian commission was given to blind the public as to the true author of this levy.

This Mansfeld now appeared in Bohemia, and, by the occupation of Pilsen, strongly fortified and favourable to the Emperor, obtained a firm footing in the country. The courage of the rebels was farther increased by succours which the Silesian States despatched to their assistance. Between these and the Imperialists, several battles were fought, far indeed from decisive, but only on that account the more destructive, which served as the prelude to a more serious war. To check the vigour of his military operations, a negotiation was entered into with the Emperor, and a disposition was shown to accept the proffered mediation of Saxony. But before the event could prove how little sincerity there was in these proposals, the Emperor was removed from the scene by death.

What now had Matthias done to justify the expectations which he had excited by the overthrow of his predecessor? Was it worth while to ascend a brother's throne through guilt, and then maintain it with so little dignity, and leave it with so little renown? As long as Matthias sat on the throne, he had to atone for the imprudence by which he had gained it. To enjoy the regal dignity a few years sooner, he had shackled the free exercise of its prerogatives. The slender portion of independence left him by the growing power of the Estates, was still farther lessened by the encroachments of his relations. Sickly and childless he saw the attention of the world turned to an ambitious heir who was impatiently anticipating his fate; and who, by his interference with the closing administration, was already opening his own.

With Matthias, the reigning line of the German House of Austria was in a manner extinct; for of all the sons of Maximilian, one only was now alive, the weak and childless Archduke Albert, in the Netherlands, who had already renounced his claims to the inheritance in favour of the line of Gratz. The Spanish House had also, in a secret bond, resigned its pretensions to the Austrian possessions in behalf of the Archduke Ferdinand of Styria, in whom the branch of Hapsburg was about to put forth new shoots, and the former greatness of Austria to experience a revival.

The father of Ferdinand was the Archduke Charles of Carniola, Carinthia, and Styria, the youngest brother of the Emperor Maximilian II.; his mother a princess of Bavaria. Having lost his father at twelve years of age, he was intrusted by the archduchess to the guardianship of her brother William, Duke of Bavaria, under whose eyes he was instructed and educated by Jesuits at the Academy of Ingolstadt. What principles he was likely to imbibe by his intercourse with a prince, who from motives of devotion had abdicated his government, may be easily conceived. Care was taken to point out to him, on the one hand, the weak indulgence of Maximilian's house towards the adherents of the new doctrines, and the consequent troubles of their dominions; on the other, the blessings of Bavaria, and the inflexible religious zeal of its rulers; between these two examples he was left to choose for himself.

Formed in this school to be a stout champion of the faith, and a prompt instrument of the church, he left Bavaria, after a residence of five years, to assume the government of his hereditary dominions. The Estates of Carniola, Carinthia, and Styria, who, before doing homage, demanded a guarantee for freedom of religion, were told that religious liberty has nothing to do with their allegiance. The oath was put to them without conditions, and unconditionally taken. Many years, however, elapsed, ere the designs which had been planned at Ingolstadt were ripe for execution. Before attempting to carry them into effect, he sought in person at Loretto the favour of the Virgin, and received the apostolic benediction in Rome at the feet of Clement VIII.

These designs were nothing less than the expulsion of Protestantism from a country where it had the advantage of numbers, and had been legally recognized by a formal act of toleration, granted by his father to the noble and knightly estates of the land. A grant so formally ratified could not be revoked without danger; but no difficulties could deter the pious pupil of the Jesuits. The example of other states, both Roman Catholic and Protestant, which within their own territories had exercised unquestioned a right of reformation, and the abuse which the Estates of Styria made of their religious liberties, would serve as a justification of this violent procedure. Under the shelter of an absurd positive law, those of equity and prudence might, it was thought, be safely despised. In the execution of these unrighteous designs, Ferdinand did, it must be owned, display no common courage and perseverance. Without tumult, and we may add, without cruelty, he suppressed the Protestant service in one town after another, and in a few years, to the astonishment of Germany, this dangerous work was brought to a successful end.

But, while the Roman Catholics admired him as a hero, and the champion of the church, the Protestants began to combine against him as against their most dangerous enemy. And yet Matthias's intention to bequeath to him the succession, met with little or no opposition in the elective states of Austria. Even the Bohemians agreed to receive him as their future king, on very favourable conditions. It was not until afterwards, when they had experienced the pernicious influence of his councils on the administration of the Emperor, that their anxiety was first excited; and then several projects, in his handwriting, which an unlucky chance threw into their hands, as they plainly evinced his disposition towards them, carried their apprehension to the utmost pitch. In particular, they were alarmed by a secret family compact with Spain, by which, in default of heirs-male of his own body, Ferdinand bequeathed to that crown the kingdom of Bohemia, without first consulting the wishes of that nation, and without regard to its right of free election. The many enemies, too, which by his reforms in Styria that prince had provoked among the Protestants, were very prejudicial to his interests in Bohemia; and some Styrian emigrants, who had taken refuge there, bringing with them into their adopted country hearts overflowing with a desire of revenge, were particularly active in exciting the flame of revolt. Thus ill-affected did Ferdinand find the Bohemians, when he succeeded Matthias.

So bad an understanding between the nation and the candidate for the throne, would have raised a storm even in the most peaceable succession; how much more so at the present moment, before the ardour of insurrection had cooled; when the nation had just recovered its dignity, and reasserted its rights; when they still held arms in their hands, and the consciousness of unity had awakened an enthusiastic reliance on their own strength; when by past success, by the promises of foreign assistance, and by visionary expectations of the future, their courage had been raised to an undoubting confidence. Disregarding the rights already conferred on Ferdinand, the Estates declared the throne vacant, and their right of election entirely unfettered. All hopes of their peaceful submission were at an end, and if Ferdinand wished still to wear the crown of Bohemia, he must choose between purchasing it at the sacrifice of all that would make a crown desirable, or winning it sword in hand.

But with what means was it to be won? Turn his eyes where he would, the fire of revolt was burning. Silesia had already joined the insurgents in Bohemia; Moravia was on the point of following its example. In Upper and Lower Austria the spirit of liberty was awake, as it had been under Rodolph, and the Estates refused to do homage. Hungary was menaced with an inroad by Prince Bethlen Gabor, on the side of Transylvania; a secret arming among the Turks spread consternation among the provinces to the eastward; and, to complete his perplexities, the Protestants also, in his hereditary dominions, stimulated by the general example, were again raising their heads. In that quarter, their numbers were overwhelming; in most places they had possession of the revenues which Ferdinand would need for the maintenance of the war. The neutral began to waver, the faithful to be discouraged, the turbulent alone to be animated and confident. One half of Germany encouraged the rebels, the other inactively awaited the issue; Spanish assistance was still very remote. The moment which had brought him every thing, threatened also to deprive him of all.

And when he now, yielding to the stern law of necessity, made overtures to the Bohemian rebels, all his proposals for peace were insolently rejected. Count Thurn, at the head of an army, entered Moravia to bring this province, which alone continued to waver, to a decision. The appearance of their friends is the signal of revolt for the Moravian Protestants. Bruenn is taken, the remainder of the country yields with free will, throughout the province government and religion are changed. Swelling as it flows, the torrent of rebellion pours down upon Austria, where a party, holding similar sentiments, receives it with a joyful concurrence. Henceforth, there should be no more distinctions of religion; equality of rights should be guaranteed to all Christian churches. They hear that a foreign force has been invited into the country to oppress the Bohemians. Let them be sought out, and the enemies of liberty pursued to the ends of the earth. Not an arm is raised in defence of the Archduke, and the rebels, at length, encamp before Vienna to besiege their sovereign.

Ferdinand had sent his children from Gratz, where they were no longer safe, to the Tyrol; he himself awaited the insurgents in his capital. A handful of soldiers was all he could oppose to the enraged multitude; these few were without pay or provisions, and therefore little to be depended on. Vienna was unprepared for a long siege. The party of the Protestants, ready at any moment to join the Bohemians, had the preponderance in the city; those in the country had already begun to levy troops against him. Already, in imagination, the Protestant populace saw the Emperor shut up in a monastery, his territories divided, and his children educated as Protestants. Confiding in secret, and surrounded by public enemies, he saw the chasm every moment widening to engulf his hopes and even himself. The Bohemian bullets were already falling upon the imperial palace, when sixteen Austrian barons forcibly entered his chamber, and inveighing against him with loud and bitter reproaches, endeavoured to force him into a confederation with the Bohemians. One of them, seizing him by the button of his doublet, demanded, in a tone of menace, "Ferdinand, wilt thou sign it?"

Who would not be pardoned had he wavered in this frightful situation? Yet Ferdinand still remembered the dignity of a Roman emperor. No alternative seemed left to him but an immediate flight or submission; laymen urged him to the one, priests to the other. If he abandoned the city, it would fall into the enemy's hands; with Vienna, Austria was lost; with Austria, the imperial throne. Ferdinand abandoned not his capital, and as little would he hear of conditions.

The Archduke is still engaged in altercation with the deputed barons, when all at once a sound of trumpets is heard in the palace square. Terror and astonishment take possession of all present; a fearful report pervades the palace; one deputy after another disappears. Many of the nobility and the citizens hastily take refuge in the camp of Thurn. This sudden change is effected by a regiment of Dampierre's cuirassiers, who at that moment marched into the city to defend the Archduke. A body of infantry soon followed; reassured by their appearance, several of the Roman Catholic citizens, and even the students themselves, take up arms. A report which arrived just at the same time from Bohemia made his deliverance complete. The Flemish general, Bucquoi, had totally defeated Count Mansfeld at Budweiss, and was marching upon Prague. The Bohemians hastily broke up their camp before Vienna to protect their own capital.

And now also the passes were free which the enemy had taken possession of, in order to obstruct Ferdinand's progress to his coronation at Frankfort. If the accession to the imperial throne was important for the plans of the King of Hungary, it was of still greater consequence at the present moment, when his nomination as Emperor would afford the most unsuspicious and decisive proof of the dignity of his person, and of the justice of his cause, while, at the same time, it would give him a hope of support from the Empire. But the same cabal which opposed him in his hereditary dominions, laboured also to counteract him in his canvass for the imperial dignity. No Austrian prince, they maintained, ought to ascend the throne; least of all Ferdinand, the bigoted persecutor of their religion, the slave of Spain and of the Jesuits. To prevent this, the crown had been offered, even during the lifetime of Matthias, to the Duke of Bavaria, and on his refusal, to the Duke of Savoy. As some difficulty was experienced in settling with the latter the conditions of acceptance, it was sought, at all events, to delay the election till some decisive blow in Austria or Bohemia should annihilate all the hopes of Ferdinand, and incapacitate him from any competition for this dignity. The members of the Union left no stone unturned to gain over from Ferdinand the Electorate of Saxony, which was bound to Austrian interests; they represented to this court the dangers with which the Protestant religion, and even the constitution of the empire, were threatened by the principles of this prince and his Spanish alliance. By the elevation of Ferdinand to the imperial throne, Germany, they further asserted, would be involved in the private quarrels of this prince, and bring upon itself the arms of Bohemia. But in spite of all opposing influences, the day of election was fixed, Ferdinand summoned to it as lawful king of Bohemia, and his electoral vote, after a fruitless resistance on the part of the Bohemian Estates, acknowledged to be good. The votes of the three ecclesiastical electorates were for him, Saxony was favourable to him, Brandenburg made no opposition, and a decided majority declared him Emperor in 1619. Thus he saw the most doubtful of his crowns placed first of all on his head; but a few days after he lost that which he had reckoned among the most certain of his possessions. While he was thus elected Emperor in Frankfort, he was in Prague deprived of the Bohemian throne.

Almost all of his German hereditary dominions had in the meantime entered into a formidable league with the Bohemians, whose insolence now exceeded all bounds. In a general Diet, the latter, on the 17th of August, 1619, proclaimed the Emperor an enemy to the Bohemian religion and liberties, who by his pernicious counsels had alienated from them the affections of the late Emperor, had furnished troops to oppress them, had given their country as a prey to foreigners, and finally, in contravention of the national rights, had bequeathed the crown, by a secret compact, to Spain: they therefore declared that he had forfeited whatever title he might otherwise have had to the crown, and immediately proceeded to a new election. As this sentence was pronounced by Protestants, their choice could not well fall upon a Roman Catholic prince, though, to save appearances, some voices were raised for Bavaria and Savoy. But the violent religious animosities which divided the evangelical and the reformed parties among the Protestants, impeded for some time the election even of a Protestant king; till at last the address and activity of the Calvinists carried the day from the numerical superiority of the Lutherans.

Among all the princes who were competitors for this dignity, the Elector Palatine Frederick V. had the best grounded claims on the confidence and gratitude of the Bohemians; and among them all, there was no one in whose case the private interests of particular Estates, and the attachment of the people, seemed to be justified by so many considerations of state. Frederick V. was of a free and lively spirit, of great goodness of heart, and regal liberality. He was the head of the Calvinistic party in Germany, the leader of the Union, whose resources were at his disposal, a near relation of the Duke of Bavaria, and a son-in-law of the King of Great Britain, who might lend him his powerful support. All these considerations were prominently and successfully brought forward by the Calvinists, and Frederick V. was chosen king by the Assembly at Prague, amidst prayers and tears of joy.

The whole proceedings of the Diet at Prague had been premeditated, and Frederick himself had taken too active a share in the matter to feel at all surprised at the offer made to him by the Bohemians. But now the immediate glitter of this throne dazzled him, and the magnitude both of his elevation and his delinquency made his weak mind to tremble. After the usual manner of pusillanimous spirits, he sought to confirm himself in his purpose by the opinions of others; but these opinions had no weight with him when they ran counter to his own cherished wishes. Saxony and Bavaria, of whom he sought advice, all his brother electors, all who compared the magnitude of the design with his capacities and resources, warned him of the danger into which he was about to rush. Even King James of England preferred to see his son-in-law deprived of this crown, than that the sacred majesty of kings should be outraged by so dangerous a precedent. But of what avail was the voice of prudence against the seductive glitter of a crown? In the moment of boldest determination, when they are indignantly rejecting the consecrated branch of a race which had governed them for two centuries, a free people throws itself into his arms. Confiding in his courage, they choose him as their leader in the dangerous career of glory and liberty. To him, as to its born champion, an oppressed religion looks for shelter and support against its persecutors. Could he have the weakness to listen to his fears, and to betray the cause of religion and liberty? This religion proclaims to him its own preponderance, and the weakness of its rival, — two-thirds of the power of Austria are now in arms against Austria itself, while a formidable confederacy, already formed in Transylvania, would, by a hostile attack, further distract even the weak remnant of its power. Could inducements such as these fail to awaken his ambition, or such hopes to animate and inflame his resolution?

A few moments of calm consideration would have sufficed to show the danger of the undertaking, and the comparative worthlessness of the prize. But the temptation spoke to his feelings; the warning only to his reason. It was his misfortune that his nearest and most influential counsellors espoused the side of his passions. The aggrandizement of their master's power opened to the ambition and avarice of his Palatine servants an unlimited field for their gratification; this anticipated triumph of their church kindled the ardour of the Calvinistic fanatic. Could a mind so weak as that of Ferdinand resist the delusions of his counsellors, who exaggerated his resources and his strength, as much as they underrated those of his enemies; or the exhortations of his preachers, who announced the effusions of their fanatical zeal as the immediate inspiration of heaven? The dreams of astrology filled his mind with visionary hopes; even love conspired, with its irresistible fascination, to complete the seduction. "Had you," demanded the Electress, "confidence enough in yourself to accept the hand of a king's daughter, and have you misgivings about taking a crown which is voluntarily offered you? I would rather eat bread at thy kingly table, than feast at thy electoral board."

Frederick accepted the Bohemian crown. The coronation was celebrated with unexampled pomp at Prague, for the nation displayed all its riches in honour of its own work. Silesia and Moravia, the adjoining provinces to Bohemia, followed their example, and did homage to Frederick. The reformed faith was enthroned in all the churches of the kingdom; the rejoicings were unbounded, their attachment to their new king bordered on adoration. Denmark and Sweden, Holland and Venice, and several of the Dutch states, acknowledged him as lawful sovereign, and Frederick now prepared to maintain his new acquisition.

His principal hopes rested on Prince Bethlen Gabor of Transylvania. This formidable enemy of Austria, and of the Roman Catholic church, not content with the principality which, with the assistance of the Turks, he had wrested from his legitimate prince, Gabriel Bathori, gladly seized this opportunity of aggrandizing himself at the expense of Austria, which had hesitated to acknowledge him as sovereign of Transylvania. An attack upon Hungary and Austria was concerted with the Bohemian rebels, and both armies were to unite before the capital. Meantime, Bethlen Gabor, under the mask of friendship, disguised the true object of his warlike preparations, artfully promising the Emperor to lure the Bohemians into the toils, by a pretended offer of assistance, and to deliver up to him alive the leaders of the insurrection. All at once, however, he appeared in a hostile attitude in Upper Hungary. Before him went terror, and devastation behind; all opposition yielded, and at Presburg he received the Hungarian crown. The Emperor's brother, who governed in Vienna, trembled for the capital. He hastily summoned General Bucquoi to his assistance, and the retreat of the Imperialists drew the Bohemians, a second time, before the walls of Vienna. Reinforced by twelve thousand Transylvanians, and soon after joined by the victorious army of Bethlen Gabor, they again menaced the capital with assault; all the country round Vienna was laid waste, the navigation of the Danube closed, all supplies cut off, and the horrors of famine were threatened. Ferdinand, hastily recalled to his capital by this urgent danger, saw himself a second time on the brink of ruin. But want of provisions, and the inclement weather, finally compelled the Bohemians to go into quarters, a defeat in Hungary recalled Bethlen Gabor, and thus once more had fortune rescued the Emperor.

In a few weeks the scene was changed, and by his prudence and activity Ferdinand improved his position as rapidly as Frederick, by indolence and impolicy, ruined his. The Estates of Lower Austria were regained to their allegiance by a confirmation of their privileges; and the few who still held out were declared guilty of 'lese-majeste' and high treason. During the election of Frankfort, he had contrived, by personal representations, to win over to his cause the ecclesiastical electors, and also Maximilian, Duke of Bavaria, at Munich. The whole issue of the war, the fate of Frederick and the Emperor, were now dependent on the part which the Union and the League should take in the troubles of Bohemia. It was evidently of importance to all the Protestants of Germany that the King of Bohemia should be supported, while it was equally the interest of the Roman Catholics to prevent the ruin of the Emperor. If the Protestants succeeded in Bohemia, all the Roman Catholic princes in Germany might tremble for their possessions; if they failed, the Emperor would give laws to Protestant Germany. Thus Ferdinand put the League, Frederick the Union, in motion. The ties of relationship and a personal attachment to the Emperor, his brother-in-law, with whom he had been educated at Ingolstadt, zeal for the Roman Catholic religion, which seemed to be in the most imminent peril, and the suggestions of the Jesuits, combined with the suspicious movements of the Union, moved the Duke of Bavaria, and all the princes of the League, to make the cause of Ferdinand their own.

According to the terms of a treaty with the Emperor, which assured to the Duke of Bavaria compensation for all the expenses of the war, or the losses he might sustain, Maximilian took, with full powers, the command of the troops of the League, which were ordered to march to the assistance of the Emperor against the Bohemian rebels. The leaders of the Union, instead of delaying by every means this dangerous coalition of the League with the Emperor, did every thing in their power to accelerate it. Could they, they thought, but once drive the Roman Catholic League to take an open part in the Bohemian war, they might reckon on similar measures from all the members and allies of the Union. Without some open step taken by the Roman Catholics against the Union, no effectual confederacy of the Protestant powers was to be looked for. They seized, therefore, the present emergency of the troubles in Bohemia to demand from the Roman Catholics the abolition of their past grievances, and full security for the future exercise of their religion. They addressed this demand, which was moreover couched in threatening language, to the Duke of Bavaria, as the head of the Roman Catholics, and they insisted on an immediate and categorical answer. Maximilian might decide for or against them, still their point was gained; his concession, if he yielded, would deprive the Roman Catholic party of its most powerful protector; his refusal would arm the whole Protestant party, and render inevitable a war in which they hoped to be the conquerors. Maximilian, firmly attached to the opposite party from so many other considerations, took the demands of the Union as a formal declaration of hostilities, and quickened his preparations. While Bavaria and the League were thus arming in the Emperor's cause, negotiations for a subsidy were opened with the Spanish court. All the difficulties with which the indolent policy of that ministry met this demand were happily surmounted by the imperial ambassador at Madrid, Count Khevenhuller. In addition to a subsidy of a million of florins, which from time to time were doled out by this court, an attack upon the Lower Palatinate, from the side of the Spanish Netherlands, was at the same time agreed upon.

During these attempts to draw all the Roman Catholic powers into the League, every exertion was made against the counter-league of the Protestants. To this end, it was important to alarm the Elector of Saxony and the other Evangelical powers, and accordingly the Union were diligent in propagating a rumour that the preparations of the League had for their object to deprive them of the ecclesiastical foundations they had secularized. A written assurance to the contrary calmed the fears of the Duke of Saxony, whom moreover private jealousy of the Palatine, and the insinuations of his chaplain, who was in the pay of Austria, and mortification at having been passed over by the Bohemians in the election to the throne, strongly inclined to the side of Austria. The fanaticism of the Lutherans could never forgive the reformed party for having drawn, as they expressed it, so many fair provinces into the gulf of Calvinism, and rejecting the Roman Antichrist only to make way for an Helvetian one.

While Ferdinand used every effort to improve the unfavourable situation of his affairs, Frederick was daily injuring his good cause. By his close and questionable connexion with the Prince of Transylvania, the open ally of the Porte, he gave offence to weak minds; and a general rumour accused him of furthering his own ambition at the expense of Christendom, and arming the Turks against Germany. His inconsiderate zeal for the Calvinistic scheme irritated the Lutherans of Bohemia, his attacks on image-worship incensed the Papists of this kingdom against him. New and oppressive imposts alienated the affections of all his subjects. The disappointed hopes of the Bohemian nobles cooled their zeal; the absence of foreign succours abated their confidence. Instead of devoting himself with untiring energies to the affairs of his kingdom, Frederick wasted his time in amusements; instead of filling his treasury by a wise economy, he squandered his revenues by a needless theatrical pomp, and a misplaced munificence. With a light-minded carelessness, he did but gaze at himself in his new dignity, and in the ill-timed desire to enjoy his crown, he forgot the more pressing duty of securing it on his head.

But greatly as men had erred in their opinion of him, Frederick himself had not less miscalculated his foreign resources. Most of the members of the Union considered the affairs of Bohemia as foreign to the real object of their confederacy; others, who were devoted to him, were overawed by fear of the Emperor. Saxony and Hesse Darmstadt had already been gained over by Ferdinand; Lower Austria, on which side a powerful diversion had been looked for, had made its submission to the Emperor; and Bethlen Gabor had concluded a truce with him. By its embassies, the court of Vienna had induced Denmark to remain inactive, and to occupy Sweden in a war with the Poles. The republic of Holland had enough to do to defend itself against the arms of the Spaniards; Venice and Saxony remained inactive; King James of England was overreached by the artifice of Spain. One friend after another withdrew; one hope vanished after another — so rapidly in a few months was every thing changed.

In the mean time, the leaders of the Union assembled an army; — the Emperor and the League did the same. The troops of the latter were assembled under the banners of Maximilian at Donauwerth, those of the Union at Ulm, under the Margrave of Anspach. The decisive moment seemed at length to have arrived which was to end these long dissensions by a vigorous blow, and irrevocably to settle the relation of the two churches in Germany. Anxiously on the stretch was the expectation of both parties. How great then was their astonishment when suddenly the intelligence of peace arrived, and both armies separated without striking a blow!

The intervention of France effected this peace, which was equally acceptable to both parties. The French cabinet, no longer swayed by the counsels of Henry the Great, and whose maxims of state were perhaps not applicable to the present condition of that kingdom, was now far less alarmed at the preponderance of Austria, than of the increase which would accrue to the strength of the Calvinists, if the Palatine house should be able to retain the throne of Bohemia. Involved at the time in a dangerous conflict with its own Calvinistic subjects, it was of the utmost importance to France that the Protestant faction in Bohemia should be suppressed before the Huguenots could copy their dangerous example. In order therefore to facilitate the Emperor's operations against the Bohemians, she offered her mediation to the Union and the League, and effected this unexpected treaty, of which the main article was, "That the Union should abandon all interference in the affairs of Bohemia, and confine the aid which they might afford to Frederick the Fifth, to his Palatine territories." To this disgraceful treaty, the Union were moved by the firmness of Maximilian, and the fear of being pressed at once by the troops of the League, and a new Imperial army which was on its march from the Netherlands.

The whole force of Bavaria and the League was now at the disposal of the Emperor to be employed against the Bohemians, who by the pacification of Ulm were abandoned to their fate. With a rapid movement, and before a rumour of the proceedings at Ulm could reach there, Maximilian appeared in Upper Austria, when the Estates, surprised and unprepared for an enemy, purchased the Emperor's pardon by an immediate and unconditional submission. In Lower Austria, the duke formed a junction with the troops from the Low Countries under Bucquoi, and without loss of time the united Imperial and Bavarian forces, amounting to 50,000 men, entered Bohemia. All the Bohemian troops, which were dispersed over Lower Austria and Moravia, were driven before them; every town which attempted resistance was quickly taken by storm; others, terrified by the report of the punishment inflicted on these, voluntarily opened their gates; nothing in short interrupted the impetuous career of Maximilian. The Bohemian army, commanded by the brave Prince Christian of Anhalt, retreated to the neighbourhood of Prague; where, under the walls of the city, Maximilian offered him battle.

The wretched condition in which he hoped to surprise the insurgents, justified the rapidity of the duke's movements, and secured him the victory. Frederick's army did not amount to 30,000 men. Eight thousand of these were furnished by the Prince of Anhalt; 10,000 were Hungarians, whom Bethlen Gabor had despatched to his assistance. An inroad of the Elector of Saxony upon Lusatia, had cut off all succours from that country, and from Silesia; the pacification of Austria put an end to all his expectations from that quarter; Bethlen Gabor, his most powerful ally, remained inactive in Transylvania; the Union had betrayed his cause to the Emperor. Nothing remained to him but his Bohemians; and they were without goodwill to his cause, and without unity and courage. The Bohemian magnates were indignant that German generals should be put over their heads; Count Mansfeld remained in Pilsen, at a distance from the camp, to avoid the mortification of serving under Anhalt and Hohenlohe. The soldiers, in want of necessaries, became dispirited; and the little discipline that was observed, gave occasion to bitter complaints from the peasantry. It was in vain that Frederick made his appearance in the camp, in the hope of reviving the courage of the soldiers by his presence, and of kindling the emulation of the nobles by his example.

The Bohemians had begun to entrench themselves on the White Mountain near Prague, when they were attacked by the Imperial and Bavarian armies, on the 8th November, 1620. In the beginning of the action, some advantages were gained by the cavalry of the Prince of Anhalt; but the superior numbers of the enemy soon neutralized them. The charge of the Bavarians and Walloons was irresistible. The Hungarian cavalry was the first to retreat. The Bohemian infantry soon followed their example; and the Germans were at last carried along with them in the general flight. Ten cannons, composing the whole of Frederick's artillery, were taken by the enemy; four thousand Bohemians fell in the flight and on the field; while of the Imperialists and soldiers of the League only a few hundred were killed. In less than an hour this decisive action was over.

Frederick was seated at table in Prague, while his army was thus cut to pieces. It is probable that he had not expected the attack on this day, since he had ordered an entertainment for it. A messenger summoned him from table, to show him from the walls the whole frightful scene. He requested a cessation of hostilities for twenty-four hours for deliberation; but eight was all the Duke of Bavaria would allow him. Frederick availed himself of these to fly by night from the capital, with his wife, and the chief officers of his army. This flight was so hurried, that the Prince of Anhalt left behind him his most private papers, and Frederick his crown. "I know now what I am," said this unfortunate prince to those who endeavoured to comfort him; "there are virtues which misfortune only can teach us, and it is in adversity alone that princes learn to know themselves."

Prague was not irretrievably lost when Frederick's pusillanimity abandoned it. The light troops of Mansfeld were still in Pilsen, and were not engaged in the action. Bethlen Gabor might at any moment have assumed an offensive attitude, and drawn off the Emperor's army to the Hungarian frontier. The defeated Bohemians might rally. Sickness, famine, and the inclement weather, might wear out the enemy; but all these hopes disappeared before the immediate alarm. Frederick dreaded the fickleness of the Bohemians, who might probably yield to the temptation to purchase, by the surrender of his person, the pardon of the Emperor.

Thurn, and those of this party who were in the same condemnation with him, found it equally inexpedient to await their destiny within the walls of Prague. They retired towards Moravia, with a view of seeking refuge in Transylvania. Frederick fled to Breslau, where, however, he only remained a short time. He removed from thence to the court of the Elector of Brandenburg, and finally took shelter in Holland.

The battle of Prague had decided the fate of Bohemia. Prague surrendered the next day to the victors; the other towns followed the example of the capital. The Estates did homage without conditions, and the same was done by those of Silesia and Moravia. The Emperor allowed three months to elapse, before instituting any inquiry into the past. Reassured by this apparent clemency, many who, at first, had fled in terror appeared again in the capital. All at once, however, the storm burst forth; forty-eight of the most active among the insurgents were arrested on the same day and hour, and tried by an extraordinary commission, composed of native Bohemians and Austrians. Of these, twenty-seven, and of the common people an immense number, expired on the scaffold. The absenting offenders were summoned to appear to their trial, and failing to do so, condemned to death, as traitors and offenders against his Catholic Majesty, their estates confiscated, and their names affixed to the gallows. The property also of the rebels who had fallen in the field was seized. This tyranny might have been borne, as it affected individuals only, and while the ruin of one enriched another; but more intolerable was the oppression which extended to the whole kingdom, without exception. All the Protestant preachers were banished from the country; the Bohemians first, and afterwards those of Germany. The 'Letter of Majesty', Ferdinand tore with his own hand, and burnt the seal. Seven years after the battle of Prague, the toleration of the Protestant religion within the kingdom was entirely revoked. But whatever violence the Emperor allowed himself against the religious privileges of his subjects, he carefully abstained from interfering with their political constitution; and while he deprived them of the liberty of thought, he magnanimously left them the prerogative of taxing themselves.

The victory of the White Mountain put Ferdinand in possession of all his dominions. It even invested him with greater authority over them than his predecessors enjoyed, since their allegiance had been unconditionally pledged to him, and no Letter of Majesty now existed to limit his sovereignty. All his wishes were now gratified, to a degree surpassing his most sanguine expectations.

It was now in his power to dismiss his allies, and disband his army. If he was just, there was an end of the war — if he was both magnanimous and just, punishment was also at an end. The fate of Germany was in his hands; the happiness and misery of millions depended on the resolution he should take. Never was so great a decision resting on a single mind; never did the blindness of one man produce so much ruin.

Book II.

The resolution which Ferdinand now adopted, gave to the war a new direction, a new scene, and new actors. From a rebellion in Bohemia, and the chastisement of rebels, a war extended first to Germany, and afterwards to Europe. It is, therefore, necessary to take a general survey of the state of affairs both in Germany and the rest of Europe.

Unequally as the territory of Germany and the privileges of its members were divided among the Roman Catholics and the Protestants, neither party could hope to maintain itself against the encroachments of its adversary otherwise than by a prudent use of its peculiar advantages, and by a politic union among themselves. If the Roman Catholics were the more numerous party, and more favoured by the constitution of the empire, the Protestants, on the other hand, had the advantage of possessing a more compact and populous line of territories, valiant princes, a warlike nobility, numerous armies, flourishing free towns, the command of the sea, and even at the worst, certainty of support from Roman Catholic states. If the Catholics could arm Spain and Italy in their favour, the republics of Venice, Holland, and England, opened their treasures to the Protestants, while the states of the North and the formidable power of Turkey, stood ready to afford them prompt assistance. Brandenburg, Saxony, and the Palatinate, opposed three Protestant to three Ecclesiastical votes in the Electoral College; while to the Elector of Bohemia, as to the Archduke of Austria, the possession of the Imperial dignity was an important check, if the Protestants properly availed themselves of it. The sword of the Union might keep within its sheath the sword of the League; or if matters actually came to a war, might make the issue of it doubtful. But, unfortunately, private interests dissolved the band of union which should have held together the Protestant members of the empire. This critical conjuncture found none but second-rate actors on the political stage, and the decisive moment was neglected because the courageous were deficient in power, and the powerful in sagacity, courage, and resolution.

The Elector of Saxony was placed at the head of the German Protestants, by the services of his ancestor Maurice, by the extent of his territories, and by the influence of his electoral vote. Upon the resolution he might adopt, the fate of the contending parties seemed to depend; and John George was not insensible to the advantages which this important situation procured him. Equally valuable as an ally, both to the Emperor and to the Protestant Union, he cautiously avoided committing himself to either party; neither trusting himself by any irrevocable declaration entirely to the gratitude of the Emperor, nor renouncing the advantages which were to be gained from his fears. Uninfected by the contagion of religious and romantic enthusiasm which hurried sovereign after sovereign to risk both crown and life on the hazard of war, John George aspired to the more solid renown of improving and advancing the interests of his territories. His cotemporaries accused him of forsaking the Protestant cause in the very midst of the storm; of preferring the aggrandizement of his house to the emancipation of his country; of exposing the whole Evangelical or Lutheran church of Germany to ruin, rather than raise an arm in defence of the Reformed or Calvinists; of injuring the common cause by his suspicious friendship more seriously than the open enmity of its avowed opponents. But it would have been well if his accusers had imitated the wise policy of the Elector. If, despite of the prudent policy, the Saxons, like all others, groaned at the cruelties which marked the Emperor's progress; if all Germany was a witness how Ferdinand deceived his confederates and trifled with his engagements; if even the Elector himself at last perceived this — the more shame to the Emperor who could so basely betray such implicit confidence.

If an excessive reliance on the Emperor, and the hope of enlarging his territories, tied the hands of the Elector of Saxony, the weak George William, Elector of Brandenburg, was still more shamefully fettered by fear of Austria, and of the loss of his dominions. What was made a reproach against these princes would have preserved to the Elector Palatine his fame and his kingdom. A rash confidence in his untried strength, the influence of French counsels, and the temptation of a crown, had seduced that unfortunate prince into an enterprise for which he had neither adequate genius nor political capacity. The partition of his territories among discordant princes, enfeebled the Palatinate, which, united, might have made a longer resistance.

This partition of territory was equally injurious to the House of Hesse, in which, between Darmstadt and Cassel, religious dissensions had occasioned a fatal division. The line of Darmstadt, adhering to the Confession of Augsburg, had placed itself under the Emperor's protection, who favoured it at the expense of the Calvinists of Cassel. While his religious confederates were shedding their blood for their faith and their liberties, the Landgrave of Darmstadt was won over by the Emperor's gold. But William of Cassel, every way worthy of his ancestor who, a century before, had defended the freedom of

Germany against the formidable Charles V., espoused the cause of danger and of honour. Superior to that pusillanimity which made far more powerful princes bow before Ferdinand's might, the Landgrave William was the first to join the hero of Sweden, and to set an example to the princes of Germany which all had hesitated to begin. The boldness of his resolve was equalled by the steadfastness of his perseverance and the valour of his exploits. He placed himself with unshrinking resolution before his bleeding country, and boldly confronted the fearful enemy, whose hands were still reeking from the carnage of Magdeburg.

The Landgrave William deserves to descend to immortality with the heroic race of Ernest. Thy day of vengeance was long delayed, unfortunate John Frederick! Noble! never-to-be-forgotten prince! Slowly but brightly it broke. Thy times returned, and thy heroic spirit descended on thy grandson. An intrepid race of princes issues from the Thuringian forests, to shame, by immortal deeds, the unjust sentence which robbed thee of the electoral crown — to avenge thy offended shade by heaps of bloody sacrifice. The sentence of the conqueror could deprive thee of thy territories, but not that spirit of patriotism which staked them, nor that chivalrous courage which, a century afterwards, was destined to shake the throne of his descendant. Thy vengeance and that of Germany whetted the sacred sword, and one heroic hand after the other wielded the irresistible steel. As men, they achieved what as sovereigns they dared not undertake; they met in a glorious cause as the valiant soldiers of liberty. Too weak in territory to attack the enemy with their own forces, they directed foreign artillery against them, and led foreign banners to victory.

The liberties of Germany, abandoned by the more powerful states, who, however, enjoyed most of the prosperity accruing from them, were defended by a few princes for whom they were almost without value. The possession of territories and dignities deadened courage; the want of both made heroes. While Saxony, Brandenburg, and the rest drew back in terror, Anhalt, Mansfeld, the Prince of Weimar and others were shedding their blood in the field. The Dukes of Pomerania, Mecklenburg, Luneburg, and Wirtemberg, and the free cities of Upper Germany, to whom the name of *emperor* was of course a formidable one, anxiously avoided a contest with such an opponent, and crouched murmuring beneath his mighty arm.

Austria and Roman Catholic Germany possessed in Maximilian of Bavaria a champion as prudent as he was powerful. Adhering throughout the war to one fixed plan, never divided between his religion and his political interests; not the slavish dependent of Austria, who was labouring for *his* advancement, and trembled before her powerful protector, Maximilian earned the territories and dignities that rewarded his exertions. The other Roman Catholic states, which were chiefly Ecclesiastical, too unwarlike to resist the multitudes whom the prosperity of their territories allured, became the victims of the war one after another, and were contented to persecute in the cabinet and in the pulpit, the enemy whom they could not openly oppose in the field. All of them, slaves either to Austria or Bavaria, sunk into insignificance by the side of Maximilian; in his hand alone their united power could be rendered available.

The formidable monarchy which Charles V. and his son had unnaturally constructed of the Netherlands, Milan, and the two Sicilies, and their distant possessions in the East and West Indies, was under Philip III. and Philip IV. fast verging to decay. Swollen to a sudden greatness by unfruitful gold, this power was now sinking under a visible decline, neglecting, as it did, agriculture, the natural support of states. The conquests in the West Indies had reduced Spain itself to poverty, while they enriched the markets of Europe; the bankers of Antwerp, Venice, and Genoa, were making profit on the gold which was still buried in the mines of Peru. For the sake of India, Spain had been depopulated, while the treasures drawn from thence were wasted in the re-conquest of Holland, in the chimerical project of changing the succession to the crown of France, and in an unfortunate attack upon England. But the pride of this court had survived its greatness, as the hate of its enemies had outlived its power. Distrust of the Protestants suggested to the ministry of Philip III. the dangerous policy of his father; and the reliance of the Roman Catholics in Germany on Spanish assistance, was as firm as their belief in the wonder-working bones of the martyrs. External splendour concealed the inward wounds at which the life-blood of this monarchy was oozing; and the belief of its strength survived, because it still maintained the lofty tone of its golden days. Slaves in their palaces, and strangers even upon their own thrones, the Spanish nominal kings still gave laws to their German relations; though it is very doubtful if the support they afforded was worth the dependence by which the emperors purchased it. The fate of Europe was decided behind the Pyrenees by ignorant monks or vindictive favourites. Yet, even in its debasement, a power must always be formidable, which yields to none in extent; which, from custom, if not from the steadfastness of its views, adhered faithfully to one system of policy; which possessed well-disciplined armies and consummate generals; which, where the sword failed, did not scruple to employ the dagger; and converted even its ambassadors into incendiaries and assassins. What it had lost in three quarters of the globe, it now sought to regain to the eastward, and all Europe was at its mercy, if it could succeed in its long cherished design of uniting with the hereditary dominions of Austria all that lay between the Alps and the Adriatic.

To the great alarm of the native states, this formidable power had gained a footing in Italy, where its continual encroachments made the neighbouring sovereigns to tremble for their own possessions. The Pope himself was in the most dangerous situation; hemmed in on both sides by the Spanish Viceroys of Naples on the one side, and that of Milan upon the other. Venice was confined between the Austrian Tyrol and the Spanish territories in Milan. Savoy was surrounded by the latter and France. Hence the wavering and equivocal policy, which from the time of Charles V. had been pursued by the Italian States. The double character which pertained to the Popes made them perpetually vacillate between two contradictory systems of policy. If the successors of St. Peter found in the Spanish princes their most obedient disciples, and the most steadfast supporters of the Papal See, yet the princes of the States of the Church had in these monarchs their most dangerous neighbours, and most formidable opponents. If, in the one capacity, their dearest wish was the destruction of the Protestants, and the triumph of Austria, in the other, they had reason to bless the arms of the Protestants, which disabled a dangerous enemy. The one or the other sentiment prevailed, according as the love of temporal dominion, or zeal for spiritual supremacy, predominated in the mind of the Pope. But the policy of Rome was, on the whole, directed to immediate dangers; and it is well known how far more powerful is the apprehension of losing a present good, than anxiety to recover a long lost possession. And thus it becomes intelligible how the Pope should first combine with Austria for the destruction of heresy, and then conspire with these very heretics for the destruction of Austria. Strangely blended are the threads of human affairs! What would have become of the Reformation, and of the liberties of Germany, if the Bishop of Rome and the Prince of Rome had had but one interest?

France had lost with its great Henry all its importance and all its weight in the political balance of Europe. A turbulent minority had destroyed all the benefits of the able administration of Henry. Incapable ministers, the creatures of court intrigue, squandered in a few years the treasures which Sully's economy and Henry's frugality had amassed. Scarce able to maintain their ground against internal factions, they were compelled to resign to other hands the helm of European affairs. The same civil war which armed Germany against itself, excited a similar commotion in France; and Louis XIII. attained majority only to wage a war with his own mother and his Protestant subjects. This party, which had been kept quiet by Henry's enlightened policy, now seized the opportunity to take up arms, and, under the command of some adventurous leaders, began to form themselves into a party within the state, and to fix on the strong and powerful town of Rochelle as the capital of their intended kingdom. Too little of a statesman to suppress, by a prudent toleration, this civil commotion in its birth, and too little master of the resources of his kingdom to direct them with energy, Louis XIII. was reduced to the degradation of purchasing the submission of the rebels by large sums of money. Though policy might incline him, in one point of view, to assist the Bohemian insurgents against Austria, the son of Henry the Fourth was now compelled to be an inactive spectator of their destruction, happy enough if the Calvinists in his own dominions did not unseasonably bethink them of their confederates beyond the Rhine. A great mind at the helm of state would have reduced the Protestants in France to obedience, while it employed them to fight for the independence of their German brethren. But Henry IV. was no more, and Richelieu had not yet revived his system of policy.

While the glory of France was thus upon the wane, the emancipated republic of Holland was completing the fabric of its greatness. The enthusiastic courage had not yet died away which, enkindled by the House of Orange, had converted this mercantile people into a nation of heroes, and had enabled them to maintain their independence in a bloody war against the Spanish monarchy. Aware how much they owed their own liberty to foreign support, these republicans were ready to assist their German brethren in a similar cause, and the more so, as both were opposed to the same enemy, and the liberty of Germany was the best warrant for that of Holland. But a republic which had still to battle for its very existence, which, with all its wonderful exertions, was scarce a match for the formidable enemy within its own territories, could not be expected to withdraw its troops from the necessary work of self-defence to employ them with a magnanimous policy in protecting foreign states.

England too, though now united with Scotland, no longer possessed, under the weak James, that influence in the affairs of Europe which the governing mind of Elizabeth had procured for it.

Convinced that the welfare of her dominions depended on the security of the Protestants, this politic princess had never swerved from the principle of promoting every enterprise which had for its object the diminution of the Austrian power. Her successor was no less devoid of capacity to comprehend, than of vigour to execute, her views. While the economical Elizabeth spared not her treasures to support the Flemings against Spain, and Henry IV. against the League, James abandoned his daughter, his son-in-law, and his grandchild, to the fury of their enemies. While he exhausted his learning to establish the divine right of kings, he allowed his own dignity to sink into the dust; while he exerted his rhetoric to prove the absolute authority of kings, he reminded the people of theirs; and by a useless profusion, sacrificed the chief of his sovereign rights — that of dispensing with his parliament, and thus depriving liberty of its organ. An innate horror at the sight of a naked sword averted him from the most just of wars; while his favourite Buckingham practised on his weakness, and his own complacent vanity rendered him an easy dupe of Spanish artifice. While his son-in-law was ruined, and the inheritance of his grandson given to others, this weak prince was imbibing, with satisfaction, the incense which was offered to him by Austria and Spain. To divert his attention from the German war, he was amused with the proposal of a Spanish marriage for his son, and the ridiculous parent encouraged the romantic youth in the foolish project of paying his addresses in person to the Spanish princess. But his son lost his bride, as his son-in-law lost the crown of Bohemia and the Palatine Electorate; and death alone saved him from the danger of closing his pacific reign by a war at home, which he never had courage to maintain, even at a distance.

The domestic disturbances which his misgovernment had gradually excited burst forth under his unfortunate son, and forced him, after some unimportant attempts, to renounce all further participation in the German war, in order to stem within his own kingdom the rage of faction.

Two illustrious monarchs, far unequal in personal reputation, but equal in power and desire of fame, made the North at this time to be respected. Under the long and active reign of Christian IV., Denmark had risen into importance. The personal qualifications of this prince, an excellent navy, a formidable army, well-ordered finances, and prudent alliances, had combined to give her prosperity at home and influence abroad. Gustavus Vasa had rescued Sweden from vassalage, reformed it by wise laws, and had introduced, for the first time, this newly-organized state into the field of European politics. What this great prince had merely sketched in rude outline, was filled up by Gustavus Adolphus, his still greater grandson.

These two kingdoms, once unnaturally united and enfeebled by their union, had been violently separated at the time of the Reformation, and this separation was the epoch of their prosperity. Injurious as this compulsory union had proved to both kingdoms, equally necessary to each apart were neighbourly friendship and harmony. On both the evangelical church leaned; both had the same seas to protect; a common interest ought to unite them against the same enemy. But the hatred which had dissolved the union of these monarchies continued long after their separation to divide the two nations. The Danish kings could not abandon their pretensions to the Swedish crown, nor the Swedes banish the remembrance of Danish oppression. The contiguous boundaries of the two kingdoms constantly furnished materials for international quarrels, while the watchful jealousy of both kings, and the unavoidable collision of their commercial interests in the North Seas, were inexhaustible sources of dispute.

Among the means of which Gustavus Vasa, the founder of the Swedish monarchy, availed himself to strengthen his new edifice, the Reformation had been one of the principal. A fundamental law of the kingdom excluded the adherents of popery from all offices of the state, and prohibited every future sovereign of Sweden from altering the religious constitution of the kingdom. But the second son and second successor of Gustavus had relapsed into popery, and his son Sigismund, also king of Poland, had been guilty of measures which menaced both the constitution and the established church. Headed by Charles, Duke of Sudermania, the third son of Gustavus, the Estates made a courageous resistance, which terminated, at last, in an open civil war between the uncle and nephew, and between the King and the people. Duke Charles, administrator of the kingdom during the absence of the king, had availed himself of Sigismund's long residence in Poland, and the just displeasure of the states, to ingratiate himself with the nation, and gradually to prepare his way to the throne. His views were not a little forwarded by Sigismund's imprudence. A general Diet ventured to abolish, in favour of the Protector, the rule of primogeniture which Gustavus had established in the succession, and placed the Duke of Sudermania on the throne, from which Sigismund, with his whole posterity, were solemnly excluded. The son of the new king (who reigned under the name of Charles IX.) was Gustavus

Adolphus, whom, as the son of a usurper, the adherents of Sigismund refused to recognize. But if the obligations between monarchy and subjects are reciprocal, and states are not to be transmitted, like a lifeless heirloom, from hand to hand, a nation acting with unanimity must have the power of renouncing their allegiance to a sovereign who has violated his obligations to them, and of filling his place by a worthier object.

Gustavus Adolphus had not completed his seventeenth year, when the Swedish throne became vacant by the death of his father. But the early maturity of his genius enabled the Estates to abridge in his favour the legal period of minority. With a glorious conquest over himself he commenced a reign which was to have victory for its constant attendant, a career which was to begin and end in success. The young Countess of Brahe, the daughter of a subject, had gained his early affections, and he had resolved to share with her the Swedish throne. But, constrained by time and circumstances, he made his attachment yield to the higher duties of a king, and heroism again took exclusive possession of a heart which was not destined by nature to confine itself within the limits of quiet domestic happiness.

Christian IV. of Denmark, who had ascended the throne before the birth of Gustavus, in an inroad upon Sweden, had gained some considerable advantages over the father of that hero. Gustavus Adolphus hastened to put an end to this destructive war, and by prudent sacrifices obtained a peace, in order to turn his arms against the Czar of Muscovy. The questionable fame of a conqueror never tempted him to spend the blood of his subjects in unjust wars; but he never shrunk from a just one. His arms were successful against Russia, and Sweden was augmented by several important provinces on the east.

In the meantime, Sigismund of Poland retained against the son the same sentiments of hostility which the father had provoked, and left no artifice untried to shake the allegiance of his subjects, to cool the ardour of his friends, and to embitter his enemies. Neither the great qualities of his rival, nor the repeated proofs of devotion which Sweden gave to her loved monarch, could extinguish in this infatuated prince the foolish hope of regaining his lost throne. All Gustavus's overtures were haughtily rejected. Unwillingly was this really peaceful king involved in a tedious war with Poland, in which the whole of Livonia and Polish Prussia were successively conquered. Though constantly victorious, Gustavus Adolphus was always the first to hold out the hand of peace.

This contest between Sweden and Poland falls somewhere about the beginning of the Thirty Years' War in Germany, with which it is in some measure connected. It was enough that Sigismund, himself a Roman Catholic, was disputing the Swedish crown with a Protestant prince, to assure him the active support of Spain and Austria; while a double relationship to the Emperor gave him a still stronger claim to his protection. It was his reliance on this powerful assistance that chiefly encouraged the King of Poland to continue the war, which had hitherto turned out so unfavourably for him, and the courts of Madrid and Vienna failed not to encourage him by high-sounding promises. While Sigismund lost one place after another in Livonia, Courland, and Prussia, he saw his ally in Germany advancing from conquest after conquest to unlimited power. No wonder then if his aversion to peace kept pace with his losses. The vehemence with which he nourished his chimerical hopes blinded him to the artful policy of his confederates, who at his expense were keeping the Swedish hero employed, in order to overturn, without opposition, the liberties of Germany, and then to seize on the exhausted North as an easy conquest. One circumstance which had not been calculated on — the magnanimity of Gustavus — overthrew this deceitful policy. An eight years' war in Poland, so far from exhausting the power of Sweden, had only served to mature the military genius of Gustavus, to inure the Swedish army to warfare, and insensibly to perfect that system of tactics by which they were afterwards to perform such wonders in Germany.

After this necessary digression on the existing circumstances of Europe, I now resume the thread of my history.

Ferdinand had regained his dominions, but had not indemnified himself for the expenses of recovering them. A sum of forty millions of florins, which the confiscations in Bohemia and Moravia had produced, would have sufficed to reimburse both himself and his allies; but the Jesuits and his favourites soon squandered this sum, large as it was. Maximilian, Duke of Bavaria, to whose victorious arm, principally, the Emperor owed the recovery of his dominions; who, in the service of religion and the Emperor, had sacrificed his near relation, had the strongest claims on his gratitude; and moreover, in a treaty which, before the war, the duke had concluded with the Emperor, he had expressly stipulated for the reimbursement of all expenses. Ferdinand felt the full weight of the obligation imposed upon him by this treaty and by these services, but he was not disposed to discharge it at his own cost. His purpose was to bestow a brilliant reward upon the duke, but without detriment to himself. How could this be done better than at the expense of the unfortunate prince who, by his revolt, had given the Emperor a right to punish him, and whose offences might be painted in colours strong enough to justify the most violent measures under the appearance of law. That, then, Maximilian may be rewarded, Frederick must be further persecuted and totally ruined; and to defray the expenses of the old war, a new one must be commenced.

But a still stronger motive combined to enforce the first. Hitherto Ferdinand had been contending for existence alone; he had been fulfilling no other duty than that of self-defence. But now, when victory gave him freedom to act, a higher duty occurred to him, and he remembered the vow which he had made at Loretto and at Rome, to his generalissima, the Holy Virgin, to extend her worship even at the risk of his crown and life. With this object, the oppression of the Protestants was inseparably connected. More favourable circumstances for its accomplishment could not offer than those which presented themselves at the close of the Bohemian war. Neither the power, nor a pretext of right, were now wanting to enable him to place the Palatinate in the hands of the Catholics, and the importance of this change to the Catholic interests in Germany would be incalculable. Thus, in rewarding the Duke of Bavaria with the spoils of his relation, he at once gratified his meanest passions and fulfilled his most exalted duties; he crushed an enemy whom he hated, and spared his avarice a painful sacrifice, while he believed he was winning a heavenly crown.

In the Emperor's cabinet, the ruin of Frederick had been resolved upon long before fortune had decided against him; but it was only after this event that they ventured to direct against him the thunders of arbitrary power. A decree of the Emperor, destitute of all the formalities required on such occasions by the laws of the Empire, pronounced the Elector, and three other princes who had borne arms for him at Silesia and Bohemia, as offenders against the imperial majesty, and disturbers of the public peace, under the ban of the empire, and deprived them of their titles and territories. The execution of this sentence against Frederick, namely the seizure of his lands, was, in further contempt of law, committed to Spain as Sovereign of the circle of Burgundy, to the Duke of Bavaria, and the League. Had the Evangelic Union been worthy of the name it bore, and of the cause which it pretended to defend, insuperable obstacles might have prevented the execution of the sentence; but it was hopeless for a power which was far from a match even for the Spanish troops in the Lower Palatinate, to contend against the united strength of the Emperor, Bavaria, and the League. The sentence of proscription pronounced upon the Elector soon detached the free cities from the Union; and the princes quickly followed their example. Fortunate in preserving their own dominions, they abandoned the Elector, their former chief, to the Emperor's mercy, renounced the Union, and vowed never to revive it again.

But while thus ingloriously the German princes deserted the unfortunate Frederick, and while Bohemia, Silesia, and Moravia submitted to the Emperor, a single man, a soldier of fortune, whose only treasure was his sword, Ernest Count Mansfeld, dared, in the Bohemian town of Pilsen, to defy the whole power of Austria. Left without assistance after the battle of Prague by the Elector, to whose service he had devoted himself, and even uncertain whether Frederick would thank him for his perseverance, he alone for some time held out against the imperialists, till the garrison, mutinying for want of pay, sold the town to the Emperor. Undismayed by this reverse, he immediately commenced new levies in the Upper Palatinate, and enlisted the disbanded troops of the Union. A new army of 20,000 men was soon assembled under his banners, the more formidable to the provinces which might be the object of its attack, because it must subsist by plunder. Uncertain where this swarm might light, the neighbouring bishops trembled for their rich possessions, which offered a tempting prey to its ravages. But, pressed by the Duke of Bavaria, who now entered the Upper Palatinate, Mansfeld was compelled to retire. Eluding, by a successful stratagem, the Bavarian general, Tilly, who was in pursuit of him, he suddenly appeared in the Lower Palatinate, and there wreaked upon the bishoprics of the Rhine the severities he had designed for those of Franconia. While the imperial and Bavarian allies thus overran Bohemia, the Spanish general, Spinola, had penetrated with a numerous army from the Netherlands into the Lower Palatinate, which, however, the pacification of Ulm permitted the Union to defend. But their measures were so badly concerted, that one place after another fell into the hands of the Spaniards; and at last, when the Union broke up, the greater part of the country was in the possession of Spain. The Spanish general, Corduba, who commanded these troops after the recall of Spinola, hastily raised the siege of Frankenthal, when Mansfeld entered the Lower Palatinate. But instead of driving the Spaniards out of this province, he hastened across the Rhine to secure for his needy troops shelter and subsistence in Alsace. The open countries on which this swarm of maurauders threw themselves were converted into frightful deserts, and only by enormous contributions could the cities purchase an exemption from plunder. Reinforced by this expedition, Mansfeld again appeared on the Rhine to cover the Lower Palatinate.

So long as such an arm fought for him, the cause of the Elector Frederick was not irretrievably lost. New prospects began to open, and misfortune raised up friends who had been silent during his prosperity. King James of England, who had looked on with indifference while his son-in-law lost the Bohemian crown, was aroused from his insensibility when the very existence of his daughter and grandson was at stake, and the victorious enemy ventured an attack upon the Electorate. Late enough, he at last opened his treasures, and hastened to afford supplies of money and troops, first to the Union, which at that time was defending the Lower Palatinate, and afterwards, when they retired, to Count Mansfeld. By his means his near relation, Christian, King of Denmark, was induced to afford his active support. At the same time, the approaching expiration of the truce between Spain and Holland deprived the Emperor of all the supplies which otherwise he might expect from the side of the Netherlands. More important still was the assistance which the Palatinate received from Transylvania and Hungary. The cessation of hostilities between Gabor and the Emperor was scarcely at an end, when this old and formidable enemy of Austria overran Hungary anew, and caused himself to be crowned king in Presburg. So rapid was his progress that, to protect Austria and Hungary, Boucquoi was obliged to evacuate Bohemia. This brave general met his death at the siege of Neuhausel, as, shortly before, the no less valiant Dampierre had fallen before Presburg. Gabor's march into the Austrian territory was irresistible; the old Count Thurn, and several other distinguished Bohemians, had united their hatred and their strength with this irreconcileable enemy of Austria. A vigorous attack on the side of Germany, while Gabor pressed the Emperor on that of Hungary, might have retrieved the fortunes of Frederick; but, unfortunately, the Bohemians and Germans had always laid down their arms when Gabor took the field; and the latter was always exhausted at the very moment that the former began to recover their vigour.

Meanwhile Frederick had not delayed to join his protector Mansfeld. In disguise he entered the Lower Palatinate, of which the possession was at that time disputed between Mansfeld and the Bavarian general, Tilly, the Upper Palatinate having been long conquered. A ray of hope shone upon him as, from the wreck of the Union, new friends came forward. A former member of the Union, George Frederick, Margrave of Baden, had for some time been engaged in assembling a military force, which soon amounted to a considerable army. Its destination was kept a secret till he suddenly took the field and joined Mansfeld. Before commencing the war, he resigned his Margraviate to his son, in the hope of eluding, by this precaution, the Emperor's revenge, if his enterprize should be unsuccessful. His neighbour, the Duke of Wirtemberg, likewise began to augment his military force. The courage of the Palatine revived, and he laboured assiduously to renew the Protestant Union. It was now time for Tilly to consult for his own safety, and he hastily summoned the Spanish troops, under Corduba, to his assistance. But while the enemy was uniting his strength, Mansfeld and the Margrave separated, and the latter was defeated by the Bavarian general near Wimpfen (1622).

To defend a king whom his nearest relation persecuted, and who was deserted even by his own father-in-law, there had come forward an adventurer without money, and whose very legitimacy was questioned. A sovereign had resigned possessions over which he reigned in peace, to hazard the uncertain fortune of war in behalf of a stranger. And now another soldier of fortune, poor in territorial possessions, but rich in illustrious ancestry, undertook the defence of a cause which the former despaired of. Christian, Duke of Brunswick, administrator of Halberstadt, seemed to have learnt from Count Mansfeld the secret of keeping in the field an army of 20,000 men without money. Impelled by youthful presumption, and influenced partly by the wish of establishing his reputation at the expense of the Roman Catholic priesthood, whom he cordially detested, and partly by a thirst for plunder, he assembled a considerable army in Lower Saxony, under the pretext of espousing the defence of Frederick, and of the liberties of Germany. "God's Friend, Priest's Foe", was the motto he chose for his coinage, which was struck out of church plate; and his conduct belied one half at least of the device.

The progress of these banditti was, as usual, marked by the most frightful devastation. Enriched by the spoils of the chapters of Lower Saxony and Westphalia, they gathered strength to plunder the bishoprics upon the Upper Rhine. Driven from thence, both by friends and foes, the Administrator approached the town of Hoechst on the Maine, which he crossed after a murderous action with Tilly, who disputed with him the passage of the river. With the loss of half his army he reached the opposite bank, where he quickly collected his shattered troops, and formed a junction with Mansfeld. Pursued by Tilly, this united host threw itself again into Alsace, to repeat their former ravages. While the Elector Frederick followed, almost like a fugitive mendicant, this swarm of plunderers which acknowledged him as its lord, and dignified itself with his name, his friends were busily endeavouring to effect a reconciliation between him and the Emperor. Ferdinand took care not to deprive them of all hope of seeing the Palatine restored to his dominion. Full of artifice and dissimulation, he pretended to be willing to enter into a negotiation, hoping thereby to cool their ardour in the field, and to prevent them from driving matters to extremity. James I., ever the dupe of Spanish cunning, contributed not a little, by his foolish intermeddling, to promote the Emperor's schemes. Ferdinand insisted that Frederick, if he would appeal to his clemency, should, first of all, lay down his arms, and James considered this demand extremely reasonable. At his instigation, the Elector dismissed his only real defenders, Count Mansfeld and the Administrator, and in Holland awaited his own fate from the mercy of the Emperor.

Mansfeld and Duke Christian were now at a loss for some new name; the cause of the Elector had not set them in motion, so his dismissal could not disarm them. War was their object; it was all the same to them in whose cause or name it was waged. After some vain attempts on the part of Mansfeld to be received into the Emperor's service, both marched into Lorraine, where the excesses of their troops spread terror even to the heart of France. Here they long waited in vain for a master willing to purchase their services; till the Dutch, pressed by the Spanish General Spinola, offered to take them into pay. After a bloody fight at Fleurus with the Spaniards, who attempted to intercept them, they reached Holland, where their appearance compelled the Spanish general forthwith to raise the siege of Bergen-op-Zoom. But even Holland was soon weary of these dangerous guests, and availed herself of the first moment to get rid of their unwelcome assistance. Mansfeld allowed his troops to recruit themselves for new enterprises in the fertile province of East Friezeland. Duke Christian, passionately enamoured of the Electress Palatine, with whom he had become acquainted in Holland, and more disposed for war than ever, led back his army into Lower Saxony, bearing that princess's glove in his hat, and on his standards the motto "All for God and Her". Neither of these adventurers had as yet run their career in this war.

All the imperial territories were now free from the enemy; the Union was dissolved; the Margrave of Baden, Duke Christian, and Mansfeld, driven from the field, and the Palatinate overrun by the executive troops of the empire. Manheim and Heidelberg were in possession of Bavaria, and Frankenthal was shortly afterwards ceded to the Spaniards. The Palatine, in a distant corner of Holland, awaited the disgraceful permission to appease, by abject submission, the vengeance of the Emperor; and an Electoral Diet was at last summoned to decide his fate. That fate, however, had been long before decided at the court of the Emperor; though now, for the first time, were circumstances favourable for giving publicity to the decision. After his past measures towards the Elector, Ferdinand believed that a sincere reconciliation was not to be hoped for. The violent course he had once begun, must be completed successfully, or recoil upon himself. What was already lost was irrecoverable; Frederick could never hope to regain his dominions; and a prince without territory and without subjects had little chance of retaining the electoral crown. Deeply as the Palatine had offended against the House of Austria, the services of the Duke of Bavaria were no less meritorious. If the House of Austria and the Roman Catholic church had much to dread from the resentment and religious rancour of the Palatine family, they had as much to hope from the gratitude and religious zeal of the Bavarian. Lastly, by the cession of the Palatine Electorate to Bavaria, the Roman Catholic religion would obtain a decisive preponderance in the Electoral College, and secure a permanent triumph in Germany.

The last circumstance was sufficient to win the support of the three Ecclesiastical Electors to this innovation; and among the Protestants the vote of Saxony was alone of any importance. But could John George be expected to dispute with the Emperor a right, without which he would expose to question his own title to the electoral dignity? To a prince whom descent, dignity, and political power placed at the head of the Protestant church in Germany, nothing, it is true, ought to be more sacred than the defence of the rights of that church against all the encroachments of the Roman Catholics. But the question here was not whether the interests of the Protestants were to be supported against the Roman Catholics, but which of two religions equally detested, the Calvinistic and the Popish, was to triumph over the other; to which of the two enemies, equally dangerous, the Palatinate was to be assigned; and in this clashing of opposite duties, it was natural that private hate and private gain should determine the event. The born protector of the liberties of Germany, and of the Protestant religion, encouraged the Emperor to dispose of the Palatinate by his imperial prerogative; and to apprehend no resistance on the part of Saxony to his measures on the mere ground of form. If the Elector was afterwards disposed to retract this consent, Ferdinand himself, by driving the Evangelical preachers from Bohemia, was the cause of this change of opinion; and, in the eyes of the Elector, the transference of the Palatine Electorate to Bavaria ceased to be illegal, as soon as Ferdinand was prevailed upon to cede Lusatia to Saxony, in consideration of six millions of dollars, as the expenses of the war.

Thus, in defiance of all Protestant Germany, and in mockery of the fundamental laws of the empire, which, as his election, he had sworn to maintain, Ferdinand at Ratisbon solemnly invested the Duke of Bavaria with the Palatinate, without prejudice, as the form ran, to the rights which the relations or descendants of Frederick might afterwards establish. That unfortunate prince thus saw himself irrevocably driven from his possessions, without having been even heard before the tribunal which condemned him — a privilege which the law allows to the meanest subject, and even to the most atrocious criminal.

This violent step at last opened the eyes of the King of England; and as the negociations for the marriage of his son with the Infanta of Spain were now broken off, James began seriously to espouse the cause of his son-in-law. A change in the French ministry had placed Cardinal Richelieu at the head of affairs, and this fallen kingdom soon began to feel that a great mind was at the helm of state. The attempts of the Spanish Viceroy in Milan to gain possession of the Valtelline, and thus to form a junction with the Austrian hereditary dominions, revived the olden dread of this power, and with it the policy of Henry the Great. The marriage of the Prince of Wales with Henrietta of France, established a close union between the two crowns; and to this alliance, Holland, Denmark, and some of the Italian states presently acceded. Its object was to expel, by force of arms, Spain from the Valtelline, and to compel Austria to reinstate Frederick; but only the first of these designs was prosecuted with vigour. James I. died, and Charles I., involved in disputes with his Parliament, could not bestow attention on the affairs of Germany. Savoy and Venice withheld their assistance; and the French minister thought it necessary to subdue the Huguenots at home, before he supported the German Protestants against the Emperor. Great as were the hopes which had been formed from this alliance, they were yet equalled by the disappointment of the event.

Mansfeld, deprived of all support, remained inactive on the Lower Rhine; and Duke Christian of Brunswick, after an unsuccessful campaign, was a second time driven out of Germany. A fresh irruption of Bethlen Gabor into Moravia, frustrated by the want of support from the Germans, terminated, like all the rest, in a formal peace with the Emperor. The Union was no more; no Protestant prince was in arms; and on the frontiers of Lower Germany, the Bavarian General Tilly, at the head of a victorious army, encamped in the Protestant territory. The movements of the Duke of Brunswick had drawn him into this quarter, and even into the circle of Lower Saxony, when he made himself master of the Administrator's magazines at Lippstadt. The necessity of observing this enemy, and preventing him from new inroads, was the pretext assigned for continuing Tilly's stay in the country. But, in truth, both Mansfeld and Duke Christian had, from want of money, disbanded their armies, and Count Tilly had no enemy to dread. Why, then, still burden the country with his presence?

It is difficult, amidst the uproar of contending parties, to distinguish the voice of truth; but certainly it was matter for alarm that the League did not lay down its arms. The premature rejoicings of the Roman Catholics, too, were calculated to increase apprehension. The Emperor and the League stood armed and victorious in Germany without a power to oppose them, should they venture to attack the Protestant states and to annul the religious treaty. Had Ferdinand been in reality far from disposed to abuse his conquests, still the defenceless position of the Protestants was most likely to suggest the temptation. Obsolete conventions could not bind a prince who thought that he owed all to religion, and believed that a religious creed would sanctify any deed, however violent. Upper Germany was already overpowered. Lower Germany alone could check his despotic authority. Here the Protestants still predominated; the church had been forcibly deprived of most of its endowments; and the present appeared a favourable moment for recovering these lost possessions. A great part of the strength of the Lower German princes consisted in these Chapters, and the plea of restoring its own to the church, afforded an excellent pretext for weakening these princes.

Unpardonable would have been their negligence, had they remained inactive in this danger. The remembrance of the ravages which Tilly's army had committed in Lower Saxony was too recent not to arouse the Estates to measures of defence. With all haste, the circle of Lower Saxony began to arm itself. Extraordinary contributions were levied, troops collected, and magazines filled. Negociations for subsidies were set on foot with Venice, Holland, and England. They deliberated, too, what power should be placed at the head of the confederacy. The kings of the Sound and the Baltic, the natural allies of this circle, would not see with indifference the Emperor treating it as a conqueror, and establishing himself as their neighbour on the shores of the North Sea. The twofold interests of religion and policy urged them to put a stop to his progress in Lower Germany. Christian IV. of Denmark, as Duke of Holstein, was himself a prince of this circle, and by considerations equally powerful, Gustavus Adolphus of Sweden was induced to join the confederacy.

These two kings vied with each other for the honour of defending Lower Saxony, and of opposing the formidable power of Austria. Each offered to raise a well-disciplined army, and to lead it in person. His victorious campaigns against Moscow and Poland gave weight to the promises of the King of Sweden. The shores of the Baltic were full of the name of Gustavus. But the fame of his rival excited the envy of the Danish monarch; and the more success he promised himself in this campaign, the less disposed was he to show any favour to his envied neighbour. Both laid their conditions and plans before the English ministry, and Christian IV. finally succeeded in outbidding his rival. Gustavus Adolphus, for his own security, had demanded the cession of some places of strength in Germany, where he himself had no territories, to afford, in case of need, a place of refuge for his troops. Christian IV. possessed Holstein and Jutland, through which, in the event of a defeat, he could always secure a retreat.

Eager to get the start of his competitor, the King of Denmark hastened to take the field. Appointed generalissimo of the circle of Lower Saxony, he soon had an army of 60,000 men in motion; the administrator of Magdeburg, and the Dukes of Brunswick and Mecklenburgh, entered into an alliance with him. Encouraged by the hope of assistance from England, and the possession of so large a force, he flattered himself he should be able to terminate the war in a single campaign.

At Vienna, it was officially notified that the only object of these preparations was the protection of the circle, and the maintenance of peace. But the negociations with Holland, England, and even France, the extraordinary exertions of the circle, and the raising of so formidable an army, seemed to have something more in view than defensive operations, and to contemplate nothing less than the complete restoration of the Elector Palatine, and the humiliation of the dreaded power of Austria.

After negociations, exhortations, commands, and threats had in vain been employed by the Emperor in order to induce the King of Denmark and the circle of Lower Saxony to lay down their arms, hostilities commenced, and Lower Germany became the theatre of war. Count Tilly, marching along the left bank of the Weser, made himself master of all the passes as far as Minden. After an unsuccessful attack on Nieuburg, he crossed the river and overran the principality of Calemberg, in which he quartered his troops. The king conducted his operations on the right bank of the river, and spread his forces over the territories of Brunswick, but having weakened his main body by too powerful detachments, he could not engage in any enterprise of importance. Aware of his opponent's superiority, he avoided a decisive action as anxiously as the general of the League sought it.

With the exception of the troops from the Spanish Netherlands, which had poured into the Lower Palatinate, the Emperor had hitherto made use only of the arms of Bavaria and the League in Germany. Maximilian conducted the war as executor of the ban of the empire, and Tilly, who commanded the army of execution, was in the Bavarian service. The Emperor owed superiority in the field to Bavaria and the League, and his fortunes were in their hands. This dependence on their goodwill, but ill accorded with the grand schemes, which the brilliant commencement of the war had led the imperial cabinet to form.

However active the League had shown itself in the Emperor's defence, while thereby it secured its own welfare, it could not be expected that it would enter as readily into his views of conquest. Or, if they still continued to lend their armies for that purpose, it was too much to be feared that they would share with the Emperor nothing but general odium, while they appropriated to themselves all advantages. A strong army under his own orders could alone free him from this debasing dependence upon Bavaria, and restore to him his former pre-eminence in Germany. But the war had already exhausted the imperial dominions, and they were unequal to the expense of such an armament. In these circumstances, nothing could be more welcome to the Emperor than the proposal with which one of his officers surprised him.

This was Count Wallenstein, an experienced officer, and the richest nobleman in Bohemia. From his earliest youth he had been in the service of the House of Austria, and several campaigns against the Turks, Venetians, Bohemians, Hungarians, and Transylvanians had established his reputation. He was present as colonel at the battle of Prague, and afterwards, as major-general, had defeated a Hungarian force in Moravia. The Emperor's gratitude was equal to his services, and a large share of the confiscated estates of the Bohemian insurgents was their reward. Possessed of immense property, excited by ambitious views, confident in his own good fortune, and still more encouraged by the existing state of circumstances, he offered, at his own expense and that of his friends, to raise and clothe an army for the Emperor, and even undertook the cost of maintaining it, if he were allowed to augment it to 50,000 men. The project was universally ridiculed as the chimerical offspring of a visionary brain; but the offer was highly valuable, if its promises should be but partially fulfilled. Certain circles in Bohemia were assigned to him as depots, with authority to appoint his own officers. In a few months he had 20,000 men under arms, with which, quitting the Austrian territories, he soon afterwards appeared on the frontiers of Lower Saxony with 30,000. The Emperor had lent this armament nothing but his name. The reputation of the general, the prospect of rapid promotion, and the hope of plunder, attracted to his standard adventurers from all quarters of Germany; and even sovereign princes, stimulated by the desire of glory or of gain, offered to raise regiments for the service of Austria.

Now, therefore, for the first time in this war, an imperial army appeared in Germany; — an event which if it was menacing to the Protestants, was scarcely more acceptable to the Catholics. Wallenstein had orders to unite his army with the troops of the League, and in conjunction with the Bavarian general to attack the King of Denmark. But long jealous of Tilly's fame, he showed no disposition to share with him the laurels of the campaign, or in the splendour of his rival's achievements to dim the lustre of his own. His plan of operations was to support the latter, but to act entirely independent of him. As he had not resources, like Tilly, for supplying the wants of his army, he was obliged to march his troops into fertile countries which had not as yet suffered from war. Disobeying, therefore, the order to form a junction with the general of the League, he marched into the territories of Halberstadt and Magdeburg, and at Dessau made himself master of the Elbe. All the lands on either bank of this river were at his command, and from them he could either attack the King of Denmark in the rear, or, if prudent, enter the territories of that prince.

Christian IV. was fully aware of the danger of his situation between two such powerful armies. He had already been joined by the administrator of Halberstadt, who had lately returned from Holland; he now also acknowledged Mansfeld, whom previously he had refused to recognise, and supported him to the best of his ability. Mansfeld amply requited this service. He alone kept at bay the army of Wallenstein upon the Elbe, and prevented its junction with that of Tilly, and a combined attack on the King of Denmark. Notwithstanding the enemy's superiority, this intrepid general even approached the bridge of Dessau, and ventured to entrench himself in presence of the imperial lines. But attacked in the rear by the whole force of the Imperialists, he was obliged to yield to superior numbers, and to abandon his post with the loss of 3,000 killed. After this defeat, Mansfeld withdrew into Brandenburg, where he soon recruited and reinforced his army; and suddenly turned into Silesia, with the view of marching from thence into Hungary; and, in conjunction with Bethlen Gabor, carrying the war into the heart of Austria. As the Austrian dominions in that quarter were entirely defenceless, Wallenstein received immediate orders to leave the King of Denmark, and if possible to intercept Mansfeld's progress through Silesia.

The diversion which this movement of Mansfeld had made in the plans of Wallenstein, enabled the king to detach a part of his force into Westphalia, to seize the bishoprics of Munster and Osnaburg. To check this movement, Tilly suddenly moved from the Weser; but the operations of Duke Christian, who threatened the territories of the League with an inroad in the direction of Hesse, and to remove thither the seat of war, recalled him as rapidly from Westphalia. In order to keep open his communication with these provinces, and to prevent the junction of the enemy with the Landgrave of Hesse, Tilly hastily seized all the tenable posts on the Werha and Fulda, and took up a strong position in Minden, at the foot of the Hessian Mountains, and at the confluence of these rivers with the Weser. He soon made himself master of Goettingen, the key of Brunswick and Hesse, and was meditating a similar attack upon Nordheim, when the king advanced upon him with his whole army. After throwing into this place the necessary supplies for a long siege, the latter attempted to open a new passage through Eichsfeld and Thuringia, into the territories of the League. He had already reached Duderstadt, when Tilly, by forced marches, came up with him. As the army of Tilly, which had been reinforced by some of Wallenstein's regiments, was superior in numbers to his own, the king, to avoid a battle, retreated towards Brunswick. But Tilly incessantly harassed his retreat, and after three days' skirmishing, he was at length obliged to await the enemy near the village of Lutter in Barenberg. The Danes began the attack with great bravery, and thrice did their intrepid monarch lead them in person against the enemy; but at length the superior numbers and discipline of the Imperialists prevailed, and the general of the League obtained a complete victory. The Danes lost sixty standards, and their whole artillery, baggage, and ammunition. Several officers of distinction and about 4,000 men were killed in the field of battle; and several companies of foot, in the flight, who had thrown themselves into the town-house of Lutter, laid down their arms and surrendered to the conqueror.

The king fled with his cavalry, and soon collected the wreck of his army which had survived this serious defeat. Tilly pursued his victory, made himself master of the Weser and Brunswick, and forced the king to retire into Bremen. Rendered more cautious by defeat, the latter now stood upon the defensive; and determined at all events to prevent the enemy from crossing the Elbe. But while he threw garrisons into every tenable place, he reduced his own diminished army to inactivity; and one after another his scattered troops were either defeated or dispersed. The forces of the League, in command of the Weser, spread themselves along the Elbe and Havel, and everywhere drove the Danes before them. Tilly himself crossing the Elbe penetrated with his victorious army into Brandenburg, while Wallenstein entered Holstein to remove the seat of war to the king's own dominions.

This general had just returned from Hungary whither he had pursued Mansfeld, without being able to obstruct his march, or prevent his junction with Bethlen Gabor. Constantly persecuted by fortune, but always superior to his fate, Mansfeld had made his way against countless difficulties, through Silesia and Hungary to Transylvania, where, after all, he was not very welcome. Relying upon the assistance of England, and a powerful diversion in Lower Saxony, Gabor had again broken the truce with the Emperor. But in place of the expected diversion in his favour, Mansfeld had drawn upon himself the whole strength of Wallenstein, and instead of bringing, required, pecuniary assistance. The want of concert in the Protestant counsels cooled Gabor's ardour; and he hastened, as usual, to avert the coming storm by a speedy peace. Firmly determined, however, to break it, with the first ray of hope, he directed Mansfeld in the mean time to apply for assistance to Venice.

Cut off from Germany, and unable to support the weak remnant of his troops in Hungary, Mansfeld sold his artillery and baggage train, and disbanded his soldiers. With a few followers, he proceeded through Bosnia and Dalmatia, towards Venice. New schemes swelled his bosom; but his career was ended. Fate, which had so restlessly sported with him throughout, now prepared for him a peaceful grave in Dalmatia. Death overtook him in the vicinity of Zara in 1626, and a short time before him died the faithful companion of his fortunes, Christian, Duke of Brunswick — two men worthy of immortality, had they but been as superior to their times as they were to their adversities.

The King of Denmark, with his whole army, was unable to cope with Tilly alone; much less, therefore, with a shattered force could he hold his ground against the two imperial generals. The Danes retired from all their posts on the Weser, the Elbe, and the Havel, and the army of Wallenstein poured like a torrent into Brandenburg, Mecklenburg, Holstein and Sleswick. That general, too proud to act in conjunction with another, had dispatched Tilly across the Elbe, to watch, as he gave out, the motions of the Dutch in that quarter; but in reality that he might terminate the war against the king, and reap for himself the fruits of Tilly's conquests. Christian had now lost all his fortresses in the German States, with the exception of Gluckstadt; his armies were defeated or dispersed; no assistance came from Germany; from England, little consolation; while his confederates in Lower Saxony were at the mercy of the conqueror. The Landgrave of Hesse Cassel had been forced by Tilly, soon after the battle of Lutter, to renounce the Danish alliance. Wallenstein's formidable appearance before Berlin reduced the Elector of Brandenburgh to submission, and compelled him to recognise, as legitimate, Maximilian's title to the Palatine Electorate. The greater part of Mecklenburgh was now overrun by imperial troops; and both dukes, as adherents of the King of Denmark, placed under the ban of the empire, and driven from their dominions. The defence of the German liberties against illegal encroachments, was punished as a crime deserving the loss of all dignities and territories; and yet this was but the prelude to the still more crying enormities which shortly followed.

The secret how Wallenstein had purposed to fulfil his extravagant designs was now manifest. He had learned the lesson from Count Mansfeld; but the scholar surpassed his master. On the principle that war must support war, Mansfeld and the Duke of Brunswick had subsisted their troops by contributions levied indiscriminately on friend and enemy; but this predatory life was attended with all the inconvenience and insecurity which accompany robbery. Like a fugitive banditti, they were obliged to steal through exasperated and vigilant enemies; to roam from one end of Germany to another; to watch their opportunity with anxiety; and to abandon the most fertile territories whenever they were defended by a superior army. If Mansfeld and Duke Christian had done such great things in the face of these difficulties, what might not be expected if the obstacles were removed; when the army raised was numerous enough to overawe in itself the most powerful states of the empire; when the name of the Emperor insured impunity to every outrage; and when, under the highest authority, and at the head of an overwhelming force, the same system of warfare was pursued, which these two adventurers had hitherto adopted at their own risk, and with only an untrained multitude?

Wallenstein had all this in view when he made his bold offer to the Emperor, which now seemed extravagant to no one. The more his army was augmented, the less cause was there to fear for its subsistence, because it could irresistibly bear down upon the refractory states; the more violent its outrages, the more probable was impunity. Towards hostile states it had the plea of right; towards the favourably disposed it could allege necessity. The inequality, too, with which it dealt out its oppressions, prevented any dangerous union among the states; while the exhaustion of their territories deprived them of the power of vengeance. Thus the whole of Germany became a kind of magazine for the imperial army, and the Emperor was enabled to deal with the other states as absolutely as with his own hereditary dominions. Universal was the clamour for redress before the imperial throne; but there was nothing to fear from the revenge of the injured princes, so long as they appealed for justice. The general discontent was directed equally against the Emperor, who had lent his name to these barbarities, and the general who exceeded his power, and openly abused the authority of his master. They applied to the Emperor for protection against the outrages of his general; but Wallenstein had no sooner felt himself absolute in the army, than he threw off his obedience to his sovereign.

The exhaustion of the enemy made a speedy peace probable; yet Wallenstein continued to augment the imperial armies until they were at least 100,000 men strong. Numberless commissions to colonelcies and inferior commands, the regal pomp of the commander-in-chief, immoderate largesses to his favourites, (for he never gave less than a thousand florins,) enormous sums lavished in corrupting the court at Vienna — all this had been effected without burdening the Emperor. These immense sums were raised by the contributions levied from the lower German provinces, where no distinction was made between friend and foe; and the territories of all princes were subjected to the same system of marching and quartering, of extortion and outrage. If credit is to be given to an extravagant contemporary statement, Wallenstein, during his seven years command, had exacted not less than sixty thousand millions of dollars from one half of Germany. The greater his extortions, the greater the rewards of his soldiers, and the greater the concourse to his standard, for the world always follows fortune. His armies flourished while all the states through which they passed withered. What cared he for the detestation of the people, and the complaints of princes? His army adored him, and the very enormity of his guilt enabled him to bid defiance to its consequences.

It would be unjust to Ferdinand, were we to lay all these irregularities to his charge. Had he foreseen that he was abandoning the German States to the mercy of his officer, he would have been sensible how dangerous to himself so absolute a general would prove. The closer the connexion became between the army, and the leader from whom flowed favour and fortune, the more the ties which united both to the Emperor were relaxed. Every thing, it is true, was done in the name of the latter; but Wallenstein only availed himself of the supreme majesty of the Emperor to crush the authority of other states. His object was to depress the princes of the empire, to destroy all gradation of rank between them and the Emperor, and to elevate the power of the latter above all competition. If the Emperor were absolute in Germany, who then would be equal to the man intrusted with the execution of his will? The height to which Wallenstein had raised the imperial authority astonished even the Emperor himself; but as the greatness of the master was entirely the work of the servant, the creation of Wallenstein would necessarily sink again into nothing upon the withdrawal of its creative hand. Not without an object, therefore, did Wallenstein labour to poison the minds of the German princes against the Emperor. The more violent their hatred of Ferdinand, the more indispensable to the Emperor would become the man who alone could render their ill-will powerless. His design unquestionably was, that his sovereign should stand in fear of no one in all Germany — besides himself, the source and engine of this despotic power.

As a step towards this end, Wallenstein now demanded the cession of Mecklenburg, to be held in pledge till the repayment of his advances for the war. Ferdinand had already created him Duke of Friedland, apparently with the view of exalting his own general over Bavaria; but an ordinary recompense would not satisfy Wallenstein's ambition. In vain was this new demand, which could be granted only at the expense of two princes of the empire, actively resisted in the Imperial Council; in vain did the Spaniards, who had long been offended by his pride, oppose his elevation. The powerful support which Wallenstein had purchased from the imperial councillors prevailed, and Ferdinand was determined, at whatever cost, to secure the devotion of so indispensable a minister. For a slight offence, one of the oldest German houses was expelled from their hereditary dominions, that a creature of the

Emperor might be enriched by their spoils (1628).

Wallenstein now began to assume the title of generalissimo of the Emperor by sea and land. Wismar was taken, and a firm footing gained on the Baltic. Ships were required from Poland and the Hanse towns to carry the war to the other side of the Baltic; to pursue the Danes into the heart of their own country, and to compel them to a peace which might prepare the way to more important conquests. The communication between the Lower German States and the Northern powers would be broken, could the Emperor place himself between them, and encompass Germany, from the Adriatic to the Sound, (the intervening kingdom of Poland being already dependent on him,) with an unbroken line of territory. If such was the Emperor's plan, Wallenstein had a peculiar interest in its execution. These possessions on the Baltic should, he intended, form the first foundation of a power, which had long been the object of his ambition, and which should enable him to throw off his dependence on the Emperor.

To effect this object, it was of extreme importance to gain possession of Stralsund, a town on the Baltic. Its excellent harbour, and the short passage from it to the Swedish and Danish coasts, peculiarly fitted it for a naval station in a war with these powers. This town, the sixth of the Hanseatic League, enjoyed great privileges under the Duke of Pomerania, and totally independent of Denmark, had taken no share in the war. But neither its neutrality, nor its privileges, could protect it against the encroachments of Wallenstein, when he had once cast a longing look upon it.

The request he made, that Stralsund should receive an imperial garrison, had been firmly and honourably rejected by the magistracy, who also refused his cunningly demanded permission to march his troops through the town, Wallenstein, therefore, now proposed to besiege it.

The independence of Stralsund, as securing the free navigation of the Baltic, was equally important to the two Northern kings. A common danger overcame at last the private jealousies which had long divided these princes. In a treaty concluded at Copenhagen in 1628, they bound themselves to assist Stralsund with their combined force, and to oppose in common every foreign power which should appear in the Baltic with hostile views. Christian IV. also threw a sufficient garrison into Stralsund, and by his personal presence animated the courage of the citizens. Some ships of war which Sigismund, King of Poland, had sent to the assistance of the imperial general, were sunk by the Danish fleet; and as Lubeck refused him the use of its shipping, this imperial generalissimo of the sea had not even ships enough to blockade this single harbour.

Nothing could appear more adventurous than to attempt the conquest of a strongly fortified seaport without first blockading its harbour. Wallenstein, however, who as yet had never experienced a check, wished to conquer nature itself, and to perform impossibilities. Stralsund, open to the sea, continued to be supplied with provisions and reinforcements; yet Wallenstein maintained his blockade on the land side, and endeavoured, by boasting menaces, to supply his want of real strength. "I will take this town," said he, "though it were fastened by a chain to the heavens." The Emperor himself, who might have cause to regret an enterprise which promised no very glorious result, joyfully availed himself of the apparent submission and acceptable propositions of the inhabitants, to order the general to retire from the town. Wallenstein despised the command, and continued to harass the besieged by incessant assaults. As the Danish garrison, already much reduced, was unequal to the fatigues of this prolonged defence, and the king was unable to detach any further troops to their support, Stralsund, with Christian's consent, threw itself under the protection of the King of Sweden. The Danish commander left the town to make way for a Swedish governor, who gloriously defended it. Here Wallenstein's good fortune forsook him; and, for the first time, his pride experienced the humiliation of relinquishing his prey, after the loss of many months and of 12,000 men. The necessity to which he reduced the town of applying for protection to Sweden, laid the foundation of a close alliance between Gustavus Adolphus and Stralsund, which greatly facilitated the entrance of the Swedes into Germany.

Hitherto invariable success had attended the arms of the Emperor and the League, and Christian IV., defeated in Germany, had sought refuge in his own islands; but the Baltic checked the further progress of the conquerors. The want of ships not only stopped the pursuit of the king, but endangered their previous acquisitions. The union of the two northern monarchs was most to be dreaded, because, so long as it lasted, it effectually prevented the Emperor and his general from acquiring a footing on the Baltic, or effecting a landing in Sweden. But if they could succeed in dissolving this union, and especially securing the friendship of the Danish king, they might hope to overpower the insulated force of Sweden. The dread of the interference of foreign powers, the insubordination of the Protestants in his own states, and still more the storm which was gradually darkening along the whole of Protestant Germany, inclined the Emperor to peace, which his general, from opposite motives, was equally desirous to effect. Far from wishing for a state of things which would reduce him from the meridian of greatness and glory to the obscurity of private life, he only wished to change the theatre of war, and by a partial peace to prolong the general confusion. The friendship of Denmark, whose neighbour he had become as Duke of Mecklenburgh, was most important for the success of his ambitious views; and he resolved, even at the sacrifice of his sovereign's interests, to secure its alliance.

By the treaty of Copenhagen, Christian IV. had expressly engaged not to conclude a separate peace with the Emperor, without the consent of Sweden. Notwithstanding, Wallenstein's proposition was readily received by him. In a conference at Lubeck in 1629, from which Wallenstein, with studied contempt, excluded the Swedish ambassadors who came to intercede for Mecklenburgh, all the conquests taken by the imperialists were restored to the Danes. The conditions imposed upon the king were, that he should interfere no farther with the affairs of Germany than was called for by his character of Duke of Holstein; that he should on no pretext harass the Chapters of Lower Germany, and should leave the Dukes of Mecklenburgh to their fate. By Christian himself had these princes been involved in the war with the Emperor; he now sacrificed them, to gain the favour of the usurper of their territories. Among the motives which had engaged him in a war with the Emperor, not the least was the restoration of his relation, the Elector Palatine — yet the name of that unfortunate prince was not even mentioned in the treaty; while in one of its articles the legitimacy of the Bavarian election was expressly recognised. Thus meanly and ingloriously did Christian IV. retire from the field.

Ferdinand had it now in his power, for the second time, to secure the tranquillity of Germany; and it depended solely on his will whether the treaty with Denmark should or should not be the basis of a general peace. From every quarter arose the cry of the unfortunate, petitioning for an end of their sufferings; the cruelties of his soldiers, and the rapacity of his generals, had exceeded all bounds. Germany, laid waste by the desolating bands of Mansfeld and the Duke of Brunswick, and by the still more terrible hordes of Tilly and Wallenstein, lay exhausted, bleeding, wasted, and sighing for repose. An anxious desire for peace was felt by all conditions, and by the Emperor himself; involved as he was in a war with France in Upper Italy, exhausted by his past warfare in Germany, and apprehensive of the day of reckoning which was approaching. But, unfortunately, the conditions on which alone the two religious parties were willing respectively to sheath the sword, were irreconcileable. The Roman Catholics wished to terminate the war to their own advantage; the Protestants advanced equal pretensions. The Emperor, instead of uniting both parties by a prudent moderation, sided with one; and thus Germany was again plunged in the horrors of a bloody war.

From the very close of the Bohemian troubles, Ferdinand had carried on a counter reformation in his hereditary dominions, in which, however, from regard to some of the Protestant Estates, he proceeded, at first, with moderation. But the victories of his generals in Lower Germany encouraged him to throw off all reserve. Accordingly he had it intimated to all the Protestants in these dominions, that they must either abandon their religion, or their native country, — a bitter and dreadful alternative, which excited the most violent commotions among his Austrian subjects. In the Palatinate, immediately after the expulsion of Frederick, the Protestant religion had been suppressed, and its professors expelled from the University of Heidelberg.

All this was but the prelude to greater changes. In the Electoral Congress held at Muehlhausen, the Roman Catholics had demanded of the Emperor that all the archbishoprics, bishoprics, mediate and immediate, abbacies and monasteries, which, since the Diet of Augsburg, had been secularized by the Protestants, should be restored to the church, in order to indemnify them for the losses and sufferings in the war. To a Roman Catholic prince so zealous as Ferdinand was, such a hint was not likely to be neglected; but he still thought it would be premature to arouse the whole Protestants of Germany by so decisive a step. Not a single Protestant prince but would be deprived, by this revocation of the religious foundations, of a part of his lands; for where these revenues had not actually been diverted to secular purposes they had been made over to the Protestant church. To this source, many princes owed the chief part of their revenues and importance. All, without exception, would be irritated by this demand for restoration. The religious treaty did not expressly deny their right to these chapters, although it did not allow it. But a possession which had now been held for nearly a century, the silence of four preceding emperors, and the law of equity, which gave them an equal right with the Roman Catholics to the foundations of their common ancestors, might be strongly pleaded by them as a valid title. Besides the actual loss of power and authority, which the surrender of these foundations would occasion, besides the inevitable confusion which would necessarily attend it, one important disadvantage to which it would lead, was, that the restoration of the Roman Catholic bishops would increase the strength of that party in the Diet by so many additional votes. Such grievous sacrifices likely to fall on the Protestants, made the Emperor apprehensive of a formidable opposition; and until the military ardour should have cooled in Germany, he had no wish to provoke a party formidable by its union, and which in the Elector of Saxony had a powerful leader. He resolved, therefore, to try the experiment at first on a small scale, in order to ascertain how it was likely to succeed on a larger one. Accordingly, some of the free cities in Upper Germany, and the Duke of Wirtemberg, received orders to surrender to the Roman Catholics several of the confiscated chapters.

The state of affairs in Saxony enabled the Emperor to make some bolder experiments in that quarter. In the bishoprics of Magdeburg and Halberstadt, the Protestant canons had not hesitated to elect bishops of their own religion. Both bishoprics, with the exception of the town of Magdeburg itself, were overrun by the troops of Wallenstein. It happened, moreover, that by the death of the Administrator Duke Christian of Brunswick, Halberstadt was vacant, as was also the Archbishopric of Magdeburg by the deposition of Christian William, a prince of the House of Brandenburgh. Ferdinand took advantage of the circumstance to restore the see of Halberstadt to a Roman Catholic bishop, and a prince of his own house. To avoid a similar coercion, the Chapter of Magdeburg hastened to elect a son of the Elector of Saxony as archbishop. But the pope, who with his arrogated authority interfered in this matter, conferred the Archbishopric of Magdeburg also on the Austrian prince. Thus, with all his pious zeal for religion, Ferdinand never lost sight of the interests of his family.

At length, when the peace of Lubeck had delivered the Emperor from all apprehensions on the side of Denmark, and the German Protestants seemed entirely powerless, the League becoming louder and more urgent in its demands, Ferdinand, in 1629, signed the Edict of Restitution, (so famous by its disastrous consequences,) which he had previously laid before the four Roman Catholic electors for their approbation. In the preamble, he claimed the prerogative, in right of his imperial authority, to interpret the meaning of the religious treaty, the ambiguities of which had already caused so many disputes, and to decide as supreme arbiter and judge between the contending parties. This prerogative he founded upon the practice of his ancestors, and its previous recognition even by Protestant states. Saxony had actually acknowledged this right of the Emperor; and it now became evident how deeply this court had injured the Protestant cause by its dependence on the House of Austria. But though the meaning of the religious treaty was really ambiguous, as a century of religious disputes sufficiently proved, yet for the Emperor, who must be either a Protestant or a Roman Catholic, and therefore an interested party, to assume the right of deciding between the disputants, was clearly a violation of an essential article of the pacification. He could not be judge in his own cause, without reducing the liberties of the empire to an empty sound.

And now, in virtue of this usurpation, Ferdinand decided, "That every secularization of a religious foundation, mediate or immediate, by the Protestants, subsequent to the date of the treaty, was contrary to its spirit, and must be revoked as a breach of it." He further decided, "That, by the religious peace, Catholic proprietors of estates were no further bound to their Protestant subjects than to allow them full liberty to quit their territories." In obedience to this decision, all unlawful possessors of benefices — the Protestant states in short without exception — were ordered, under pain of the ban of the empire, immediately to surrender their usurped possessions to the imperial commissioners.

This sentence applied to no less than two archbishoprics and twelve bishoprics, besides innumerable abbacies. The edict came like a thunderbolt on the whole of Protestant Germany; dreadful even in its immediate consequences; but yet more so from the further calamities it seemed to threaten. The Protestants were now convinced that the suppression of their religion had been resolved on by the Emperor and the League, and that the overthrow of German liberty would soon follow. Their remonstrances were unheeded; the commissioners were named, and an army assembled to enforce obedience. The edict was first put in force in Augsburg, where the treaty was concluded; the city was again placed under the government of its bishop, and six Protestant churches in the town were closed. The Duke of Wirtemberg was, in like manner, compelled to surrender his abbacies. These severe measures, though they alarmed the Protestant states, were yet insufficient to rouse them to an active resistance. Their fear of the Emperor was too strong, and many were disposed to quiet submission. The hope of attaining their end by gentle measures, induced the Roman Catholics likewise to delay for a year the execution of the edict, and this saved the Protestants; before the end of that period, the success of the Swedish arms had totally changed the state of affairs.

In a Diet held at Ratisbon, at which Ferdinand was present in person (in 1630), the necessity of taking some measures for the immediate restoration of a general peace to Germany, and for the removal of all grievances, was debated. The complaints of the Roman Catholics were scarcely less numerous than those of the Protestants, although Ferdinand had flattered himself that by the Edict of Restitution he had secured the members of the League, and its leader by the gift of the electoral dignity, and the cession of great part of the Palatinate. But the good understanding between the Emperor and the princes of the League had rapidly declined since the employment of Wallenstein. Accustomed to give law to Germany, and even to sway the Emperor's own destiny, the haughty Elector of Bavaria now at once saw himself supplanted by the imperial general, and with that of the League, his own importance completely undermined. Another had now stepped in to reap the fruits of his victories, and to bury his past services in oblivion. Wallenstein's imperious character, whose dearest triumph was in degrading the authority of the princes, and giving an odious latitude to that of the Emperor, tended not a little to augment the irritation of the Elector. Discontented with the Emperor, and distrustful of his intentions, he had entered into an alliance with France, which the other members of the League were suspected of favouring. A fear of the Emperor's plans of aggrandizement, and discontent with existing evils, had extinguished among them all feelings of gratitude. Wallenstein's exactions had become altogether intolerable. Brandenburg estimated its losses at twenty, Pomerania at ten, Hesse Cassel at seven millions of dollars, and the rest in proportion. The cry for redress was loud, urgent, and universal; all prejudices were hushed; Roman Catholics and Protestants were united on this point. The terrified Emperor was assailed on all sides by petitions against Wallenstein, and his ear filled with the most fearful descriptions of his outrages. Ferdinand was not naturally cruel. If not totally innocent of the atrocities which were practised in Germany under the shelter of his name, he was ignorant of their extent; and he was not long in yielding to the representation of the princes, and reduced his standing army by eighteen thousand cavalry. While this reduction took place, the Swedes were actively preparing an expedition into Germany, and the greater part of the disbanded Imperialists enlisted under their banners.

The Emperor's concessions only encouraged the Elector of Bavaria to bolder demands. So long as the Duke of Friedland retained the supreme command, his triumph over the Emperor was incomplete. The princes of the League were meditating a severe revenge on Wallenstein for that haughtiness with which he had treated them all alike. His dismissal was demanded by the whole college of electors, and even by Spain, with a degree of unanimity and urgency which astonished the Emperor. The anxiety with which Wallenstein's enemies pressed for his dismissal, ought to have convinced the Emperor of the importance of his services. Wallenstein, informed of the cabals which were forming against him in Ratisbon, lost no time in opening the eyes of the Emperor to the real views of the Elector of Bavaria. He himself appeared in Ratisbon, with a pomp which threw his master into the shade, and increased the hatred of his opponents.

Long was the Emperor undecided. The sacrifice demanded was a painful one. To the Duke of Friedland alone he owed his preponderance; he felt how much he would lose in yielding him to the indignation of the princes. But at this moment, unfortunately, he was under the necessity of conciliating the Electors. His son Ferdinand had already been chosen King of Hungary, and he was endeavouring to procure his election as his successor in the empire. For this purpose, the support of Maximilian was indispensable. This consideration was the weightiest, and to oblige the Elector of Bavaria he scrupled not to sacrifice his most valuable servant.

At the Diet at Ratisbon, there were present ambassadors from France, empowered to adjust the differences which seemed to menace a war in Italy between the Emperor and their sovereign. Vincent, Duke of Mantua and Montferrat, dying without issue, his next relation, Charles, Duke of Nevers, had taken possession of this inheritance, without doing homage to the Emperor as liege lord of the principality. Encouraged by the support of France and Venice, he refused to surrender these territories into the hands of the imperial commissioners, until his title to them should be decided. On the other hand, Ferdinand had taken up arms at the instigation of the Spaniards, to whom, as possessors of Milan, the near neighbourhood of a vassal of France was peculiarly alarming, and who welcomed this prospect of making, with the assistance of the Emperor, additional conquests in Italy. In spite of all the exertions of Pope Urban VIII. to avert a war in that country, Ferdinand marched a German army across the Alps, and threw the Italian states into a general consternation. His arms had been successful throughout Germany, and exaggerated fears revived the olden apprehension of Austria's projects of universal monarchy. All the horrors of the German war now spread like a deluge over those favoured countries which the Po waters; Mantua was taken by storm, and the surrounding districts given up to the ravages of a lawless soldiery. The curse of Italy was thus added to the maledictions upon the

Emperor which resounded through Germany; and even in the Roman Conclave, silent prayers were offered for the success of the Protestant arms.

Alarmed by the universal hatred which this Italian campaign had drawn upon him, and wearied out by the urgent remonstrances of the Electors, who zealously supported the application of the French ambassador, the Emperor promised the investiture to the new Duke of Mantua.

This important service on the part of Bavaria, of course, required an equivalent from France. The adjustment of the treaty gave the envoys of Richelieu, during their residence in Ratisbon, the desired opportunity of entangling the Emperor in dangerous intrigues, of inflaming the discontented princes of the League still more strongly against him, and of turning to his disadvantage all the transactions of the Diet. For this purpose Richelieu had chosen an admirable instrument in Father Joseph, a Capuchin friar, who accompanied the ambassadors without exciting the least suspicion. One of his principal instructions was assiduously to bring about the dismissal of Wallenstein. With the general who had led it to victory, the army of Austria would lose its principal strength; many armies could not compensate for the loss of this individual. It would therefore be a masterstroke of policy, at the very moment when a victorious monarch, the absolute master of his operations, was arming against the Emperor, to remove from the head of the imperial armies the only general who, by ability and military experience, was able to cope with the French king. Father Joseph, in the interests of Bavaria, undertook to overcome the irresolution of the Emperor, who was now in a manner besieged by the Spaniards and the Electoral Council. "It would be expedient," he thought, "to gratify the Electors on this occasion, and thereby facilitate his son's election to the Roman Crown. This object once gained, Wallenstein could at any time resume his former station." The artful Capuchin was too sure of his man to touch upon this ground of consolation.

The voice of a monk was to Ferdinand II. the voice of God. "Nothing on earth," writes his own confessor, "was more sacred in his eyes than a priest. If it could happen, he used to say, that an angel and a Regular were to meet him at the same time and place, the Regular should receive his first, and the angel his second obeisance." Wallenstein's dismissal was determined upon.

In return for this pious concession, the Capuchin dexterously counteracted the Emperor's scheme to procure for the King of Hungary the further dignity of King of the Romans. In an express clause of the treaty just concluded, the French ministers engaged in the name of their sovereign to observe a complete neutrality between the Emperor and his enemies; while, at the same time, Richelieu was actually negociating with the King of Sweden to declare war, and pressing upon him the alliance of his master. The latter, indeed, disavowed the lie as soon as it had served its purpose, and Father Joseph, confined to a convent, must atone for the alleged offence of exceeding his instructions. Ferdinand perceived, when too late, that he had been imposed upon. "A wicked Capuchin," he was heard to say, "has disarmed me with his rosary, and thrust nothing less than six electoral crowns into his cowl."

Artifice and trickery thus triumphed over the Emperor, at the moment when he was believed to be omnipotent in Germany, and actually was so in the field. With the loss of 18,000 men, and of a general who alone was worth whole armies, he left Ratisbon without gaining the end for which he had made such sacrifices. Before the Swedes had vanquished him in the field, Maximilian of Bavaria and Father Joseph had given him a mortal blow. At this memorable Diet at Ratisbon the war with Sweden was resolved upon, and that of Mantua terminated. Vainly had the princes present at it interceded for the Dukes of Mecklenburgh; and equally fruitless had been an application by the English ambassadors for a pension to the Palatine Frederick.

Wallenstein was at the head of an army of nearly a hundred thousand men who adored him, when the sentence of his dismissal arrived. Most of the officers were his creatures: — with the common soldiers his hint was law. His ambition was boundless, his pride indomitable, his imperious spirit could not brook an injury unavenged. One moment would now precipitate him from the height of grandeur into the obscurity of a private station. To execute such a sentence upon such a delinquent seemed to require more address than it cost to obtain it from the judge. Accordingly, two of Wallenstein's most intimate friends were selected as heralds of these evil tidings, and instructed to soften them as much as possible, by flattering assurances of the continuance of the Emperor's favour.

Wallenstein had ascertained the purport of their message before the imperial ambassadors arrived. He had time to collect himself, and his countenance exhibited an external calmness, while grief and rage were storming in his bosom. He had made up his mind to obey. The Emperor's decision had taken him by surprise before circumstances were ripe, or his preparations complete, for the bold measures he had contemplated. His extensive estates were scattered over Bohemia and Moravia; and by their confiscation, the Emperor might at once destroy the sinews of his power. He looked, therefore, to the future for revenge; and in this hope he was encouraged by the predictions of an Italian astrologer, who led his imperious spirit like a child in leading strings. Seni had read in the stars, that his master's brilliant career was not yet ended; and that bright and glorious prospects still awaited him. It was, indeed, unnecessary to consult the stars to foretell that an enemy, Gustavus Adolphus, would ere long render indispensable the services of such a general as Wallenstein.

"The Emperor is betrayed," said Wallenstein to the messengers; "I pity but forgive him. It is plain that the grasping spirit of the Bavarian dictates to him. I grieve that, with so much weakness, he has sacrificed me, but I will obey." He dismissed the emissaries with princely presents; and in a humble letter besought the continuance of the Emperor's favour, and of the dignities he had bestowed upon him.

The murmurs of the army were universal, on hearing of the dismissal of their general; and the greater part of his officers immediately quitted the imperial service. Many followed him to his estates in Bohemia and Moravia; others he attached to his interests by pensions, in order to command their services when the opportunity should offer.

But repose was the last thing that Wallenstein contemplated when he returned to private life. In his retreat, he surrounded himself with a regal pomp, which seemed to mock the sentence of degradation. Six gates led to the palace he inhabited in Prague, and a hundred houses were pulled down to make way for his courtyard. Similar palaces were built on his other numerous estates. Gentlemen of the noblest houses contended for the honour of serving him, and even imperial chamberlains resigned the golden key to the Emperor, to fill a similar office under Wallenstein. He maintained sixty pages, who were instructed by the ablest masters. His antichamber was protected by fifty life guards. His table never consisted of less than 100 covers, and his seneschal was a person of distinction. When he travelled, his baggage and suite accompanied him in a hundred wagons, drawn by six or four horses; his court followed in sixty carriages, attended by fifty led horses. The pomp of his liveries, the splendour of his equipages, and the decorations of his apartments, were in keeping with all the rest. Six barons and as many knights, were in constant attendance about his person, and ready to execute his slightest order. Twelve patrols went their rounds about his palace, to prevent any disturbance. His busy genius required silence. The noise of coaches was to be kept away from his residence, and the streets leading to it were frequently blocked up with chains. His own circle was as silent as the approaches to his palace; dark, reserved, and impenetrable, he was more sparing of his words than of his gifts; while the little that he spoke was harsh and imperious. He never smiled, and the coldness of his temperament was proof against sensual seductions. Ever occupied with grand schemes, he despised all those idle amusements in which so many waste their lives. The correspondence he kept up with the whole of Europe was chiefly managed by himself, and, that as little as possible might be trusted to the silence of others, most of the letters were written by his own hand. He was a man of large stature, thin, of a sallow complexion, with short red hair, and small sparkling eyes. A gloomy and forbidding seriousness sat upon his brow; and his magnificent presents alone retained the trembling crowd of his dependents.

In this stately obscurity did Wallenstein silently, but not inactively, await the hour of revenge. The victorious career of Gustavus Adolphus soon gave him a presentiment of its approach. Not one of his lofty schemes had been abandoned; and the Emperor's ingratitude had loosened the curb of his ambition. The dazzling splendour of his private life bespoke high soaring projects; and, lavish as a king, he seemed already to reckon among his certain possessions those which he contemplated with hope.

After Wallenstein's dismissal, and the invasion of Gustavus Adolphus, a new generalissimo was to be appointed; and it now appeared advisable to unite both the imperial army and that of the League under one general. Maximilian of Bavaria sought this appointment, which would have enabled him to dictate to the Emperor, who, from a conviction of this, wished to procure the command for his eldest son, the King of Hungary. At last, in order to avoid offence to either of the competitors, the appointment was given to Tilly, who now exchanged the Bavarian for the Austrian service. The imperial army in Germany, after the retirement of Wallenstein, amounted to about 40,000 men; that of the League to nearly the same number, both commanded by excellent officers, trained by the experience of several campaigns, and proud of a long series of victories. With such a force, little apprehension was felt at the invasion of the King of Sweden, and the less so as it commanded both Pomerania and Mecklenburg, the only countries through which he could enter Germany.

After the unsuccessful attempt of the King of Denmark to check the Emperor's progress, Gustavus Adolphus was the only prince in Europe from whom oppressed liberty could look for protection — the only one who, while he was personally qualified to conduct such an enterprise, had both political motives to recommend and wrongs to justify it. Before the commencement of the war in Lower Saxony, important political interests induced him, as well as the King of Denmark, to offer his services and his army for the defence of Germany; but the offer of the latter had, to his own misfortune, been preferred. Since that time, Wallenstein and the Emperor had adopted measures which must have been equally offensive to him as a man and as a king. Imperial troops had been despatched to the aid of the Polish king, Sigismund, to defend Prussia against the Swedes. When the king complained to Wallenstein of this act of hostility, he received for answer, "The Emperor has more soldiers than he wants for himself, he must help his friends." The Swedish ambassadors had been insolently ordered by Wallenstein to withdraw from the conference at Lubeck; and when, unawed by this command, they were courageous enough to remain, contrary to the law of nations, he had threatened them with violence. Ferdinand had also insulted the Swedish flag, and intercepted the king's despatches to Transylvania. He also threw every obstacle in the way of a peace betwixt Poland and Sweden, supported the pretensions of Sigismund to the Swedish throne, and denied the right of Gustavus to the title of king. Deigning no regard to the repeated remonstrances of Gustavus, he rather aggravated the offence by new grievances, than acceded the required satisfaction.

So many personal motives, supported by important considerations, both of policy and religion, and seconded by pressing invitations from Germany, had their full weight with a prince, who was naturally the more jealous of his royal prerogative the more it was questioned, who was flattered by the glory he hoped to gain as Protector of the Oppressed, and passionately loved war as the element of his genius. But, until a truce or peace with Poland should set his hands free, a new and dangerous war was not to be thought of.

Cardinal Richelieu had the merit of effecting this truce with Poland. This great statesman, who guided the helm of Europe, while in France he repressed the rage of faction and the insolence of the nobles, pursued steadily, amidst the cares of a stormy administration, his plan of lowering the ascendancy of the House of Austria. But circumstances opposed considerable obstacles to the execution of his designs; and even the greatest minds cannot, with impunity, defy the prejudices of the age. The minister of a Roman Catholic king, and a Cardinal, he was prevented by the purple he bore from joining the enemies of that church in an open attack on a power which had the address to sanctify its ambitious encroachments under the name of religion. The external deference which Richelieu was obliged to pay to the narrow views of his contemporaries limited his exertions to secret negociations, by which he endeavoured to gain the hand of others to accomplish the enlightened projects of his own mind. After a fruitless attempt to prevent the peace between Denmark and the Emperor, he had recourse to Gustavus Adolphus, the hero of his age. No exertion was spared to bring this monarch to a favourable decision, and at the same time to facilitate the execution of it. Charnasse, an unsuspected agent of the Cardinal, proceeded to Polish Prussia, where Gustavus Adolphus was conducting the war against Sigismund, and alternately visited these princes, in order to persuade them to a truce or peace. Gustavus had been long inclined to it, and the French minister succeeded at last in opening the eyes of Sigismund to his true interests, and to the deceitful policy of the Emperor. A truce for six years was agreed on, Gustavus being allowed to retain all his conquests. This treaty gave him also what he had so long desired, the liberty of directing his arms against the Emperor. For this the French ambassador offered him the alliance of his sovereign and considerable subsidies. But Gustavus Adolphus was justly apprehensive lest the acceptance of the assistance should make him dependent upon France, and fetter him in his career of conquest, while an alliance with a Roman Catholic power might excite distrust among the Protestants.

If the war was just and necessary, the circumstances under which it was undertaken were not less promising. The name of the Emperor, it is true, was formidable, his resources inexhaustible, his power hitherto invincible. So dangerous a contest would have dismayed any other than Gustavus. He saw all the obstacles and dangers which opposed his undertaking, but he knew also the means by which, as he hoped, they might be conquered. His army, though not numerous, was well disciplined, inured to hardship by a severe climate and campaigns, and trained to victory in the war with Poland. Sweden, though poor in men and money, and overtaxed by an eight years' war, was devoted to its monarch with an enthusiasm which assured him of the ready support of his subjects. In Germany, the name of the Emperor was at least as much hated as feared. The Protestant princes only awaited the arrival of a deliverer to throw off his intolerable yoke, and openly declare for the Swedes. Even the Roman Catholic states would welcome an antagonist to the Emperor, whose opposition might control his overwhelming influence. The first victory gained on German ground would be decisive. It would encourage those princes who still hesitated to declare themselves, strengthen the cause of his adherents, augment his troops, and open resources for the maintenance of the campaign. If the greater part of the German states were impoverished by oppression, the flourishing Hanse towns had escaped, and they could not hesitate, by a small voluntary sacrifice, to avert the general ruin. As the imperialists should be driven from the different provinces, their armies would diminish, since they were subsisting on the countries in which they were encamped. The strength, too, of the Emperor had been lessened by ill-timed detachments to Italy and the Netherlands; while Spain, weakened by the loss of the Manilla galleons, and engaged in a serious war in the Netherlands, could afford him little support. Great Britain, on the other hand, gave the King of Sweden hope of considerable subsidies; and France, now at peace with itself, came forward with the most favourable offers.

But the strongest pledge for the success of his undertaking Gustavus found — in himself. Prudence demanded that he should embrace all the foreign assistance he could, in order to guard his enterprise from the imputation of rashness; but all his confidence and courage were entirely derived from himself. He was indisputably the greatest general of his age, and the bravest soldier in the army which he had formed. Familiar with the tactics of Greece and Rome, he had discovered a more effective system of warfare, which was adopted as a model by the most eminent commanders of subsequent times. He reduced the unwieldy squadrons of cavalry, and rendered their movements more light and rapid; and, with the same view, he widened the intervals between his battalions. Instead of the usual array in a single line, he disposed his forces in two lines, that the second might advance in the event of the first giving way.

He made up for his want of cavalry, by placing infantry among the horse; a practice which frequently decided the victory. Europe first learned from him the importance of infantry. All Germany was astonished at the strict discipline which, at the first, so creditably distinguished the Swedish army within their territories; all disorders were punished with the utmost severity, particularly impiety, theft, gambling, and duelling. The Swedish articles of war enforced frugality. In the camp, the King's tent not excepted, neither silver nor gold was to be seen. The general's eye looked as vigilantly to the morals as to the martial bravery of his soldiers; every regiment was ordered to form round its chaplain for morning and evening prayers. In all these points the lawgiver was also an example. A sincere and ardent piety exalted his courage. Equally free from the coarse infidelity which leaves the passions of the barbarian without a control, — and from the grovelling superstition of Ferdinand, who humbled himself to the dust before the Supreme Being, while he haughtily trampled on his fellow-creature — in the height of his success he was ever a man and a Christian — in the height of his devotion, a king and a hero. The hardships of war he shared with the meanest soldier in his army; maintained a calm serenity amidst the hottest fury of battle; his glance was omnipresent, and he intrepidly forgot the danger while he exposed himself to the greatest peril. His natural courage, indeed, too often made him forget the duty of a general; and the life of a king ended in the death of a common soldier. But such a leader was followed to victory alike by the coward and the brave, and his eagle glance marked every heroic deed which his example had inspired. The fame of their sovereign excited in the nation an enthusiastic sense of their own importance; proud of their king, the peasant in Finland and Gothland joyfully contributed his pittance; the soldier willingly shed his blood; and the lofty energy which his single mind had imparted to the nation long survived its creator.

The necessity of the war was acknowledged, but the best plan of conducting it was a matter of much question. Even to the bold Chancellor Oxenstiern, an offensive war appeared too daring a measure; the resources of his poor and conscientious master, appeared to him too slender to compete with those of a despotic sovereign, who held all Germany at his command. But the minister's timid scruples were overruled by the hero's penetrating prudence. "If we await the enemy in Sweden," said Gustavus, "in the event of a defeat every thing would be lost, by a fortunate commencement in Germany everything would be gained. The sea is wide, and we have a long line of coast in Sweden to defend. If the enemy's fleet should escape us, or our own be defeated, it would, in either case, be impossible to prevent the enemy's landing. Every thing depends on the retention of Stralsund. So long as this harbour is open to us, we shall both command the Baltic, and secure a retreat from Germany. But to protect this port, we must not remain in Sweden, but advance at once into Pomerania. Let us talk no more, then, of a defensive war, by which we should sacrifice our greatest advantages. Sweden must not be doomed to behold a hostile banner; if we are vanquished in Germany, it will be time enough to follow your plan."

Gustavus resolved to cross the Baltic and attack the Emperor. His preparations were made with the utmost expedition, and his precautionary measures were not less prudent than the resolution itself was bold and magnanimous. Before engaging in so distant a war, it was necessary to secure Sweden against its neighbours. At a personal interview with the King of Denmark at Markaroed, Gustavus assured himself of the friendship of that monarch; his frontier on the side of Moscow was well guarded; Poland might be held in check from Germany, if it betrayed any design of infringing the truce. Falkenberg, a Swedish ambassador, who visited the courts of Holland and Germany, obtained the most flattering promises from several Protestant princes, though none of them yet possessed courage or self-devotion enough to enter into a formal alliance with him. Lubeck and Hamburg engaged to advance him money, and to accept Swedish copper in return. Emissaries were also despatched to the Prince of Transylvania, to excite that implacable enemy of Austria to arms.

In the mean time, Swedish levies were made in Germany and the Netherlands, the regiments increased to their full complement, new ones raised, transports provided, a fleet fitted out, provisions, military stores, and money collected. Thirty ships of war were in a short time prepared, 15,000 men equipped, and 200 transports were ready to convey them across the Baltic. A greater force Gustavus Adolphus was unwilling to carry into Germany, and even the maintenance of this exceeded the revenues of his kingdom. But however small his army, it was admirable in all points of discipline, courage, and experience, and might serve as the nucleus of a more powerful armament, if it once gained the German frontier, and its first attempts were attended with success. Oxenstiern, at once general and chancellor, was posted with 10,000 men in Prussia, to protect that province against Poland. Some regular troops, and a considerable body of militia, which served as a nursery for the main body, remained in Sweden, as a defence against a sudden invasion by any treacherous neighbour.

These were the measures taken for the external defence of the kingdom. Its internal administration was provided for with equal care. The government was intrusted to the Council of State, and the finances to the Palatine John Casimir, the brother-in-law of the King, while his wife, tenderly as he was attached to her, was excluded from all share in the government, for which her limited talents incapacitated her. He set his house in order like a dying man. On the 20th May, 1630, when all his measures were arranged, and all was ready for his departure, the King appeared in the Diet at Stockholm, to bid the States a solemn farewell. Taking in his arms his daughter Christina, then only four years old, who, in the cradle, had been acknowledged as his successor, he presented her to the States as the future sovereign, exacted from them a renewal of the oath of allegiance to her, in case he should never more return; and then read the ordinances for the government of the kingdom during his absence, or the minority of his daughter. The whole assembly was dissolved in tears, and the King himself was some time before he could attain sufficient composure to deliver his farewell address to the States.

"Not lightly or wantonly," said he, "am I about to involve myself and you in this new and dangerous war; God is my witness that *I* do not fight to gratify my own ambition. But the Emperor has wronged me most shamefully in the person of my ambassadors. He has supported my enemies, persecuted my friends and brethren, trampled my religion in the dust, and even stretched his revengeful arm against my crown. The oppressed states of Germany call loudly for aid, which, by God's help, we will give them.

"I am fully sensible of the dangers to which my life will be exposed. I have never yet shrunk from them, nor is it likely that I shall escape them all. Hitherto, Providence has wonderfully protected me, but I shall at last fall in defence of my country. I commend you to the protection of Heaven. Be just, be conscientious, act uprightly, and we shall meet again in eternity.

"To you, my Counsellors of State, I address myself first. May God enlighten you, and fill you with wisdom, to promote the welfare of my people. You, too, my brave nobles, I commend to the divine protection. Continue to prove yourselves the worthy successors of those Gothic heroes, whose bravery humbled to the dust the pride of ancient Rome. To you, ministers of religion, I recommend moderation and unity; be yourselves examples of the virtues which you preach, and abuse not your influence over the minds of my people. On you, deputies of the burgesses, and the peasantry, I entreat the blessing of heaven; may your industry be rewarded by a prosperous harvest; your stores plenteously filled, and may you be crowned abundantly with all the blessings of this life. For the prosperity of all my subjects, absent and present, I offer my warmest prayers to Heaven. I bid you all a sincere — it may be — an eternal farewell."

The embarkation of the troops took place at Elfsknaben, where the fleet lay at anchor. An immense concourse flocked thither to witness this magnificent spectacle. The hearts of the spectators were agitated by varied emotions, as they alternately considered the vastness of the enterprise, and the greatness of the leader. Among the superior officers who commanded in this army were Gustavus Horn, the Rhinegrave Otto Lewis, Henry Matthias, Count Thurn, Ottenberg, Baudissen, Banner, Teufel, Tott, Mutsenfahl, Falkenberg, Kniphausen, and other distinguished names. Detained by contrary winds, the fleet did not sail till June, and on the 24th of that month reached the Island of Rugen in Pomerania.

Gustavus Adolphus was the first who landed. In the presence of his suite, he knelt on the shore of Germany to return thanks to the Almighty for the safe arrival of his fleet and his army. He landed his troops on the Islands of Wollin and Usedom; upon his approach, the imperial garrisons abandoned their entrenchments and fled. He advanced rapidly on Stettin, to secure this important place before the appearance of the Imperialists. Bogislaus XIV., Duke of Pomerania, a feeble and superannuated prince, had been long tired out by the outrages committed by the latter within his territories; but too weak to resist, he had contented himself with murmurs. The appearance of his deliverer, instead of animating his courage, increased his fear and anxiety. Severely as his country had suffered from the Imperialists, the risk of incurring the Emperor's vengeance prevented him from declaring openly for the Swedes. Gustavus Adolphus, who was encamped under the walls of the town, summoned the city to receive a Swedish garrison. Bogislaus appeared in person in the camp of Gustavus, to deprecate this condition. "I come to you," said Gustavus, "not as an enemy but a friend. I wage no war against Pomerania, nor against the German empire, but against the enemies of both. In my hands this duchy shall be sacred; and it shall be restored to you at the conclusion of the campaign, by me, with more certainty, than by any other. Look to the traces of the imperial force within your territories, and to mine in Usedom; and decide whether you will have the Emperor or me as your friend. What have you to expect, if the Emperor should make himself master of your capital? Will he deal with you more leniently than I? Or is it your intention to stop my progress? The case is pressing: decide at once, and do not compel me to have recourse to more violent measures."

The alternative was a painful one. On the one side, the King of Sweden was before his gates with a formidable army; on the other, he saw the inevitable vengeance of the Emperor, and the fearful example of so many German princes, who were now wandering in misery, the victims of that revenge. The more immediate danger decided his resolution. The gates of Stettin were opened to the king; the Swedish troops entered; and the Austrians, who were advancing by rapid marches, anticipated. The capture of this place procured for the king a firm footing in Pomerania, the command of the Oder, and a magazine for his troops. To prevent a charge of treachery, Bogislaus was careful to excuse this step to the Emperor on the plea of necessity; but aware of Ferdinand's implacable disposition, he entered into a close alliance with his new protector. By this league with Pomerania, Gustavus secured a powerful friend in Germany, who covered his rear, and maintained his communication with Sweden.

As Ferdinand was already the aggressor in Prussia, Gustavus Adolphus thought himself absolved from the usual formalities, and commenced hostilities without any declaration of war. To the other European powers, he justified his conduct in a manifesto, in which he detailed the grounds which had led him to take up arms. Meanwhile he continued his progress in Pomerania, while he saw his army daily increasing. The troops which had fought under Mansfeld, Duke Christian of Brunswick, the King of Denmark, and Wallenstein, came in crowds, both officers and soldiers, to join his victorious standard.

At the Imperial court, the invasion of the king of Sweden at first excited far less attention than it merited. The pride of Austria, extravagantly elated by its unheard-of successes, looked down with contempt upon a prince, who, with a handful of men, came from an obscure corner of Europe, and who owed his past successes, as they imagined, entirely to the incapacity of a weak opponent. The depreciatory representation which Wallenstein had artfully given of the Swedish power, increased the Emperor's security; for what had he to fear from an enemy, whom his general undertook to drive with such ease from Germany? Even the rapid progress of Gustavus Adolphus in Pomerania, could not entirely dispel this prejudice, which the mockeries of the courtiers continued to feed. He was called in Vienna the Snow King, whom the cold of the north kept together, but who would infallibly melt as he advanced southward. Even the electors, assembled in Ratisbon, disregarded his representations; and, influenced by an abject complaisance to Ferdinand, refused him even the title of king. But while they mocked him in Ratisbon and Vienna, in Mecklenburg and Pomerania, one strong town after another fell into his hands.

Notwithstanding this contempt, the Emperor thought it proper to offer to adjust his differences with Sweden by negociation, and for that purpose sent plenipotentiaries to Denmark. But their instructions showed how little he was in earnest in these proposals, for he still continued to refuse to Gustavus the title of king. He hoped by this means to throw on the king of Sweden the odium of being the aggressor, and thereby to ensure the support of the States of the empire. The conference at Dantzic proved, as might be expected, fruitless, and the animosity of both parties was increased to its utmost by an intemperate correspondence.

An imperial general, Torquato Conti, who commanded in Pomerania, had, in the mean time, made a vain attempt to wrest Stettin from the Swedes. The Imperialists were driven out from one place after another; Damm, Stargard, Camin, and Wolgast, soon fell into the hands of Gustavus. To revenge himself upon the Duke of Pomerania, the imperial general permitted his troops, upon his retreat, to exercise every barbarity on the unfortunate inhabitants of Pomerania, who had already suffered but too severely from his avarice. On pretence of cutting off the resources of the Swedes, the whole country was laid waste and plundered; and often when the Imperialists were unable any longer to maintain a place, it was laid in ashes, in order to leave the enemy nothing but ruins. But these barbarities only served to place in a more favourable light the opposite conduct of the Swedes, and to win all hearts to their humane monarch. The Swedish soldier paid for all he required; no private property was injured on his march. The Swedes consequently were received with open arms both in town and country, whilst every Imperialist that fell into the hands of the Pomeranian peasantry was ruthlessly murdered. Many Pomeranians entered into the service of Sweden, and the estates of this exhausted country willingly voted the king a contribution of 100,000 florins.

Torquato Conti, who, with all his severity of character, was a consummate general, endeavoured to render Stettin useless to the king of Sweden, as he could not deprive him of it. He entrenched himself upon the Oder, at Gartz, above Stettin, in order, by commanding that river, to cut off the water communication of the town with the rest of Germany. Nothing could induce him to attack the King of Sweden, who was his superior in numbers, while the latter was equally cautious not to storm the strong entrenchments of the Imperialists. Torquato, too deficient in troops and money to act upon the offensive against the king, hoped by this plan of operations to give time for Tilly to hasten to the defence of Pomerania, and then, in conjunction with that general, to attack the Swedes. Seizing the opportunity of the temporary absence of Gustavus, he made a sudden attempt upon Stettin, but the Swedes were not unprepared for him. A vigorous attack of the Imperialists was firmly repulsed, and Torquato was forced to retire with great loss. For this auspicious commencement of the war, however, Gustavus was, it must be owned, as much indebted to his good fortune as to his military talents. The imperial troops in Pomerania had been greatly reduced since Wallenstein's dismissal; moreover, the outrages they had committed were now severely revenged upon them; wasted and exhausted, the country no longer afforded them a subsistence. All discipline was at an end; the orders of the officers were disregarded, while their numbers daily decreased by desertion, and by a general mortality, which the piercing cold of a strange climate had produced among them.

Under these circumstances, the imperial general was anxious to allow his troops the repose of winter quarters, but he had to do with an enemy to whom the climate of Germany had no winter. Gustavus had taken the precaution of providing his soldiers with dresses of sheep-skin, to enable them to keep the field even in the most inclement season. The imperial plenipotentiaries, who came to treat with him for a cessation of hostilities, received this discouraging answer: "The Swedes are soldiers in winter as well as in summer, and not disposed to oppress the unfortunate peasantry. The Imperialists may act as they think proper, but they need not expect to remain undisturbed." Torquato Conti soon after resigned a command, in which neither riches nor reputation were to be gained.

In this inequality of the two armies, the advantage was necessarily on the side of the Swedes. The Imperialists were incessantly harassed in their winter quarters; Greifenhagen, an important place upon the Oder, taken by storm, and the towns of Gartz and Piritz were at last abandoned by the enemy. In the whole of Pomerania, Greifswald, Demmin, and Colberg alone remained in their hands, and these the king made great preparations to besiege. The enemy directed their retreat towards Brandenburg, in which much of their artillery and baggage, and many prisoners fell into the hands of the pursuers.

By seizing the passes of Riebnitz and Damgarden, Gustavus had opened a passage into Mecklenburg, whose inhabitants were invited to return to their allegiance under their legitimate sovereigns, and to expel the adherents of Wallenstein. The Imperialists, however, gained the important town of Rostock by stratagem, and thus prevented the farther advance of the king, who was unwilling to divide his forces. The exiled dukes of Mecklenburg had ineffectually employed the princes assembled at Ratisbon to intercede with the Emperor: in vain they had endeavoured to soften Ferdinand, by renouncing the alliance of the king, and every idea of resistance. But, driven to despair by the Emperor's inflexibility, they openly espoused the side of Sweden, and raising troops, gave the command of them to Francis Charles Duke of Saxe-Lauenburg. That general made himself master of several strong places on the Elbe, but lost them afterwards to the Imperial General Pappenheim, who was despatched to oppose him. Soon afterwards, besieged by the latter in the town of Ratzeburg, he was compelled to surrender with all his troops. Thus ended the attempt which these unfortunate princes made to recover their territories; and it was reserved for the victorious arm of Gustavus Adolphus to render them that brilliant service.

The Imperialists had thrown themselves into Brandenburg, which now became the theatre of the most barbarous atrocities. These outrages were inflicted upon the subjects of a prince who had never injured the Emperor, and whom, moreover, he was at the very time inciting to take up arms against the King of Sweden. The sight of the disorders of their soldiers, which want of money compelled them to wink at, and of authority over their troops, excited the disgust even of the imperial generals; and, from very shame, their commander-in-chief, Count Schaumburg, wished to resign.

Without a sufficient force to protect his territories, and left by the Emperor, in spite of the most pressing remonstrances, without assistance, the Elector of Brandenburg at last issued an edict, ordering his subjects to repel force by force, and to put to death without mercy every Imperial soldier who should henceforth be detected in plundering. To such a height had the violence of outrage and the misery of the government risen, that nothing was left to the sovereign, but the desperate extremity of sanctioning private vengeance by a formal law.

The Swedes had pursued the Imperialists into Brandenburg; and only the Elector's refusal to open to him the fortress of Custrin for his march, obliged the king to lay aside his design of besieging Frankfort on the Oder. He therefore returned to complete the conquest of Pomerania, by the capture of Demmin and Colberg. In the mean time, Field-Marshal Tilly was advancing to the defence of Brandenburg.

This general, who could boast as yet of never having suffered a defeat, the conqueror of Mansfeld, of Duke Christian of Brunswick, of the Margrave of Baden, and the King of Denmark, was now in the Swedish monarch to meet an opponent worthy of his fame. Descended of a noble family in Liege, Tilly had formed his military talents in the wars of the Netherlands, which was then the great school for generals. He soon found an opportunity of distinguishing himself under Rodolph II. in Hungary, where he rapidly rose from one step to another. After the peace, he entered into the service of Maximilian of Bavaria, who made him commander-in-chief with absolute powers. Here, by his excellent regulations, he was the founder of the Bavarian army; and to him, chiefly, Maximilian was indebted for his superiority in the field. Upon the termination of the Bohemian war, he was appointed commander of the troops of the League; and, after Wallenstein's dismissal, generalissimo of the imperial armies. Equally stern towards his soldiers and implacable towards his enemies, and as gloomy and impenetrable as Wallenstein, he was greatly his superior in probity and disinterestedness. A bigoted zeal for religion, and a bloody spirit of persecution, co-operated, with the natural ferocity of his character, to make him the terror of the Protestants. A strange and terrific aspect bespoke his character: of low stature, thin, with hollow cheeks, a long nose, a broad and wrinkled forehead, large whiskers, and a pointed chin; he was generally attired in a Spanish doublet of green satin, with slashed sleeves, with a small high peaked hat upon his head, surmounted by a red feather which hung down to his back. His whole aspect recalled to recollection the Duke of Alva, the scourge of the Flemings, and his actions were far from effacing the impression. Such was the general who was now to be opposed to the hero of the north.

Tilly was far from undervaluing his antagonist, "The King of Sweden," said he in the Diet at Ratisbon, "is an enemy both prudent and brave, inured to war, and in the flower of his age. His plans are excellent, his resources considerable; his subjects enthusiastically attached to him. His army, composed of Swedes, Germans, Livonians, Finlanders, Scots and English, by its devoted obedience to their leader, is blended into one nation: he is a gamester in playing with whom not to have lost is to have won a great deal."

The progress of the King of Sweden in Brandenburg and Pomerania, left the new generalissimo no time to lose; and his presence was now urgently called for by those who commanded in that quarter. With all expedition, he collected the imperial troops which were dispersed over the empire; but it required time to obtain from the exhausted and impoverished provinces the necessary supplies. At last, about the middle of winter, he appeared at the head of 20,000 men, before Frankfort on the Oder, where he was joined by Schaumburg. Leaving to this general the defence of Frankfort, with a sufficient garrison, he hastened to Pomerania, with a view of saving Demmin, and relieving Colberg, which was already hard pressed by the Swedes. But even before he had left Brandenburg, Demmin, which was but poorly defended by the Duke of Savelli, had surrendered to the king, and Colberg, after a five months' siege, was starved into a capitulation. As the passes in Upper Pomerania were well guarded, and the king's camp near Schwedt defied attack, Tilly abandoned his offensive plan of operations, and retreated towards the Elbe to besiege Magdeburg.

The capture of Demmin opened to the king a free passage into Mecklenburg; but a more important enterprise drew his arms into another quarter. Scarcely had Tilly commenced his retrograde movement, when suddenly breaking up his camp at Schwedt, the king marched his whole force against Frankfort on the Oder. This town, badly fortified, was defended by a garrison of 8,000 men, mostly composed of those ferocious bands who had so cruelly ravaged Pomerania and Brandenburg. It was now attacked with such impetuosity, that on the third day it was taken by storm. The Swedes, assured of victory, rejected every offer of capitulation, as they were resolved to exercise the dreadful right of retaliation. For Tilly, soon after his arrival, had surrounded a Swedish detachment, and, irritated by their obstinate resistance, had cut them in pieces to a man. This cruelty was not forgotten by the Swedes. "New Brandenburg Quarter", they replied to the Imperialists who begged their lives, and slaughtered them without mercy. Several thousands were either killed or taken, and many were drowned in the Oder, the rest fled to Silesia. All their artillery fell into the hands of the Swedes. To satisfy the rage of his troops, Gustavus Adolphus was under the necessity of giving up the town for three hours to plunder.

While the king was thus advancing from one conquest to another, and, by his success, encouraging the Protestants to active resistance, the Emperor proceeded to enforce the Edict of Restitution, and, by his exorbitant pretensions, to exhaust the patience of the states. Compelled by necessity, he continued the violent course which he had begun with such arrogant confidence; the difficulties into which his arbitrary conduct had plunged him, he could only extricate himself from by measures still more arbitrary. But in so complicated a body as the German empire, despotism must always create the most dangerous convulsions. With astonishment, the princes beheld the constitution of the empire overthrown, and the state of nature to which matters were again verging, suggested to them the idea of self-defence, the only means of protection in such a state of things. The steps openly taken by the Emperor against the Lutheran church, had at last removed the veil from the eyes of John George, who had been so long the dupe of his artful policy. Ferdinand, too, had personally offended him by the exclusion of his son from the archbishopric of Magdeburg; and field-marshal Arnheim, his new favourite and minister, spared no pains to increase the resentment of his master. Arnheim had formerly been an imperial general under Wallenstein, and being still zealously attached to him, he was eager to avenge his old benefactor and himself on the Emperor, by detaching Saxony from the Austrian interests. Gustavus Adolphus, supported by the Protestant states, would be invincible; a consideration which already filled the Emperor with alarm. The example of Saxony would probably influence others, and the Emperor's fate seemed now in a manner to depend upon the Elector's decision. The artful favourite impressed upon his master this idea of his own importance, and advised him to terrify the Emperor, by threatening an alliance with Sweden, and thus to extort from his fears, what he had sought in vain from his gratitude. The favourite, however, was far from wishing him actually to enter into the Swedish alliance, but, by holding aloof from both parties, to maintain his own importance and independence. Accordingly, he laid before him a plan, which only wanted a more able hand to carry it into execution, and recommended him, by heading the Protestant party, to erect a third power in Germany, and thereby maintain the balance between Sweden and Austria.

This project was peculiarly flattering to the Saxon Elector, to whom the idea of being dependent upon Sweden, or of longer submitting to the tyranny of the Emperor, was equally hateful. He could not, with indifference, see the control of German affairs wrested from him by a foreign prince; and incapable as he was of taking a principal part, his vanity would not condescend to act a subordinate one. He resolved, therefore, to draw every possible advantage from the progress of Gustavus, but to pursue, independently, his own separate plans. With this view, he consulted with the Elector of Brandenburg, who, from similar causes, was ready to act against the Emperor, but, at the same time, was jealous of Sweden. In a Diet at Torgau, having assured himself of the support of his Estates, he invited the Protestant States of the empire to a general convention, which took place at Leipzig, on the 6th February 1631. Brandenburg, Hesse Cassel, with several princes, counts, estates of the empire, and Protestant bishops were present, either personally or by deputy, at this assembly, which the chaplain to the Saxon Court, Dr. Hoe von Hohenegg, opened with a vehement discourse from the pulpit. The

Emperor had, in vain, endeavoured to prevent this self-appointed convention, whose object was evidently to provide for its own defence, and which the presence of the Swedes in the empire, rendered more than usually alarming. Emboldened by the progress of Gustavus Adolphus, the assembled princes asserted their rights, and after a session of two months broke up, with adopting a resolution which placed the Emperor in no slight embarrassment. Its import was to demand of the Emperor, in a general address, the revocation of the Edict of Restitution, the withdrawal of his troops from their capitals and fortresses, the suspension of all existing proceedings, and the abolition of abuses; and, in the mean time, to raise an army of 40,000 men, to enable them to redress their own grievances, if the Emperor should still refuse satisfaction.

A further incident contributed not a little to increase the firmness of the Protestant princes. The King of Sweden had, at last, overcome the scruples which had deterred him from a closer alliance with France, and, on the 13th January 1631, concluded a formal treaty with this crown. After a serious dispute respecting the treatment of the Roman Catholic princes of the empire, whom France took under her protection, and against whom Gustavus claimed the right of retaliation, and after some less important differences with regard to the title of majesty, which the pride of France was loth to concede to the King of Sweden, Richelieu yielded the second, and Gustavus Adolphus the first point, and the treaty was signed at Beerwald in Neumark. The contracting parties mutually covenanted to defend each other with a military force, to protect their common friends, to restore to their dominions the deposed princes of the empire, and to replace every thing, both on the frontier and in the interior of Germany, on the same footing on which it stood before the commencement of the war. For this end, Sweden engaged to maintain an army of 30,000 men in Germany, and France agreed to furnish the Swedes with an annual subsidy of 400,000 dollars. If the arms of Gustavus were successful, he was to respect the Roman Catholic religion and the constitution of the empire in all the conquered places, and to make no attempt against either. All Estates and princes whether Protestant or Roman Catholic, either in Germany or in other countries, were to be invited to become parties to the treaty; neither France nor Sweden was to conclude a separate peace without the knowledge and consent of the other; and the treaty itself was to continue in force for five years.

Great as was the struggle to the King of Sweden to receive subsidies from France, and sacrifice his independence in the conduct of the war, this alliance with France decided his cause in Germany. Protected, as he now was, by the greatest power in Europe, the German states began to feel confidence in his undertaking, for the issue of which they had hitherto good reason to tremble. He became truly formidable to the Emperor. The Roman Catholic princes too, who, though they were anxious to humble Austria, had witnessed his progress with distrust, were less alarmed now that an alliance with a Roman Catholic power ensured his respect for their religion. And thus, while Gustavus Adolphus protected the Protestant religion and the liberties of Germany against the aggression of Ferdinand, France secured those liberties, and the Roman Catholic religion, against Gustavus himself, if the intoxication of success should hurry him beyond the bounds of moderation.

The King of Sweden lost no time in apprizing the members of the confederacy of Leipzig of the treaty concluded with France, and inviting them to a closer union with himself. The application was seconded by France, who spared no pains to win over the Elector of Saxony. Gustavus was willing to be content with secret support, if the princes should deem it too bold a step as yet to declare openly in his favour. Several princes gave him hopes of his proposals being accepted on the first favourable opportunity; but the Saxon Elector, full of jealousy and distrust towards the King of Sweden, and true to the selfish policy he had pursued, could not be prevailed upon to give a decisive answer.

The resolution of the confederacy of Leipzig, and the alliance betwixt France and Sweden, were news equally disagreeable to the Emperor. Against them he employed the thunder of imperial ordinances, and the want of an army saved France from the full weight of his displeasure. Remonstrances were addressed to all the members of the confederacy, strongly prohibiting them from enlisting troops. They retorted with explanations equally vehement, justified their conduct upon the principles of natural right, and continued their preparations.

Meantime, the imperial generals, deficient both in troops and money, found themselves reduced to the disagreeable alternative of losing sight either of the King of Sweden, or of the Estates of the empire, since with a divided force they were not a match for either. The movements of the Protestants called their attention to the interior of the empire, while the progress of the king in Brandenburg, by threatening the hereditary possessions of Austria, required them to turn their arms to that quarter. After the conquest of Frankfort, the king had advanced upon Landsberg on the Warta, and Tilly, after a fruitless attempt to relieve it, had again returned to Magdeburg, to prosecute with vigour the siege of that town.

The rich archbishopric, of which Magdeburg was the capital, had long been in the possession of princes of the house of Brandenburg, who introduced the Protestant religion into the province. Christian William, the last administrator, had, by his alliance with Denmark, incurred the ban of the empire, on which account the chapter, to avoid the Emperor's displeasure, had formally deposed him. In his place they had elected Prince John Augustus, the second son of the Elector of Saxony, whom the Emperor rejected, in order to confer the archbishopric on his son Leopold. The Elector of Saxony complained ineffectually to the imperial court; but Christian William of Brandenburg took more active measures. Relying on the attachment of the magistracy and inhabitants of Brandenburg, and excited by chimerical hopes, he thought himself able to surmount all the obstacles which the vote of the chapter, the competition of two powerful rivals, and the Edict of Restitution opposed to his restoration. He went to Sweden, and, by the promise of a diversion in Germany, sought to obtain assistance from Gustavus. He was dismissed by that monarch not without hopes of effectual protection, but with the advice to act with caution.

Scarcely had Christian William been informed of the landing of his protector in Pomerania, than he entered Magdeburg in disguise. Appearing suddenly in the town council, he reminded the magistrates of the ravages which both town and country had suffered from the imperial troops, of the pernicious designs of Ferdinand, and the danger of the Protestant church. He then informed them that the moment of deliverance was at hand, and that Gustavus Adolphus offered them his alliance and assistance. Magdeburg, one of the most flourishing towns in Germany, enjoyed under the government of its magistrates a republican freedom, which inspired its citizens with a brave heroism. Of this they had already given proofs, in the bold defence of their rights against Wallenstein, who, tempted by their wealth, made on them the most extravagant demands. Their territory had been given up to the fury of his troops, though Magdeburg itself had escaped his vengeance. It was not difficult, therefore, for the Administrator to gain the concurrence of men in whose minds the rememberance of these outrages was still recent. An alliance was formed between the city and the Swedish king, by which Magdeburg granted to the king a free passage through its gates and territories, with liberty of enlisting soldiers within its boundaries, and on the other hand, obtained promises of effectual protection for its religion and its privileges.

The Administrator immediately collected troops and commenced hostilities, before Gustavus Adolphus was near enough to co-operate with him. He defeated some imperial detachments in the neighbourhood, made a few conquests, and even surprised Halle. But the approach of an imperial army obliged him to retreat hastily, and not without loss, to Magdeburg. Gustavus Adolphus, though displeased with his premature measures, sent Dietrich Falkenberg, an experienced officer, to direct the Administrator's military operations, and to assist him with his counsel. Falkenberg was named by the magistrates governor of the town during the war. The Prince's army was daily augmented by recruits from the neighbouring towns; and he was able for some months to maintain a petty warfare with success.

At length Count Pappenheim, having brought his expedition against the Duke of Saxe-Lauenburg to a close, approached the town. Driving the troops of the Administrator from their entrenchments, he cut off his communication with Saxony, and closely invested the place. He was soon followed by Tilly, who haughtily summoned the Elector forthwith to comply with the Edict of Restitution, to submit to the Emperor's orders, and surrender Magdeburg. The Prince's answer was spirited and resolute, and obliged Tilly at once to have recourse to arms.

In the meanwhile, the siege was prolonged, by the progress of the King of Sweden, which called the Austrian general from before the place; and the jealousy of the officers, who conducted the operations in his absence, delayed, for some months, the fall of Magdeburg. On the 30th March 1631, Tilly returned, to push the siege with vigour.

The outworks were soon carried, and Falkenberg, after withdrawing the garrisons from the points which he could no longer hold, destroyed the bridge over the Elbe. As his troops were barely sufficient to defend the extensive fortifications, the suburbs of Sudenburg and Neustadt were abandoned to the enemy, who immediately laid them in ashes. Pappenheim, now separated from Tilly, crossed the Elbe at Schonenbeck, and attacked the town from the opposite side.

The garrison, reduced by the defence of the outworks, scarcely exceeded 2000 infantry and a few hundred horse; a small number for so extensive and irregular a fortress. To supply this deficiency, the citizens were armed — a desperate expedient, which produced more evils than those it prevented. The citizens, at best but indifferent soldiers, by their disunion threw the town into confusion. The poor complained that they were exposed to every hardship and danger, while the rich, by hiring substitutes, remained at home in safety. These rumours broke out at last in an open mutiny; indifference succeeded to zeal; weariness and negligence took the place of vigilance and foresight. Dissension, combined with growing scarcity, gradually produced a feeling of despondence, many began to tremble at the desperate nature of their undertaking, and the magnitude of the power to which they were opposed. But religious zeal, an ardent love of liberty, an invincible hatred to the Austrian yoke, and the expectation of speedy relief, banished as yet the idea of a surrender; and divided as they were in every thing else, they were united in the resolve to defend themselves to the last extremity.

Their hopes of succour were apparently well founded. They knew that the confederacy of Leipzig was arming; they were aware of the near approach of Gustavus Adolphus. Both were alike interested in the preservation of Magdeburg; and a few days might bring the King of Sweden before its walls. All this was also known to Tilly, who, therefore, was anxious to make himself speedily master of the place. With this view, he had despatched a trumpeter with letters to the Administrator, the commandant, and the magistrates, offering terms of capitulation; but he received for answer, that they would rather die than surrender. A spirited sally of the citizens, also convinced him that their courage was as earnest as their words, while the king's arrival at Potsdam, with the incursions of the Swedes as far as Zerbst, filled him with uneasiness, but raised the hopes of the garrison. A second trumpeter was now despatched; but the more moderate tone of his demands increased the confidence of the besieged, and unfortunately their negligence also.

The besiegers had now pushed their approaches as far as the ditch, and vigorously cannonaded the fortifications from the abandoned batteries. One tower was entirely overthrown, but this did not facilitate an assault, as it fell sidewise upon the wall, and not into the ditch. Notwithstanding the continual bombardment, the walls had not suffered much; and the fire balls, which were intended to set the town in flames, were deprived of their effect by the excellent precautions adopted against them. But the ammunition of the besieged was nearly expended, and the cannon of the town gradually ceased to answer the fire of the Imperialists. Before a new supply could be obtained, Magdeburg would be either relieved, or taken. The hopes of the besieged were on the stretch, and all eyes anxiously directed towards the quarter in which the Swedish banners were expected to appear. Gustavus Adolphus was near enough to reach Magdeburg within three days; security grew with hope, which all things contributed to augment. On the 9th of May, the fire of the Imperialists was suddenly stopped, and the cannon withdrawn from several of the batteries. A deathlike stillness reigned in the Imperial camp. The besieged were convinced that deliverance was at hand. Both citizens and soldiers left their posts upon the ramparts early in the morning, to indulge themselves, after their long toils, with the refreshment of sleep, but it was indeed a dear sleep, and a frightful awakening.

Tilly had abandoned the hope of taking the town, before the arrival of the Swedes, by the means which he had hitherto adopted; he therefore determined to raise the siege, but first to hazard a general assault. This plan, however, was attended with great difficulties, as no breach had been effected, and the works were scarcely injured. But the council of war assembled on this occasion, declared for an assault, citing the example of Maestricht, which had been taken early in the morning, while the citizens and soldiers were reposing themselves. The attack was to be made simultaneously on four points; the night betwixt the 9th and 10th of May, was employed in the necessary preparations. Every thing was ready and awaiting the signal, which was to be given by cannon at five o'clock in the morning. The signal, however, was not given for two hours later, during which Tilly, who was still doubtful of success, again consulted the council of war. Pappenheim was ordered to attack the works of the new town, where the attempt was favoured by a sloping rampart, and a dry ditch of moderate depth. The citizens and soldiers had mostly left the walls, and the few who remained were overcome with sleep. This general, therefore, found little difficulty in mounting the wall at the head of his troops.

Falkenberg, roused by the report of musketry, hastened from the town-house, where he was employed in despatching Tilly's second trumpeter, and hurried with all the force he could hastily assemble towards the gate of the new town, which was already in the possession of the enemy. Beaten back, this intrepid general flew to another quarter, where a second party of the enemy were preparing to scale the walls. After an ineffectual resistance he fell in the commencement of the action. The roaring of musketry, the pealing of the alarm-bells, and the growing tumult apprised the awakening citizens of their danger. Hastily arming themselves, they rushed in blind confusion against the enemy. Still some hope of repulsing the besiegers remained; but the governor being killed, their efforts were without plan and co-operation, and at last their ammunition began to fail them. In the meanwhile, two other gates, hitherto unattacked, were stripped of their defenders, to meet the urgent danger within the town. The enemy quickly availed themselves of this confusion to attack these posts. The resistance was nevertheless spirited and obstinate, until four imperial regiments, at length, masters of the ramparts, fell upon the garrison in the rear, and completed their rout. Amidst the general tumult, a brave captain, named Schmidt, who still headed a few of the more resolute against the enemy, succeeded in driving them to the gates; here he fell mortally wounded, and with him expired the hopes of Magdeburg. Before noon, all the works were carried, and the town was in the enemy's hands.

Two gates were now opened by the storming party for the main body, and Tilly marched in with part of his infantry. Immediately occupying the principal streets, he drove the citizens with pointed cannon into their dwellings, there to await their destiny. They were not long held in suspense; a word from Tilly decided the fate of Magdeburg.

Even a more humane general would in vain have recommended mercy to such soldiers; but Tilly never made the attempt. Left by their general's silence masters of the lives of all the citizens, the soldiery broke into the houses to satiate their most brutal appetites. The prayers of innocence excited some compassion in the hearts of the Germans, but none in the rude breasts of Pappenheim's Walloons. Scarcely had the savage cruelty commenced, when the other gates were thrown open, and the cavalry, with the fearful hordes of the Croats, poured in upon the devoted inhabitants.

Here commenced a scene of horrors for which history has no language — poetry no pencil. Neither innocent childhood, nor helpless old age; neither youth, sex, rank, nor beauty, could disarm the fury of the conquerors. Wives were abused in the arms of their husbands, daughters at the feet of their parents; and the defenceless sex exposed to the double sacrifice of virtue and life. No situation, however obscure, or however sacred, escaped the rapacity of the enemy. In a single church fifty-three women were found beheaded. The Croats amused themselves with throwing children into the flames; Pappenheim's Walloons with stabbing infants at the mother's breast. Some officers of the League, horror-struck at this dreadful scene, ventured to remind Tilly that he had it in his power to stop the carnage. "Return in an hour," was his answer; "I will see what I can do; the soldier must have some reward for his danger and toils." These horrors lasted with unabated fury, till at last the smoke and flames proved a check to the plunderers. To augment the confusion and to divert the resistance of the inhabitants, the Imperialists had, in the commencement of the assault, fired the town in several places. The wind rising rapidly, spread the flames, till the blaze became universal. Fearful, indeed, was the tumult amid clouds of smoke, heaps of dead bodies, the clash of swords, the crash of falling ruins, and streams of blood. The atmosphere glowed; and the intolerable heat forced at last even the murderers to take refuge in their camp. In less than twelve hours, this strong, populous, and flourishing city, one of the finest in Germany, was reduced to ashes, with the exception of two churches and a few houses. The Administrator, Christian William, after receiving several wounds, was taken prisoner, with three of the burgomasters; most of the officers and magistrates had already met an enviable death. The avarice of the officers had saved 400 of the richest citizens, in the hope of extorting from them an exorbitant ransom. But this humanity was confined to the officers of the League, whom the ruthless barbarity of the Imperialists caused to be regarded as guardian angels.

Scarcely had the fury of the flames abated, when the Imperialists returned to renew the pillage amid the ruins and ashes of the town. Many were suffocated by the smoke; many found rich booty in the cellars, where the citizens had concealed their more valuable effects. On the 13th of May, Tilly himself appeared in the town, after the streets had been cleared of ashes and dead bodies. Horrible and revolting to humanity was the scene that presented itself. The living crawling from under the dead, children wandering about with heart-rending cries, calling for their parents; and infants still sucking the breasts of their lifeless mothers. More than 6,000 bodies were thrown into the Elbe to clear the streets; a much greater number had been consumed by the flames. The whole number of the slain was reckoned at not less than 30,000.

The entrance of the general, which took place on the 14th, put a stop to the plunder, and saved the few who had hitherto contrived to escape. About a thousand people were taken out of the cathedral, where they had remained three days and two nights, without food, and in momentary fear of death. Tilly promised them quarter, and commanded bread to be distributed among them. The next day, a solemn mass was performed in the cathedral, and 'Te Deum' sung amidst the discharge of artillery. The imperial general rode through the streets, that he might be able, as an eyewitness, to inform his master that no such conquest had been made since the destruction of Troy and Jerusalem. Nor was this an exaggeration, whether we consider the greatness, importance, and prosperity of the city razed, or the fury of its ravagers.

In Germany, the tidings of the dreadful fate of Magdeburg caused triumphant joy to the Roman Catholics, while it spread terror and consternation among the Protestants. Loudly and generally they complained against the king of Sweden, who, with so strong a force, and in the very neighbourhood, had left an allied city to its fate. Even the most reasonable deemed his inaction inexplicable; and lest he should lose irretrievably the good will of the people, for whose deliverance he had engaged in this war, Gustavus was under the necessity of publishing to the world a justification of his own conduct.

He had attacked, and on the 16th April, carried Landsberg, when he was apprised of the danger of Magdeburg. He resolved immediately to march to the relief of that town; and he moved with all his cavalry, and ten regiments of infantry towards the Spree. But the position which he held in Germany, made it necessary that he should not move forward without securing his rear. In traversing a country where he was surrounded by suspicious friends and dangerous enemies, and where a single premature movement might cut off his communication with his own kingdom, the utmost vigilance and caution were necessary. The Elector of Brandenburg had already opened the fortress of Custrin to the flying Imperialists, and closed the gates against their pursuers. If now Gustavus should fail in his attack upon Tilly, the Elector might again open his fortresses to the Imperialists, and the king, with an enemy both in front and rear, would be irrecoverably lost. In order to prevent this contingency, he demanded that the Elector should allow him to hold the fortresses of Custrin and Spandau, till the siege of Magdeburg should be raised.

Nothing could be more reasonable than this demand. The services which Gustavus had lately rendered the Elector, by expelling the Imperialists from Brandenburg, claimed his gratitude, while the past conduct of the Swedes in Germany entitled them to confidence. But by the surrender of his fortresses, the Elector would in some measure make the King of Sweden master of his country; besides that, by such a step, he must at once break with the Emperor, and expose his States to his future vengeance. The Elector's struggle with himself was long and violent, but pusillanimity and self-interest for awhile prevailed. Unmoved by the fate of Magdeburg, cold in the cause of religion and the liberties of Germany, he saw nothing but his own danger; and this anxiety was greatly stimulated by his minister Von Schwartzenburgh, who was secretly in the pay of Austria. In the mean time, the Swedish troops approached Berlin, and the king took up his residence with the Elector. When he witnessed the timorous hesitation of that prince, he could not restrain his indignation: "My road is to Magdeburg," said he; "not for my own advantage, but for that of the Protestant religion. If no one will stand by me, I shall immediately retreat, conclude a peace with the Emperor, and return to Stockholm. I am convinced that Ferdinand will readily grant me whatever conditions I may require. But if Magdeburg is once lost, and the Emperor relieved from all fear of me, then it is for you to look to yourselves and the consequences." This timely threat, and perhaps, too, the aspect of the Swedish army, which was strong enough to obtain by force what was refused to entreaty, brought at last the Elector to his senses, and Spandau was delivered into the hands of the Swedes.

The king had now two routes to Magdeburg; one westward led through an exhausted country, and filled with the enemy's troops, who might dispute with him the passage of the Elbe; the other more to the southward, by Dessau and Wittenberg, where bridges were to be found for crossing the Elbe, and where supplies could easily be drawn from Saxony. But he could not avail himself of the latter without the consent of the Elector, whom Gustavus had good reason to distrust. Before setting out on his march, therefore, he demanded from that prince a free passage and liberty for purchasing provisions for his troops. His application was refused, and no remonstrances could prevail on the Elector to abandon his system of neutrality. While the point was still in dispute, the news of the dreadful fate of Magdeburg arrived.

Tilly announced its fall to the Protestant princes in the tone of a conqueror, and lost no time in making the most of the general consternation. The influence of the Emperor, which had sensibly declined during the rapid progress of Gustavus, after this decisive blow rose higher than ever; and the change was speedily visible in the imperious tone he adopted towards the Protestant states. The decrees of the Confederation of Leipzig were annulled by a proclamation, the Convention itself suppressed by an imperial decree, and all the refractory states threatened with the fate of Magdeburg. As the executor of this imperial mandate, Tilly immediately ordered troops to march against the Bishop of Bremen, who was a member of the Confederacy, and had himself enlisted soldiers. The terrified bishop immediately gave up his forces to Tilly, and signed the revocation of the acts of the Confederation. An imperial army, which had lately returned from Italy, under the command of Count Furstenberg, acted in the same manner towards the Administrator of Wirtemberg. The duke was compelled to submit to the Edict of Restitution, and all the decrees of the Emperor, and even to pay a monthly subsidy of 100,000 dollars, for the maintenance of the imperial troops. Similar burdens were inflicted upon Ulm and Nuremberg, and the entire circles of Franconia and Swabia. The hand of the Emperor was stretched in terror over all Germany. The sudden preponderance, more in appearance, perhaps, than in reality, which he had obtained by this blow, carried him beyond the bounds even of the moderation which he had hitherto observed, and misled him into hasty and violent measures, which at last turned the wavering resolution of the German princes in favour of Gustavus Adolphus. Injurious as the immediate consequences of the fall of Magdeburg were to the Protestant cause, its remoter effects were most advantageous. The past surprise made way for active resentment, despair inspired courage, and the German freedom rose, like a phoenix, from the ashes of Magdeburg.

Among the princes of the Leipzig Confederation, the Elector of Saxony and the Landgrave of Hesse were the most powerful; and, until they were disarmed, the universal authority of the Emperor was unconfirmed. Against the Landgrave, therefore, Tilly first directed his attack, and marched straight from Magdeburg into Thuringia. During this march, the territories of Saxe Ernest and Schwartzburg were laid waste, and Frankenhausen plundered before the very eyes of Tilly, and laid in ashes with impunity. The unfortunate peasant paid dear for his master's attachment to the interests of Sweden. Erfurt, the key of Saxony and Franconia, was threatened with a siege, but redeemed itself by a voluntary contribution of money and provisions. From thence, Tilly despatched his emissaries to the Landgrave, demanding of him the immediate disbanding of his army, a renunciation of the league of Leipzig, the reception of imperial garrisons into his territories and fortresses, with the necessary contributions, and the declaration of friendship or hostility. Such was the treatment which a prince of the Empire was compelled to submit to from a servant of the Emperor. But these extravagant demands acquired a formidable weight from the power which supported them; and the dreadful fate of Magdeburg, still fresh in the memory of the Landgrave, tended still farther to enforce them. Admirable, therefore, was the intrepidity of the Landgrave's answer: "To admit foreign troops into his capital and fortresses, the Landgrave is not disposed; his troops he requires for his own purposes; as for an attack, he can defend himself. If General Tilly wants money or provisions, let him go to Munich, where there is plenty of both." The irruption of two bodies of imperial troops into Hesse Cassel was the immediate result of this spirited reply, but the Landgrave gave them so warm a reception that they could effect nothing; and just as Tilly was preparing to follow with his whole army, to punish the unfortunate country for the firmness of its sovereign, the movements of the King of Sweden recalled him to another quarter.

Gustavus Adolphus had learned the fall of Magdeburg with deep regret; and the demand now made by the Elector, George William, in terms of their agreement, for the restoration of Spandau, greatly increased this feeling. The loss of Magdeburg had rather augmented than lessened the reasons which made the possession of this fortress so desirable; and the nearer became the necessity of a decisive battle between himself and Tilly, the more unwilling he felt to abandon the only place which, in the event of a defeat, could ensure him a refuge. After a vain endeavour, by entreaties and representations, to bring over the Elector to his views, whose coldness and lukewarmness daily increased, he gave orders to his general to evacuate Spandau, but at the same time declared to the Elector that he would henceforth regard him as an enemy.

To give weight to this declaration, he appeared with his whole force before Berlin. "I will not be worse treated than the imperial generals," was his reply to the ambassadors whom the bewildered Elector despatched to his camp. "Your master has received them into his territories, furnished them with all necessary supplies, ceded to them every place which they required, and yet, by all these concessions, he could not prevail upon them to treat his subjects with common humanity. All that I require of him is security, a moderate sum of money, and provisions for my troops; in return, I promise to protect his country, and to keep the war at a distance from him. On these points, however, I must insist; and my brother, the Elector, must instantly determine to have me as a friend, or to see his capital plundered." This decisive tone produced a due impression; and the cannon pointed against the town put an end to the doubts of George William. In a few days, a treaty was signed, by which the Elector engaged to furnish a monthly subsidy of 30,000 dollars, to leave Spandau in the king's hands, and to open Custrin at all times to the Swedish troops. This now open alliance of the Elector of Brandenburg with the Swedes, excited no less displeasure at Vienna, than did formerly the similar procedure of the Duke of

Pomerania; but the changed fortune which now attended his arms, obliged the Emperor to confine his resentment to words.

The king's satisfaction, on this favourable event, was increased by the agreeable intelligence that Griefswald, the only fortress which the Imperialists still held in Pomerania, had surrendered, and that the whole country was now free of the enemy. He appeared once more in this duchy, and was gratified at the sight of the general joy which he had caused to the people. A year had elapsed since Gustavus first entered Germany, and this event was now celebrated by all Pomerania as a national festival. Shortly before, the Czar of Moscow had sent ambassadors to congratulate him, to renew his alliance, and even to offer him troops. He had great reason to rejoice at the friendly disposition of Russia, as it was indispensable to his interests that Sweden itself should remain undisturbed by any dangerous neighbour during the war in which he himself was engaged. Soon after, his queen, Maria Eleonora, landed in Pomerania, with a reinforcement of 8000 Swedes; and the arrival of 6000 English, under the Marquis of Hamilton, requires more particular notice because this is all that history mentions of the English during the Thirty Years' War.

During Tilly's expedition into Thuringia, Pappenheim commanded in Magdeburg; but was unable to prevent the Swedes from crossing the Elbe at various points, routing some imperial detachments, and seizing several posts. He himself, alarmed at the approach of the King of Sweden, anxiously recalled Tilly, and prevailed upon him to return by rapid marches to Magdeburg. Tilly encamped on this side of the river at Wolmerstadt; Gustavus on the same side, near Werben, not far from the confluence of the Havel and the Elbe. His very arrival portended no good to Tilly. The Swedes routed three of his regiments, which were posted in villages at some distance from the main body, carried off half their baggage, and burned the remainder. Tilly in vain advanced within cannon shot of the king's camp, and offered him battle. Gustavus, weaker by one-half than his adversary, prudently declined it; and his position was too strong for an attack. Nothing more ensued but a distant cannonade, and a few skirmishes, in which the Swedes had invariably the advantage. In his retreat to Wolmerstadt, Tilly's army was weakened by numerous desertions. Fortune seemed to have forsaken him since the carnage of Magdeburg.

The King of Sweden, on the contrary, was followed by uninterrupted success. While he himself was encamped in Werben, the whole of Mecklenburg, with the exception of a few towns, was conquered by his General Tott and the Duke Adolphus Frederick; and he enjoyed the satisfaction of reinstating both dukes in their dominions. He proceeded in person to Gustrow, where the reinstatement was solemnly to take place, to give additional dignity to the ceremony by his presence. The two dukes, with their deliverer between them, and attended by a splendid train of princes, made a public entry into the city, which the joy of their subjects converted into an affecting solemnity. Soon after his return to Werben, the Landgrave of Hesse Cassel appeared in his camp, to conclude an offensive and defensive alliance; the first sovereign prince in Germany, who voluntarily and openly declared against the Emperor, though not wholly uninfluenced by strong motives. The Landgrave bound himself to act against the king's enemies as his own, to open to him his towns and territory, and to furnish his army with provisions and necessaries. The king, on the other hand, declared himself his ally and protector; and engaged to conclude no peace with the Emperor without first obtaining for the Landgrave a full redress of grievances. Both parties honourably performed their agreement. Hesse Cassel adhered to the Swedish alliance during the whole of this tedious war; and at the peace of Westphalia had no reason to regret the friendship of Sweden.

Tilly, from whom this bold step on the part of the Landgrave was not long concealed, despatched Count Fugger with several regiments against him; and at the same time endeavoured to excite his subjects to rebellion by inflammatory letters. But these made as little impression as his troops, which subsequently failed him so decidedly at the battle of Breitenfeld. The Estates of Hesse could not for a moment hesitate between their oppressor and their protector.

But the imperial general was far more disturbed by the equivocal conduct of the Elector of Saxony, who, in defiance of the imperial prohibition, continued his preparations, and adhered to the confederation of Leipzig. At this conjuncture, when the proximity of the King of Sweden made a decisive battle ere long inevitable, it appeared extremely dangerous to leave Saxony in arms, and ready in a moment to declare for the enemy. Tilly had just received a reinforcement of 25,000 veteran troops under Furstenberg, and, confident in his strength, he hoped either to disarm the Elector by the mere terror of his arrival, or at least to conquer him with little difficulty. Before quitting his camp at Wolmerstadt, he commanded the Elector, by a special messenger, to open his territories to the imperial troops; either to disband his own, or to join them to the imperial army; and to assist, in conjunction with himself, in driving the King of Sweden out of Germany. While he reminded him that, of all the German states, Saxony had hitherto been most respected, he threatened it, in case of refusal, with the most destructive ravages.

But Tilly had chosen an unfavourable moment for so imperious a requisition. The ill-treatment of his religious and political confederates, the destruction of Magdeburg, the excesses of the Imperialists in Lusatia, all combined to incense the Elector against the Emperor. The approach, too, of Gustavus Adolphus, (however slender his claims were to the protection of that prince,) tended to fortify his resolution. He accordingly forbade the quartering of the imperial soldiers in his territories, and announced his firm determination to persist in his warlike preparations. However surprised he should be, he added, "to see an imperial army on its march against his territories, when that army had enough to do in watching the operations of the King of Sweden, nevertheless he did not expect, instead of the promised and well merited rewards, to be repaid with ingratitude and the ruin of his country." To Tilly's deputies, who were entertained in a princely style, he gave a still plainer answer on the occasion. "Gentlemen," said he, "I perceive that the Saxon confectionery, which has been so long kept back, is at length to be set upon the table. But as it is usual to mix with it nuts and garnish of all kinds, take care of your teeth."

Tilly instantly broke up his camp, and, with the most frightful devastation, advanced upon Halle; from this place he renewed his demands on the Elector, in a tone still more urgent and threatening. The previous policy of this prince, both from his own inclination, and the persuasions of his corrupt ministers had been to promote the interests of the Emperor, even at the expense of his own sacred obligations, and but very little tact had hitherto kept him inactive. All this but renders more astonishing the infatuation of the Emperor or his ministers in abandoning, at so critical a moment, the policy they had hitherto adopted, and by extreme measures, incensing a prince so easily led. Was this the very object which Tilly had in view? Was it his purpose to convert an equivocal friend into an open enemy, and thus to relieve himself from the necessity of that indulgence in the treatment of this prince, which the secret instructions of the Emperor had hitherto imposed upon him? Or was it the Emperor's wish, by driving the Elector to open hostilities, to get quit of his obligations to him, and so cleverly to break off at once the difficulty of a reckoning? In either case, we must be equally surprised at the daring presumption of Tilly, who hesitated not, in presence of one formidable enemy, to provoke another; and at his negligence in permitting, without opposition, the union of the two.

The Saxon Elector, rendered desperate by the entrance of Tilly into his territories, threw himself, though not without a violent struggle, under the protection of Sweden.

Immediately after dismissing Tilly's first embassy, he had despatched his field-marshal Arnheim in all haste to the camp of Gustavus, to solicit the prompt assistance of that monarch whom he had so long neglected. The king concealed the inward satisfaction he felt at this long wished for result. "I am sorry for the Elector," said he, with dissembled coldness, to the ambassador; "had he heeded my repeated remonstrances, his country would never have seen the face of an enemy, and Magdeburg would not have fallen. Now, when necessity leaves him no alternative, he has recourse to my assistance. But tell him, that I cannot, for the sake of the Elector of Saxony, ruin my own cause, and that of my confederates. What pledge have I for the sincerity of a prince whose minister is in the pay of Austria, and who will abandon me as soon as the Emperor flatters him, and withdraws his troops from his frontiers? Tilly, it is true, has received a strong reinforcement; but this shall not prevent me from meeting him with confidence, as soon as I have covered my rear."

The Saxon minister could make no other reply to these reproaches, than that it was best to bury the past in oblivion.

He pressed the king to name the conditions, on which he would afford assistance to Saxony, and offered to guarantee their acceptance. "I require," said Gustavus, "that the Elector shall cede to me the fortress of Wittenberg, deliver to me his eldest sons as hostages, furnish my troops with three months' pay, and deliver up to me the traitors among his ministry."

"Not Wittenberg alone," said the Elector, when he received this answer, and hurried back his minister to the Swedish camp, "not Wittenberg alone, but Torgau, and all Saxony, shall be open to him; my whole family shall be his hostages, and if that is insufficient, I will place myself in his hands. Return and inform him I am ready to deliver to him any traitors he shall name, to furnish his army with the money he requires, and to venture my life and fortune in the good cause.

The king had only desired to test the sincerity of the Elector's new sentiments. Convinced of it, he now retracted these harsh demands. "The distrust," said he, "which was shown to myself when advancing to the relief of Magdeburg, had naturally excited mine; the Elector's present confidence demands a return. I am satisfied, provided he grants my army one month's pay, and even for this advance I hope to indemnify him."

Immediately upon the conclusion of the treaty, the king crossed the Elbe, and next day joined the Saxons. Instead of preventing this junction, Tilly had advanced against Leipzig, which he summoned to receive an imperial garrison. In hopes of speedy relief, Hans Von der Pforta, the commandant, made preparations for his defence, and laid the suburb towards Halle in ashes. But the ill condition of the fortifications made resistance vain, and on the second day the gates were opened. Tilly had fixed his head quarters in the house of a grave-digger, the only one still standing in the suburb of Halle: here he signed the capitulation, and here, too, he arranged his attack on the King of Sweden. Tilly grew pale at the representation of the death's head and cross bones, with which the proprietor had decorated his house; and, contrary to all expectation, Leipzig experienced moderate treatment.

Meanwhile, a council of war was held at Torgau, between the King of Sweden and the Elector of Saxony, at which the Elector of Brandenburg was also present. The resolution which should now be adopted, was to decide irrevocably the fate of Germany and the Protestant religion, the happiness of nations and the destiny of their princes. The anxiety of suspense which, before every decisive resolve, oppresses even the hearts of heroes, appeared now for a moment to overshadow the great mind of Gustavus Adolphus. "If we decide upon battle," said he, "the stake will be nothing less than a crown and two electorates. Fortune is changeable, and the inscrutable decrees of Heaven may, for our sins, give the victory to our enemies. My kingdom, it is true, even after the loss of my life and my army, would still have a hope left. Far removed from the scene of action, defended by a powerful fleet, a well-guarded frontier, and a warlike population, it would at least be safe from the worst consequences of a defeat. But what chances of escape are there for you, with an enemy so close at hand?" Gustavus Adolphus displayed the modest diffidence of a hero, whom an overweening belief of his own strength did not blind to the greatness of his danger; John George, the confidence of a weak man, who knows that he has a hero by his side. Impatient to rid his territories as soon as possible of the oppressive presence of two armies, he burned for a battle, in which he had no former laurels to lose. He was ready to march with his Saxons alone against Leipzig, and attack Tilly. At last Gustavus acceded to his opinion; and it was resolved that the attack should be made without delay, before the arrival of the reinforcements, which were on their way, under Altringer and Tiefenbach. The united Swedish and Saxon armies now crossed the Mulda, while the Elector returned homeward.

Early on the morning of the 7th September, 1631, the hostile armies came in sight of each other. Tilly, who, since he had neglected the opportunity of overpowering the Saxons before their union with the Swedes, was disposed to await the arrival of the reinforcements, had taken up a strong and advantageous position not far from Leipzig, where he expected he should be able to avoid the battle. But the impetuosity of Pappenheim obliged him, as soon as the enemy were in motion, to alter his plans, and to move to the left, in the direction of the hills which run from the village of Wahren towards Lindenthal. At the foot of these heights, his army was drawn up in a single line, and his artillery placed upon the heights behind, from which it could sweep the whole extensive plain of Breitenfeld. The Swedish and Saxon army advanced in two columns, having to pass the Lober near Podelwitz, in Tilly's front.

To defend the passage of this rivulet, Pappenheim advanced at the head of 2000 cuirassiers, though after great reluctance on the part of Tilly, and with express orders not to commence a battle. But, in disobedience to this command, Pappenheim attacked the vanguard of the Swedes, and after a brief struggle was driven to retreat. To check the progress of the enemy, he set fire to Podelwitz, which, however, did not prevent the two columns from advancing and forming in order of battle.

On the right, the Swedes drew up in a double line, the infantry in the centre, divided into such small battalions as could be easily and rapidly manoeuvred without breaking their order; the cavalry upon their wings, divided in the same manner into small squadrons, interspersed with bodies of musqueteers, so as both to give an appearance of greater numerical force, and to annoy the enemy's horse. Colonel Teufel commanded the centre, Gustavus Horn the left, while the right was led by the king in person, opposed to Count Pappenheim.

On the left, the Saxons formed at a considerable distance from the Swedes, — by the advice of

Gustavus, which was justified by the event. The order of battle had been arranged between the Elector and his field-marshal, and the king was content with merely signifying his approval. He was anxious apparently to separate the Swedish prowess from that of the Saxons, and fortune did not confound them.

The enemy was drawn up under the heights towards the west, in one immense line, long enough to outflank the Swedish army, — the infantry being divided in large battalions, the cavalry in equally unwieldy squadrons. The artillery being on the heights behind, the range of its fire was over the heads of his men. From this position of his artillery, it was evident that Tilly's purpose was to await rather than to attack the enemy; since this arrangement rendered it impossible for him to do so without exposing his men to the fire of his own cannons. Tilly himself commanded the centre, Count Furstenberg the right wing, and Pappenheim the left. The united troops of the Emperor and the League on this day did not amount to 34,000 or 35,000 men; the Swedes and Saxons were about the same number. But had a million been confronted with a million it could only have rendered the action more bloody, certainly not more important and decisive. For this day Gustavus had crossed the Baltic, to court danger in a distant country, and expose his crown and life to the caprice of fortune. The two greatest generals of the time, both hitherto invincible, were now to be matched against each other in a contest which both had long avoided; and on this field of battle the hitherto untarnished laurels of one leader must droop for ever. The two parties in Germany had beheld the approach of this day with fear and trembling; and the whole age awaited with deep anxiety its issue, and posterity was either to bless or deplore it for ever.

Tilly's usual intrepidity and resolution seemed to forsake him on this eventful day. He had formed no regular plan for giving battle to the King, and he displayed as little firmness in avoiding it. Contrary to his own judgment, Pappenheim had forced him to action. Doubts which he had never before felt, struggled in his bosom; gloomy forebodings clouded his ever-open brow; the shade of Magdeburg seemed to hover over him.

A cannonade of two hours commenced the battle; the wind, which was from the west, blew thick clouds of smoke and dust from the newly-ploughed and parched fields into the faces of the Swedes. This compelled the king insensibly to wheel northwards, and the rapidity with which this movement was executed left no time to the enemy to prevent it.

Tilly at last left his heights, and began the first attack upon the Swedes; but to avoid their hot fire, he filed off towards the right, and fell upon the Saxons with such impetuosity that their line was broken, and the whole army thrown into confusion. The Elector himself retired to Eilenburg, though a few regiments still maintained their ground upon the field, and by a bold stand saved the honour of Saxony. Scarcely had the confusion began ere the Croats commenced plundering, and messengers were despatched to Munich and Vienna with the news of the victory.

Pappenheim had thrown himself with the whole force of his cavalry upon the right wing of the Swedes, but without being able to make it waver. The king commanded here in person, and under him General Banner. Seven times did Pappenheim renew the attack, and seven times was he repulsed. He fled at last with great loss, and abandoned the field to his conqueror.

In the mean time, Tilly, having routed the remainder of the Saxons, attacked with his victorious troops the left wing of the Swedes. To this wing the king, as soon as he perceived that the Saxons were thrown into disorder, had, with a ready foresight, detached a reinforcement of three regiments to cover its flank, which the flight of the Saxons had left exposed. Gustavus Horn, who commanded here, showed the enemy's cuirassiers a spirited resistance, which the infantry, interspersed among the squadrons of horse, materially assisted. The enemy were already beginning to relax the vigour of their attack, when Gustavus Adolphus appeared to terminate the contest. The left wing of the Imperialists had been routed; and the king's division, having no longer any enemy to oppose, could now turn their arms wherever it would be to the most advantage. Wheeling, therefore, with his right wing and main body to the left, he attacked the heights on which the enemy's artillery was planted. Gaining possession of them in a short time, he turned upon the enemy the full fire of their own cannon.

The play of artillery upon their flank, and the terrible onslaught of the Swedes in front, threw this hitherto invincible army into confusion. A sudden retreat was the only course left to Tilly, but even this was to be made through the midst of the enemy. The whole army was in disorder, with the exception of four regiments of veteran soldiers, who never as yet had fled from the field, and were resolved not to do so now. Closing their ranks, they broke through the thickest of the victorious army, and gained a small thicket, where they opposed a new front to the Swedes, and maintained their resistance till night, when their number was reduced to six hundred men. With them fled the wreck of Tilly's army, and the battle was decided.

Amid the dead and the wounded, Gustavus Adolphus threw himself on his knees; and the first joy of his victory gushed forth in fervent prayer. He ordered his cavalry to pursue the enemy as long as the darkness of the night would permit. The pealing of the alarm-bells set the inhabitants of all the neighbouring villages in motion, and utterly lost was the unhappy fugitive who fell into their hands. The king encamped with the rest of his army between the field of battle and Leipzig, as it was impossible to attack the town the same night. Seven thousand of the enemy were killed in the field, and more than 5,000 either wounded or taken prisoners. Their whole artillery and camp fell into the hands of the Swedes, and more than a hundred standards and colours were taken. Of the Saxons about 2,000 had fallen, while the loss of the Swedes did not exceed 700. The rout of the Imperialists was so complete, that Tilly, on his retreat to Halle and Halberstadt, could not rally above 600 men, or Pappenheim more than 1,400 — so rapidly was this formidable army dispersed, which so lately was the terror of Italy and Germany.

Tilly himself owed his escape merely to chance. Exhausted by his wounds, he still refused to surrender to a Swedish captain of horse, who summoned him to yield; but who, when he was on the point of putting him to death, was himself stretched on the ground by a timely pistol-shot. But more grievous than danger or wounds was the pain of surviving his reputation, and of losing in a single day the fruits of a long life. All former victories were as nothing, since he had failed in gaining the one that should have crowned them all. Nothing remained of all his past exploits, but the general execration which had followed them. From this period, he never recovered his cheerfulness or his good fortune. Even his last consolation, the hope of revenge, was denied to him, by the express command of the Emperor not to risk a decisive battle.

The disgrace of this day is to be ascribed principally to three mistakes; his planting the cannon on the hills behind him, his afterwards abandoning these heights, and his allowing the enemy, without opposition, to form in order of battle. But how easily might those mistakes have been rectified, had it not been for the cool presence of mind and superior genius of his adversary!

Tilly fled from Halle to Halberstadt, where he scarcely allowed time for the cure of his wounds, before he hurried towards the Weser to recruit his force by the imperial garrisons in Lower Saxony.

The Elector of Saxony had not failed, after the danger was over, to appear in Gustavus's camp. The king thanked him for having advised a battle; and the Elector, charmed at his friendly reception, promised him, in the first transports of joy, the Roman crown. Gustavus set out next day for Merseburg, leaving the Elector to recover Leipzig. Five thousand Imperialists, who had collected together after the defeat, and whom he met on his march, were either cut in pieces or taken prisoners, of whom again the greater part entered into his service. Merseburg quickly surrendered; Halle was soon after taken, whither the Elector of Saxony, after making himself master of Leipzig, repaired to meet the king, and to concert their future plan of operations.

The victory was gained, but only a prudent use of it could render it decisive. The imperial armies were totally routed, Saxony free from the enemy, and Tilly had retired into Brunswick. To have followed him thither would have been to renew the war in Lower Saxony, which had scarcely recovered from the ravages of the last. It was therefore determined to carry the war into the enemy's country, which, open and defenceless as far as Vienna, invited attack. On their right, they might fall upon the territories of the Roman Catholic princes, or penetrate, on the left, into the hereditary dominions of Austria, and make the Emperor tremble in his palace. Both plans were resolved on; and the question that now remained was to assign its respective parts. Gustavus Adolphus, at the head of a victorious army, had little resistance to apprehend in his progress from Leipzig to Prague, Vienna, and Presburg. As to Bohemia, Moravia, Austria, and Hungary, they had been stripped of their defenders, while the oppressed Protestants in these countries were ripe for a revolt. Ferdinand was no longer secure in his capital: Vienna, on the first terror of surprise, would at once open its gates. The loss of his territories would deprive the enemy of the resources by which alone the war could be maintained; and Ferdinand would, in all probability, gladly accede, on the hardest conditions, to a peace which would remove a formidable enemy from the heart of his dominions. This bold plan of operations was flattering to a conqueror, and success perhaps might have justified it. But Gustavus Adolphus, as prudent as he was brave, and more a statesman than a conqueror, rejected it, because he had a higher end in view, and would not trust the issue either to bravery or good fortune alone.

By marching towards Bohemia, Franconia and the Upper Rhine would be left to the Elector of Saxony. But Tilly had already begun to recruit his shattered army from the garrisons in Lower Saxony, and was likely to be at the head of a formidable force upon the Weser, and to lose no time in marching against the enemy. To so experienced a general, it would not do to oppose an Arnheim, of whose military skill the battle of Leipzig had afforded but equivocal proof; and of what avail would be the rapid and brilliant career of the king in Bohemia and Austria, if Tilly should recover his superiority in the Empire, animating the courage of the Roman Catholics, and disarming, by a new series of victories, the allies and confederates of the king? What would he gain by expelling the Emperor from his hereditary dominions, if Tilly succeeded in conquering for that Emperor the rest of Germany? Could he hope to reduce the Emperor more than had been done, twelve years before, by the insurrection of Bohemia, which had failed to shake the firmness or exhaust the resources of that prince, and from which he had risen more formidable than ever?

Less brilliant, but more solid, were the advantages which he had to expect from an incursion into the territories of the League. In this quarter, his appearance in arms would be decisive. At this very conjuncture, the princes were assembled in a Diet at Frankfort, to deliberate upon the Edict of Restitution, where Ferdinand employed all his artful policy to persuade the intimidated Protestants to accede to a speedy and disadvantageous arrangement. The advance of their protector could alone encourage them to a bold resistance, and disappoint the Emperor's designs. Gustavus Adolphus hoped, by his presence, to unite the discontented princes, or by the terror of his arms to detach them from the Emperor's party. Here, in the centre of Germany, he could paralyse the nerves of the imperial power, which, without the aid of the League, must soon fall — here, in the neighbourhood of France, he could watch the movements of a suspicious ally; and however important to his secret views it was to cultivate the friendship of the Roman Catholic electors, he saw the necessity of making himself first of all master of their fate, in order to establish, by his magnanimous forbearance, a claim to their gratitude.

He accordingly chose the route to Franconia and the Rhine; and left the conquest of Bohemia to the Elector of Saxony.

Book III.

The glorious battle of Leipzig effected a great change in the conduct of Gustavus Adolphus, as well as in the opinion which both friends and foes entertained of him. Successfully had he confronted the greatest general of the age, and had matched the strength of his tactics and the courage of his Swedes against the elite of the imperial army, the most experienced troops in Europe. From this moment he felt a firm confidence in his own powers — self-confidence has always been the parent of great actions. In all his subsequent operations more boldness and decision are observable; greater determination, even amidst the most unfavourable circumstances, a more lofty tone towards his adversaries, a more dignified bearing towards his allies, and even in his clemency, something of the forbearance of a conqueror. His natural courage was farther heightened by the pious ardour of his imagination. He saw in his own cause that of heaven, and in the defeat of Tilly beheld the decisive interference of Providence against his enemies, and in himself the instrument of divine vengeance. Leaving his crown and his country far behind, he advanced on the wings of victory into the heart of Germany, which for centuries had seen no foreign conqueror within its bosom. The warlike spirit of its inhabitants, the vigilance of its numerous princes, the artful confederation of its states, the number of its strong castles, its many and broad rivers, had long restrained the ambition of its neighbours; and frequently as its extensive frontier had been attacked, its interior had been free from hostile invasion. The Empire had hitherto enjoyed the equivocal privilege of being its own enemy, though invincible from without. Even now, it was merely the disunion of its members, and the intolerance of religious zeal, that paved the way for the Swedish invader. The bond of union between the states, which alone had rendered the Empire invincible, was now dissolved; and Gustavus derived from Germany itself the power by which he subdued it. With as much courage as prudence, he availed himself of all that the favourable moment afforded; and equally at home in the cabinet and the field, he tore asunder the web of the artful policy, with as much ease, as he shattered walls with the thunder of his cannon. Uninterruptedly he pursued his conquests from one end of Germany to the other, without breaking the line of posts which commanded a secure retreat at any moment; and whether on the banks of the Rhine, or at the mouth of the Lech, alike maintaining his communication with his hereditary dominions.

The consternation of the Emperor and the League at Tilly's defeat at Leipzig, was scarcely greater than the surprise and embarrassment of the allies of the King of Sweden at his unexpected success. It was beyond both their expectations and their wishes. Annihilated in a moment was that formidable army which, while it checked his progress and set bounds to his ambition, rendered him in some measure dependent on themselves. He now stood in the heart of Germany, alone, without a rival or without an adversary who was a match for him. Nothing could stop his progress, or check his pretensions, if the intoxication of success should tempt him to abuse his victory. If formerly they had dreaded the Emperor's irresistible power, there was no less cause now to fear every thing for the Empire, from the violence of a foreign conqueror, and for the Catholic Church, from the religious zeal of a Protestant king. The distrust and jealousy of some of the combined powers, which a stronger fear of the Emperor had for a time repressed, now revived; and scarcely had Gustavus Adolphus merited, by his courage and success, their confidence, when they began covertly to circumvent all his plans. Through a continual struggle with the arts of enemies, and the distrust of his own allies, must his victories henceforth be won; yet resolution, penetration, and prudence made their way through all impediments. But while his success excited the jealousy of his more powerful allies, France and Saxony, it gave courage to the weaker, and emboldened them openly to declare their sentiments and join his party. Those who could neither vie with Gustavus Adolphus in importance, nor suffer from his ambition, expected the more from the magnanimity of their powerful ally, who enriched them with the spoils of their enemies, and protected them against the oppression of their stronger neighbours. His strength covered their weakness, and, inconsiderable in themselves, they acquired weight and influence from their union with the Swedish hero. This was the case with most of the free cities, and particularly with the weaker Protestant states. It was these that introduced the king into the heart of Germany; these covered his rear, supplied his troops with necessaries, received them into their fortresses, while they exposed their own lives in his battles. His prudent regard to their national pride, his popular deportment, some brilliant acts of justice, and his respect for the laws, were so many ties by which he bound the German Protestants to his cause; while the crying atrocities of the Imperialists, the Spaniards, and the troops of Lorraine, powerfully contributed to set his own conduct and that of his army in a favourable light.

If Gustavus Adolphus owed his success chiefly to his own genius, at the same time, it must be owned, he was greatly favoured by fortune and by circumstances. Two great advantages gave him a decided superiority over the enemy. While he removed the scene of war into the lands of the League, drew their youth as recruits, enriched himself with booty, and used the revenues of their fugitive princes as his own, he at once took from the enemy the means of effectual resistance, and maintained an expensive war with little cost to himself. And, moreover, while his opponents, the princes of the League, divided among themselves, and governed by different and often conflicting interests, acted without unanimity, and therefore without energy; while their generals were deficient in authority, their troops in obedience, the operations of their scattered armies without concert; while the general was separated from the lawgiver and the statesman; these several functions were united in Gustavus Adolphus, the only source from which authority flowed, the sole object to which the eye of the warrior turned; the soul of his party, the inventor as well as the executor of his plans. In him, therefore, the Protestants had a centre of unity and harmony, which was altogether wanting to their opponents. No wonder, then, if favoured by such advantages, at the head of such an army, with such a genius to direct it, and guided by such political prudence, Gustavus Adolphus was irresistible.

With the sword in one hand, and mercy in the other, he traversed Germany as a conqueror, a lawgiver, and a judge, in as short a time almost as the tourist of pleasure. The keys of towns and fortresses were delivered to him, as if to the native sovereign. No fortress was inaccessible; no river checked his victorious career. He conquered by the very terror of his name. The Swedish standards were planted along the whole stream of the Maine: the Lower Palatinate was free, the troops of Spain and Lorraine had fled across the Rhine and the Moselle. The Swedes and Hessians poured like a torrent into the territories of Mentz, of Wurtzburg, and Bamberg, and three fugitive bishops, at a distance from their sees, suffered dearly for their unfortunate attachment to the Emperor. It was now the turn for Maximilian, the leader of the League, to feel in his own dominions the miseries he had inflicted upon others. Neither the terrible fate of his allies, nor the peaceful overtures of Gustavus, who, in the midst of conquest, ever held out the hand of friendship, could conquer the obstinacy of this prince. The torrent of war now poured into Bavaria. Like the banks of the Rhine, those of the Lecke and the Donau were crowded with Swedish troops. Creeping into his fortresses, the defeated Elector abandoned to the ravages of the foe his dominions, hitherto unscathed by war, and on which the bigoted violence of the Bavarians seemed to invite retaliation. Munich itself opened its gates to the invincible monarch, and the fugitive Palatine, Frederick V., in the forsaken residence of his rival, consoled himself for a time for the loss of his dominions.

While Gustavus Adolphus was extending his conquests in the south, his generals and allies were gaining similar triumphs in the other provinces. Lower Saxony shook off the yoke of Austria, the enemy abandoned Mecklenburg, and the imperial garrisons retired from the banks of the Weser and the Elbe. In Westphalia and the Upper Rhine, William, Landgrave of Hesse, rendered himself formidable; the Duke of Weimar in Thuringia, and the French in the Electorate of Treves; while to the eastward the whole kingdom of Bohemia was conquered by the Saxons. The Turks were preparing to attack Hungary, and in the heart of Austria a dangerous insurrection was threatened. In vain did the Emperor look around to the courts of Europe for support; in vain did he summon the Spaniards to his assistance, for the bravery of the Flemings afforded them ample employment beyond the Rhine; in vain did he call upon the Roman court and the whole church to come to his rescue. The offended Pope sported, in pompous processions and idle anathemas, with the embarrassments of Ferdinand, and instead of the desired subsidy he was shown the devastation of Mantua.

On all sides of his extensive monarchy hostile arms surrounded him. With the states of the League, now overrun by the enemy, those ramparts were thrown down, behind which Austria had so long defended herself, and the embers of war were now smouldering upon her unguarded frontiers. His most zealous allies were disarmed; Maximilian of Bavaria, his firmest support, was scarce able to defend himself. His armies, weakened by desertion and repeated defeat, and dispirited by continued misfortunes had unlearnt, under beaten generals, that warlike impetuosity which, as it is the consequence, so it is the guarantee of success. The danger was extreme, and extraordinary means alone could raise the imperial power from the degradation into which it was fallen.

The most urgent want was that of a general; and the only one from whom he could hope for the revival of his former splendour, had been removed from his command by an envious cabal. So low had the Emperor now fallen, that he was forced to make the most humiliating proposals to his injured subject and servant, and meanly to press upon the imperious Duke of Friedland the acceptance of the powers which no less meanly had been taken from him. A new spirit began from this moment to animate the expiring body of Austria; and a sudden change in the aspect of affairs bespoke the firm hand which guided them. To the absolute King of Sweden, a general equally absolute was now opposed; and one victorious hero was confronted with another. Both armies were again to engage in the doubtful struggle; and the prize of victory, already almost secured in the hands of Gustavus Adolphus, was to be the object of another and a severer trial. The storm of war gathered around Nuremberg; before its walls the hostile armies encamped; gazing on each other with dread and respect, longing for, and yet shrinking from, the moment that was to close them together in the shock of battle. The eyes of Europe turned to the scene in curiosity and alarm, while Nuremberg, in dismay, expected soon to lend its name to a more decisive battle than that of Leipzig. Suddenly the clouds broke, and the storm rolled away from Franconia, to burst upon the plains of Saxony. Near Lutzen fell the thunder that had menaced Nuremberg; the victory, half lost, was purchased by the death of the king. Fortune, which had never forsaken him in his lifetime, favoured the King of Sweden even in his death, with the rare privilege of falling in the fulness of his glory and an untarnished fame. By a timely death, his protecting genius rescued him from the inevitable fate of man — that of forgetting moderation in the intoxication of success, and justice in the plenitude of power. It may be doubted whether, had he lived longer, he would still have deserved the tears which Germany shed over his grave, or maintained his title to the admiration with which posterity regards him, as the first and only *just* conqueror that the world has produced. The untimely fall of their great leader seemed to threaten the ruin of his party; but to the Power which rules the world, no loss of a single man is irreparable. As the helm of war dropped from the hand of the falling hero, it was seized by two great statesmen, Oxenstiern and Richelieu. Destiny still pursued its relentless course, and for full sixteen years longer the flames of war blazed over the ashes of the long-forgotten king and soldier.

I may now be permitted to take a cursory retrospect of Gustavus Adolphus in his victorious career; glance at the scene in which he alone was the great actor; and then, when Austria becomes reduced to extremity by the successes of the Swedes, and by a series of disasters is driven to the most humiliating and desperate expedients, to return to the history of the Emperor.

As soon as the plan of operations had been concerted at Halle, between the King of Sweden and the Elector of Saxony; as soon as the alliance had been concluded with the neighbouring princes of Weimar and Anhalt, and preparations made for the recovery of the bishopric of Magdeburg, the king began his march into the empire. He had here no despicable foe to contend with. Within the empire, the Emperor was still powerful; throughout Franconia, Swabia, and the Palatinate, imperial garrisons were posted, with whom the possession of every place of importance must be disputed sword in hand. On the Rhine he was opposed by the Spaniards, who had overrun the territory of the banished Elector Palatine, seized all its strong places, and would everywhere dispute with him the passage over that river. On his rear was Tilly, who was fast recruiting his force, and would soon be joined by the auxiliaries from Lorraine. Every Papist presented an inveterate foe, while his connexion with France did not leave him at liberty to act with freedom against the Roman Catholics. Gustavus had foreseen all these obstacles, but at the same time the means by which they were to be overcome. The strength of the Imperialists was broken and divided among different garrisons, while he would bring against them one by one his whole united force. If he was to be opposed by the fanaticism of the Roman Catholics, and the awe in which the lesser states regarded the Emperor's power, he might depend on the active support of the Protestants, and their hatred to Austrian oppression. The ravages of the Imperialist and Spanish troops also powerfully aided him in these quarters; where the ill-treated husbandman and citizen sighed alike for a deliverer, and where the mere change of yoke seemed to promise a relief. Emissaries were despatched to gain over to the Swedish side the principal free cities, particularly Nuremberg and Frankfort. The first that lay in the king's march, and which he could not leave unoccupied in his rear, was Erfurt. Here the Protestant party among the citizens opened to him, without a blow, the gates of the town and the citadel. From the inhabitants of this, as of every important place which afterwards submitted, he exacted an oath of allegiance, while he secured its possession by a sufficient garrison. To his ally, Duke William of Weimar, he intrusted the command of an army to be raised in Thuringia. He also left his queen in Erfurt, and promised to increase its privileges. The Swedish army now crossed the Thuringian forest in two columns, by Gotha and Arnstadt, and having delivered, in its march, the county of Henneberg from the Imperialists, formed a junction on the third day near Koenigshofen, on the frontiers of Franconia.

Francis, Bishop of Wurtzburg, the bitter enemy of the Protestants, and the most zealous member of the League, was the first to feel the indignation of Gustavus Adolphus. A few threats gained for the Swedes possession of his fortress of Koenigshofen, and with it the key of the whole province. At the news of this rapid conquest, dismay seized all the Roman Catholic towns of the circle. The Bishops of Wurtzburg and Bamberg trembled in their castles; they already saw their sees tottering, their churches profaned, and their religion degraded. The malice of his enemies had circulated the most frightful representations of the persecuting spirit and the mode of warfare pursued by the Swedish king and his soldiers, which neither the repeated assurances of the king, nor the most splendid examples of humanity and toleration, ever entirely effaced. Many feared to suffer at the hands of another what in similar circumstances they were conscious of inflicting themselves. Many of the richest Roman Catholics hastened to secure by flight their property, their religion, and their persons, from the sanguinary fanaticism of the Swedes. The bishop himself set the example. In the midst of the alarm, which his bigoted zeal had caused, he abandoned his dominions, and fled to Paris, to excite, if possible, the French ministry against the common enemy of religion.

The further progress of Gustavus Adolphus in the ecclesiastical territories agreed with this brilliant commencement. Schweinfurt, and soon afterwards Wurtzburg, abandoned by their Imperial garrisons, surrendered; but Marienberg he was obliged to carry by storm. In this place, which was believed to be impregnable, the enemy had collected a large store of provisions and ammunition, all of which fell into the hands of the Swedes. The king found a valuable prize in the library of the Jesuits, which he sent to Upsal, while his soldiers found a still more agreeable one in the prelate's well-filled cellars; his treasures the bishop had in good time removed. The whole bishopric followed the example of the capital, and submitted to the Swedes. The king compelled all the bishop's subjects to swear allegiance to himself; and, in the absence of the lawful sovereign, appointed a regency, one half of whose members were Protestants. In every Roman Catholic town which Gustavus took, he opened the churches to the Protestant people, but without retaliating on the Papists the cruelties which they had practised on the former. On such only as sword in hand refused to submit, were the fearful rights of war enforced; and for the occasional acts of violence committed by a few of the more lawless soldiers, in the blind rage of the first attack, their humane leader is not justly responsible. Those who were peaceably disposed, or defenceless, were treated with mildness. It was a sacred principle of Gustavus to spare the blood of his enemies, as well as that of his own troops.

On the first news of the Swedish irruption, the Bishop of Wurtzburg, without regarding the treaty which he had entered into with the King of Sweden, had earnestly pressed the general of the League to hasten to the assistance of the bishopric. That defeated commander had, in the mean time, collected on the Weser the shattered remnant of his army, reinforced himself from the garrisons of Lower Saxony, and effected a junction in Hesse with Altringer and Fugger, who commanded under him. Again at the head of a considerable force, Tilly burned with impatience to wipe out the stain of his first defeat by a splendid victory. From his camp at Fulda, whither he had marched with his army, he earnestly requested permission from the Duke of Bavaria to give battle to Gustavus Adolphus. But, in the event of Tilly's defeat, the League had no second army to fall back upon, and Maximilian was too cautious to risk again the fate of his party on a single battle. With tears in his eyes, Tilly read the commands of his superior, which compelled him to inactivity. Thus his march to Franconia was delayed, and Gustavus Adolphus gained time to overrun the whole bishopric. It was in vain that Tilly, reinforced at Aschaffenburg by a body of 12,000 men from Lorraine, marched with an overwhelming force to the relief of Wurtzburg. The town and citadel were already in the hands of the Swedes, and Maximilian of Bavaria was generally blamed (and not without cause, perhaps) for having, by his scruples, occasioned the loss of the bishopric. Commanded to avoid a battle, Tilly contented himself with checking the farther advance of the enemy; but he could save only a few of the towns from the impetuosity of the Swedes. Baffled in an attempt to reinforce the weak garrison of Hanau, which it was highly important to the Swedes to gain, he crossed the Maine, near Seligenstadt, and took the direction of the Bergstrasse, to protect the Palatinate from the conqueror.

Tilly, however, was not the sole enemy whom Gustavus Adolphus met in Franconia, and drove before him. Charles, Duke of Lorraine, celebrated in the annals of the time for his unsteadiness of character, his vain projects, and his misfortunes, ventured to raise a weak arm against the Swedish hero, in the hope of obtaining from the Emperor the electoral dignity. Deaf to the suggestions of a rational policy, he listened only to the dictates of heated ambition; by supporting the Emperor, he exasperated France, his formidable neighbour; and in the pursuit of a visionary phantom in another country, left undefended his own dominions, which were instantly overrun by a French army. Austria willingly conceded to him, as well as to the other princes of the League, the honour of being ruined in her cause. Intoxicated with vain hopes, this prince collected a force of 17,000 men, which he proposed to lead in person against the Swedes. If these troops were deficient in discipline and courage, they were at least attractive by the splendour of their accoutrements; and however sparing they were of their prowess against the foe, they were liberal enough with it against the defenceless citizens and peasantry, whom they were summoned to defend. Against the bravery, and the formidable discipline of the Swedes this splendidly attired army, however, made no long stand. On the first advance of the Swedish cavalry a panic seized them, and they were driven without difficulty from their cantonments in Wurtzburg; the defeat of a few regiments occasioned a general rout, and the scattered remnant sought a covert from the Swedish valour in the towns beyond the Rhine. Loaded with shame and ridicule, the duke hurried home by Strasburg, too fortunate in escaping, by a submissive written apology, the indignation of his conqueror, who had first beaten him out of the field, and then called upon him to account for his hostilities. It is related upon this occasion that, in a village on the Rhine a peasant struck the horse of the duke as he rode past, exclaiming, "Haste, Sir, you must go quicker to escape the great King of Sweden!"

The example of his neighbours' misfortunes had taught the Bishop of Bamberg prudence. To avert the plundering of his territories, he made offers of peace, though these were intended only to delay the king's course till the arrival of assistance. Gustavus Adolphus, too honourable himself to suspect dishonesty in another, readily accepted the bishop's proposals, and named the conditions on which he was willing to save his territories from hostile treatment. He was the more inclined to peace, as he had no time to lose in the conquest of Bamberg, and his other designs called him to the Rhine. The rapidity with which he followed up these plans, cost him the loss of those pecuniary supplies which, by a longer residence in Franconia, he might easily have extorted from the weak and terrified bishop. This artful prelate broke off the negotiation the instant the storm of war passed away from his own territories. No sooner had Gustavus marched onwards than he threw himself under the protection of Tilly, and received the troops of the Emperor into the very towns and fortresses, which shortly before he had shown himself ready to open to the Swedes. By this stratagem, however, he only delayed for a brief interval the ruin of his bishopric. A Swedish general who had been left in Franconia, undertook to punish the perfidy of the bishop; and the ecclesiastical territory became the seat of war, and was ravaged alike by friends and foes.

The formidable presence of the Imperialists had hitherto been a check upon the Franconian States; but their retreat, and the humane conduct of the Swedish king, emboldened the nobility and other inhabitants of this circle to declare in his favour. Nuremberg joyfully committed itself to his protection; and the Franconian nobles were won to his cause by flattering proclamations, in which he condescended to apologize for his hostile appearance in the dominions. The fertility of Franconia, and the rigorous honesty of the Swedish soldiers in their dealings with the inhabitants, brought abundance to the camp of the king. The high esteem which the nobility of the circle felt for Gustavus, the respect and admiration with which they regarded his brilliant exploits, the promises of rich booty which the service of this monarch held out, greatly facilitated the recruiting of his troops; a step which was made necessary by detaching so many garrisons from the main body. At the sound of his drums, recruits flocked to his standard from all quarters.

The king had scarcely spent more time in conquering Franconia, than he would have required to cross it. He now left behind him Gustavus Horn, one of his best generals, with a force of 8,000 men, to complete and retain his conquest. He himself with his main army, reinforced by the late recruits, hastened towards the Rhine in order to secure this frontier of the empire from the Spaniards; to disarm the ecclesiastical electors, and to obtain from their fertile territories new resources for the prosecution of the war. Following the course of the Maine, he subjected, in the course of his march, Seligenstadt, Aschaffenburg, Steinheim, the whole territory on both sides of the river. The imperial garrisons seldom awaited his approach, and never attempted resistance. In the meanwhile one of his colonels had been fortunate enough to take by surprise the town and citadel of Hanau, for whose preservation Tilly had shown such anxiety. Eager to be free of the oppressive burden of the Imperialists, the Count of Hanau gladly placed himself under the milder yoke of the King of Sweden.

Gustavus Adolphus now turned his whole attention to Frankfort, for it was his constant maxim to cover his rear by the friendship and possession of the more important towns. Frankfort was among the free cities which, even from Saxony, he had endeavoured to prepare for his reception; and he now called upon it, by a summons from Offenbach, to allow him a free passage, and to admit a Swedish garrison. Willingly would this city have dispensed with the necessity of choosing between the King of Sweden and the Emperor; for, whatever party they might embrace, the inhabitants had a like reason to fear for their privileges and trade. The Emperor's vengeance would certainly fall heavily upon them, if they were in a hurry to submit to the King of Sweden, and afterwards he should prove unable to protect his adherents in Germany. But still more ruinous for them would be the displeasure of an irresistible conqueror, who, with a formidable army, was already before their gates, and who might punish their opposition by the ruin of their commerce and prosperity. In vain did their deputies plead the danger which menaced their fairs, their privileges, perhaps their constitution itself, if, by espousing the party of the Swedes, they were to incur the Emperor's displeasure. Gustavus Adolphus expressed to them his astonishment that, when the liberties of Germany and the Protestant religion were at stake, the citizens of Frankfort should talk of their annual fairs, and postpone for temporal interests the great cause of their country and their conscience. He had, he continued, in a menacing tone, found the keys of every town and fortress, from the Isle of Rugen to the Maine, and knew also where to find a key to Frankfort; the safety of Germany, and the freedom of the Protestant Church, were, he assured them, the sole objects of his invasion; conscious of the justice of his cause, he was determined not to allow any obstacle to impede his progress. "The inhabitants of Frankfort, he was well aware, wished to stretch out only a finger to him, but he must have the whole hand in order to have something to grasp." At the head of the army, he closely followed the deputies as they carried back his answer, and in order of battle awaited, near Saxenhausen, the decision of the council.

If Frankfort hesitated to submit to the Swedes, it was solely from fear of the Emperor; their own inclinations did not allow them a moment to doubt between the oppressor of Germany and its protector. The menacing preparations amidst which Gustavus Adolphus now compelled them to decide, would lessen the guilt of their revolt in the eyes of the Emperor, and by an appearance of compulsion justify the step which they willingly took. The gates were therefore opened to the King of Sweden, who marched his army through this imperial town in magnificent procession, and in admirable order. A garrison of 600 men was left in Saxenhausen; while the king himself advanced the same evening, with the rest of his army, against the town of Hoechst in Mentz, which surrendered to him before night.

While Gustavus was thus extending his conquests along the Maine, fortune crowned also the efforts of his generals and allies in the north of Germany. Rostock, Wismar, and Doemitz, the only strong places in the Duchy of Mecklenburg which still sighed under the yoke of the Imperialists, were recovered by their legitimate sovereign, the Duke John Albert, under the Swedish general, Achatius Tott. In vain did the imperial general, Wolf Count von Mansfeld, endeavour to recover from the Swedes the territories of Halberstadt, of which they had taken possession immediately upon the victory of Leipzig; he was even compelled to leave Magdeburg itself in their hands. The Swedish general, Banner, who with 8,000 men remained upon the Elbe, closely blockaded that city, and had defeated several imperial regiments which had been sent to its relief. Count Mansfeld defended it in person with great resolution; but his garrison being too weak to oppose for any length of time the numerous force of the besiegers, he was already about to surrender on conditions, when Pappenheim advanced to his assistance, and gave employment elsewhere to the Swedish arms. Magdeburg, however, or rather the wretched huts that peeped out miserably from among the ruins of that once great town, was afterwards voluntarily abandoned by the Imperialists, and immediately taken possession of by the Swedes.

Even Lower Saxony, encouraged by the progress of the king, ventured to raise its head from the disasters of the unfortunate Danish war. They held a congress at Hamburg, and resolved upon raising three regiments, which they hoped would be sufficient to free them from the oppressive garrisons of the Imperialists. The Bishop of Bremen, a relation of Gustavus Adolphus, was not content even with this; but assembled troops of his own, and terrified the unfortunate monks and priests of the neighbourhood, but was quickly compelled by the imperial general, Count Gronsfeld, to lay down his arms. Even George, Duke of Lunenburg, formerly a colonel in the Emperor's service, embraced the party of Gustavus, for whom he raised several regiments, and by occupying the attention of the Imperialists in Lower Saxony, materially assisted him.

But more important service was rendered to the king by the Landgrave William of Hesse Cassel, whose victorious arms struck with terror the greater part of Westphalia and Lower Saxony, the bishopric of Fulda, and even the Electorate of Cologne. It has been already stated that immediately after the conclusion of the alliance between the Landgrave and Gustavus Adolphus at Werben, two imperial generals, Fugger and Altringer, were ordered by Tilly to march into Hesse, to punish the Landgrave for his revolt from the Emperor. But this prince had as firmly withstood the arms of his enemies, as his subjects had the proclamations of Tilly inciting them to rebellion, and the battle of Leipzig presently relieved him of their presence. He availed himself of their absence with courage and resolution; in a short time, Vach, Muenden and Hoexter surrendered to him, while his rapid advance alarmed the bishoprics of Fulda, Paderborn, and the ecclesiastical territories which bordered on Hesse. The terrified states hastened by a speedy submission to set limits to his progress, and by considerable contributions to purchase exemption from plunder. After these successful enterprises, the Landgrave united his victorious army with that of Gustavus Adolphus, and concerted with him at Frankfort their future plan of operations.

In this city, a number of princes and ambassadors were assembled to congratulate Gustavus on his success, and either to conciliate his favour or to appease his indignation. Among them was the fugitive King of Bohemia, the Palatine Frederick V., who had hastened from Holland to throw himself into the arms of his avenger and protector. Gustavus gave him the unprofitable honour of greeting him as a crowned head, and endeavoured, by a respectful sympathy, to soften his sense of his misfortunes. But great as the advantages were, which Frederick had promised himself from the power and good fortune of his protector; and high as were the expectations he had built on his justice and magnanimity, the chance of this unfortunate prince's reinstatement in his kingdom was as distant as ever. The inactivity and contradictory politics of the English court had abated the zeal of Gustavus Adolphus, and an irritability which he could not always repress, made him on this occasion forget the glorious vocation of protector of the oppressed, in which, on his invasion of Germany, he had so loudly announced himself.

The terrors of the king's irresistible strength, and the near prospect of his vengeance, had also compelled George, Landgrave of Hesse Darmstadt, to a timely submission. His connection with the Emperor, and his indifference to the Protestant cause, were no secret to the king, but he was satisfied with laughing at so impotent an enemy. As the Landgrave knew his own strength and the political situation of Germany so little, as to offer himself as mediator between the contending parties, Gustavus used jestingly to call him the peacemaker. He was frequently heard to say, when at play he was winning from the Landgrave, "that the money afforded double satisfaction, as it was Imperial coin." To his affinity with the Elector of Saxony, whom Gustavus had cause to treat with forbearance, the Landgrave was indebted for the favourable terms he obtained from the king, who contented himself with the surrender of his fortress of Russelheim, and his promise of observing a strict neutrality during the war. The Counts of Westerwald and Wetteran also visited the King in Frankfort, to offer him their assistance against the Spaniards, and to conclude an alliance, which was afterwards of great service to him. The town of Frankfort itself had reason to rejoice at the presence of this monarch, who took their commerce under his protection, and by the most effectual measures restored the fairs, which had been greatly interrupted by the war.

The Swedish army was now reinforced by ten thousand Hessians, which the Landgrave of Casse commanded. Gustavus Adolphus had already invested Koenigstein; Kostheim and Floersheim surrendered after a short siege; he was in command of the Maine; and transports were preparing with all speed at Hoechst to carry his troops across the Rhine. These preparations filled the Elector of Mentz, Anselm Casimir, with consternation; and he no longer doubted but that the storm of war would next fall upon him. As a partisan of the Emperor, and one of the most active members of the League, he could expect no better treatment than his confederates, the Bishops of Wurtzburg and Bamberg, had already experienced. The situation of his territories upon the Rhine made it necessary for the enemy to secure them, while the fertility afforded an irresistible temptation to a necessitous army. Miscalculating his own strength and that of his adversaries, the Elector flattered himself that he was able to repel force by force, and weary out the valour of the Swedes by the strength of his fortresses. He ordered the fortifications of his capital to be repaired with all diligence, provided it with every necessary for sustaining a long siege, and received into the town a garrison of 2,000 Spaniards, under Don Philip de Sylva. To prevent the approach of the Swedish transports, he endeavoured to close the mouth of the Maine by driving piles, and sinking large heaps of stones and vessels. He himself, however, accompanied by the Bishop of Worms, and carrying with him his most precious effects, took refuge in Cologne, and abandoned his capital and territories to the rapacity of a tyrannical garrison. But these preparations, which bespoke less of true courage than of weak and overweening confidence, did not prevent the Swedes from marching against Mentz, and making serious preparations for an attack upon the city. While one body of their troops poured into the Rheingau, routed the Spaniards who remained there, and levied contributions on the inhabitants, another laid the Roman Catholic towns in Westerwald and Wetterau under similar contributions. The main army had encamped at Cassel, opposite Mentz; and Bernhard, Duke of Weimar, made himself master of the Maeusethurm and the Castle of Ehrenfels, on the other side of the Rhine. Gustavus was now actively preparing to cross the river, and to blockade the town on the land side, when the movements of Tilly in Franconia suddenly called him from the siege, and obtained for the Elector a short repose.

The danger of Nuremberg, which, during the absence of Gustavus Adolphus on the Rhine, Tilly had made a show of besieging, and, in the event of resistance, threatened with the cruel fate of Magdeburg, occasioned the king suddenly to retire from before Mentz. Lest he should expose himself a second time to the reproaches of Germany, and the disgrace of abandoning a confederate city to a ferocious enemy, he hastened to its relief by forced marches. On his arrival at Frankfort, however, he heard of its spirited resistance, and of the retreat of Tilly, and lost not a moment in prosecuting his designs against Mentz. Failing in an attempt to cross the Rhine at Cassel, under the cannon of the besieged, he directed his march towards the Bergstrasse, with a view of approaching the town from an opposite quarter. Here he quickly made himself master of all the places of importance, and at Stockstadt, between Gernsheim and Oppenheim, appeared a second time upon the banks of the Rhine. The whole of the Bergstrasse was abandoned by the Spaniards, who endeavoured obstinately to defend the other bank of the river. For this purpose, they had burned or sunk all the vessels in the neighbourhood, and arranged a formidable force on the banks, in case the king should attempt the passage at that place.

On this occasion, the king's impetuosity exposed him to great danger of falling into the hands of the enemy. In order to reconnoitre the opposite bank, he crossed the river in a small boat; he had scarcely landed when he was attacked by a party of Spanish horse, from whose hands he only saved himself by a precipitate retreat. Having at last, with the assistance of the neighbouring fishermen, succeeded in procuring a few transports, he despatched two of them across the river, bearing Count Brahe and 300 Swedes. Scarcely had this officer time to entrench himself on the opposite bank, when he was attacked by 14 squadrons of Spanish dragoons and cuirassiers. Superior as the enemy was in number, Count Brahe, with his small force, bravely defended himself, and gained time for the king to support him with fresh troops. The Spaniards at last retired with the loss of 600 men, some taking refuge in Oppenheim, and others in Mentz. A lion of marble on a high pillar, holding a naked sword in his paw, and a helmet on his head, was erected seventy years after the event, to point out to the traveller the spot where the immortal monarch crossed the great river of Germany.

Gustavus Adolphus now conveyed his artillery and the greater part of his troops over the river, and laid siege to Oppenheim, which, after a brave resistance, was, on the 8th December, 1631, carried by storm. Five hundred Spaniards, who had so courageously defended the place, fell indiscriminately a sacrifice to the fury of the Swedes. The crossing of the Rhine by Gustavus struck terror into the Spaniards and Lorrainers, who had thought themselves protected by the river from the vengeance of the Swedes. Rapid flight was now their only security; every place incapable of an effectual defence was immediately abandoned. After a long train of outrages on the defenceless citizens, the troops of Lorraine evacuated Worms, which, before their departure, they treated with wanton cruelty. The Spaniards hastened to shut themselves up in Frankenthal, where they hoped to defy the victorious arms of Gustavus Adolphus.

The king lost no time in prosecuting his designs against Mentz, into which the flower of the Spanish troops had thrown themselves. While he advanced on the left bank of the Rhine, the Landgrave of Hesse Cassel moved forward on the other, reducing several strong places on his march. The besieged Spaniards, though hemmed in on both sides, displayed at first a bold determination, and threw, for several days, a shower of bombs into the Swedish camp, which cost the king many of his bravest soldiers. But notwithstanding, the Swedes continually gained ground, and had at last advanced so close to the ditch that they prepared seriously for storming the place. The courage of the besieged now began to droop. They trembled before the furious impetuosity of the Swedish soldiers, of which Marienberg, in Wurtzburg, had afforded so fearful an example. The same dreadful fate awaited Mentz, if taken by storm; and the enemy might even be easily tempted to revenge the carnage of Magdeburg on this rich and magnificent residence of a Roman Catholic prince. To save the town, rather than their own lives, the Spanish garrison capitulated on the fourth day, and obtained from the magnanimity of Gustavus a safe conduct to Luxembourg; the greater part of them, however, following the example of many others, enlisted in the service of Sweden.

On the 13th December, 1631, the king made his entry into the conquered town, and fixed his quarters in the palace of the Elector. Eighty pieces of cannon fell into his hands, and the citizens were obliged to redeem their property from pillage, by a payment of 80,000 florins. The benefits of this redemption did not extend to the Jews and the clergy, who were obliged to make large and separate contributions for themselves. The library of the Elector was seized by the king as his share, and presented by him to his chancellor, Oxenstiern, who intended it for the Academy of Westerrah, but the vessel in which it was shipped to Sweden foundered at sea.

After the loss of Mentz, misfortune still pursued the Spaniards on the Rhine. Shortly before the capture of that city, the Landgrave of Hesse Cassel had taken Falkenstein and Reifenberg, and the fortress of Koningstein surrendered to the Hessians. The Rhinegrave, Otto Louis, one of the king's generals, defeated nine Spanish squadrons who were on their march for Frankenthal, and made himself master of the most important towns upon the Rhine, from Boppart to Bacharach. After the capture of the fortress of Braunfels, which was effected by the Count of Wetterau, with the co-operation of the Swedes, the Spaniards quickly lost every place in Wetterau, while in the Palatinate they retained few places besides Frankenthal. Landau and Kronweisenberg openly declared for the Swedes; Spires offered troops for the king's service; Manheim was gained through the prudence of the Duke Bernard of Weimar, and the negligence of its governor, who, for this misconduct, was tried before the council of war, at Heidelberg, and beheaded.

The king had protracted the campaign into the depth of winter, and the severity of the season was perhaps one cause of the advantage his soldiers gained over those of the enemy. But the exhausted troops now stood in need of the repose of winter quarters, which, after the surrender of Mentz, Gustavus assigned to them, in its neighbourhood. He himself employed the interval of inactivity in the field, which the season of the year enjoined, in arranging, with his chancellor, the affairs of his cabinet, in treating for a neutrality with some of his enemies, and adjusting some political disputes which had sprung up with a neighbouring ally. He chose the city of Mentz for his winter quarters, and the settlement of these state affairs, and showed a greater partiality for this town, than seemed consistent with the interests of the German princes, or the shortness of his visit to the Empire. Not content with strongly fortifying it, he erected at the opposite angle which the Maine forms with the Rhine, a new citadel, which was named Gustavusburg from its founder, but which is better known under the title of Pfaffenraub or Pfaffenzwang[1].

While Gustavus Adolphus made himself master of the Rhine, and threatened the three neighbouring electorates with his victorious arms, his vigilant enemies in Paris and St. Germain's made use of every artifice to deprive him of the support of France, and, if possible, to involve him in a war with that power. By his sudden and equivocal march to the Rhine, he had surprised his friends, and furnished his enemies with the means of exciting a distrust of his intentions. After the conquest of Wurtzburg, and of the greater part of Franconia, the road into Bavaria and Austria lay open to him through Bamberg and the Upper Palatinate; and the expectation was as general, as it was natural, that he would not delay to attack the Emperor and the Duke of Bavaria in the very centre of their power, and, by the reduction of his two principal enemies, bring the war immediately to an end. But to the surprise of both parties, Gustavus left the path which general expectation had thus marked out for him; and instead of advancing to the right, turned to the left, to make the less important and more innocent princes of the Rhine feel his power, while he gave time to his more formidable opponents to recruit their strength. Nothing but the paramount design of reinstating the unfortunate Palatine, Frederick V., in the possession of his territories, by the expulsion of the Spaniards, could seem to account for this strange step; and the belief that Gustavus was about to effect that restoration, silenced for a while the suspicions of his friends and the calumnies of his enemies. But the Lower Palatinate was now almost entirely cleared of the enemy; and yet Gustavus continued to form new schemes of conquest on the Rhine, and to withhold the reconquered country from the Palatine, its rightful owner. In vain did the English ambassador remind him of what justice demanded, and what his own solemn engagement made a duty of honour; Gustavus replied to these demands with bitter complaints of the inactivity of the English court, and prepared to carry his victorious standard into Alsace, and even into Lorraine.

A distrust of the Swedish monarch was now loud and open, while the malice of his enemies busily circulated the most injurious reports as to his intentions. Richelieu, the minister of Louis XIII., had long witnessed with anxiety the king's progress towards the French frontier, and the suspicious temper of Louis rendered him but too accessible to the evil surmises which the occasion gave rise to. France was at this time involved in a civil war with her Protestant subjects, and the fear was not altogether groundless, that the approach of a victorious monarch of their party might revive their drooping spirit, and encourage them to a more desperate resistance. This might be the case, even if Gustavus Adolphus was far from showing a disposition to encourage them, or to act unfaithfully towards his ally, the King of France. But the vindictive Bishop of Wurtzburg, who was anxious to avenge the loss of his dominions, the envenomed rhetoric of the Jesuits and the active zeal of the Bavarian minister, represented this dreaded alliance between the Huguenots and the Swedes as an undoubted fact, and filled the timid mind of Louis with the most alarming fears. Not merely chimerical politicians, but

[1]Priests' plunder; alluding to the means by which the expense of its erection had been defrayed. —

many of the best informed Roman Catholics, fully believed that the king was on the point of breaking into the heart of France, to make common cause with the Huguenots, and to overturn the Catholic religion within the kingdom. Fanatical zealots already saw him, with his army, crossing the Alps, and dethroning the Viceregent of Christ in Italy. Such reports no doubt soon refute themselves; yet it cannot be denied that Gustavus, by his manoeuvres on the Rhine, gave a dangerous handle to the malice of his enemies, and in some measure justified the suspicion that he directed his arms, not so much against the Emperor and the Duke of Bavaria, as against the Roman Catholic religion itself.

The general clamour of discontent which the Jesuits raised in all the Catholic courts, against the alliance between France and the enemy of the church, at last compelled Cardinal Richelieu to take a decisive step for the security of his religion, and at once to convince the Roman Catholic world of the zeal of France, and of the selfish policy of the ecclesiastical states of Germany. Convinced that the views of the King of Sweden, like his own, aimed solely at the humiliation of the power of Austria, he hesitated not to promise to the princes of the League, on the part of Sweden, a complete neutrality, immediately they abandoned their alliance with the Emperor and withdrew their troops. Whatever the resolution these princes should adopt, Richelieu would equally attain his object. By their separation from the Austrian interest, Ferdinand would be exposed to the combined attack of France and Sweden; and Gustavus Adolphus, freed from his other enemies in Germany, would be able to direct his undivided force against the hereditary dominions of Austria. In that event, the fall of Austria was inevitable, and this great object of Richelieu's policy would be gained without injury to the church. If, on the other hand, the princes of the League persisted in their opposition, and adhered to the Austrian alliance, the result would indeed be more doubtful, but still France would have sufficiently proved to all Europe the sincerity of her attachment to the Catholic cause, and performed her duty as a member of the Roman Church. The princes of the League would then appear the sole authors of those evils, which the continuance of the war would unavoidably bring upon the Roman Catholics of Germany; they alone, by their wilful and obstinate adherence to the Emperor, would frustrate the measures employed for their protection, involve the church in danger, and themselves in ruin.

Richelieu pursued this plan with greater zeal, the more he was embarrassed by the repeated demands of the Elector of Bavaria for assistance from France; for this prince, as already stated, when he first began to entertain suspicions of the Emperor, entered immediately into a secret alliance with France, by which, in the event of any change in the Emperor's sentiments, he hoped to secure the possession of the Palatinate. But though the origin of the treaty clearly showed against what enemy it was directed, Maximilian now thought proper to make use of it against the King of Sweden, and did not hesitate to demand from France that assistance against her ally, which she had simply promised against Austria. Richelieu, embarrassed by this conflicting alliance with two hostile powers, had no resource left but to endeavour to put a speedy termination to their hostilities; and as little inclined to sacrifice Bavaria, as he was disabled, by his treaty with Sweden, from assisting it, he set himself, with all diligence, to bring about a neutrality, as the only means of fulfilling his obligations to both. For this purpose, the Marquis of Breze was sent, as his plenipotentiary, to the King of Sweden at Mentz, to learn his sentiments on this point, and to procure from him favourable conditions for the allied princes. But if Louis XIII. had powerful motives for wishing for this neutrality, Gustavus Adolphus had as grave reasons for desiring the contrary. Convinced by numerous proofs that the hatred of the princes of the League to the Protestant religion was invincible, their aversion to the foreign power of the Swedes inextinguishable, and their attachment to the House of Austria irrevocable, he apprehended less danger from their open hostility, than from a neutrality which was so little in unison with their real inclinations; and, moreover, as he was constrained to carry on the war in Germany at the expense of the enemy, he manifestly sustained great loss if he diminished their number without increasing that of his friends. It was not surprising, therefore, if Gustavus evinced little inclination to purchase the neutrality of the League, by which he was likely to gain so little, at the expense of the advantages he had already obtained.

The conditions, accordingly, upon which he offered to adopt the neutrality towards Bavaria were severe, and suited to these views. He required of the whole League a full and entire cessation from all hostilities; the recall of their troops from the imperial army, from the conquered towns, and from all the Protestant countries; the reduction of their military force; the exclusion of the imperial armies from their territories, and from supplies either of men, provisions, or ammunition. Hard as the conditions were, which the victor thus imposed upon the vanquished, the French mediator flattered himself he should be able to induce the Elector of Bavaria to accept them. In order to give time for an accommodation, Gustavus had agreed to a cessation of hostilities for a fortnight. But at the very time when this monarch was receiving from the French agents repeated assurances of the favourable progress of the negociation, an intercepted letter from the Elector to Pappenheim, the imperial general in Westphalia, revealed the perfidy of that prince, as having no other object in view by the whole negociation, than to gain time for his measures of defence. Far from intending to fetter his military operations by a truce with Sweden, the artful prince hastened his preparations, and employed the leisure which his enemy afforded him, in making the most active dispositions for resistance. The negociation accordingly failed, and served only to increase the animosity of the Bavarians and the Swedes.

Tilly's augmented force, with which he threatened to overrun Franconia, urgently required the king's presence in that circle; but it was necessary to expel previously the Spaniards from the Rhine, and to cut off their means of invading Germany from the Netherlands. With this view, Gustavus Adolphus had made an offer of neutrality to the Elector of Treves, Philip von Zeltern, on condition that the fortress of Hermanstein should be delivered up to him, and a free passage granted to his troops through Coblentz. But unwillingly as the Elector had beheld the Spaniards within his territories, he was still less disposed to commit his estates to the suspicious protection of a heretic, and to make the Swedish conqueror master of his destinies. Too weak to maintain his independence between two such powerful competitors, he took refuge in the protection of France. With his usual prudence, Richelieu profited by the embarrassments of this prince to augment the power of France, and to gain for her an important ally on the German frontier. A numerous French army was despatched to protect the territory of Treves, and a French garrison was received into Ehrenbreitstein. But the object which had moved the Elector to this bold step was not completely gained, for the offended pride of Gustavus Adolphus was not appeased till he had obtained a free passage for his troops through Treves.

Pending these negociations with Treves and France, the king's generals had entirely cleared the territory of Mentz of the Spanish garrisons, and Gustavus himself completed the conquest of this district by the capture of Kreutznach. To protect these conquests, the chancellor Oxenstiern was left with a division of the army upon the Middle Rhine, while the main body, under the king himself, began its march against the enemy in Franconia.

The possession of this circle had, in the mean time, been disputed with variable success, between Count Tilly and the Swedish General Horn, whom Gustavus had left there with 8,000 men; and the Bishopric of Bamberg, in particular, was at once the prize and the scene of their struggle. Called away to the Rhine by his other projects, the king had left to his general the chastisement of the bishop, whose perfidy had excited his indignation, and the activity of Horn justified the choice. In a short time, he subdued the greater part of the bishopric; and the capital itself, abandoned by its imperial garrison, was carried by storm. The banished bishop urgently demanded assistance from the Elector of Bavaria, who was at length persuaded to put an end to Tilly's inactivity. Fully empowered by his master's order to restore the bishop to his possessions, this general collected his troops, who were scattered over the Upper Palatinate, and with an army of 20,000 men advanced upon Bamberg. Firmly resolved to maintain his conquest even against this overwhelming force, Horn awaited the enemy within the walls of Bamberg; but was obliged to yield to the vanguard of Tilly what he had thought to be able to dispute with his whole army. A panic which suddenly seized his troops, and which no presence of mind of their general could check, opened the gates to the enemy, and it was with difficulty that the troops, baggage, and artillery, were saved. The reconquest of Bamberg was the fruit of this victory; but Tilly, with all his activity, was unable to overtake the Swedish general, who retired in good order behind the Maine. The king's appearance in Franconia, and his junction with Gustavus Horn at Kitzingen, put a stop to Tilly's conquests, and compelled him to provide for his own safety by a rapid retreat.

The king made a general review of his troops at Aschaffenburg. After his junction with Gustavus Horn, Banner, and Duke William of Weimar, they amounted to nearly 40,000 men. His progress through Franconia was uninterrupted; for Tilly, far too weak to encounter an enemy so superior in numbers, had retreated, by rapid marches, towards the Danube. Bohemia and Bavaria were now equally near to the king, and, uncertain whither his victorious course might be directed, Maximilian could form no immediate resolution. The choice of the king, and the fate of both provinces, now depended on the road that should be left open to Count Tilly. It was dangerous, during the approach of so formidable an enemy, to leave Bavaria undefended, in order to protect Austria; still more dangerous, by receiving Tilly into Bavaria, to draw thither the enemy also, and to render it the seat of a destructive war. The cares of the sovereign finally overcame the scruples of the statesman, and Tilly received orders, at all hazards, to cover the frontiers of Bavaria with his army.

Nuremberg received with triumphant joy the protector of the Protestant religion and German freedom, and the enthusiasm of the citizens expressed itself on his arrival in loud transports of admiration and joy. Even Gustavus could not contain his astonishment, to see himself in this city, which was the very centre of Germany, where he had never expected to be able to penetrate. The noble appearance of his person, completed the impression produced by his glorious exploits, and the condescension with which he received the congratulations of this free city won all hearts. He now confirmed the alliance he had concluded with it on the shores of the Baltic, and excited the citizens to zealous activity and fraternal unity against the common enemy. After a short stay in Nuremberg, he followed his army to the Danube, and appeared unexpectedly before the frontier town of Donauwerth. A numerous Bavarian garrison defended the place; and their commander, Rodolph Maximilian, Duke of Saxe Lauenburg, showed at first a resolute determination to defend it till the arrival of Tilly. But the vigour with which Gustavus Adolphus prosecuted the siege, soon compelled him to take measures for a speedy and secure retreat, which amidst a tremendous fire from the Swedish artillery he successfully executed.

The conquest of Donauwerth opened to the king the further side of the Danube, and now the small river Lech alone separated him from Bavaria. The immediate danger of his dominions aroused all Maximilian's activity; and however little he had hitherto disturbed the enemy's progress to his frontier, he now determined to dispute as resolutely the remainder of their course. On the opposite bank of the Lech, near the small town of Rain, Tilly occupied a strongly fortified camp, which, surrounded by three rivers, bade defiance to all attack. All the bridges over the Lech were destroyed; the whole course of the stream protected by strong garrisons as far as Augsburg; and that town itself, which had long betrayed its impatience to follow the example of Nuremberg and Frankfort, secured by a Bavarian garrison, and the disarming of its inhabitants. The Elector himself, with all the troops he could collect, threw himself into Tilly's camp, as if all his hopes centred on this single point, and here the good fortune of the Swedes was to suffer shipwreck for ever.

Gustavus Adolphus, after subduing the whole territory of Augsburg, on his own side of the river, and opening to his troops a rich supply of necessaries from that quarter, soon appeared on the bank opposite the Bavarian entrenchments. It was now the month of March, when the river, swollen by frequent rains, and the melting of the snow from the mountains of the Tyrol, flowed full and rapid between its steep banks. Its boiling current threatened the rash assailants with certain destruction, while from the opposite side the enemy's cannon showed their murderous mouths. If, in despite of the fury both of fire and water, they should accomplish this almost impossible passage, a fresh and vigorous enemy awaited the exhausted troops in an impregnable camp; and when they needed repose and refreshment they must prepare for battle. With exhausted powers they must ascend the hostile entrenchments, whose strength seemed to bid defiance to every assault. A defeat sustained upon this shore would be attended with inevitable destruction, since the same stream which impeded their advance would also cut off their retreat, if fortune should abandon them.

The Swedish council of war, which the king now assembled, strongly urged upon him all these considerations, in order to deter him from this dangerous undertaking. The most intrepid were appalled, and a troop of honourable warriors, who had grown gray in the field, did not hesitate to express their alarm. But the king's resolution was fixed. "What!" said he to Gustavus Horn, who spoke for the rest, "have we crossed the Baltic, and so many great rivers of Germany, and shall we now be checked by a brook like the Lech?" Gustavus had already, at great personal risk, reconnoitred the whole country, and discovered that his own side of the river was higher than the other, and consequently gave a considerable advantage to the fire of the Swedish artillery over that of the enemy. With great presence of mind he determined to profit by this circumstance. At the point where the left bank of the Lech forms an angle with the right, he immediately caused three batteries to be erected, from which 72 field-pieces maintained a cross fire upon the enemy. While this tremendous cannonade drove the Bavarians from the opposite bank, he caused to be erected a bridge over the river with all possible rapidity. A thick smoke, kept up by burning wood and wet straw, concealed for some time the progress of the work from the enemy, while the continued thunder of the cannon overpowered the noise of the axes. He kept alive by his own example the courage of his troops, and discharged more than 60 cannon with his own hand. The cannonade was returned by the Bavarians with equal vivacity for two hours, though with less effect, as the Swedish batteries swept the lower opposite bank, while their height served as a breast-work to their own troops. In vain, therefore, did the Bavarians attempt to destroy these works; the superior fire of the Swedes threw them into disorder, and the bridge was completed under their very eyes. On this dreadful day, Tilly did every thing in his power to encourage his troops; and no danger could drive him from the bank. At length he found the death which he sought, a cannon ball shattered his leg; and Altringer, his brave companion-in-arms, was, soon after, dangerously wounded in the head. Deprived of the animating presence of their two generals, the Bavarians gave way at last, and Maximilian, in spite of his own judgment, was driven to adopt a pusillanimous resolve. Overcome by the persuasions of the dying Tilly, whose wonted firmness was overpowered by the near approach of death, he gave up his impregnable position for lost; and the discovery by the Swedes of a ford, by which their cavalry were on the point of passing, accelerated his inglorious retreat. The same night, before a single soldier of the enemy had crossed the Lech, he broke up his camp, and, without giving time for the King to harass him in his march, retreated in good order to Neuburgh and Ingolstadt. With astonishment did Gustavus Adolphus, who completed the passage of the river on the following day behold the hostile camp abandoned; and the Elector's flight surprised him still more, when he saw the strength of the position he had quitted. "Had I been the Bavarian," said he, "though a cannon ball had carried away my beard and chin, never would I have abandoned a position like this, and laid open my territory to my enemies."

Bavaria now lay exposed to the conqueror; and, for the first time, the tide of war, which had hitherto only beat against its frontier, now flowed over its long spared and fertile fields. Before, however, the King proceeded to the conquest of these provinces, he delivered the town of Augsburg from the yoke of Bavaria; exacted an oath of allegiance from the citizens; and to secure its observance, left a garrison in the town. He then advanced, by rapid marches, against Ingolstadt, in order, by the capture of this important fortress, which the Elector covered with the greater part of his army, to secure his conquests in Bavaria, and obtain a firm footing on the Danube.

Shortly after the appearance of the Swedish King before Ingolstadt, the wounded Tilly, after experiencing the caprice of unstable fortune, terminated his career within the walls of that town. Conquered by the superior generalship of Gustavus Adolphus, he lost, at the close of his days, all the laurels of his earlier victories, and appeased, by a series of misfortunes, the demands of justice, and the avenging manes of Magdeburg. In his death, the Imperial army and that of the League sustained an irreparable loss; the Roman Catholic religion was deprived of its most zealous defender, and Maximilian of Bavaria of the most faithful of his servants, who sealed his fidelity by his death, and even in his dying moments fulfilled the duties of a general. His last message to the Elector was an urgent advice to take possession of Ratisbon, in order to maintain the command of the Danube, and to keep open the communication with Bohemia.

With the confidence which was the natural fruit of so many victories, Gustavus Adolphus commenced the siege of Ingolstadt, hoping to gain the town by the fury of his first assault. But the strength of its fortifications, and the bravery of its garrison, presented obstacles greater than any he had had to encounter since the battle of Breitenfeld, and the walls of Ingolstadt were near putting an end to his career. While reconnoitring the works, a 24-pounder killed his horse under him, and he fell to the ground, while almost immediately afterwards another ball struck his favourite, the young Margrave of Baden, by his side. With perfect self-possession the king rose, and quieted the fears of his troops by immediately mounting another horse.

The occupation of Ratisbon by the Bavarians, who, by the advice of Tilly, had surprised this town by stratagem, and placed in it a strong garrison, quickly changed the king's plan of operations. He had flattered himself with the hope of gaining this town, which favoured the Protestant cause, and to find in it an ally as devoted to him as Nuremberg, Augsburg, and Frankfort. Its seizure by the Bavarians seemed to postpone for a long time the fulfilment of his favourite project of making himself master of the Danube, and cutting off his adversaries' supplies from Bohemia. He suddenly raised the siege of Ingolstadt, before which he had wasted both his time and his troops, and penetrated into the interior of Bavaria, in order to draw the Elector into that quarter for the defence of his territories, and thus to strip the Danube of its defenders.

The whole country, as far as Munich, now lay open to the conqueror. Mosburg, Landshut, and the whole territory of Freysingen, submitted; nothing could resist his arms. But if he met with no regular force to oppose his progress, he had to contend against a still more implacable enemy in the heart of every Bavarian — religious fanaticism. Soldiers who did not believe in the Pope were, in this country, a new and unheard-of phenomenon; the blind zeal of the priests represented them to the peasantry as monsters, the children of hell, and their leader as Antichrist. No wonder, then, if they thought themselves released from all the ties of nature and humanity towards this brood of Satan, and justified in committing the most savage atrocities upon them. Woe to the Swedish soldier who fell into their hands! All the torments which inventive malice could devise were exercised upon these unhappy victims; and the sight of their mangled bodies exasperated the army to a fearful retaliation. Gustavus Adolphus, alone, sullied the lustre of his heroic character by no act of revenge; and the aversion which the Bavarians felt towards his religion, far from making him depart from the obligations of humanity towards that unfortunate people, seemed to impose upon him the stricter duty to honour his religion by a more constant clemency.

The approach of the king spread terror and consternation in the capital, which, stripped of its defenders, and abandoned by its principal inhabitants, placed all its hopes in the magnanimity of the conqueror. By an unconditional and voluntary surrender, it hoped to disarm his vengeance; and sent deputies even to Freysingen to lay at his feet the keys of the city. Strongly as the king might have been tempted by the inhumanity of the Bavarians, and the hostility of their sovereign, to make a dreadful use of the rights of victory; pressed as he was by Germans to avenge the fate of Magdeburg on the capital of its destroyer, this great prince scorned this mean revenge; and the very helplessness of his enemies disarmed his severity. Contented with the more noble triumph of conducting the Palatine Frederick with the pomp of a victor into the very palace of the prince who had been the chief instrument of his ruin, and the usurper of his territories, he heightened the brilliancy of his triumphal entry by the brighter splendour of moderation and clemency.

The King found in Munich only a forsaken palace, for the Elector's treasures had been transported to Werfen. The magnificence of the building astonished him; and he asked the guide who showed the apartments who was the architect. "No other," replied he, "than the Elector himself." — "I wish," said the King, "I had this architect to send to Stockholm." "That," he was answered, "the architect will take care to prevent." When the arsenal was examined, they found nothing but carriages, stripped of their cannon. The latter had been so artfully concealed under the floor, that no traces of them remained; and but for the treachery of a workman, the deceit would not have been detected. "Rise up from the dead," said the King, "and come to judgment." The floor was pulled up, and 140 pieces of cannon discovered, some of extraordinary calibre, which had been principally taken in the Palatinate and Bohemia. A treasure of 30,000 gold ducats, concealed in one of the largest, completed the pleasure which the King received from this valuable acquisition.

A far more welcome spectacle still would have been the Bavarian army itself; for his march into the heart of Bavaria had been undertaken chiefly with the view of luring them from their entrenchments. In this expectation he was disappointed. No enemy appeared; no entreaties, however urgent, on the part of his subjects, could induce the Elector to risk the remainder of his army to the chances of a battle. Shut up in Ratisbon, he awaited the reinforcements which Wallenstein was bringing from Bohemia; and endeavoured, in the mean time, to amuse his enemy and keep him inactive, by reviving the negociation for a neutrality. But the King's distrust, too often and too justly excited by his previous conduct, frustrated this design; and the intentional delay of Wallenstein abandoned Bavaria to the Swedes.

Thus far had Gustavus advanced from victory to victory, without meeting with an enemy able to cope with him. A part of Bavaria and Swabia, the Bishoprics of Franconia, the Lower Palatinate, and the Archbishopric of Mentz, lay conquered in his rear. An uninterrupted career of conquest had conducted him to the threshold of Austria; and the most brilliant success had fully justified the plan of operations which he had formed after the battle of Breitenfeld. If he had not succeeded to his wish in promoting a confederacy among the Protestant States, he had at least disarmed or weakened the League, carried on the war chiefly at its expense, lessened the Emperor's resources, emboldened the weaker States, and while he laid under contribution the allies of the Emperor, forced a way through their territories into Austria itself. Where arms were unavailing, the greatest service was rendered by the friendship of the free cities, whose affections he had gained, by the double ties of policy and religion; and, as long as he should maintain his superiority in the field, he might reckon on every thing from their zeal. By his conquests on the Rhine, the Spaniards were cut off from the Lower Palatinate, even if the state of the war in the Netherlands left them at liberty to interfere in the affairs of Germany. The Duke of Lorraine, too, after his unfortunate campaign, had been glad to adopt a neutrality. Even the numerous garrisons he had left behind him, in his progress through Germany, had not diminished his army; and, fresh and vigorous as when he first began his march, he now stood in the centre of Bavaria, determined and prepared to carry the war into the heart of Austria.

While Gustavus Adolphus thus maintained his superiority within the empire, fortune, in another quarter, had been no less favourable to his ally, the Elector of Saxony. By the arrangement concerted between these princes at Halle, after the battle of Leipzig, the conquest of Bohemia was intrusted to the Elector of Saxony, while the King reserved for himself the attack upon the territories of the League. The first fruits which the Elector reaped from the battle of Breitenfeld, was the reconquest of Leipzig, which was shortly followed by the expulsion of the Austrian garrisons from the entire circle. Reinforced by the troops who deserted to him from the hostile garrisons, the Saxon General, Arnheim, marched towards Lusatia, which had been overrun by an Imperial General, Rudolph von Tiefenbach, in order to chastise the Elector for embracing the cause of the enemy. He had already commenced in this weakly defended province the usual course of devastation, taken several towns, and terrified Dresden itself by his approach, when his destructive progress was suddenly stopped, by an express mandate from the Emperor to spare the possessions of the King of Saxony.

Ferdinand had perceived too late the errors of that policy, which reduced the Elector of Saxony to extremities, and forcibly driven this powerful monarch into an alliance with Sweden. By moderation, equally ill-timed, he now wished to repair if possible the consequences of his haughtiness; and thus committed a second error in endeavouring to repair the first. To deprive his enemy of so powerful an ally, he had opened, through the intervention of Spain, a negociation with the Elector; and in order to facilitate an accommodation, Tiefenbach was ordered immediately to retire from Saxony. But these concessions of the Emperor, far from producing the desired effect, only revealed to the Elector the embarrassment of his adversary and his own importance, and emboldened him the more to prosecute the advantages he had already obtained. How could he, moreover, without becoming chargeable with the most shameful ingratitude, abandon an ally to whom he had given the most solemn assurances of fidelity, and to whom he was indebted for the preservation of his dominions, and even of his Electoral dignity?

The Saxon army, now relieved from the necessity of marching into Lusatia, advanced towards Bohemia, where a combination of favourable circumstances seemed to ensure them an easy victory. In this kingdom, the first scene of this fatal war, the flames of dissension still smouldered beneath the ashes, while the discontent of the inhabitants was fomented by daily acts of oppression and tyranny. On every side, this unfortunate country showed signs of a mournful change. Whole districts had changed their proprietors, and groaned under the hated yoke of Roman Catholic masters, whom the favour of the Emperor and the Jesuits had enriched with the plunder and possessions of the exiled Protestants. Others, taking advantage themselves of the general distress, had purchased, at a low rate, the confiscated estates. The blood of the most eminent champions of liberty had been shed upon the scaffold; and such as by a timely flight avoided that fate, were wandering in misery far from their native land, while the obsequious slaves of despotism enjoyed their patrimony. Still more insupportable than the oppression of these petty tyrants, was the restraint of conscience which was imposed without distinction on all the Protestants of that kingdom. No external danger, no opposition on the part of the nation, however steadfast, not even the fearful lessons of past experience could check in the Jesuits the rage of proselytism; where fair means were ineffectual, recourse was had to military force to bring the deluded wanderers within the pale of the church. The inhabitants of Joachimsthal, on the frontiers between Bohemia and Meissen, were the chief sufferers from this violence. Two imperial commissaries, accompanied by as many Jesuits, and supported by fifteen musketeers, made their appearance in this peaceful valley to preach the gospel to the heretics. Where the rhetoric of the former was ineffectual, the forcibly quartering the latter upon the houses, and threats of banishment and fines were tried. But on this occasion, the good cause prevailed, and the bold resistance of this small district compelled the Emperor disgracefully to recall his mandate of conversion. The example of the court had, however, afforded a precedent to the Roman Catholics of the empire, and seemed to justify every act of oppression which their insolence tempted them to wreak upon the Protestants. It is not surprising, then, if this persecuted party was favourable to a revolution, and saw with pleasure their deliverers on the frontiers.

The Saxon army was already on its march towards Prague, the imperial garrisons everywhere retired before them. Schloeckenau, Tetschen, Aussig, Leutmeritz, soon fell into the enemy's hands, and every Roman Catholic place was abandoned to plunder. Consternation seized all the Papists of the Empire; and conscious of the outrages which they themselves had committed on the Protestants, they did not venture to abide the vengeful arrival of a Protestant army. All the Roman Catholics, who had anything to lose, fled hastily from the country to the capital, which again they presently abandoned. Prague was unprepared for an attack, and was too weakly garrisoned to sustain a long siege. Too late had the Emperor resolved to despatch Field-Marshal Tiefenbach to the defence of this capital. Before the imperial orders could reach the head-quarters of that general, in Silesia, the Saxons were already close to Prague, the Protestant inhabitants of which showed little zeal, while the weakness of the garrison left no room to hope a long resistance. In this fearful state of embarrassment, the Roman Catholics of Prague looked for security to Wallenstein, who now lived in that city as a private individual. But far from lending his military experience, and the weight of his name, towards its defence, he seized the favourable opportunity to satiate his thirst for revenge. If he did not actually invite the Saxons to Prague, at least his conduct facilitated its capture. Though unprepared, the town might still hold out until succours could arrive; and an imperial colonel, Count Maradas, showed serious intentions of undertaking its defence. But without command and authority, and having no support but his own zeal and courage, he did not dare to venture upon such a step without the advice of a superior. He therefore consulted the Duke of Friedland, whose approbation might supply the want of authority from the Emperor, and to whom the Bohemian generals were referred by an express edict of the court in the last extremity. He, however, artfully excused himself, on the plea of holding no official appointment, and his long retirement from the political world; while he weakened the resolution of the subalterns by the scruples which he suggested, and painted in the strongest colours. At last, to render the consternation general and complete, he quitted the capital with his whole court, however little he had to fear from its capture; and the city was lost, because, by his departure, he showed that he despaired of its safety. His example was followed by all the Roman Catholic nobility, the generals with their troops, the clergy, and all the officers of the crown. All night the people were employed in saving their persons and effects. The roads to Vienna were crowded with fugitives, who scarcely recovered from their consternation till they reached the imperial city. Maradas himself, despairing of the safety of Prague, followed the rest, and led his small detachment to Tabor, where he awaited the event.

Profound silence reigned in Prague, when the Saxons next morning appeared before it; no preparations were made for defence; not a single shot from the walls announced an intention of resistance. On the contrary, a crowd of spectators from the town, allured by curiosity, came flocking round, to behold the foreign army; and the peaceful confidence with which they advanced, resembled a friendly salutation, more than a hostile reception. From the concurrent reports of these people, the Saxons learned that the town had been deserted by the troops, and that the government had fled to Budweiss. This unexpected and inexplicable absence of resistance excited Arnheim's distrust the more, as the speedy approach of the Silesian succours was no secret to him, and as he knew that the Saxon army was too indifferently provided with materials for undertaking a siege, and by far too weak in numbers to attempt to take the place by storm. Apprehensive of stratagem, he redoubled his vigilance; and he continued in this conviction until Wallenstein's house-steward, whom he discovered among the crowd, confirmed to him this intelligence. "The town is ours without a blow!" exclaimed he in astonishment to his officers, and immediately summoned it by a trumpeter.

The citizens of Prague, thus shamefully abandoned by their defenders, had long taken their resolution; all that they had to do was to secure their properties and liberties by an advantageous capitulation. No sooner was the treaty signed by the Saxon general, in his master's name, than the gates were opened, without farther opposition; and upon the 11th of November, 1631, the army made their triumphal entry. The Elector soon after followed in person, to receive the homage of those whom he had newly taken under his protection; for it was only in the character of protector that the three towns of Prague had surrendered to him. Their allegiance to the Austrian monarchy was not to be dissolved by the step they had taken. In proportion as the Papists' apprehensions of reprisals on the part of the Protestants had been exaggerated, so was their surprise great at the moderation of the Elector, and the discipline of his troops. Field-Marshal Arnheim plainly evinced, on this occasion, his respect for Wallenstein. Not content with sparing his estates on his march, he now placed guards over his palace, in Prague, to prevent the plunder of any of his effects. The Roman Catholics of the town were allowed the fullest liberty of conscience; and of all the churches they had wrested from the Protestants, four only were now taken back from them. From this general indulgence, none were excluded but the Jesuits, who were generally considered as the authors of all past grievances, and thus banished the kingdom.

John George belied not the submission and dependence with which the terror of the imperial name inspired him; nor did he indulge at Prague, in a course of conduct which would assuredly have been pursued against himself in Dresden, by imperial generals, such as Tilly or Wallenstein. He carefully distinguished between the enemy with whom he was at war, and the head of the Empire, to whom he owed obedience. He did not venture to touch the household furniture of the latter, while, without scruple, he appropriated and transported to Dresden the cannon of the former. He did not take up his residence in the imperial palace, but the house of Lichtenstein; too modest to use the apartments of one whom he had deprived of a kingdom. Had this trait been related of a great man and a hero, it would irresistibly excite our admiration; but the character of this prince leaves us in doubt whether this moderation ought to be ascribed to a noble self-command, or to the littleness of a weak mind, which even good fortune could not embolden, and liberty itself could not strip of its habituated fetters.

The surrender of Prague, which was quickly followed by that of most of the other towns, effected a great and sudden change in Bohemia. Many of the Protestant nobility, who had hitherto been wandering about in misery, now returned to their native country; and Count Thurn, the famous author of the Bohemian insurrection, enjoyed the triumph of returning as a conqueror to the scene of his crime and his condemnation. Over the very bridge where the heads of his adherents, exposed to view, held out a fearful picture of the fate which had threatened himself, he now made his triumphal entry; and to remove these ghastly objects was his first care. The exiles again took possession of their properties, without thinking of recompensing for the purchase money the present possessors, who had mostly taken to flight. Even though they had received a price for their estates, they seized on every thing which had once been their own; and many had reason to rejoice at the economy of the late possessors. The lands and cattle had greatly improved in their hands; the apartments were now decorated with the most costly furniture; the cellars, which had been left empty, were richly filled; the stables supplied; the magazines stored with provisions. But distrusting the constancy of that good fortune, which had so unexpectedly smiled upon them, they hastened to get quit of these insecure possessions, and to convert their immoveable into transferable property.

The presence of the Saxons inspired all the Protestants of the kingdom with courage; and, both in the country and the capital, crowds flocked to the newly opened Protestant churches. Many, whom fear alone had retained in their adherence to Popery, now openly professed the new doctrine; and many of the late converts to Roman Catholicism gladly renounced a compulsory persuasion, to follow the earlier conviction of their conscience. All the moderation of the new regency, could not restrain the manifestation of that just displeasure, which this persecuted people felt against their oppressors. They made a fearful and cruel use of their newly recovered rights; and, in many parts of the kingdom, their hatred of the religion which they had been compelled to profess, could be satiated only by the blood of its adherents.

Meantime the succours which the imperial generals, Goetz and Tiefenbach, were conducting from Silesia, had entered Bohemia, where they were joined by some of Tilly's regiments, from the Upper Palatinate. In order to disperse them before they should receive any further reinforcement, Arnheim advanced with part of his army from Prague, and made a vigorous attack on their entrenchments near Limburg, on the Elbe. After a severe action, not without great loss, he drove the enemy from their fortified camp, and forced them, by his heavy fire, to recross the Elbe, and to destroy the bridge which they had built over that river. Nevertheless, the Imperialists obtained the advantage in several skirmishes, and the Croats pushed their incursions to the very gates of Prague. Brilliant and promising as the opening of the Bohemian campaign had been, the issue by no means satisfied the expectations of Gustavus Adolphus. Instead of vigorously following up their advantages, by forcing a passage to the Swedish army through the conquered country, and then, with it, attacking the imperial power in its centre, the Saxons weakened themselves in a war of skirmishes, in which they were not always successful, while they lost the time which should have been devoted to greater undertakings. But the Elector's subsequent conduct betrayed the motives which had prevented him from pushing his advantage over the Emperor, and by consistent measures promoting the plans of the King of Sweden.

The Emperor had now lost the greater part of Bohemia, and the Saxons were advancing against Austria, while the Swedish monarch was rapidly moving to the same point through Franconia, Swabia, and Bavaria. A long war had exhausted the strength of the Austrian monarchy, wasted the country, and diminished its armies. The renown of its victories was no more, as well as the confidence inspired by constant success; its troops had lost the obedience and discipline to which those of the Swedish monarch owed all their superiority in the field. The confederates of the Emperor were disarmed, or their fidelity shaken by the danger which threatened themselves. Even Maximilian of Bavaria, Austria's most powerful ally, seemed disposed to yield to the seductive proposition of neutrality; while his suspicious alliance with France had long been a subject of apprehension to the Emperor. The bishops of Wurtzburg and Bamberg, the Elector of Mentz, and the Duke of Lorraine, were either expelled from their territories, or threatened with immediate attack; Treves had placed itself under the protection of France. The bravery of the Hollanders gave full employment to the Spanish arms in the Netherlands; while Gustavus had driven them from the Rhine. Poland was still fettered by the truce which subsisted between that country and Sweden. The Hungarian frontier was threatened by the Transylvanian Prince, Ragotsky, a successor of Bethlen Gabor, and the inheritor of his restless mind; while the Porte was making great preparation to profit by the favourable conjuncture for aggression. Most of the Protestant states, encouraged by their protector's success, were openly and actively declaring against the Emperor. All the resources which had been obtained by the violent and oppressive extortions of Tilly and Wallenstein were exhausted; all these depots, magazines, and rallying-points, were now lost to the Emperor; and the war could no longer be carried on as before at the cost of others. To complete his embarrassment, a dangerous insurrection broke out in the territory of the Ens, where the ill-timed religious zeal of the government had provoked the Protestants to resistance; and thus fanaticism lit its torch within the empire, while a foreign enemy was already on its frontier. After so long a continuance of good fortune, such brilliant victories and extensive conquests, such fruitless effusion of blood, the Emperor saw himself a second time on the brink of that abyss, into which he was so near falling at the commencement of his reign. If Bavaria should embrace the neutrality; if Saxony should resist the tempting offers he had held out; and France resolve to attack the Spanish power at the same time in the Netherlands, in Italy and in Catalonia, the ruin of Austria would be complete; the allied powers would divide its spoils, and the political system of Germany would undergo a total change.

The chain of these disasters began with the battle of Breitenfeld, the unfortunate issue of which plainly revealed the long decided decline of the Austrian power, whose weakness had hitherto been concealed under the dazzling glitter of a grand name. The chief cause of the Swedes' superiority in the field, was evidently to be ascribed to the unlimited power of their leader, who concentrated in himself the whole strength of his party; and, unfettered in his enterprises by any higher authority, was complete master of every favourable opportunity, could control all his means to the accomplishment of his ends, and was responsible to none but himself. But since Wallenstein's dismissal, and Tilly's defeat, the very reverse of this course was pursued by the Emperor and the League. The generals wanted authority over their troops, and liberty of acting at their discretion; the soldiers were deficient in discipline and obedience; the scattered corps in combined operation; the states in attachment to the cause; the leaders in harmony among themselves, in quickness to resolve, and firmness to execute. What gave the Emperor's enemy so decided an advantage over him, was not so much their superior power, as their manner of using it. The League and the Emperor did not want means, but a mind capable of directing them with energy and effect. Even had Count Tilly not lost his old renown, distrust of Bavaria would not allow the Emperor to place the fate of Austria in the hands of one who had never concealed his attachment to the Bavarian Elector. The urgent want which Ferdinand felt, was for a general possessed of sufficient experience to form and to command an army, and willing at the same time to dedicate his services, with blind devotion, to the Austrian monarchy.

This choice now occupied the attention of the Emperor's privy council, and divided the opinions of its members. In order to oppose one monarch to another, and by the presence of their sovereign to animate the courage of the troops, Ferdinand, in the ardour of the moment, had offered himself to be the leader of his army; but little trouble was required to overturn a resolution which was the offspring of despair alone, and which yielded at once to calm reflection. But the situation which his dignity, and the duties of administration, prevented the Emperor from holding, might be filled by his son, a youth of talents and bravery, and of whom the subjects of Austria had already formed great expectations. Called by his birth to the defence of a monarchy, of whose crowns he wore two already, Ferdinand III., King of Hungary and Bohemia, united, with the natural dignity of heir to the throne, the respect of the army, and the attachment of the people, whose co-operation was indispensable to him in the conduct of the war. None but the beloved heir to the crown could venture to impose new burdens on a people already severely oppressed; his personal presence with the army could alone suppress the pernicious jealousies of the several leaders, and by the influence of his name, restore the neglected discipline of the troops to its former rigour. If so young a leader was devoid of the maturity of judgment, prudence, and military experience which practice alone could impart, this deficiency might be supplied by a judicious choice of counsellors and assistants, who, under the cover of his name, might be vested with supreme authority.

But plausible as were the arguments with which a part of the ministry supported this plan, it was met by difficulties not less serious, arising from the distrust, perhaps even the jealousy, of the Emperor, and also from the desperate state of affairs. How dangerous was it to entrust the fate of the monarchy to a youth, who was himself in need of counsel and support! How hazardous to oppose to the greatest general of his age, a tyro, whose fitness for so important a post had never yet been tested by experience; whose name, as yet unknown to fame, was far too powerless to inspire a dispirited army with the assurance of future victory! What a new burden on the country, to support the state a royal leader was required to maintain, and which the prejudices of the age considered as inseparable from his presence with the army! How serious a consideration for the prince himself, to commence his political career, with an office which must make him the scourge of his people, and the oppressor of the territories which he was hereafter to rule.

But not only was a general to be found for the army; an army must also be found for the general. Since the compulsory resignation of Wallenstein, the Emperor had defended himself more by the assistance of Bavaria and the League, than by his own armies; and it was this dependence on equivocal allies, which he was endeavouring to escape, by the appointment of a general of his own. But what possibility was there of raising an army out of nothing, without the all-powerful aid of gold, and the inspiriting name of a victorious commander; above all, an army which, by its discipline, warlike spirit, and activity, should be fit to cope with the experienced troops of the northern conqueror? In all Europe, there was but one man equal to this, and that one had been mortally affronted.

The moment had at last arrived, when more than ordinary satisfaction was to be done to the wounded pride of the Duke of Friedland. Fate itself had been his avenger, and an unbroken chain of disasters, which had assailed Austria from the day of his dismissal, had wrung from the Emperor the humiliating confession, that with this general he had lost his right arm. Every defeat of his troops opened afresh this wound; every town which he lost, revived in the mind of the deceived monarch the memory of his own weakness and ingratitude. It would have been well for him, if, in the offended general, he had only lost a leader of his troops, and a defender of his dominions; but he was destined to find in him an enemy, and the most dangerous of all, since he was least armed against the stroke of treason.

Removed from the theatre of war, and condemned to irksome inaction, while his rivals gathered laurels on the field of glory, the haughty duke had beheld these changes of fortune with affected composure, and concealed, under a glittering and theatrical pomp, the dark designs of his restless genius. Torn by burning passions within, while all without bespoke calmness and indifference, he brooded over projects of ambition and revenge, and slowly, but surely, advanced towards his end. All that he owed to the Emperor was effaced from his mind; what he himself had done for the Emperor was imprinted in burning characters on his memory. To his insatiable thirst for power, the Emperor's ingratitude was welcome, as it seemed to tear in pieces the record of past favours, to absolve him from every obligation towards his former benefactor. In the disguise of a righteous retaliation, the projects dictated by his ambition now appeared to him just and pure. In proportion as the external circle of his operations was narrowed, the world of hope expanded before him, and his dreamy imagination revelled in boundless projects, which, in any mind but such as his, madness alone could have given birth to. His services had raised him to the proudest height which it was possible for a man, by his own efforts, to attain. Fortune had denied him nothing which the subject and the citizen could lawfully enjoy. Till the moment of his dismissal, his demands had met with no refusal, his ambition had met with no check; but the blow which, at the diet of Ratisbon, humbled him, showed him the difference between *original* and *deputed* power, the distance between the subject and his sovereign. Roused from the intoxication of his own greatness by this sudden reverse of fortune, he compared the authority which he had possessed, with that which had deprived him of it; and his ambition marked the steps which it had yet to surmount upon the ladder of fortune. From the moment he had so bitterly experienced the weight of sovereign power, his efforts were directed to attain it for himself; the wrong which he himself had suffered made him a robber. Had he not been outraged by injustice, he might have obediently moved in his orbit round the majesty of the throne, satisfied with the glory of being the brightest of its satellites. It was only when violently forced from its sphere, that his wandering star threw in disorder the system to which it belonged, and came in destructive collision with its sun.

Gustavus Adolphus had overrun the north of Germany; one place after another was lost; and at Leipzig, the flower of the Austrian army had fallen. The intelligence of this defeat soon reached the ears of Wallenstein, who, in the retired obscurity of a private station in Prague, contemplated from a calm distance the tumult of war. The news, which filled the breasts of the Roman Catholics with dismay, announced to him the return of greatness and good fortune. For him was Gustavus Adolphus labouring. Scarce had the king begun to gain reputation by his exploits, when Wallenstein lost not a moment to court his friendship, and to make common cause with this successful enemy of Austria. The banished Count Thurn, who had long entered the service of Sweden, undertook to convey Wallenstein's congratulations to the king, and to invite him to a close alliance with the duke. Wallenstein required 15,000 men from the king; and with these, and the troops he himself engaged to raise, he undertook to conquer Bohemia and Moravia, to surprise Vienna, and drive his master, the Emperor, before him into Italy. Welcome as was this unexpected proposition, its extravagant promises were naturally calculated to excite suspicion. Gustavus Adolphus was too good a judge of merit to reject with coldness the offers of one who might be so important a friend. But when Wallenstein, encouraged by the favourable reception of his first message, renewed it after the battle of Breitenfeld, and pressed for a decisive answer, the prudent monarch hesitated to trust his reputation to the chimerical projects of so daring an adventurer, and to commit so large a force to the honesty of a man who felt no shame in openly avowing himself a traitor. He excused himself, therefore, on the plea of the weakness of his army which, if diminished by so large a detachment, would certainly suffer in its march through the empire; and thus, perhaps, by excess of caution, lost an opportunity of putting an immediate end to the war. He afterwards endeavoured to renew the negociation; but the favourable moment was past, and Wallenstein's offended pride never forgave the first neglect.

But the king's hesitation, perhaps, only accelerated the breach, which their characters made inevitable sooner or later. Both framed by nature to give laws, not to receive them, they could not long have co-operated in an enterprise, which eminently demanded mutual submission and sacrifices. Wallenstein was *nothing* where he was not *everything*; he must either act with unlimited power, or not at all. So cordially, too, did Gustavus dislike control, that he had almost renounced his advantageous alliance with France, because it threatened to fetter his own independent judgment. Wallenstein was lost to a party, if he could not lead; the latter was, if possible, still less disposed to obey the instructions of another. If the pretensions of a rival would be so irksome to the Duke of Friedland, in the conduct of combined operations, in the division of the spoil they would be insupportable. The proud monarch might condescend to accept the assistance of a rebellious subject against the Emperor, and to reward his valuable services with regal munificence; but he never could so far lose sight of his own dignity, and the majesty of royalty, as to bestow the recompense which the extravagant ambition of Wallenstein demanded; and requite an act of treason, however useful, with a crown. In him, therefore, even if all Europe should tacitly acquiesce, Wallenstein had reason to expect the most decided and formidable opponent to his views on the Bohemian crown; and in all Europe he was the only one who could enforce his opposition. Constituted Dictator in Germany by Wallenstein himself, he might turn his arms against him, and consider himself bound by no obligations to one who was himself a traitor. There was no room for a Wallenstein under such an ally; and it was, apparently, this conviction, and not any supposed designs upon the imperial throne, that he alluded to, when, after the death of the King of Sweden, he exclaimed, "It is well for him and me that he is gone. The German Empire does not require two such leaders."

His first scheme of revenge on the house of Austria had indeed failed; but the purpose itself remained unalterable; the choice of means alone was changed. What he had failed in effecting with the King of Sweden, he hoped to obtain with less difficulty and more advantage from the Elector of Saxony. Him he was as certain of being able to bend to his views, as he had always been doubtful of Gustavus Adolphus. Having always maintained a good understanding with his old friend Arnheim, he now made use of him to bring about an alliance with Saxony, by which he hoped to render himself equally formidable to the Emperor and the King of Sweden. He had reason to expect that a scheme, which, if successful, would deprive the Swedish monarch of his influence in Germany, would be welcomed by the Elector of Saxony, who he knew was jealous of the power and offended at the lofty pretensions of Gustavus Adolphus. If he succeeded in separating Saxony from the Swedish alliance, and in establishing, conjointly with that power, a third party in the Empire, the fate of the war would be placed in his hand; and by this single step he would succeed in gratifying his revenge against the Emperor, revenging the neglect of the Swedish monarch, and on the ruin of both, raising the edifice of his own greatness.

But whatever course he might follow in the prosecution of his designs, he could not carry them into effect without an army entirely devoted to him. Such a force could not be secretly raised without its coming to the knowledge of the imperial court, where it would naturally excite suspicion, and thus frustrate his design in the very outset. From the army, too, the rebellious purposes for which it was destined, must be concealed till the very moment of execution, since it could scarcely be expected that they would at once be prepared to listen to the voice of a traitor, and serve against their legitimate sovereign. Wallenstein, therefore, must raise it publicly and in name of the Emperor, and be placed at its head, with unlimited authority, by the Emperor himself. But how could this be accomplished, otherwise than by his being appointed to the command of the army, and entrusted with full powers to conduct the war. Yet neither his pride, nor his interest, permitted him to sue in person for this post, and as a suppliant to accept from the favour of the Emperor a limited power, when an unlimited authority might be extorted from his fears. In order to make himself the master of the terms on which he would resume the command of the army, his course was to wait until the post should be forced upon him. This was the advice he received from Arnheim, and this the end for which he laboured with profound policy and restless activity.

Convinced that extreme necessity would alone conquer the Emperor's irresolution, and render powerless the opposition of his bitter enemies, Bavaria and Spain, he henceforth occupied himself in promoting the success of the enemy, and in increasing the embarrassments of his master. It was apparently by his instigation and advice, that the Saxons, when on the route to Lusatia and Silesia, had turned their march towards Bohemia, and overrun that defenceless kingdom, where their rapid conquests was partly the result of his measures. By the fears which he affected to entertain, he paralyzed every effort at resistance; and his precipitate retreat caused the delivery of the capital to the enemy. At a conference with the Saxon general, which was held at Kaunitz under the pretext of negociating for a peace, the seal was put to the conspiracy, and the conquest of Bohemia was the first fruits of this mutual understanding. While Wallenstein was thus personally endeavouring to heighten the perplexities of Austria, and while the rapid movements of the Swedes upon the Rhine effectually promoted his designs, his friends and bribed adherents in Vienna uttered loud complaints of the public calamities, and represented the dismissal of the general as the sole cause of all these misfortunes. "Had Wallenstein commanded, matters would never have come to this," exclaimed a thousand voices; while their opinions found supporters, even in the Emperor's privy council.

Their repeated remonstrances were not needed to convince the embarrassed Emperor of his general's merits, and of his own error. His dependence on Bavaria and the League had soon become insupportable; but hitherto this dependence permitted him not to show his distrust, or irritate the Elector by the recall of Wallenstein. But now when his necessities grew every day more pressing, and the weakness of Bavaria more apparent, he could no longer hesitate to listen to the friends of the duke, and to consider their overtures for his restoration to command. The immense riches Wallenstein possessed, the universal reputation he enjoyed, the rapidity with which six years before he had assembled an army of 40,000 men, the little expense at which he had maintained this formidable force, the actions he had performed at its head, and lastly, the zeal and fidelity he had displayed for his master's honour, still lived in the Emperor's recollection, and made Wallenstein seem to him the ablest instrument to restore the balance between the belligerent powers, to save Austria, and preserve the Catholic religion. However sensibly the imperial pride might feel the humiliation, in being forced to make so unequivocal an admission of past errors and present necessity; however painful it was to descend to humble entreaties, from the height of imperial command; however doubtful the fidelity of so deeply injured and implacable a character; however loudly and urgently the Spanish minister and the Elector of Bavaria protested against this step, the immediate pressure of necessity finally overcame every other consideration, and the friends of the duke were empowered to consult him on the subject, and to hold out the prospect of his restoration.

Informed of all that was transacted in the Emperor's cabinet to his advantage, Wallenstein possessed sufficient self-command to conceal his inward triumph and to assume the mask of indifference. The moment of vengeance was at last come, and his proud heart exulted in the prospect of repaying with interest the injuries of the Emperor. With artful eloquence, he expatiated upon the happy tranquillity of a private station, which had blessed him since his retirement from a political stage. Too long, he said, had he tasted the pleasures of ease and independence, to sacrifice to the vain phantom of glory, the uncertain favour of princes. All his desire of power and distinction were extinct: tranquillity and repose were now the sole object of his wishes. The better to conceal his real impatience, he declined the Emperor's invitation to the court, but at the same time, to facilitate the negociations, came to Znaim in Moravia.

At first, it was proposed to limit the authority to be intrusted to him, by the presence of a superior, in order, by this expedient, to silence the objections of the Elector of Bavaria. The imperial deputies, Questenberg and Werdenberg, who, as old friends of the duke, had been employed in this delicate mission, were instructed to propose that the King of Hungary should remain with the army, and learn the art of war under Wallenstein. But the very mention of his name threatened to put a period to the whole negociation. "No! never," exclaimed Wallenstein, "will I submit to a colleague in my office. No — not even if it were God himself, with whom I should have to share my command." But even when this obnoxious point was given up, Prince Eggenberg, the Emperor's minister and favourite, who had always been the steady friend and zealous champion of Wallenstein, and was therefore expressly sent to him, exhausted his eloquence in vain to overcome the pretended reluctance of the duke. "The Emperor," he admitted, "had, in Wallenstein, thrown away the most costly jewel in his crown: but unwillingly and compulsorily only had he taken this step, which he had since deeply repented of; while his esteem for the duke had remained unaltered, his favour for him undiminished. Of these sentiments he now gave the most decisive proof, by reposing unlimited confidence in his fidelity and capacity to repair the mistakes of his predecessors, and to change the whole aspect of affairs. It would be great and noble to sacrifice his just indignation to the good of his country; dignified and worthy of him to refute the evil calumny of his enemies by the double warmth of his zeal. This victory over himself," concluded the prince, "would crown his other unparalleled services to the empire, and render him the greatest man of his age."

These humiliating confessions, and flattering assurances, seemed at last to disarm the anger of the duke; but not before he had disburdened his heart of his reproaches against the Emperor, pompously dwelt upon his own services, and humbled to the utmost the monarch who solicited his assistance, did he condescend to listen to the attractive proposals of the minister. As if he yielded entirely to the force of their arguments, he condescended with a haughty reluctance to that which was the most ardent wish of his heart; and deigned to favour the ambassadors with a ray of hope. But far from putting an end to the Emperor's embarrassments, by giving at once a full and unconditional consent, he only acceded to a part of his demands, that he might exalt the value of that which still remained, and was of most importance. He accepted the command, but only for three months; merely for the purpose of raising, but not of leading, an army. He wished only to show his power and ability in its organization, and to display before the eyes of the Emperor, the greatness of that assistance, which he still retained in his hands. Convinced that an army raised by his name alone, would, if deprived of its creator, soon sink again into nothing, he intended it to serve only as a decoy to draw more important concessions from his master. And yet Ferdinand congratulated himself, even in having gained so much as he had.

Wallenstein did not long delay to fulfil those promises which all Germany regarded as chimerical, and which Gustavus Adolphus had considered as extravagant. But the foundation for the present enterprise had been long laid, and he now only put in motion the machinery, which many years had been prepared for the purpose. Scarcely had the news spread of Wallenstein's levies, when, from every quarter of the Austrian monarchy, crowds of soldiers repaired to try their fortunes under this experienced general. Many, who had before fought under his standards, had been admiring eye-witnesses of his great actions, and experienced his magnanimity, came forward from their retirement, to share with him a second time both booty and glory. The greatness of the pay he promised attracted thousands, and the plentiful supplies the soldier was likely to enjoy at the cost of the peasant, was to the latter an irresistible inducement to embrace the military life at once, rather than be the victim of its oppression. All the Austrian provinces were compelled to assist in the equipment. No class was exempt from taxation — no dignity or privilege from capitation. The Spanish court, as well as the King of Hungary, agreed to contribute a considerable sum. The ministers made large presents, while Wallenstein himself advanced 200,000 dollars from his own income to hasten the armament. The poorer officers he supported out of his own revenues; and, by his own example, by brilliant promotions, and still more brilliant promises, he induced all, who were able, to raise troops at their own expense. Whoever raised a corps at his own cost was to be its commander. In the appointment of officers, religion made no difference. Riches, bravery and experience were more regarded than creed. By this uniform treatment of different religious sects, and still more by his express declaration, that his present levy had nothing to do with religion, the Protestant subjects of the empire were tranquillized, and reconciled to bear their share of the public burdens. The duke, at the same time, did not omit to treat, in his own name, with foreign states for men and money. He prevailed on the Duke of Lorraine, a second time, to espouse the cause of the Emperor. Poland was urged to supply him with Cossacks, and Italy with warlike necessaries. Before the three months were expired, the army which was assembled in Moravia, amounted to no less than 40,000 men, chiefly drawn from the unconquered parts of Bohemia, from Moravia, Silesia, and the German provinces of the House of Austria. What to every one had appeared impracticable, Wallenstein, to the astonishment of all Europe, had in a short time effected. The charm of his name, his treasures, and his genius, had assembled thousands in arms, where before Austria had only looked for hundreds. Furnished, even to superfluity, with all necessaries, commanded by experienced officers, and inflamed by enthusiasm which assured itself of victory, this newly created army only awaited the signal of their leader to show themselves, by the bravery of their deeds, worthy of his choice.

The duke had fulfilled his promise, and the troops were ready to take the field; he then retired, and left to the Emperor to choose a commander. But it would have been as easy to raise a second army like the first, as to find any other commander for it than Wallenstein. This promising army, the last hope of the

Emperor, was nothing but an illusion, as soon as the charm was dissolved which had called it into existence; by Wallenstein it had been raised, and, without him, it sank like a creation of magic into its original nothingness. Its officers were either bound to him as his debtors, or, as his creditors, closely connected with his interests, and the preservation of his power. The regiments he had entrusted to his own relations, creatures, and favourites. He, and he alone, could discharge to the troops the extravagant promises by which they had been lured into his service. His pledged word was the only security on which their bold expectations rested; a blind reliance on his omnipotence, the only tie which linked together in one common life and soul the various impulses of their zeal. There was an end of the good fortune of each individual, if he retired, who alone was the voucher of its fulfilment.

However little Wallenstein was serious in his refusal, he successfully employed this means to terrify the Emperor into consenting to his extravagant conditions. The progress of the enemy every day increased the pressure of the Emperor's difficulties, while the remedy was also close at hand; a word from him might terminate the general embarrassment. Prince Eggenberg at length received orders, for the third and last time, at any cost and sacrifice, to induce his friend, Wallenstein, to accept the command.

He found him at Znaim in Moravia, pompously surrounded by the troops, the possession of which he made the Emperor so earnestly to long for. As a suppliant did the haughty subject receive the deputy of his sovereign. "He never could trust," he said, "to a restoration to command, which he owed to the Emperor's necessities, and not to his sense of justice. He was now courted, because the danger had reached its height, and safety was hoped for from his arm only; but his successful services would soon cause the servant to be forgotten, and the return of security would bring back renewed ingratitude. If he deceived the expectations formed of him, his long earned renown would be forfeited; even if he fulfilled them, his repose and happiness must be sacrificed. Soon would envy be excited anew, and the dependent monarch would not hesitate, a second time, to make an offering of convenience to a servant whom he could now dispense with. Better for him at once, and voluntarily, to resign a post from which sooner or later the intrigues of his enemies would expel him. Security and content were to be found in the bosom of private life; and nothing but the wish to oblige the Emperor had induced him, reluctantly enough, to relinquish for a time his blissful repose."

Tired of this long farce, the minister at last assumed a serious tone, and threatened the obstinate duke with the Emperor's resentment, if he persisted in his refusal. "Low enough had the imperial dignity," he added, "stooped already; and yet, instead of exciting his magnanimity by its condescension, had only flattered his pride and increased his obstinacy. If this sacrifice had been made in vain, he would not answer, but that the suppliant might be converted into the sovereign, and that the monarch might not avenge his injured dignity on his rebellious subject. However greatly Ferdinand may have erred, the Emperor at least had a claim to obedience; the man might be mistaken, but the monarch could not confess his error. If the Duke of Friedland had suffered by an unjust decree, he might yet be recompensed for all his losses; the wound which it had itself inflicted, the hand of Majesty might heal. If he asked security for his person and his dignities, the Emperor's equity would refuse him no reasonable demand. Majesty contemned, admitted not of any atonement; disobedience to its commands cancelled the most brilliant services. The Emperor required his services, and as emperor he demanded them. Whatever price Wallenstein might set upon them, the Emperor would readily agree to; but he demanded obedience, or the weight of his indignation should crush the refractory servant."

Wallenstein, whose extensive possessions within the Austrian monarchy were momentarily exposed to the power of the Emperor, was keenly sensible that this was no idle threat; yet it was not fear that at last overcame his affected reluctance. This imperious tone of itself, was to his mind a plain proof of the weakness and despair which dictated it, while the Emperor's readiness to yield all his demands, convinced him that he had attained the summit of his wishes. He now made a show of yielding to the persuasions of Eggenberg; and left him, in order to write down the conditions on which he accepted the command.

Not without apprehension, did the minister receive the writing, in which the proudest of subjects had prescribed laws to the proudest of sovereigns. But however little confidence he had in the moderation of his friend, the extravagant contents of his writing surpassed even his worst expectations. Wallenstein required the uncontrolled command over all the German armies of Austria and Spain, with unlimited powers to reward and punish. Neither the King of Hungary, nor the Emperor himself, were to appear in the army, still less to exercise any act of authority over it. No commission in the army, no pension or letter of grace, was to be granted by the Emperor without Wallenstein's approval. All the conquests and confiscations that should take place, were to be placed entirely at Wallenstein's disposal, to the exclusion of every other tribunal. For his ordinary pay, an imperial hereditary estate was to be assigned him, with another of the conquered estates within the empire for his extraordinary expenses. Every Austrian province was to be opened to him if he required it in case of retreat. He farther demanded the assurance of the possession of the Duchy of Mecklenburg, in the event of a future peace; and a formal and timely intimation, if it should be deemed necessary a second time to deprive him of the command.

In vain the minister entreated him to moderate his demands, which, if granted, would deprive the Emperor of all authority over his own troops, and make him absolutely dependent on his general. The value placed on his services had been too plainly manifested to prevent him dictating the price at which they were to be purchased. If the pressure of circumstances compelled the Emperor to grant these demands, it was more than a mere feeling of haughtiness and desire of revenge which induced the duke to make them. His plans of rebellion were formed, to their success, every one of the conditions for which Wallenstein stipulated in this treaty with the court, was indispensable. Those plans required that the Emperor should be deprived of all authority in Germany, and be placed at the mercy of his general; and this object would be attained, the moment Ferdinand subscribed the required conditions. The use which Wallenstein intended to make of his army, (widely different indeed from that for which it was entrusted to him,) brooked not of a divided power, and still less of an authority superior to his own. To be the sole master of the will of his troops, he must also be the sole master of their destinies; insensibly to supplant his sovereign, and to transfer permanently to his own person the rights of sovereignty, which were only lent to him for a time by a higher authority, he must cautiously keep the latter out of the view of the army. Hence his obstinate refusal to allow any prince of the house of Austria to be present with the army. The liberty of free disposal of all the conquered and confiscated estates in the empire, would also afford him fearful means of purchasing dependents and instruments of his plans, and of acting the dictator in Germany more absolutely than ever any Emperor did in time of peace. By the right to use any of the Austrian provinces as a place of refuge, in case of need, he had full power to hold the Emperor a prisoner by means of his own forces, and within his own dominions; to exhaust the strength and resources of these countries, and to undermine the power of Austria in its very foundation.

Whatever might be the issue, he had equally secured his own advantage, by the conditions he had extorted from the Emperor. If circumstances proved favourable to his daring project, this treaty with the Emperor facilitated its execution; if on the contrary, the course of things ran counter to it, it would at least afford him a brilliant compensation for the failure of his plans. But how could he consider an agreement valid, which was extorted from his sovereign, and based upon treason? How could he hope to bind the Emperor by a written agreement, in the face of a law which condemned to death every one who should have the presumption to impose conditions upon him? But this criminal was the most indispensable man in the empire, and Ferdinand, well practised in dissimulation, granted him for the present all he required.

At last, then, the imperial army had found a commander-in-chief worthy of the name. Every other authority in the army, even that of the Emperor himself, ceased from the moment Wallenstein assumed the commander's baton, and every act was invalid which did not proceed from him. From the banks of the Danube, to those of the Weser and the Oder, was felt the life-giving dawning of this new star; a new spirit seemed to inspire the troops of the emperor, a new epoch of the war began. The Papists form fresh hopes, the Protestant beholds with anxiety the changed course of affairs.

The greater the price at which the services of the new general had been purchased, the greater justly were the expectations from those which the court of the Emperor entertained. But the duke was in no hurry to fulfil these expectations. Already in the vicinity of Bohemia, and at the head of a formidable force, he had but to show himself there, in order to overpower the exhausted force of the Saxons, and brilliantly to commence his new career by the reconquest of that kingdom. But, contented with harassing the enemy with indecisive skirmishes of his Croats, he abandoned the best part of that kingdom to be plundered, and moved calmly forward in pursuit of his own selfish plans. His design was, not to conquer the Saxons, but to unite with them. Exclusively occupied with this important object, he remained inactive in the hope of conquering more surely by means of negociation. He left no expedient untried, to detach this prince from the Swedish alliance; and Ferdinand himself, ever inclined to an accommodation with this prince, approved of this proceeding. But the great debt which Saxony owed to Sweden, was as yet too freshly remembered to allow of such an act of perfidy; and even had the Elector been disposed to yield to the temptation, the equivocal character of Wallenstein, and the bad character of Austrian policy, precluded any reliance in the integrity of its promises. Notorious already as a treacherous statesman, he met not with faith upon the very occasion when perhaps he intended to act honestly; and, moreover, was denied, by circumstances, the opportunity of proving the sincerity of his intentions, by the disclosure of his real motives.

He, therefore, unwillingly resolved to extort, by force of arms, what he could not obtain by negociation. Suddenly assembling his troops, he appeared before Prague ere the Saxons had time to advance to its relief. After a short resistance, the treachery of some Capuchins opens the gates to one of his regiments; and the garrison, who had taken refuge in the citadel, soon laid down their arms upon disgraceful conditions. Master of the capital, he hoped to carry on more successfully his negociations at the Saxon court; but even while he was renewing his proposals to Arnheim, he did not hesitate to give them weight by striking a decisive blow. He hastened to seize the narrow passes between Aussig and Pirna, with a view of cutting off the retreat of the Saxons into their own country; but the rapidity of Arnheim's operations fortunately extricated them from the danger. After the retreat of this general, Egra and Leutmeritz, the last strongholds of the Saxons, surrendered to the conqueror: and the whole kingdom was restored to its legitimate sovereign, in less time than it had been lost.

Wallenstein, less occupied with the interests of his master, than with the furtherance of his own plans, now purposed to carry the war into Saxony, and by ravaging his territories, compel the Elector to enter into a private treaty with the Emperor, or rather with himself. But, however little accustomed he was to make his will bend to circumstances, he now perceived the necessity of postponing his favourite scheme for a time, to a more pressing emergency. While he was driving the Saxons from Bohemia, Gustavus Adolphus had been gaining the victories, already detailed, on the Rhine and the Danube, and carried the war through Franconia and Swabia, to the frontiers of Bavaria. Maximilian, defeated on the Lech, and deprived by death of Count Tilly, his best support, urgently solicited the Emperor to send with all speed the Duke of Friedland to his assistance, from Bohemia, and by the defence of Bavaria, to avert the danger from Austria itself. He also made the same request to Wallenstein, and entreated him, till he could himself come with the main force, to despatch in the mean time a few regiments to his aid. Ferdinand seconded the request with all his influence, and one messenger after another was sent to Wallenstein, urging him to move towards the Danube.

It now appeared how completely the Emperor had sacrificed his authority, in surrendering to another the supreme command of his troops. Indifferent to Maximilian's entreaties, and deaf to the Emperor's repeated commands, Wallenstein remained inactive in Bohemia, and abandoned the Elector to his fate. The remembrance of the evil service which Maximilian had rendered him with the Emperor, at the Diet at Ratisbon, was deeply engraved on the implacable mind of the duke, and the Elector's late attempts to prevent his reinstatement, were no secret to him. The moment of revenging this affront had now arrived, and Maximilian was doomed to pay dearly for his folly, in provoking the most revengeful of men. Wallenstein maintained, that Bohemia ought not to be left exposed, and that Austria could not be better protected, than by allowing the Swedish army to waste its strength before the Bavarian fortress. Thus, by the arm of the Swedes, he chastised his enemy; and while one place after another fell into their hands, he allowed the Elector vainly to await his arrival in Ratisbon. It was only when the complete subjugation of Bohemia left him without excuse, and the conquests of Gustavus Adolphus in Bavaria threatened Austria itself, that he yielded to the pressing entreaties of the Elector and the Emperor, and determined to effect the long-expected union with the former; an event, which, according to the general anticipation of the Roman Catholics, would decide the fate of the campaign.

Gustavus Adolphus, too weak in numbers to cope even with Wallenstein's force alone, naturally dreaded the junction of such powerful armies, and the little energy he used to prevent it, was the occasion of great surprise. Apparently he reckoned too much on the hatred which alienated the leaders, and seemed to render their effectual co-operation improbable; when the event contradicted his views, it was too late to repair his error. On the first certain intelligence he received of their designs, he hastened to the Upper Palatinate, for the purpose of intercepting the Elector: but the latter had already arrived there, and the junction had been effected at Egra.

This frontier town had been chosen by Wallenstein, for the scene of his triumph over his proud rival. Not content with having seen him, as it were, a suppliant at his feet, he imposed upon him the hard condition of leaving his territories in his rear exposed to the enemy, and declaring by this long march to meet him, the necessity and distress to which he was reduced. Even to this humiliation, the haughty prince patiently submitted. It had cost him a severe struggle to ask for protection of the man who, if his own wishes had been consulted, would never have had the power of granting it: but having once made up his mind to it, he was ready to bear all the annoyances which were inseparable from that resolve, and sufficiently master of himself to put up with petty grievances, when an important end was in view.

But whatever pains it had cost to effect this junction, it was equally difficult to settle the conditions on which it was to be maintained. The united army must be placed under the command of one individual, if any object was to be gained by the union, and each general was equally averse to yield to the superior authority of the other. If Maximilian rested his claim on his electoral dignity, the nobleness of his descent, and his influence in the empire, Wallenstein's military renown, and the unlimited command conferred on him by the Emperor, gave an equally strong title to it. If it was deeply humiliating to the pride of the former to serve under an imperial subject, the idea of imposing laws on so imperious a spirit, flattered in the same degree the haughtiness of Wallenstein. An obstinate dispute ensued, which, however, terminated in a mutual compromise to Wallenstein's advantage. To him was assigned the unlimited command of both armies, particularly in battle, while the Elector was deprived of all power of altering the order of battle, or even the route of the army. He retained only the bare right of punishing and rewarding his own troops, and the free use of these, when not acting in conjunction with the Imperialists.

After these preliminaries were settled, the two generals at last ventured upon an interview; but not until they had mutually promised to bury the past in oblivion, and all the outward formalities of a reconciliation had been settled. According to agreement, they publicly embraced in the sight of their troops, and made mutual professions of friendship, while in reality the hearts of both were overflowing with malice. Maximilian, well versed in dissimulation, had sufficient command over himself, not to betray in a single feature his real feelings; but a malicious triumph sparkled in the eyes of Wallenstein, and the constraint which was visible in all his movements, betrayed the violence of the emotion which overpowered his proud soul.

The combined Imperial and Bavarian armies amounted to nearly 60,000 men, chiefly veterans. Before this force, the King of Sweden was not in a condition to keep the field. As his attempt to prevent their junction had failed, he commenced a rapid retreat into Franconia, and awaited there for some decisive movement on the part of the enemy, in order to form his own plans. The position of the combined armies between the frontiers of Saxony and Bavaria, left it for some time doubtful whether they would remove the war into the former, or endeavour to drive the Swedes from the Danube, and deliver Bavaria. Saxony had been stripped of troops by Arnheim, who was pursuing his conquests in Silesia; not without a secret design, it was generally supposed, of favouring the entrance of the Duke of Friedland into that electorate, and of thus driving the irresolute John George into peace with the Emperor. Gustavus Adolphus himself, fully persuaded that Wallenstein's views were directed against Saxony, hastily despatched a strong reinforcement to the assistance of his confederate, with the intention, as soon as circumstances would allow, of following with the main body. But the movements of Wallenstein's army soon led him to suspect that he himself was the object of attack; and the Duke's march through the Upper Palatinate, placed the matter beyond a doubt. The question now was, how to provide for his own security, and the prize was no longer his supremacy, but his very existence. His fertile genius must now supply the means, not of conquest, but of preservation. The approach of the enemy had surprised him before he had time to concentrate his troops, which were scattered all over Germany, or to summon his allies to his aid. Too weak to meet the enemy in the field, he had no choice left, but either to throw himself into Nuremberg, and run the risk of being shut up in its walls, or to sacrifice that city, and await a reinforcement under the cannon of Donauwerth. Indifferent to danger or difficulty, while he obeyed the call of humanity or honour, he chose the first without hesitation, firmly resolved to bury himself with his whole army under the ruins of Nuremberg, rather than to purchase his own safety by the sacrifice of his confederates.

Measures were immediately taken to surround the city and suburbs with redoubts, and to form an entrenched camp. Several thousand workmen immediately commenced this extensive work, and an heroic determination to hazard life and property in the common cause, animated the inhabitants of Nuremberg. A trench, eight feet deep and twelve broad, surrounded the whole fortification; the lines were defended by redoubts and batteries, the gates by half moons. The river Pegnitz, which flows through Nuremberg, divided the whole camp into two semicircles, whose communication was secured by several bridges. About three hundred pieces of cannon defended the town-walls and the intrenchments. The peasantry from the neighbouring villages, and the inhabitants of Nuremberg, assisted the Swedish soldiers so zealously, that on the seventh day the army was able to enter the camp, and, in a fortnight, this great work was completed.

While these operations were carried on without the walls, the magistrates of Nuremberg were busily occupied in filling the magazines with provisions and ammunition for a long siege. Measures were taken, at the same time, to secure the health of the inhabitants, which was likely to be endangered by the conflux of so many people; cleanliness was enforced by the strictest regulations. In order, if necessary, to support the King, the youth of the city were embodied and trained to arms, the militia of the town considerably reinforced, and a new regiment raised, consisting of four-and-twenty names, according to the letters of the alphabet. Gustavus had, in the mean time, called to his assistance his allies, Duke William of Weimar, and the Landgrave of Hesse Cassel; and ordered his generals on the Rhine, in Thuringia and Lower Saxony, to commence their march immediately, and join him with their troops in Nuremberg. His army, which was encamped within the lines, did not amount to more than 16,000 men, scarcely a third of the enemy.

The Imperialists had, in the mean time, by slow marches, advanced to Neumark, where Wallenstein made a general review. At the sight of this formidable force, he could not refrain from indulging in a childish boast: "In four days," said he, "it will be shown whether I or the King of Sweden is to be master of the world." Yet, notwithstanding his superiority, he did nothing to fulfil his promise; and even let slip the opportunity of crushing his enemy, when the latter had the hardihood to leave his lines to meet him. "Battles enough have been fought," was his answer to those who advised him to attack the King, "it is now time to try another method." Wallenstein's well-founded reputation required not any of those rash enterprises on which younger soldiers rush, in the hope of gaining a name. Satisfied that the enemy's despair would dearly sell a victory, while a defeat would irretrievably ruin the Emperor's affairs, he resolved to wear out the ardour of his opponent by a tedious blockade, and by thus depriving him of every opportunity of availing himself of his impetuous bravery, take from him the very advantage which had hitherto rendered him invincible. Without making any attack, therefore, he erected a strong fortified camp on the other side of the Pegnitz, and opposite Nuremberg; and, by this well chosen position, cut off from the city and the camp of Gustavus all supplies from Franconia, Swabia, and Thuringia. Thus he held in siege at once the city and the King, and flattered himself with the hope of slowly, but surely, wearing out by famine and pestilence the courage of his opponent whom he had no wish to encounter in the field.

Little aware, however, of the resources and the strength of his adversary, Wallenstein had not taken sufficient precautions to avert from himself the fate he was designing for others. From the whole of the neighbouring country, the peasantry had fled with their property; and what little provision remained, must be obstinately contested with the Swedes. The King spared the magazines within the town, as long as it was possible to provision his army from without; and these forays produced constant skirmishes between the Croats and the Swedish cavalry, of which the surrounding country exhibited the most melancholy traces. The necessaries of life must be obtained sword in hand; and the foraging parties could not venture out without a numerous escort. And when this supply failed, the town opened its magazines to the King, but Wallenstein had to support his troops from a distance. A large convoy from Bavaria was on its way to him, with an escort of a thousand men. Gustavus Adolphus having received intelligence of its approach, immediately sent out a regiment of cavalry to intercept it; and the darkness of the night favoured the enterprise. The whole convoy, with the town in which it was, fell into the hands of the Swedes; the Imperial escort was cut to pieces; about 1,200 cattle carried off; and a thousand waggons, loaded with bread, which could not be brought away, were set on fire. Seven regiments, which Wallenstein had sent forward to Altdorp to cover the entrance of the long and anxiously expected convoy, were attacked by the King, who had, in like manner, advanced to cover the retreat of his cavalry, and routed after an obstinate action, being driven back into the Imperial camp, with the loss of 400 men. So many checks and difficulties, and so firm and unexpected a resistance on the part of the King, made the Duke of Friedland repent that he had declined to hazard a battle. The strength of the Swedish camp rendered an attack impracticable; and the armed youth of Nuremberg served the King as a nursery from which he could supply his loss of troops. The want of provisions, which began to be felt in the Imperial camp as strongly as in the Swedish, rendered it uncertain which party would be first compelled to give way.

Fifteen days had the two armies now remained in view of each other, equally defended by inaccessible entrenchments, without attempting anything more than slight attacks and unimportant skirmishes. On both sides, infectious diseases, the natural consequence of bad food, and a crowded population, had occasioned a greater loss than the sword. And this evil daily increased. But at length, the long expected succours arrived in the Swedish camp; and by this strong reinforcement, the King was now enabled to obey the dictates of his native courage, and to break the chains which had hitherto fettered him.

In obedience to his requisitions, the Duke of Weimar had hastily drawn together a corps from the garrisons in Lower Saxony and Thuringia, which, at Schweinfurt in Franconia, was joined by four Saxon regiments, and at Kitzingen by the corps of the Rhine, which the Landgrave of Hesse, and the Palatine of Birkenfeld, despatched to the relief of the King. The Chancellor, Oxenstiern, undertook to lead this force to its destination. After being joined at Windsheim by the Duke of Weimar himself, and the Swedish General Banner, he advanced by rapid marches to Bruck and Eltersdorf, where he passed the Rednitz, and reached the Swedish camp in safety. This reinforcement amounted to nearly 50,000 men, and was attended by a train of 60 pieces of cannon, and 4,000 baggage waggons. Gustavus now saw himself at the head of an army of nearly 70,000 strong, without reckoning the militia of Nuremberg, which, in case of necessity, could bring into the field about 30,000 fighting men; a formidable force, opposed to another not less formidable. The war seemed at length compressed to the point of a single battle, which was to decide its fearful issue. With divided sympathies, Europe looked with anxiety to this scene, where the whole strength of the two contending parties was fearfully drawn, as it were, to a focus.

If, before the arrival of the Swedish succours, a want of provisions had been felt, the evil was now fearfully increased to a dreadful height in both camps, for Wallenstein had also received reinforcements from Bavaria. Besides the 120,000 men confronted to each other, and more than 50,000 horses, in the two armies, and besides the inhabitants of Nuremberg, whose number far exceeded the Swedish army, there were in the camp of Wallenstein about 15,000 women, with as many drivers, and nearly the same number in that of the Swedes. The custom of the time permitted the soldier to carry his family with him to the field. A number of prostitutes followed the Imperialists; while, with the view of preventing such excesses, Gustavus's care for the morals of his soldiers promoted marriages. For the rising generation, who had this camp for their home and country, regular military schools were established, which educated a race of excellent warriors, by which means the army might in a manner recruit itself in the course of a long campaign. No wonder, then, if these wandering nations exhausted every territory in which they encamped, and by their immense consumption raised the necessaries of life to an exorbitant price. All the mills of Nuremberg were insufficient to grind the corn required for each day; and 15,000 pounds of bread, which were daily delivered, by the town into the Swedish camp, excited, without allaying, the hunger of the soldiers. The laudable exertions of the magistrates of Nuremberg could not prevent the greater part of the horses from dying for want of forage, while the increasing mortality in the camp consigned more than a hundred men daily to the grave.

To put an end to these distresses, Gustavus Adolphus, relying on his numerical superiority, left his lines on the 25th day, forming before the enemy in order of battle, while he cannonaded the duke's camp from three batteries erected on the side of the Rednitz. But the duke remained immoveable in his entrenchments, and contented himself with answering this challenge by a distant fire of cannon and musketry. His plan was to wear out the king by his inactivity, and by the force of famine to overcome his resolute determination; and neither the remonstrances of Maximilian, and the impatience of his army, nor the ridicule of his opponent, could shake his purpose. Gustavus, deceived in his hope of forcing a battle, and compelled by his increasing necessities, now attempted impossibilities, and resolved to storm a position which art and nature had combined to render impregnable.

Intrusting his own camp to the militia of Nuremberg, on the fifty-eighth day of his encampment, (the festival of St. Bartholomew,) he advanced in full order of battle, and passing the Rednitz at Furth, easily drove the enemy's outposts before him. The main army of the Imperialists was posted on the steep heights between the Biber and the Rednitz, called the Old Fortress and Altenberg; while the camp itself, commanded by these eminences, spread out immeasurably along the plain. On these heights, the whole of the artillery was placed. Deep trenches surrounded inaccessible redoubts, while thick barricadoes, with pointed palisades, defended the approaches to the heights, from the summits of which, Wallenstein calmly and securely discharged the lightnings of his artillery from amid the dark thunder-clouds of smoke. A destructive fire of musketry was maintained behind the breastworks, and a hundred pieces of cannon threatened the desperate assailant with certain destruction. Against this dangerous post Gustavus now directed his attack; five hundred musketeers, supported by a few infantry, (for a greater number could not act in the narrow space,) enjoyed the unenvied privilege of first throwing themselves into the open jaws of death. The assault was furious, the resistance obstinate. Exposed to the whole fire of the enemy's artillery, and infuriate by the prospect of inevitable death, these determined warriors rushed forward to storm the heights; which, in an instant, converted into a flaming volcano, discharged on them a shower of shot. At the same moment, the heavy cavalry rushed forward into the openings which the artillery had made in the close ranks of the assailants, and divided them; till the intrepid band, conquered by the strength of nature and of man, took to flight, leaving a hundred dead upon the field. To Germans had Gustavus yielded this post of honour. Exasperated at their retreat, he now led on his Finlanders to the attack, thinking, by their northern courage, to shame the cowardice of the Germans. But they, also, after a similar hot reception, yielded to the superiority of the enemy; and a third regiment succeeded them to experience the same fate. This was replaced by a fourth, a fifth, and a sixth; so that, during a ten hours' action, every regiment was brought to the attack to retire with bloody loss from the contest. A thousand mangled bodies covered the field; yet Gustavus undauntedly maintained the attack, and Wallenstein held his position unshaken.

In the mean time, a sharp contest had taken place between the imperial cavalry and the left wing of the Swedes, which was posted in a thicket on the Rednitz, with varying success, but with equal intrepidity and loss on both sides. The Duke of Friedland and Prince Bernard of Weimar had each a horse shot under them; the king himself had the sole of his boot carried off by a cannon ball. The combat was maintained with undiminished obstinacy, till the approach of night separated the combatants. But the Swedes had advanced too far to retreat without hazard. While the king was seeking an officer to convey to the regiments the order to retreat, he met Colonel Hepburn, a brave Scotchman, whose native courage alone had drawn him from the camp to share in the dangers of the day. Offended with the king for having not long before preferred a younger officer for some post of danger, he had rashly vowed never again to draw his sword for the king. To him Gustavus now addressed himself, praising his courage, and requesting him to order the regiments to retreat. "Sire," replied the brave soldier, "it is the only service I cannot refuse to your Majesty; for it is a hazardous one," — and immediately hastened to carry the command. One of the heights above the old fortress had, in the heat of the action, been carried by the Duke of Weimar. It commanded the hills and the whole camp. But the heavy rain which fell during the night, rendered it impossible to draw up the cannon; and this post, which had been gained with so much bloodshed, was also voluntarily abandoned. Diffident of fortune, which forsook him on this decisive day, the king did not venture the following morning to renew the attack with his exhausted troops; and vanquished for the first time, even because he was not victor, he led back his troops over the Rednitz. Two thousand dead which he left behind him on the field, testified to the extent of his loss; and the Duke of Friedland remained unconquered within his lines.

For fourteen days after this action, the two armies still continued in front of each other, each in the hope that the other would be the first to give way. Every day reduced their provisions, and as scarcity became greater, the excesses of the soldiers rendered furious, exercised the wildest outrages on the peasantry. The increasing distress broke up all discipline and order in the Swedish camp; and the German regiments, in particular, distinguished themselves for the ravages they practised indiscriminately on friend and foe. The weak hand of a single individual could not check excesses, encouraged by the silence, if not the actual example, of the inferior officers. These shameful breaches of discipline, on the maintenance of which he had hitherto justly prided himself, severely pained the king; and the vehemence with which he reproached the German officers for their negligence, bespoke the liveliness of his emotion. "It is you yourselves, Germans," said he, "that rob your native country, and ruin your own confederates in the faith. As God is my judge, I abhor you, I loathe you; my heart sinks within me whenever I look upon you. Ye break my orders; ye are the cause that the world curses me, that the tears of poverty follow me, that complaints ring in my ear — 'The king, our friend, does us more harm than even our worst enemies.' On your account I have stripped my own kingdom of its treasures, and spent upon you more than 40 tons of gold[2]; while from your German empire I have not received the least aid. I gave you a share of all that God had given to me; and had ye regarded my orders, I would have gladly shared with you all my future acquisitions. Your want of discipline convinces me of your evil intentions, whatever cause I might otherwise have to applaud your bravery."

Nuremberg had exerted itself, almost beyond its power, to subsist for eleven weeks the vast crowd which was compressed within its boundaries; but its means were at length exhausted, and the king's more numerous party was obliged to determine on a retreat. By the casualties of war and sickness, Nuremberg had lost more than 10,000 of its inhabitants, and Gustavus Adolphus nearly 20,000 of his soldiers. The fields around the city were trampled down, the villages lay in ashes, the plundered peasantry lay faint and dying on the highways; foul odours infected the air, and bad food, the exhalations from so dense a population, and so many putrifying carcasses, together with the heat of the dog-days, produced a desolating pestilence which raged among men and beasts, and long after the retreat of both armies, continued to load the country with misery and distress. Affected by the general distress, and despairing of conquering the steady determination of the Duke of Friedland, the king broke up his camp on the 8th September, leaving in Nuremberg a sufficient garrison. He advanced in

[2]A ton of gold in Sweden amounts to 100,000 rix dollars. —

full order of battle before the enemy, who remained motionless, and did not attempt in the least to harass his retreat. His route lay by the Aisch and Windsheim towards Neustadt, where he halted five days to refresh his troops, and also to be near to Nuremberg, in case the enemy should make an attempt upon the town. But Wallenstein, as exhausted as himself, had only awaited the retreat of the Swedes to commence his own. Five days afterwards, he broke up his camp at Zirndorf, and set it on fire. A hundred columns of smoke, rising from all the burning villages in the neighbourhood, announced his retreat, and showed the city the fate it had escaped. His march, which was directed on Forchheim, was marked by the most frightful ravages; but he was too far advanced to be overtaken by the king. The latter now divided his army, which the exhausted country was unable to support, and leaving one division to protect Franconia, with the other he prosecuted in person his conquests in Bavaria.

In the mean time, the imperial Bavarian army had marched into the Bishopric of Bamberg, where the Duke of Friedland a second time mustered his troops. He found this force, which so lately had amounted to 60,000 men, diminished by the sword, desertion, and disease, to about 24,000, and of these a fourth were Bavarians. Thus had the encampments before Nuremberg weakened both parties more than two great battles would have done, apparently without advancing the termination of the war, or satisfying, by any decisive result, the expectations of Europe. The king's conquests in Bavaria, were, it is true, checked for a time by this diversion before Nuremberg, and Austria itself secured against the danger of immediate invasion; but by the retreat of the king from that city, he was again left at full liberty to make Bavaria the seat of war. Indifferent towards the fate of that country, and weary of the restraint which his union with the Elector imposed upon him, the Duke of Friedland eagerly seized the opportunity of separating from this burdensome associate, and prosecuting, with renewed earnestness, his favourite plans. Still adhering to his purpose of detaching Saxony from its Swedish alliance, he selected that country for his winter quarters, hoping by his destructive presence to force the Elector the more readily into his views.

No conjuncture could be more favourable for his designs. The Saxons had invaded Silesia, where, reinforced by troops from Brandenburgh and Sweden, they had gained several advantages over the Emperor's troops. Silesia would be saved by a diversion against the Elector in his own territories, and the attempt was the more easy, as Saxony, left undefended during the war in Silesia, lay open on every side to attack. The pretext of rescuing from the enemy an hereditary dominion of Austria, would silence the remonstrances of the Elector of Bavaria, and, under the mask of a patriotic zeal for the Emperor's interests, Maximilian might be sacrificed without much difficulty. By giving up the rich country of Bavaria to the Swedes, he hoped to be left unmolested by them in his enterprise against Saxony, while the increasing coldness between Gustavus and the Saxon Court, gave him little reason to apprehend any extraordinary zeal for the deliverance of John George. Thus a second time abandoned by his artful protector, the Elector separated from Wallenstein at Bamberg, to protect his defenceless territory with the small remains of his troops, while the imperial army, under Wallenstein, directed its march through Bayreuth and Coburg towards the Thuringian Forest.

An imperial general, Holk, had previously been sent into Vogtland with 6,000 men, to waste this defenceless province with fire and sword, he was soon followed by Gallas, another of the Duke's generals, and an equally faithful instrument of his inhuman orders. Finally, Pappenheim, too, was recalled from Lower Saxony, to reinforce the diminished army of the duke, and to complete the miseries of the devoted country. Ruined churches, villages in ashes, harvests wilfully destroyed, families plundered, and murdered peasants, marked the progress of these barbarians, under whose scourge the whole of Thuringia, Vogtland, and Meissen, lay defenceless. Yet this was but the prelude to greater sufferings, with which Wallenstein himself, at the head of the main army, threatened Saxony. After having left behind him fearful monuments of his fury, in his march through Franconia and Thuringia, he arrived with his whole army in the Circle of Leipzig, and compelled the city, after a short resistance, to surrender. His design was to push on to Dresden, and by the conquest of the whole country, to prescribe laws to the Elector. He had already approached the Mulda, threatening to overpower the Saxon army which had advanced as far as Torgau to meet him, when the King of Sweden's arrival at Erfurt gave an unexpected check to his operations. Placed between the Saxon and Swedish armies, which were likely to be farther reinforced by the troops of George, Duke of Luneburg, from Lower Saxony, he hastily retired upon Meresberg, to form a junction there with Count Pappenheim, and to repel the further advance of the Swedes.

Gustavus Adolphus had witnessed, with great uneasiness, the arts employed by Spain and Austria to detach his allies from him. The more important his alliance with Saxony, the more anxiety the inconstant temper of John George caused him. Between himself and the Elector, a sincere friendship could never subsist. A prince, proud of his political importance, and accustomed to consider himself as the head of his party, could not see without annoyance the interference of a foreign power in the affairs of the Empire; and nothing, but the extreme danger of his dominions, could overcome the aversion with which he had long witnessed the progress of this unwelcome intruder. The increasing influence of the king in Germany, his authority with the Protestant states, the unambiguous proofs which he gave of his ambitious views, which were of a character calculated to excite the jealousies of all the states of the Empire, awakened in the Elector's breast a thousand anxieties, which the imperial emissaries did not fail skilfully to keep alive and cherish. Every arbitrary step on the part of the King, every demand, however reasonable, which he addressed to the princes of the Empire, was followed by bitter complaints from the Elector, which seemed to announce an approaching rupture. Even the generals of the two powers, whenever they were called upon to act in common, manifested the same jealousy as divided their leaders. John George's natural aversion to war, and a lingering attachment to Austria, favoured the efforts of Arnheim; who, maintaining a constant correspondence with Wallenstein, laboured incessantly to effect a private treaty between his master and the Emperor; and if his representations were long disregarded, still the event proved that they were not altogether without effect.

Gustavus Adolphus, naturally apprehensive of the consequences which the defection of so powerful an ally would produce on his future prospects in Germany, spared no pains to avert so pernicious an event; and his remonstrances had hitherto had some effect upon the Elector. But the formidable power with which the Emperor seconded his seductive proposals, and the miseries which, in the case of hesitation, he threatened to accumulate upon Saxony, might at length overcome the resolution of the Elector, should he be left exposed to the vengeance of his enemies; while an indifference to the fate of so powerful a confederate, would irreparably destroy the confidence of the other allies in their protector. This consideration induced the king a second time to yield to the pressing entreaties of the Elector, and to sacrifice his own brilliant prospects to the safety of this ally. He had already resolved upon a second attack on Ingoldstadt; and the weakness of the Elector of Bavaria gave him hopes of soon forcing this exhausted enemy to accede to a neutrality. An insurrection of the peasantry in Upper Austria, opened to him a passage into that country, and the capital might be in his possession, before Wallenstein could have time to advance to its defence. All these views he now gave up for the sake of an ally, who, neither by his services nor his fidelity, was worthy of the sacrifice; who, on the pressing occasions of common good, had steadily adhered to his own selfish projects; and who was important, not for the services he was expected to render, but merely for the injuries he had it in his power to inflict. Is it possible, then, to refrain from indignation, when we know that, in this expedition, undertaken for the benefit of such an ally, the great king was destined to terminate his career?

Rapidly assembling his troops in Franconia, he followed the route of Wallenstein through Thuringia. Duke Bernard of Weimar, who had been despatched to act against Pappenheim, joined the king at Armstadt, who now saw himself at the head of 20,000 veterans. At Erfurt he took leave of his queen, who was not to behold him, save in his coffin, at Weissenfels. Their anxious adieus seemed to forbode an eternal separation.

He reached Naumburg on the 1st November, 1632, before the corps, which the Duke of Friedland had despatched for that purpose, could make itself master of that place. The inhabitants of the surrounding country flocked in crowds to look upon the hero, the avenger, the great king, who, a year before, had first appeared in that quarter, like a guardian angel. Shouts of joy everywhere attended his progress; the people knelt before him, and struggled for the honour of touching the sheath of his sword, or the hem of his garment. The modest hero disliked this innocent tribute which a sincerely grateful and admiring multitude paid him. "Is it not," said he, "as if this people would make a God of me? Our affairs prosper, indeed; but I fear the vengeance of Heaven will punish me for this presumption, and soon enough reveal to this deluded multitude my human weakness and mortality!" How amiable does Gustavus appear before us at this moment, when about to leave us for ever! Even in the plenitude of success, he honours an avenging Nemesis, declines that homage which is due only to the Immortal, and strengthens his title to our tears, the nearer the moment approaches that is to call them forth!

In the mean time, the Duke of Friedland had determined to advance to meet the king, as far as Weissenfels, and even at the hazard of a battle, to secure his winter-quarters in Saxony. His inactivity before Nuremberg had occasioned a suspicion that he was unwilling to measure his powers with those of the Hero of the North, and his hard-earned reputation would be at stake, if, a second time, he should decline a battle. His present superiority in numbers, though much less than what it was at the beginning of the siege of Nuremberg, was still enough to give him hopes of victory, if he could compel the king to give battle before his junction with the Saxons. But his present reliance was not so much in his numerical superiority, as in the predictions of his astrologer Seni, who had read in the stars that the good fortune of the Swedish monarch would decline in the month of November. Besides, between Naumburg and Weissenfels there was also a range of narrow defiles, formed by a long mountainous ridge, and the river Saal, which ran at their foot, along which the Swedes could not advance without difficulty, and which might, with the assistance of a few troops, be rendered almost impassable. If attacked there, the king would have no choice but either to penetrate with great danger through the defiles, or commence a laborious retreat through Thuringia, and to expose the greater part of his army to a march through a desert country, deficient in every necessary for their support. But the rapidity with which Gustavus Adolphus had taken possession of Naumburg, disappointed this plan, and it was now Wallenstein himself who awaited the attack.

But in this expectation he was disappointed; for the king, instead of advancing to meet him at Weissenfels, made preparations for entrenching himself near Naumburg, with the intention of awaiting there the reinforcements which the Duke of Lunenburg was bringing up. Undecided whether to advance against the king through the narrow passes between Weissenfels and Naumburg, or to remain inactive in his camp, he called a council of war, in order to have the opinion of his most experienced generals. None of these thought it prudent to attack the king in his advantageous position. On the other hand, the preparations which the latter made to fortify his camp, plainly showed that it was not his intention soon to abandon it. But the approach of winter rendered it impossible to prolong the campaign, and by a continued encampment to exhaust the strength of the army, already so much in need of repose. All voices were in favour of immediately terminating the campaign: and, the more so, as the important city of Cologne upon the Rhine was threatened by the Dutch, while the progress of the enemy in Westphalia and the Lower Rhine called for effective reinforcements in that quarter. Wallenstein yielded to the weight of these arguments, and almost convinced that, at this season, he had no reason to apprehend an attack from the King, he put his troops into winter-quarters, but so that, if necessary, they might be rapidly assembled. Count Pappenheim was despatched, with great part of the army, to the assistance of Cologne, with orders to take possession, on his march, of the fortress of Moritzburg, in the territory of Halle. Different corps took up their winter-quarters in the neighbouring towns, to watch, on all sides, the motions of the enemy. Count Colloredo guarded the castle of Weissenfels, and Wallenstein himself encamped with the remainder not far from Merseburg, between Flotzgaben and the Saal, from whence he purposed to march to Leipzig, and to cut off the communication between the Saxons and the Swedish army.

Scarcely had Gustavus Adolphus been informed of Pappenheim's departure, when suddenly breaking up his camp at Naumburg, he hastened with his whole force to attack the enemy, now weakened to one half. He advanced, by rapid marches, towards Weissenfels, from whence the news of his arrival quickly reached the enemy, and greatly astonished the Duke of Friedland. But a speedy resolution was now necessary; and the measures of Wallenstein were soon taken. Though he had little more than 12,000 men to oppose to the 20,000 of the enemy, he might hope to maintain his ground until the return of Pappenheim, who could not have advanced farther than Halle, five miles distant. Messengers were hastily despatched to recall him, while Wallenstein moved forward into the wide plain between the Canal and Lutzen, where he awaited the King in full order of battle, and, by this position, cut off his communication with Leipzig and the Saxon auxiliaries.

Three cannon shots, fired by Count Colloredo from the castle of Weissenfels, announced the king's approach; and at this concerted signal, the light troops of the Duke of Friedland, under the command of the Croatian General Isolani, moved forward to possess themselves of the villages lying upon the Rippach. Their weak resistance did not impede the advance of the enemy, who crossed the Rippach, near the village of that name, and formed in line below Lutzen, opposite the Imperialists. The high road which goes from Weissenfels to Leipzig, is intersected between Lutzen and Markranstadt by the canal which extends from Zeitz to Merseburg, and unites the Elster with the Saal. On this canal, rested the left wing of the Imperialists, and the right of the King of Sweden; but so that the cavalry of both extended themselves along the opposite side. To the northward, behind Lutzen, was Wallenstein's right wing, and to the south of that town was posted the left wing of the Swedes; both armies fronted the high road, which ran between them, and divided their order of battle; but the evening before the battle, Wallenstein, to the great disadvantage of his opponent, had possessed himself of this highway, deepened the trenches which ran along its sides, and planted them with musketeers, so as to make the crossing of it both difficult and dangerous. Behind these, again, was erected a battery of seven large pieces of cannon, to support the fire from the trenches; and at the windmills, close behind Lutzen, fourteen smaller field pieces were ranged on an eminence, from which they could sweep the greater part of the plain. The infantry, divided into no more than five unwieldy brigades, was drawn up at the distance of 300 paces from the road, and the cavalry covered the flanks. All the baggage was sent to Leipzig, that it might not impede the movements of the army; and the ammunition-waggons alone remained, which were placed in rear of the line. To conceal the weakness of the Imperialists, all the camp-followers and sutlers were mounted, and posted on the left wing, but only until Pappenheim's troops arrived. These arrangements were made during the darkness of the night; and when the morning dawned, all was ready for the reception of the enemy.

On the evening of the same day, Gustavus Adolphus appeared on the opposite plain, and formed his troops in the order of attack. His disposition was the same as that which had been so successful the year before at Leipzig. Small squadrons of horse were interspersed among the divisions of the infantry, and troops of musketeers placed here and there among the cavalry. The army was arranged in two lines, the canal on the right and in its rear, the high road in front, and the town on the left. In the centre, the infantry was formed, under the command of Count Brahe; the cavalry on the wings; the artillery in front. To the German hero, Bernard, Duke of Weimar, was intrusted the command of the German cavalry of the left wing; while, on the right, the king led on the Swedes in person, in order to excite the emulation of the two nations to a noble competition. The second line was formed in the same manner; and behind these was placed the reserve, commanded by Henderson, a Scotchman.

In this position, they awaited the eventful dawn of morning, to begin a contest, which long delay, rather than the probability of decisive consequences, and the picked body, rather than the number of the combatants, was to render so terrible and remarkable. The strained expectation of Europe, so disappointed before Nuremberg, was now to be gratified on the plains of Lutzen. During the whole course of the war, two such generals, so equally matched in renown and ability, had not before been pitted against each other. Never, as yet, had daring been cooled by so awful a hazard, or hope animated by so glorious a prize. Europe was next day to learn who was her greatest general: — to-morrow, the leader, who had hitherto been invincible, must acknowledge a victor. This morning was to place it beyond a doubt, whether the victories of Gustavus at Leipzig and on the Lech, were owing to his own military genius, or to the incompetency of his opponent; whether the services of Wallenstein were to vindicate the Emperor's choice, and justify the high price at which they had been purchased. The victory was as yet doubtful, but certain were the labour and the bloodshed by which it must be earned. Every private in both armies, felt a jealous share in their leader's reputation, and under every corslet beat the same emotions that inflamed the bosoms of the generals. Each army knew the enemy to which it was to be opposed: and the anxiety which each in vain attempted to repress, was a convincing proof of their opponent's strength.

At last the fateful morning dawned; but an impenetrable fog, which spread over the plain, delayed the attack till noon. Kneeling in front of his lines, the king offered up his devotions; and the whole army, at the same moment dropping on their knees, burst into a moving hymn, accompanied by the military music. The king then mounted his horse, and clad only in a leathern doublet and surtout, (for a wound he had formerly received prevented his wearing armour,) rode along the ranks, to animate the courage of his troops with a joyful confidence, which, however, the forboding presentiment of his own bosom contradicted. "God with us!" was the war-cry of the Swedes; "Jesus Maria!" that of the Imperialists. About eleven the fog began to disperse, and the enemy became visible. At the same moment Lutzen was seen in flames, having been set on fire by command of the duke, to prevent his being outflanked on that side. The charge was now sounded; the cavalry rushed upon the enemy, and the infantry advanced against the trenches.

Received by a tremendous fire of musketry and heavy artillery, these intrepid battalions maintained the attack with undaunted courage, till the enemy's musketeers abandoned their posts, the trenches were passed, the battery carried and turned against the enemy. They pressed forward with irresistible impetuosity; the first of the five imperial brigades was immediately routed, the second soon after, and the third put to flight. But here the genius of Wallenstein opposed itself to their progress. With the rapidity of lightning he was on the spot to rally his discomfited troops; and his powerful word was itself sufficient to stop the flight of the fugitives. Supported by three regiments of cavalry, the vanquished brigades, forming anew, faced the enemy, and pressed vigorously into the broken ranks of the Swedes. A murderous conflict ensued. The nearness of the enemy left no room for fire-arms, the fury of the attack no time for loading; man was matched to man, the useless musket exchanged for the sword and pike, and science gave way to desperation. Overpowered by numbers, the wearied Swedes at last retire beyond the trenches; and the captured battery is again lost by the retreat. A thousand mangled bodies already strewed the plain, and as yet not a single step of ground had been won.

In the mean time, the king's right wing, led by himself, had fallen upon the enemy's left. The first impetuous shock of the heavy Finland cuirassiers dispersed the lightly-mounted Poles and Croats, who were posted here, and their disorderly flight spread terror and confusion among the rest of the cavalry. At this moment notice was brought the king, that his infantry were retreating over the trenches, and also that his left wing, exposed to a severe fire from the enemy's cannon posted at the windmills was beginning to give way. With rapid decision he committed to General Horn the pursuit of the enemy's left, while he flew, at the head of the regiment of Steinbock, to repair the disorder of his right wing. His noble charger bore him with the velocity of lightning across the trenches, but the squadrons that followed could not come on with the same speed, and only a few horsemen, among whom was Francis Albert, Duke of Saxe Lauenburg, were able to keep up with the king. He rode directly to the place where his infantry were most closely pressed, and while he was reconnoitring the enemy's line for an exposed point of attack, the shortness of his sight unfortunately led him too close to their ranks. An imperial Gefreyter[3], remarking that every one respectfully made way for him as he rode along, immediately ordered a musketeer to take aim at him. "Fire at him yonder," said he, "that must be a man of consequence." The soldier fired, and the king's left arm was shattered. At that moment his squadron came hurrying up, and a confused cry of "the king bleeds! the king is shot!" spread terror and consternation through all the ranks. "It is nothing — follow me," cried the king, collecting his whole strength; but overcome by pain, and nearly fainting, he requested the Duke of Lauenburg, in French, to lead him unobserved out of the tumult. While the duke proceeded towards the right wing with the king, making a long circuit to keep this discouraging sight from the disordered infantry, his majesty received a second shot through the back, which deprived him of his remaining strength. "Brother," said he, with a dying voice, "I have enough! look only to your own life." At the same moment he fell from his horse pierced by several more shots; and abandoned by all his attendants, he breathed his last amidst the plundering hands of the Croats. His charger, flying without its rider, and covered with blood, soon made known to the Swedish cavalry the fall of their king. They rushed madly forward to rescue his sacred remains from the hands of the enemy. A murderous conflict ensued over the body, till his mangled remains were buried beneath a heap of slain.

The mournful tidings soon ran through the Swedish army; but instead of destroying the courage of these brave troops, it but excited it into a new, a wild, and consuming flame. Life had lessened in value, now that the most sacred life of all was gone; death had no terrors for the lowly since the anointed head was not spared. With the fury of lions the Upland, Smaeland, Finland, East and West Gothland regiments rushed a second time upon the left wing of the enemy, which, already making but feeble resistance to General Horn, was now entirely beaten from the field. Bernard, Duke of Saxe-Weimar, gave to the bereaved Swedes a noble leader in his own person; and the spirit of Gustavus led his victorious squadrons anew. The left wing quickly formed again, and vigorously pressed the right of the Imperialists. The artillery at the windmills, which had maintained so murderous a fire upon the Swedes, was captured and turned against the enemy. The centre, also, of the Swedish infantry, commanded by the duke and Knyphausen, advanced a second time against the trenches, which they successfully passed, and retook the battery of seven cannons. The attack was now renewed with redoubled fury upon the heavy battalions of the enemy's centre; their resistance became gradually less, and chance conspired with Swedish valour to complete the defeat. The imperial powder-waggons took fire, and, with a tremendous explosion, grenades and bombs filled the air. The enemy, now in confusion, thought they were attacked in the rear, while the Swedish brigades pressed them in front. Their courage began to fail them. Their left wing was already beaten, their right wavering, and their artillery in the enemy's hands. The battle seemed to be almost decided; another moment would decide the fate of the day, when Pappenheim appeared on the field, with his cuirassiers and dragoons; all the advantages already gained were lost, and the battle was to be fought anew.

The order which recalled that general to Lutzen had reached him in Halle, while his troops were still plundering the town. It was impossible to collect the scattered infantry with that rapidity, which the urgency of the order, and Pappenheim's impatience required. Without waiting for it, therefore, he ordered eight regiments of cavalry to mount; and at their head he galloped at full speed for Lutzen, to share in the battle. He arrived in time to witness the flight of the imperial right wing, which Gustavus Horn was driving from the field, and to be at first involved in their rout. But with rapid presence of

[3]Gefreyter, a person exempt from watching duty, nearly corresponding to the corporal.

mind he rallied the flying troops, and led them once more against the enemy. Carried away by his wild bravery, and impatient to encounter the king, who he supposed was at the head of this wing, he burst furiously upon the Swedish ranks, which, exhausted by victory, and inferior in numbers, were, after a noble resistance, overpowered by this fresh body of enemies. Pappenheim's unexpected appearance revived the drooping courage of the Imperialists, and the Duke of Friedland quickly availed himself of the favourable moment to re-form his line. The closely serried battalions of the Swedes were, after a tremendous conflict, again driven across the trenches; and the battery, which had been twice lost, again rescued from their hands. The whole yellow regiment, the finest of all that distinguished themselves in this dreadful day, lay dead on the field, covering the ground almost in the same excellent order which, when alive, they maintained with such unyielding courage. The same fate befel another regiment of Blues, which Count Piccolomini attacked with the imperial cavalry, and cut down after a desperate contest. Seven times did this intrepid general renew the attack; seven horses were shot under him, and he himself was pierced with six musket balls; yet he would not leave the field, until he was carried along in the general rout of the whole army. Wallenstein himself was seen riding through his ranks with cool intrepidity, amidst a shower of balls, assisting the distressed, encouraging the valiant with praise, and the wavering by his fearful glance. Around and close by him his men were falling thick, and his own mantle was perforated by several shots. But avenging destiny this day protected that breast, for which another weapon was reserved; on the same field where the noble Gustavus expired, Wallenstein was not allowed to terminate his guilty career.

Less fortunate was Pappenheim, the Telamon of the army, the bravest soldier of Austria and the church. An ardent desire to encounter the king in person, carried this daring leader into the thickest of the fight, where he thought his noble opponent was most surely to be met. Gustavus had also expressed a wish to meet his brave antagonist, but these hostile wishes remained ungratified; death first brought together these two great heroes. Two musket-balls pierced the breast of Pappenheim; and his men forcibly carried him from the field. While they were conveying him to the rear, a murmur reached him, that he whom he had sought, lay dead upon the plain. When the truth of the report was confirmed to him, his look became brighter, his dying eye sparkled with a last gleam of joy. "Tell the Duke of Friedland," said he, "that I lie without hope of life, but that I die happy, since I know that the implacable enemy of my religion has fallen on the same day."

With Pappenheim, the good fortune of the Imperialists departed. The cavalry of the left wing, already beaten, and only rallied by his exertions, no sooner missed their victorious leader, than they gave up everything for lost, and abandoned the field of battle in spiritless despair. The right wing fell into the same confusion, with the exception of a few regiments, which the bravery of their colonels Gotz, Terzky, Colloredo, and Piccolomini, compelled to keep their ground. The Swedish infantry, with prompt determination, profited by the enemy's confusion. To fill up the gaps which death had made in the front line, they formed both lines into one, and with it made the final and decisive charge. A third time they crossed the trenches, and a third time they captured the battery. The sun was setting when the two lines closed. The strife grew hotter as it drew to an end; the last efforts of strength were mutually exerted, and skill and courage did their utmost to repair in these precious moments the fortune of the day. It was in vain; despair endows every one with superhuman strength; no one can conquer, no one will give way. The art of war seemed to exhaust its powers on one side, only to unfold some new and untried masterpiece of skill on the other. Night and darkness at last put an end to the fight, before the fury of the combatants was exhausted; and the contest only ceased, when no one could any longer find an antagonist. Both armies separated, as if by tacit agreement; the trumpets sounded, and each party claiming the victory, quitted the field.

The artillery on both sides, as the horses could not be found, remained all night upon the field, at once the reward and the evidence of victory to him who should hold it. Wallenstein, in his haste to leave Leipzig and Saxony, forgot to remove his part. Not long after the battle was ended, Pappenheim's infantry, who had been unable to follow the rapid movements of their general, and who amounted to six regiments, marched on the field, but the work was done. A few hours earlier, so considerable a reinforcement would perhaps have decided the day in favour of the Imperialists; and, even now, by remaining on the field, they might have saved the duke's artillery, and made a prize of that of the Swedes. But they had received no orders to act; and, uncertain as to the issue of the battle, they retired to Leipzig, where they hoped to join the main body.

The Duke of Friedland had retreated thither, and was followed on the morrow by the scattered remains of his army, without artillery, without colours, and almost without arms. The Duke of Weimar, it appears, after the toils of this bloody day, allowed the Swedish army some repose, between Lutzen and Weissenfels, near enough to the field of battle to oppose any attempt the enemy might make to recover it. Of the two armies, more than 9,000 men lay dead; a still greater number were wounded, and among the Imperialists, scarcely a man escaped from the field uninjured. The entire plain from Lutzen to the Canal was strewed with the wounded, the dying, and the dead. Many of the principal nobility had fallen on both sides. Even the Abbot of Fulda, who had mingled in the combat as a spectator, paid for his curiosity and his ill-timed zeal with his life. History says nothing of prisoners; a further proof of the animosity of the combatants, who neither gave nor took quarter.

Pappenheim died the next day of his wounds at Leipzig; an irreparable loss to the imperial army, which this brave warrior had so often led on to victory. The battle of Prague, where, together with Wallenstein, he was present as colonel, was the beginning of his heroic career. Dangerously wounded, with a few troops, he made an impetuous attack on a regiment of the enemy, and lay for several hours mixed with the dead upon the field, beneath the weight of his horse, till he was discovered by some of his own men in plundering. With a small force he defeated, in three different engagements, the rebels in Upper Austria, though 40,000 strong. At the battle of Leipzig, he for a long time delayed the defeat of Tilly by his bravery, and led the arms of the Emperor on the Elbe and the Weser to victory. The wild impetuous fire of his temperament, which no danger, however apparent, could cool, or impossibilities check, made him the most powerful arm of the imperial force, but unfitted him for acting at its head. The battle of Leipzig, if Tilly may be believed, was lost through his rash ardour. At the destruction of Magdeburg, his hands were deeply steeped in blood; war rendered savage and ferocious his disposition, which had been cultivated by youthful studies and various travels. On his forehead, two red streaks, like swords, were perceptible, with which nature had marked him at his very birth. Even in his later years, these became visible, as often as his blood was stirred by passion; and superstition easily persuaded itself, that the future destiny of the man was thus impressed upon the forehead of the child. As a faithful servant of the House of Austria, he had the strongest claims on the gratitude of both its lines, but he did not survive to enjoy the most brilliant proof of their regard. A messenger was already on his way from Madrid, bearing to him the order of the Golden Fleece, when death overtook him at Leipzig.

Though Te Deum, in all Spanish and Austrian lands, was sung in honour of a victory, Wallenstein himself, by the haste with which he quitted Leipzig, and soon after all Saxony, and by renouncing his original design of fixing there his winter quarters, openly confessed his defeat. It is true he made one more feeble attempt to dispute, even in his flight, the honour of victory, by sending out his Croats next morning to the field; but the sight of the Swedish army drawn up in order of battle, immediately dispersed these flying bands, and Duke Bernard, by keeping possession of the field, and soon after by the capture of Leipzig, maintained indisputably his claim to the title of victor.

But it was a dear conquest, a dearer triumph! It was not till the fury of the contest was over, that the full weight of the loss sustained was felt, and the shout of triumph died away into a silent gloom of despair. He, who had led them to the charge, returned not with them; there he lay upon the field which he had won, mingled with the dead bodies of the common crowd. After a long and almost fruitless search, the corpse of the king was discovered, not far from the great stone, which, for a hundred years before, had stood between Lutzen and the Canal, and which, from the memorable disaster of that day, still bears the name of the Stone of the Swede. Covered with blood and wounds, so as scarcely to be recognised, trampled beneath the horses' hoofs, stripped by the rude hands of plunderers of its ornaments and clothes, his body was drawn from beneath a heap of dead, conveyed to Weissenfels, and there delivered up to the lamentations of his soldiers, and the last embraces of his queen. The first tribute had been paid to revenge, and blood had atoned for the blood of the monarch; but now affection assumes its rights, and tears of grief must flow for the man. The universal sorrow absorbs all individual woes. The generals, still stupefied by the unexpected blow, stood speechless and motionless around his bier, and no one trusted himself enough to contemplate the full extent of their loss.

The Emperor, we are told by Khevenhuller, showed symptoms of deep, and apparently sincere feeling, at the sight of the king's doublet stained with blood, which had been stripped from him during the battle, and carried to Vienna. "Willingly," said he, "would I have granted to the unfortunate prince a longer life, and a safe return to his kingdom, had Germany been at peace." But when a trait, which is nothing more than a proof of a yet lingering humanity, and which a mere regard to appearances and even self-love, would have extorted from the most insensible, and the absence of which could exist only in the most inhuman heart, has, by a Roman Catholic writer of modern times and acknowledged merit, been made the subject of the highest eulogium, and compared with the magnanimous tears of

Alexander, for the fall of Darius, our distrust is excited of the other virtues of the writer's hero, and what is still worse, of his own ideas of moral dignity. But even such praise, whatever its amount, is much for one, whose memory his biographer has to clear from the suspicion of being privy to the assassination of a king.

It was scarcely to be expected, that the strong leaning of mankind to the marvellous, would leave to the common course of nature the glory of ending the career of Gustavus Adolphus. The death of so formidable a rival was too important an event for the Emperor, not to excite in his bitter opponent a ready suspicion, that what was so much to his interests, was also the result of his instigation. For the execution, however, of this dark deed, the Emperor would require the aid of a foreign arm, and this it was generally believed he had found in Francis Albert, Duke of Saxe Lauenburg. The rank of the latter permitted him a free access to the king's person, while it at the same time seemed to place him above the suspicion of so foul a deed. This prince, however, was in fact not incapable of this atrocity, and he had moreover sufficient motives for its commission.

Francis Albert, the youngest of four sons of Francis II, Duke of Lauenburg, and related by the mother's side to the race of Vasa, had, in his early years, found a most friendly reception at the Swedish court. Some offence which he had committed against Gustavus Adolphus, in the queen's chamber, was, it is said, repaid by this fiery youth with a box on the ear; which, though immediately repented of, and amply apologized for, laid the foundation of an irreconcileable hate in the vindictive heart of the duke. Francis Albert subsequently entered the imperial service, where he rose to the command of a regiment, and formed a close intimacy with Wallenstein, and condescended to be the instrument of a secret negociation with the Saxon court, which did little honour to his rank. Without any sufficient cause being assigned, he suddenly quitted the Austrian service, and appeared in the king's camp at Nuremberg, to offer his services as a volunteer. By his show of zeal for the Protestant cause, and prepossessing and flattering deportment, he gained the heart of the king, who, warned in vain by Oxenstiern, continued to lavish his favour and friendship on this suspicious new comer. The battle of Lutzen soon followed, in which Francis Albert, like an evil genius, kept close to the king's side and did not leave him till he fell. He owed, it was thought, his own safety amidst the fire of the enemy, to a green sash which he wore, the colour of the Imperialists. He was at any rate the first to convey to his friend Wallenstein the intelligence of the king's death. After the battle, he exchanged the Swedish service for the Saxon; and, after the murder of Wallenstein, being charged with being an accomplice of that general, he only escaped the sword of justice by abjuring his faith. His last appearance in life was as commander of an imperial army in Silesia, where he died of the wounds he had received before Schweidnitz. It requires some effort to believe in the innocence of a man, who had run through a career like this, of the act charged against him; but, however great may be the moral and physical possibility of his committing such a crime, it must still be allowed that there are no certain grounds for imputing it to him. Gustavus Adolphus, it is well known, exposed himself to danger, like the meanest soldier in his army, and where thousands fell, he, too, might naturally meet his death. How it reached him, remains indeed buried in mystery; but here, more than anywhere, does the maxim apply, that where the ordinary course of things is fully sufficient to account for the fact, the honour of human nature ought not to be stained by any suspicion of moral atrocity.

But by whatever hand he fell, his extraordinary destiny must appear a great interposition of Providence. History, too often confined to the ungrateful task of analyzing the uniform play of human passions, is occasionally rewarded by the appearance of events, which strike like a hand from heaven, into the nicely adjusted machinery of human plans, and carry the contemplative mind to a higher order of things. Of this kind, is the sudden retirement of Gustavus Adolphus from the scene; — stopping for a time the whole movement of the political machine, and disappointing all the calculations of human prudence. Yesterday, the very soul, the great and animating principle of his own creation; to-day, struck unpitiably to the ground in the very midst of his eagle flight; untimely torn from a whole world of great designs, and from the ripening harvest of his expectations, he left his bereaved party disconsolate; and the proud edifice of his past greatness sunk into ruins. The Protestant party had identified its hopes with its invincible leader, and scarcely can it now separate them from him; with him, they now fear all good fortune is buried. But it was no longer the benefactor of Germany who fell at Lutzen: the beneficent part of his career, Gustavus Adolphus had already terminated; and now the greatest service which he could render to the liberties of Germany was — to die. The all-engrossing power of an individual was at an end, but many came forward to essay their strength; the equivocal assistance of an over-powerful protector, gave place to a more noble self-exertion on the part of the Estates; and those who were formerly the mere instruments of his aggrandizement, now began to work for themselves. They now looked to their own exertions for the emancipation, which could not be received without danger from the hand of the mighty; and the Swedish power, now incapable of sinking into the oppressor, was henceforth restricted to the more modest part of an ally.

The ambition of the Swedish monarch aspired unquestionably to establish a power within Germany, and to attain a firm footing in the centre of the empire, which was inconsistent with the liberties of the Estates. His aim was the imperial crown; and this dignity, supported by his power, and maintained by his energy and activity, would in his hands be liable to more abuse than had ever been feared from the House of Austria. Born in a foreign country, educated in the maxims of arbitrary power, and by principles and enthusiasm a determined enemy to Popery, he was ill qualified to maintain inviolate the constitution of the German States, or to respect their liberties. The coercive homage which Augsburg, with many other cities, was forced to pay to the Swedish crown, bespoke the conqueror, rather than the protector of the empire; and this town, prouder of the title of a royal city, than of the higher dignity of the freedom of the empire, flattered itself with the anticipation of becoming the capital of his future kingdom. His ill-disguised attempts upon the Electorate of Mentz, which he first intended to bestow upon the Elector of Brandenburg, as the dower of his daughter Christina, and afterwards destined for his chancellor and friend Oxenstiern, evinced plainly what liberties he was disposed to take with the constitution of the empire. His allies, the Protestant princes, had claims on his gratitude, which could be satisfied only at the expense of their Roman Catholic neighbours, and particularly of the immediate Ecclesiastical Chapters; and it seems probable a plan was early formed for dividing the conquered provinces, (after the precedent of the barbarian hordes who overran the German empire,) as a common spoil, among the German and Swedish confederates. In his treatment of the Elector Palatine, he entirely belied the magnanimity of the hero, and forgot the sacred character of a protector. The Palatinate was in his hands, and the obligations both of justice and honour demanded its full and immediate restoration to the legitimate sovereign. But, by a subtlety unworthy of a great mind, and disgraceful to the honourable title of protector of the oppressed, he eluded that obligation. He treated the Palatinate as a conquest wrested from the enemy, and thought that this circumstance gave him a right to deal with it as he pleased. He surrendered it to the Elector as a favour, not as a debt; and that, too, as a Swedish fief, fettered by conditions which diminished half its value, and degraded this unfortunate prince into a humble vassal of Sweden. One of these conditions obliged the Elector, after the conclusion of the war, to furnish, along with the other princes, his contribution towards the maintenance of the Swedish army, a condition which plainly indicates the fate which, in the event of the ultimate success of the king, awaited Germany. His sudden disappearance secured the liberties of Germany, and saved his reputation, while it probably spared him the mortification of seeing his own allies in arms against him, and all the fruits of his victories torn from him by a disadvantageous peace. Saxony was already disposed to abandon him, Denmark viewed his success with alarm and jealousy; and even France, the firmest and most potent of his allies, terrified at the rapid growth of his power and the imperious tone which he assumed, looked around at the very moment he past the Lech, for foreign alliances, in order to check the progress of the Goths, and restore to Europe the balance of power.

Book IV.

The weak bond of union, by which Gustavus Adolphus contrived to hold together the Protestant members of the empire, was dissolved by his death: the allies were now again at liberty, and their alliance, to last, must be formed anew. By the former event, if unremedied, they would lose all the advantages they had gained at the cost of so much bloodshed, and expose themselves to the inevitable danger of becoming one after the other the prey of an enemy, whom, by their union alone, they had been able to oppose and to master. Neither Sweden, nor any of the states of the empire, was singly a match with the Emperor and the League; and, by seeking a peace under the present state of things, they would necessarily be obliged to receive laws from the enemy. Union was, therefore, equally indispensable, either for concluding a peace or continuing the war. But a peace, sought under the present circumstances, could not fail to be disadvantageous to the allied powers. With the death of Gustavus Adolphus, the enemy had formed new hopes; and however gloomy might be the situation of his affairs after the battle of Lutzen, still the death of his dreaded rival was an event too disastrous to the allies, and too favourable for the Emperor, not to justify him in entertaining the most brilliant expectations, and not to encourage him to the prosecution of the war. Its inevitable consequence, for the moment at least, must be want of union among the allies, and what might not the Emperor and the League gain from such a division of their enemies? He was not likely to sacrifice such prospects, as the present turn of affairs held out to him, for any peace, not highly beneficial to himself; and such a peace the allies would not be disposed to accept. They naturally determined, therefore, to continue the war, and for this purpose, the maintenance of the existing union was acknowledged to be indispensable.

But how was this union to be renewed? and whence were to be derived the necessary means for continuing the war? It was not the power of Sweden, but the talents and personal influence of its late king, which had given him so overwhelming an influence in Germany, so great a command over the minds of men; and even he had innumerable difficulties to overcome, before he could establish among the states even a weak and wavering alliance. With his death vanished all, which his personal qualities alone had rendered practicable; and the mutual obligation of the states seemed to cease with the hopes on which it had been founded. Several impatiently threw off the yoke which had always been irksome; others hastened to seize the helm which they had unwillingly seen in the hands of Gustavus, but which, during his lifetime, they did not dare to dispute with him. Some were tempted, by the seductive promises of the Emperor, to abandon the alliance; others, oppressed by the heavy burdens of a fourteen years' war, longed for the repose of peace, upon any conditions, however ruinous. The generals of the army, partly German princes, acknowledged no common head, and no one would stoop to receive orders from another. Unanimity vanished alike from the cabinet and the field, and their common weal was threatened with ruin, by the spirit of disunion.

Gustavus had left no male heir to the crown of Sweden: his daughter Christina, then six years old, was the natural heir. The unavoidable weakness of a regency, suited ill with that energy and resolution, which Sweden would be called upon to display in this trying conjuncture. The wide reaching mind of Gustavus Adolphus had raised this unimportant, and hitherto unknown kingdom, to a rank among the powers of Europe, which it could not retain without the fortune and genius of its author, and from which it could not recede, without a humiliating confession of weakness. Though the German war had been conducted chiefly on the resources of Germany, yet even the small contribution of men and money, which Sweden furnished, had sufficed to exhaust the finances of that poor kingdom, and the peasantry groaned beneath the imposts necessarily laid upon them. The plunder gained in Germany enriched only a few individuals, among the nobles and the soldiers, while Sweden itself remained poor as before. For a time, it is true, the national glory reconciled the subject to these burdens, and the sums exacted, seemed but as a loan placed at interest, in the fortunate hand of Gustavus Adolphus, to be richly repaid by the grateful monarch at the conclusion of a glorious peace. But with the king's death this hope vanished, and the deluded people now loudly demanded relief from their burdens.

But the spirit of Gustavus Adolphus still lived in the men to whom he had confided the administration of the kingdom. However dreadful to them, and unexpected, was the intelligence of his death, it did not deprive them of their manly courage; and the spirit of ancient Rome, under the invasion of Brennus and Hannibal, animated this noble assembly. The greater the price, at which these hard-gained advantages had been purchased, the less readily could they reconcile themselves to renounce them: not unrevenged was a king to be sacrificed. Called on to choose between a doubtful and exhausting war, and a profitable but disgraceful peace, the Swedish council of state boldly espoused the side of danger and honour; and with agreeable surprise, men beheld this venerable senate acting with all the energy and enthusiasm of youth. Surrounded with watchful enemies, both within and without, and threatened on every side with danger, they armed themselves against them all, with equal prudence and heroism, and laboured to extend their kingdom, even at the moment when they had to struggle for its existence.

The decease of the king, and the minority of his daughter Christina, renewed the claims of Poland to the Swedish throne; and King Ladislaus, the son of Sigismund, spared no intrigues to gain a party in Sweden. On this ground, the regency lost no time in proclaiming the young queen, and arranging the administration of the regency. All the officers of the kingdom were summoned to do homage to their new princess; all correspondence with Poland prohibited, and the edicts of previous monarchs against the heirs of Sigismund, confirmed by a solemn act of the nation. The alliance with the Czar of Muscovy was carefully renewed, in order, by the arms of this prince, to keep the hostile Poles in check. The death of Gustavus Adolphus had put an end to the jealousy of Denmark, and removed the grounds of alarm which had stood in the way of a good understanding between the two states. The representations by which the enemy sought to stir up Christian IV. against Sweden were no longer listened to; and the strong wish the Danish monarch entertained for the marriage of his son Ulrick with the young princess, combined, with the dictates of a sounder policy, to incline him to a neutrality. At the same time, England, Holland, and France came forward with the gratifying assurances to the regency of continued friendship and support, and encouraged them, with one voice, to prosecute with activity the war, which hitherto had been conducted with so much glory. Whatever reason France might have to congratulate itself on the death of the Swedish conqueror, it was as fully sensible of the expediency of maintaining the alliance with Sweden. Without exposing itself to great danger, it could not allow the power of Sweden to sink in Germany. Want of resources of its own, would either drive Sweden to conclude a hasty and disadvantageous peace with Austria, and then all the past efforts to lower the ascendancy of this dangerous power would be thrown away; or necessity and despair would drive the armies to extort from the Roman Catholic states the means of support, and France would then be regarded as the betrayer of those very states, who had placed themselves under her powerful protection. The death of Gustavus, far from breaking up the alliance between France and Sweden, had only rendered it more necessary for both, and more profitable for France. Now, for the first time, since he was dead who had stretched his protecting arm over Germany, and guarded its frontiers against the encroaching designs of France, could the latter safely pursue its designs upon Alsace, and thus be enabled to sell its aid to the German Protestants at a dearer rate.

Strengthened by these alliances, secured in its interior, and defended from without by strong frontier garrisons and fleets, the regency did not delay an instant to continue a war, by which Sweden had little of its own to lose, while, if success attended its arms, one or more of the German provinces might be won, either as a conquest, or indemnification of its expenses. Secure amidst its seas, Sweden, even if driven out of Germany, would scarcely be exposed to greater peril, than if it voluntarily retired from the contest, while the former measure was as honourable, as the latter was disgraceful. The more boldness the regency displayed, the more confidence would they inspire among their confederates, the more respect among their enemies, and the more favourable conditions might they anticipate in the event of peace. If they found themselves too weak to execute the wide-ranging projects of Gustavus, they at least owed it to this lofty model to do their utmost, and to yield to no difficulty short of absolute necessity. Alas, that motives of self-interest had too great a share in this noble determination, to demand our unqualified admiration! For those who had nothing themselves to suffer from the calamities of war, but were rather to be enriched by it, it was an easy matter to resolve upon its continuation; for the German empire was, in the end, to defray the expenses; and the provinces on which they reckoned, would be cheaply purchased with the few troops they sacrificed to them, and with the generals who were placed at the head of armies, composed for the most part of Germans, and with the honourable superintendence of all the operations, both military and political.

But this superintendence was irreconcileable with the distance of the Swedish regency from the scene of action, and with the slowness which necessarily accompanies all the movements of a council.

To one comprehensive mind must be intrusted the management of Swedish interests in Germany, and with full powers to determine at discretion all questions of war and peace, the necessary alliances, or the acquisitions made. With dictatorial power, and with the whole influence of the crown which he was to represent, must this important magistrate be invested, in order to maintain its dignity, to enforce united and combined operations, to give effect to his orders, and to supply the place of the monarch whom he succeeded. Such a man was found in the Chancellor Oxenstiern, the first minister, and what is more, the friend of the deceased king, who, acquainted with all the secrets of his master, versed in the politics of Germany, and in the relations of all the states of Europe, was unquestionably the fittest instrument to carry out the plans of Gustavus Adolphus in their full extent.

Oxenstiern was on his way to Upper Germany, in order to assemble the four Upper Circles, when the news of the king's death reached him at Hanau. This was a heavy blow, both to the friend and the statesman. Sweden, indeed, had lost but a king, Germany a protector; but Oxenstiern, the author of his fortunes, the friend of his soul, and the object of his admiration. Though the greatest sufferer in the general loss, he was the first who by his energy rose from the blow, and the only one qualified to repair it. His penetrating glance foresaw all the obstacles which would oppose the execution of his plans, the discouragement of the estates, the intrigues of hostile courts, the breaking up of the confederacy, the jealousy of the leaders, and the dislike of princes of the empire to submit to foreign authority. But even this deep insight into the existing state of things, which revealed the whole extent of the evil, showed him also the means by which it might be overcome. It was essential to revive the drooping courage of the weaker states, to meet the secret machinations of the enemy, to allay the jealousy of the more powerful allies, to rouse the friendly powers, and France in particular, to active assistance; but above all, to repair the ruined edifice of the German alliance, and to reunite the scattered strength of the party by a close and permanent bond of union. The dismay which the loss of their leader occasioned the German Protestants, might as readily dispose them to a closer alliance with Sweden, as to a hasty peace with the Emperor; and it depended entirely upon the course pursued, which of these alternatives they would adopt. Every thing might be lost by the slightest sign of despondency; nothing, but the confidence which Sweden showed in herself, could kindle among the Germans a noble feeling of self-confidence. All the attempts of Austria, to detach these princes from the Swedish alliance, would be unavailing, the moment their eyes became opened to their true interests, and they were instigated to a public and formal breach with the Emperor.

Before these measures could be taken, and the necessary points settled between the regency and their minister, a precious opportunity of action would, it is true, be lost to the Swedish army, of which the enemy would be sure to take the utmost advantage. It was, in short, in the power of the Emperor totally to ruin the Swedish interest in Germany, and to this he was actually invited by the prudent councils of the Duke of Friedland. Wallenstein advised him to proclaim a universal amnesty, and to meet the Protestant states with favourable conditions. In the first consternation produced by the fall of Gustavus Adolphus, such a declaration would have had the most powerful effects, and probably would have brought the wavering states back to their allegiance. But blinded by this unexpected turn of fortune, and infatuated by Spanish counsels, he anticipated a more brilliant issue from war, and, instead of listening to these propositions of an accommodation, he hastened to augment his forces. Spain, enriched by the grant of the tenth of the ecclesiastical possessions, which the pope confirmed, sent him considerable supplies, negociated for him at the Saxon court, and hastily levied troops for him in Italy to be employed in Germany. The Elector of Bavaria also considerably increased his military force; and the restless disposition of the Duke of Lorraine did not permit him to remain inactive in this favourable change of fortune. But while the enemy were thus busy to profit by the disaster of Sweden, Oxenstiern was diligent to avert its most fatal consequences.

Less apprehensive of open enemies, than of the jealousy of the friendly powers, he left Upper Germany, which he had secured by conquests and alliances, and set out in person to prevent a total defection of the Lower German states, or, what would have been almost equally ruinous to Sweden, a private alliance among themselves. Offended at the boldness with which the chancellor assumed the direction of affairs, and inwardly exasperated at the thought of being dictated to by a Swedish nobleman, the Elector of Saxony again meditated a dangerous separation from Sweden; and the only question in his mind was, whether he should make full terms with the Emperor, or place himself at the head of the Protestants and form a third party in Germany. Similar ideas were cherished by Duke Ulric of Brunswick, who, indeed, showed them openly enough by forbidding the Swedes from recruiting within his dominions, and inviting the Lower Saxon states to Luneburg, for the purpose of forming a confederacy among themselves. The Elector of Brandenburg, jealous of the influence which Saxony was likely to attain in Lower Germany, alone manifested any zeal for the interests of the Swedish throne, which, in thought, he already destined for his son. At the court of Saxony, Oxenstiern was no doubt honourably received; but, notwithstanding the personal efforts of the Elector of Brandenburg, empty promises of continued friendship were all which he could obtain. With the Duke of Brunswick he was more successful, for with him he ventured to assume a bolder tone. Sweden was at the time in possession of the See of Magdeburg, the bishop of which had the power of assembling the Lower Saxon circle. The chancellor now asserted the rights of the crown, and by this spirited proceeding, put a stop for the present to this dangerous assembly designed by the duke. The main object, however, of his present journey and of his future endeavours, a general confederacy of the Protestants, miscarried entirely, and he was obliged to content himself with some unsteady alliances in the Saxon circles, and with the weaker assistance of Upper Germany.

As the Bavarians were too powerful on the Danube, the assembly of the four Upper Circles, which should have been held at Ulm, was removed to Heilbronn, where deputies of more than twelve cities of the empire, with a brilliant crowd of doctors, counts, and princes, attended. The ambassadors of foreign powers likewise, France, England, and Holland, attended this Congress, at which Oxenstiern appeared in person, with all the splendour of the crown whose representative he was. He himself opened the proceedings, and conducted the deliberations. After receiving from all the assembled estates assurances of unshaken fidelity, perseverance, and unity, he required of them solemnly and formally to declare the Emperor and the league as enemies. But desirable as it was for Sweden to exasperate the ill-feeling between the emperor and the estates into a formal rupture, the latter, on the other hand, were equally indisposed to shut out the possibility of reconciliation, by so decided a step, and to place themselves entirely in the hands of the Swedes. They maintained, that any formal declaration of war was useless and superfluous, where the act would speak for itself, and their firmness on this point silenced at last the chancellor. Warmer disputes arose on the third and principal article of the treaty, concerning the means of prosecuting the war, and the quota which the several states ought to furnish for the support of the army. Oxenstiern's maxim, to throw as much as possible of the common burden on the states, did not suit very well with their determination to give as little as possible. The Swedish chancellor now experienced, what had been felt by thirty emperors before him, to their cost, that of all difficult undertakings, the most difficult was to extort money from the Germans. Instead of granting the necessary sums for the new armies to be raised, they eloquently dwelt upon the calamities occasioned by the former, and demanded relief from the old burdens, when they were required to submit to new. The irritation which the chancellor's demand for money raised among the states, gave rise to a thousand complaints; and the outrages committed by the troops, in their marches and quarters, were dwelt upon with a startling minuteness and truth.

In the service of two absolute monarchs, Oxenstiern had but little opportunity to become accustomed to the formalities and cautious proceedings of republican deliberations, or to bear opposition with patience. Ready to act, the instant the necessity of action was apparent, and inflexible in his resolution, when he had once taken it, he was at a loss to comprehend the inconsistency of most men, who, while they desire the end, are yet averse to the means. Prompt and impetuous by nature, he was so on this occasion from principle; for every thing depended on concealing the weakness of Sweden, under a firm and confident speech, and by assuming the tone of a lawgiver, really to become so. It was nothing wonderful, therefore, if, amidst these interminable discussions with German doctors and deputies, he was entirely out of his sphere, and if the deliberateness which distinguishes the character of the Germans in their public deliberations, had driven him almost to despair. Without respecting a custom, to which even the most powerful of the emperors had been obliged to conform, he rejected all written deliberations which suited so well with the national slowness of resolve. He could not conceive how ten days could be spent in debating a measure, which with himself was decided upon its bare suggestion. Harshly, however, as he treated the States, he found them ready enough to assent to his fourth motion, which concerned himself. When he pointed out the necessity of giving a head and a director to the new confederation, that honour was unanimously assigned to Sweden, and he himself was humbly requested to give to the common cause the benefit of his enlightened experience, and to take upon himself the burden of the supreme command. But in order to prevent his abusing the great powers thus conferred upon him, it was proposed, not without French influence, to appoint a number of overseers, in fact, under the name of assistants, to control the expenditure of the common treasure, and to consult with him as to the levies, marches, and quarterings of the troops. Oxenstiern long and strenuously resisted this limitation of his authority, which could not fail to trammel him in the execution of every enterprise requiring promptitude or secrecy, and at last succeeded, with difficulty, in obtaining so far a modification of it, that his management in affairs of war was to be uncontrolled. The chancellor finally approached the delicate point of the indemnification which Sweden was to expect at the conclusion of the war, from the gratitude of the allies, and flattered himself with the hope that Pomerania, the main object of Sweden, would be assigned to her, and that he would obtain from the provinces, assurances of effectual cooperation in its acquisition. But he could obtain nothing more than a vague assurance, that in a general peace the interests of all parties would be attended to. That on this point, the caution of the estates was not owing to any regard for the constitution of the empire, became manifest from the liberality they evinced towards the chancellor, at the expense of the most sacred laws of the empire. They were ready to grant him the archbishopric of Mentz, (which he already held as a conquest,) and only with difficulty did the French ambassador succeed in preventing a step, which was as impolitic as it was disgraceful. Though on the whole, the result of the congress had fallen far short of Oxenstiern's expectations, he had at least gained for himself and his crown his main object, namely, the direction of the whole confederacy; he had also succeeded in strengthening the bond of union between the four upper circles, and obtained from the states a yearly contribution of two millions and a half of dollars, for the maintenance of the army.

These concessions on the part of the States, demanded some return from Sweden. A few weeks after the death of Gustavus Adolphus, sorrow ended the days of the unfortunate Elector Palatine. For eight months he had swelled the pomp of his protector's court, and expended on it the small remainder of his patrimony. He was, at last, approaching the goal of his wishes, and the prospect of a brighter future was opening, when death deprived him of his protector. But what he regarded as the greatest calamity, was highly favourable to his heirs. Gustavus might venture to delay the restoration of his dominions, or to load the gift with hard conditions; but Oxenstiern, to whom the friendship of England, Holland, and Brandenburg, and the good opinion of the Reformed States were indispensable, felt the necessity of immediately fulfilling the obligations of justice. At this assembly, at Heilbronn, therefore, he engaged to surrender to Frederick's heirs the whole Palatinate, both the part already conquered, and that which remained to be conquered, with the exception of Manheim, which the Swedes were to hold, until they should be indemnified for their expenses. The Chancellor did not confine his liberality to the family of the Palatine alone; the other allied princes received proofs, though at a later period, of the gratitude of Sweden, which, however, she dispensed at little cost to herself.

Impartiality, the most sacred obligation of the historian, here compels us to an admission, not much to the honour of the champions of German liberty. However the Protestant Princes might boast of the justice of their cause, and the sincerity of their conviction, still the motives from which they acted were selfish enough; and the desire of stripping others of their possessions, had at least as great a share in the commencement of hostilities, as the fear of being deprived of their own. Gustavus soon found that he might reckon much more on these selfish motives, than on their patriotic zeal, and did not fail to avail himself of them. Each of his confederates received from him the promise of some possession, either already wrested, or to be afterwards taken from the enemy; and death alone prevented him from fulfilling these engagements. What prudence had suggested to the king, necessity now prescribed to his successor. If it was his object to continue the war, he must be ready to divide the spoil among the allies, and promise them advantages from the confusion which it was his object to continue. Thus he promised to the Landgrave of Hesse, the abbacies of Paderborn, Corvey, Munster, and Fulda; to Duke Bernard of Weimar, the Franconian Bishoprics; to the Duke of Wirtemberg, the Ecclesiastical domains, and the Austrian counties lying within his territories, all under the title of fiefs of Sweden. This spectacle, so strange and so dishonourable to the German character, surprised the Chancellor, who found it difficult to repress his contempt, and on one occasion exclaimed, "Let it be writ in our records, for an everlasting memorial, that a German prince made such a request of a Swedish nobleman, and that the Swedish nobleman granted it to the German upon German ground!"

After these successful measures, he was in a condition to take the field, and prosecute the war with fresh vigour. Soon after the victory at Lutzen, the troops of Saxony and Lunenburg united with the Swedish main body; and the Imperialists were, in a short time, totally driven from Saxony. The united army again divided: the Saxons marched towards Lusatia and Silesia, to act in conjunction with Count Thurn against the Austrians in that quarter; a part of the Swedish army was led by the Duke of Weimar into Franconia, and the other by George, Duke of Brunswick, into Westphalia and Lower Saxony.

The conquests on the Lech and the Danube, during Gustavus's expedition into Saxony, had been maintained by the Palatine of Birkenfeld, and the Swedish General Banner, against the Bavarians; but unable to hold their ground against the victorious progress of the latter, supported as they were by the bravery and military experience of the Imperial General Altringer, they were under the necessity of summoning the Swedish General Horn to their assistance, from Alsace. This experienced general having captured the towns of Benfeld, Schlettstadt, Colmar, and Hagenau, committed the defence of them to the Rhinegrave Otto Louis, and hastily crossed the Rhine to form a junction with Banner's army. But although the combined force amounted to more than 16,000, they could not prevent the enemy from obtaining a strong position on the Swabian frontier, taking Kempten, and being joined by seven regiments from Bohemia. In order to retain the command of the important banks of the Lech and the

Danube, they were under the necessity of recalling the Rhinegrave Otto Louis from Alsace, where he had, after the departure of Horn, found it difficult to defend himself against the exasperated peasantry. With his army, he was now summoned to strengthen the army on the Danube; and as even this reinforcement was insufficient, Duke Bernard of Weimar was earnestly pressed to turn his arms into this quarter.

Duke Bernard, soon after the opening of the campaign of 1633, had made himself master of the town and territory of Bamberg, and was now threatening Wurtzburg. But on receiving the summons of General Horn, without delay he began his march towards the Danube, defeated on his way a Bavarian army under John de Werth, and joined the Swedes near Donauwerth. This numerous force, commanded by excellent generals, now threatened Bavaria with a fearful inroad. The bishopric of Eichstadt was completely overrun, and Ingoldstadt was on the point of being delivered up by treachery to the Swedes. Altringer, fettered in his movements by the express order of the Duke of Friedland, and left without assistance from Bohemia, was unable to check the progress of the enemy. The most favourable circumstances combined to further the progress of the Swedish arms in this quarter, when the operations of the army were at once stopped by a mutiny among the officers.

All the previous successes in Germany were owing altogether to arms; the greatness of Gustavus himself was the work of the army, the fruit of their discipline, their bravery, and their persevering courage under numberless dangers and privations. However wisely his plans were laid in the cabinet, it was to the army ultimately that he was indebted for their execution; and the expanding designs of the general did but continually impose new burdens on the soldiers. All the decisive advantages of the war, had been violently gained by a barbarous sacrifice of the soldiers' lives in winter campaigns, forced marches, stormings, and pitched battles; for it was Gustavus's maxim never to decline a battle, so long as it cost him nothing but men. The soldiers could not long be kept ignorant of their own importance, and they justly demanded a share in the spoil which had been won by their own blood. Yet, frequently, they hardly received their pay; and the rapacity of individual generals, or the wants of the state, generally swallowed up the greater part of the sums raised by contributions, or levied upon the conquered provinces. For all the privations he endured, the soldier had no other recompense than the doubtful chance either of plunder or promotion, in both of which he was often disappointed. During the lifetime of Gustavus Adolphus, the combined influence of fear and hope had suppressed any open complaint, but after his death, the murmurs were loud and universal; and the soldiery seized the most dangerous moment to impress their superiors with a sense of their importance. Two officers, Pfuhl and Mitschefal, notorious as restless characters, even during the King's life, set the example in the camp on the Danube, which in a few days was imitated by almost all the officers of the army. They solemnly bound themselves to obey no orders, till these arrears, now outstanding for months, and even years, should be paid up, and a gratuity, either in money or lands, made to each man, according to his services. "Immense sums," they said, "were daily raised by contributions, and all dissipated by a few. They were called out to serve amidst frost and snow, and no reward requited their incessant labours. The soldiers' excesses at Heilbronn had been blamed, but no one ever talked of their services. The world rung with the tidings of conquests and victories, but it was by their hands that they had been fought and won."

The number of the malcontents daily increased; and they even attempted by letters, (which were fortunately intercepted,) to seduce the armies on the Rhine and in Saxony. Neither the representations of Bernard of Weimar, nor the stern reproaches of his harsher associate in command, could suppress this mutiny, while the vehemence of Horn seemed only to increase the insolence of the insurgents. The conditions they insisted on, were that certain towns should be assigned to each regiment for the payment of arrears. Four weeks were allowed to the Swedish Chancellor to comply with these demands; and in case of refusal, they announced that they would pay themselves, and never more draw a sword for Sweden.

These pressing demands, made at the very time when the military chest was exhausted, and credit at a low ebb, greatly embarrassed the chancellor. The remedy, he saw, must be found quickly, before the contagion should spread to the other troops, and he should be deserted by all his armies at once. Among all the Swedish generals, there was only one of sufficient authority and influence with the soldiers to put an end to this dispute. The Duke of Weimar was the favourite of the army, and his prudent moderation had won the good-will of the soldiers, while his military experience had excited their admiration. He now undertook the task of appeasing the discontented troops; but, aware of his importance, he embraced the opportunity to make advantageous stipulations for himself, and to make the embarrassment of the chancellor subservient to his own views.

Gustavus Adolphus had flattered him with the promise of the Duchy of Franconia, to be formed out of the Bishoprics of Wurtzburg and Bamberg, and he now insisted on the performance of this pledge. He at the same time demanded the chief command, as generalissimo of Sweden. The abuse which the Duke of Weimar thus made of his influence, so irritated Oxenstiern, that, in the first moment of his displeasure, he gave him his dismissal from the Swedish service. But he soon thought better of it, and determined, instead of sacrificing so important a leader, to attach him to the Swedish interests at any cost. He therefore granted to him the Franconian bishoprics, as a fief of the Swedish crown, reserving, however, the two fortresses of Wurtzburg and Koenigshofen, which were to be garrisoned by the Swedes; and also engaged, in name of the Swedish crown, to secure these territories to the duke. His demand of the supreme authority was evaded on some specious pretext. The duke did not delay to display his gratitude for this valuable grant, and by his influence and activity soon restored tranquillity to the army. Large sums of money, and still more extensive estates, were divided among the officers, amounting in value to about five millions of dollars, and to which they had no other right but that of conquest. In the mean time, however, the opportunity for a great undertaking had been lost, and the united generals divided their forces to oppose the enemy in other quarters.

Gustavus Horn, after a short inroad into the Upper Palatinate, and the capture of Neumark, directed his march towards the Swabian frontier, where the Imperialists, strongly reinforced, threatened Wuertemberg. At his approach, the enemy retired to the Lake of Constance, but only to show the Swedes the road into a district hitherto unvisited by war. A post on the entrance to Switzerland, would be highly serviceable to the Swedes, and the town of Kostnitz seemed peculiarly well fitted to be a point of communication between him and the confederated cantons. Accordingly, Gustavus Horn immediately commenced the siege of it; but destitute of artillery, for which he was obliged to send to Wirtemberg, he could not press the attack with sufficient vigour, to prevent the enemy from throwing supplies into the town, which the lake afforded them convenient opportunity of doing. He, therefore, after an ineffectual attempt, quitted the place and its neighbourhood, and hastened to meet a more threatening danger upon the Danube.

At the Emperor's instigation, the Cardinal Infante, the brother of Philip IV. of Spain, and the Viceroy of Milan, had raised an army of 14,000 men, intended to act upon the Rhine, independently of Wallenstein, and to protect Alsace. This force now appeared in Bavaria, under the command of the Duke of Feria, a Spaniard; and, that they might be directly employed against the Swedes, Altringer was ordered to join them with his corps. Upon the first intelligence of their approach, Horn had summoned to his assistance the Palsgrave of Birkenfeld, from the Rhine; and being joined by him at Stockach, boldly advanced to meet the enemy's army of 30,000 men.

The latter had taken the route across the Danube into Swabia, where Gustavus Horn came so close upon them, that the two armies were only separated from each other by half a German mile. But, instead of accepting the offer of battle, the Imperialists moved by the Forest towns towards Briesgau and Alsace, where they arrived in time to relieve Breysack, and to arrest the victorious progress of the Rhinegrave, Otto Louis. The latter had, shortly before, taken the Forest towns, and, supported by the Palatine of Birkenfeld, who had liberated the Lower Palatinate and beaten the Duke of Lorraine out of the field, had once more given the superiority to the Swedish arms in that quarter. He was now forced to retire before the superior numbers of the enemy; but Horn and Birkenfeld quickly advanced to his support, and the Imperialists, after a brief triumph, were again expelled from Alsace. The severity of the autumn, in which this hapless retreat had to be conducted, proved fatal to most of the Italians; and their leader, the Duke of Feria, died of grief at the failure of his enterprise.

In the mean time, Duke Bernard of Weimar had taken up his position on the Danube, with eighteen regiments of infantry and 140 squadrons of horse, to cover Franconia, and to watch the movements of the Imperial-Bavarian army upon that river. No sooner had Altringer departed, to join the Italians under Feria, than Bernard, profiting by his absence, hastened across the Danube, and with the rapidity of lightning appeared before Ratisbon. The possession of this town would ensure the success of the Swedish designs upon Bavaria and Austria; it would establish them firmly on the Danube, and provide a safe refuge in case of defeat, while it alone could give permanence to their conquests in that quarter. To defend Ratisbon, was the urgent advice which the dying Tilly left to the Elector; and Gustavus Adolphus had lamented it as an irreparable loss, that the Bavarians had anticipated him in taking possession of this place. Indescribable, therefore, was the consternation of Maximilian, when Duke Bernard suddenly appeared before the town, and prepared in earnest to besiege it.

The garrison consisted of not more than fifteen companies, mostly newly-raised soldiers; although that number was more than sufficient to weary out an enemy of far superior force, if supported by well-disposed and warlike inhabitants. But this was not the greatest danger which the Bavarian garrison had to contend against. The Protestant inhabitants of Ratisbon, equally jealous of their civil and religious freedom, had unwillingly submitted to the yoke of Bavaria, and had long looked with impatience for the appearance of a deliverer. Bernard's arrival before the walls filled them with lively joy; and there was much reason to fear that they would support the attempts of the besiegers without, by exciting a tumult within. In this perplexity, the Elector addressed the most pressing entreaties to the Emperor and the Duke of Friedland to assist him, were it only with 5,000 men. Seven messengers in succession were despatched by Ferdinand to Wallenstein, who promised immediate succours, and even announced to the Elector the near advance of 12,000 men under Gallas; but at the same time forbade that general, under pain of death, to march. Meanwhile the Bavarian commandant of Ratisbon, in the hope of speedy assistance, made the best preparations for defence, armed the Roman Catholic peasants, disarmed and carefully watched the Protestant citizens, lest they should attempt any hostile design against the garrison. But as no relief arrived, and the enemy's artillery incessantly battered the walls, he consulted his own safety, and that of the garrison, by an honourable capitulation, and abandoned the Bavarian officials and ecclesiastics to the conqueror's mercy.

The possession of Ratisbon, enlarged the projects of the duke, and Bavaria itself now appeared too narrow a field for his bold designs. He determined to penetrate to the frontiers of Austria, to arm the Protestant peasantry against the Emperor, and restore to them their religious liberty. He had already taken Straubingen, while another Swedish army was advancing successfully along the northern bank of the Danube. At the head of his Swedes, bidding defiance to the severity of the weather, he reached the mouth of the Iser, which he passed in the presence of the Bavarian General Werth, who was encamped on that river. Passau and Lintz trembled for their fate; the terrified Emperor redoubled his entreaties and commands to Wallenstein, to hasten with all speed to the relief of the hard-pressed Bavarians. But here the victorious Bernard, of his own accord, checked his career of conquest. Having in front of him the river Inn, guarded by a number of strong fortresses, and behind him two hostile armies, a disaffected country, and the river Iser, while his rear was covered by no tenable position, and no entrenchment could be made in the frozen ground, and threatened by the whole force of Wallenstein, who had at last resolved to march to the Danube, by a timely retreat he escaped the danger of being cut off from Ratisbon, and surrounded by the enemy. He hastened across the Iser to the Danube, to defend the conquests he had made in the Upper Palatinate against Wallenstein, and fully resolved not to decline a battle, if necessary, with that general. But Wallenstein, who was not disposed for any great exploits on the Danube, did not wait for his approach; and before the Bavarians could congratulate themselves on his arrival, he suddenly withdrew again into Bohemia. The duke thus ended his victorious campaign, and allowed his troops their well-earned repose in winter quarters upon an enemy's country.

While in Swabia the war was thus successfully conducted by Gustavus Horn, and on the Upper and Lower Rhine by the Palatine of Birkenfeld, General Baudissen, and the Rhinegrave Otto Louis, and by Duke Bernard on the Danube; the reputation of the Swedish arms was as gloriously sustained in Lower Saxony and Westphalia by the Duke of Lunenburg and the Landgrave of Hesse Cassel. The fortress of Hamel was taken by Duke George, after a brave defence, and a brilliant victory obtained over the imperial General Gronsfeld, by the united Swedish and Hessian armies, near Oldendorf. Count Wasaburg, a natural son of Gustavus Adolphus, showed himself in this battle worthy of his descent. Sixteen pieces of cannon, the whole baggage of the Imperialists, together with 74 colours, fell into the hands of the Swedes; 3,000 of the enemy perished on the field, and nearly the same number were taken prisoners. The town of Osnaburg surrendered to the Swedish Colonel Knyphausen, and Paderborn to the Landgrave of Hesse; while, on the other hand, Bueckeburg, a very important place for the Swedes, fell into the hands of the Imperialists. The Swedish banners were victorious in almost every quarter of Germany; and the year after the death of Gustavus, left no trace of the loss which had been sustained in the person of that great leader.

In a review of the important events which signalized the campaign of 1633, the inactivity of a man, of whom the highest expectations had been formed, justly excites astonishment. Among all the generals who distinguished themselves in this campaign, none could be compared with Wallenstein, in experience, talents, and reputation; and yet, after the battle of Lutzen, we lose sight of him entirely. The fall of his great rival had left the whole theatre of glory open to him; all Europe was now attentively awaiting those exploits, which should efface the remembrance of his defeat, and still prove to the world his military superiority. Nevertheless, he continued inactive in Bohemia, while the Emperor's losses in Bavaria, Lower Saxony, and the Rhine, pressingly called for his presence — a conduct equally unintelligible to friend and foe — the terror, and, at the same time, the last hope of the Emperor. After the defeat of Lutzen he had hastened into Bohemia, where he instituted the strictest inquiry into the conduct of his officers in that battle. Those whom the council of war declared guilty of misconduct, were put to death without mercy, those who had behaved with bravery, rewarded with princely munificence, and the memory of the dead honoured by splendid monuments. During the winter, he oppressed the imperial provinces by enormous contributions, and exhausted the Austrian territories by his winter quarters, which he purposely avoided taking up in an enemy's country. And in the spring of 1633, instead of being the first to open the campaign, with this well-chosen and well-appointed army, and to make a worthy display of his great abilities, he was the last who appeared in the field; and even then, it was an hereditary province of Austria, which he selected as the seat of war.

Of all the Austrian provinces, Silesia was most exposed to danger. Three different armies, a Swedish under Count Thurn, a Saxon under Arnheim and the Duke of Lauenburg, and one of Brandenburg under Borgsdorf, had at the same time carried the war into this country; they had already taken possession of the most important places, and even Breslau had embraced the cause of the allies. But this crowd of commanders and armies was the very means of saving this province to the Emperor; for the jealousy of the generals, and the mutual hatred of the Saxons and the Swedes, never allowed them to act with unanimity. Arnheim and Thurn contended for the chief command; the troops of Brandenburg and Saxony combined against the Swedes, whom they looked upon as troublesome strangers who ought to be got rid of as soon as possible. The Saxons, on the contrary, lived on a very intimate footing with the Imperialists, and the officers of both these hostile armies often visited and entertained each other. The Imperialists were allowed to remove their property without hindrance, and many did not affect to conceal that they had received large sums from Vienna. Among such equivocal allies, the Swedes saw themselves sold and betrayed; and any great enterprise was out of the question, while so bad an understanding prevailed between the troops. General Arnheim, too, was absent the greater part of the time; and when he at last returned, Wallenstein was fast approaching the frontiers with a formidable force.

His army amounted to 40,000 men, while to oppose him the allies had only 24,000. They nevertheless resolved to give him battle, and marched to Munsterberg, where he had formed an intrenched camp. But Wallenstein remained inactive for eight days; he then left his intrenchments, and marched slowly and with composure to the enemy's camp. But even after quitting his position, and when the enemy, emboldened by his past delay, manfully prepared to receive him, he declined the opportunity of fighting. The caution with which he avoided a battle was imputed to fear; but the well-established reputation of Wallenstein enabled him to despise this suspicion. The vanity of the allies allowed them not to see that he purposely saved them a defeat, because a victory at that time would not have served his own ends. To convince them of his superior power, and that his inactivity proceeded not from any fear of them, he put to death the commander of a castle that fell into his hands, because he had refused at once to surrender an untenable place.

For nine days, did the two armies remain within musket-shot of each other, when Count Terzky, from the camp of the Imperialists, appeared with a trumpeter in that of the allies, inviting General Arnheim to a conference. The purport was, that Wallenstein, notwithstanding his superiority, was willing to agree to a cessation of arms for six weeks. "He was come," he said, "to conclude a lasting peace with the Swedes, and with the princes of the empire, to pay the soldiers, and to satisfy every one. All this was in his power; and if the Austrian court hesitated to confirm his agreement, he would unite with the allies, and (as he privately whispered to Arnheim) hunt the Emperor to the devil." At the second conference, he expressed himself still more plainly to Count Thurn. "All the privileges of the Bohemians," he engaged, "should be confirmed anew, the exiles recalled and restored to their estates, and he himself would be the first to resign his share of them. The Jesuits, as the authors of all past grievances, should be banished, the Swedish crown indemnified by stated payments, and all the superfluous troops on both sides employed against the Turks." The last article explained the whole mystery. "If," he continued, "*He* should obtain the crown of Bohemia, all the exiles would have reason to applaud his generosity; perfect toleration of religions should be established within the kingdom, the Palatine family be reinstated in its rights, and he would accept the Margraviate of Moravia as a compensation for Mecklenburg. The allied armies would then, under his command, advance upon Vienna, and sword in hand, compel the Emperor to ratify the treaty."

Thus was the veil at last removed from the schemes, over which he had brooded for years in mysterious silence. Every circumstance now convinced him that not a moment was to be lost in its execution. Nothing but a blind confidence in the good fortune and military genius of the Duke of Friedland, had induced the Emperor, in the face of the remonstrances of Bavaria and Spain, and at the expense of his own reputation, to confer upon this imperious leader such an unlimited command. But this belief in Wallenstein's being invincible, had been much weakened by his inaction, and almost entirely overthrown by the defeat at Lutzen. His enemies at the imperial court now renewed their intrigues; and the Emperor's disappointment at the failure of his hopes, procured for their remonstrances a favourable reception. Wallenstein's whole conduct was now reviewed with the most malicious criticism; his ambitious haughtiness, his disobedience to the Emperor's orders, were recalled to the recollection of that jealous prince, as well as the complaints of the Austrian subjects against his boundless oppression; his fidelity was questioned, and alarming hints thrown out as to his secret views. These insinuations, which the conduct of the duke seemed but too well to justify, failed not to make a deep impression on Ferdinand; but the step had been taken, and the great power with which Wallenstein had been invested, could not be taken from him without danger. Insensibly to diminish that power, was the only course that now remained, and, to effect this, it must in the first place be divided; but, above all, the Emperor's present dependence on the good will of his general put an end to. But even this right had been resigned in his engagement with Wallenstein, and the Emperor's own handwriting secured him against every attempt to unite another general with him in the command, or to exercise any immediate act of authority over the troops. As this disadvantageous contract could neither be kept nor broken, recourse was had to artifice. Wallenstein was Imperial Generalissimo in Germany, but his command extended no further, and he could not presume to exercise any authority over a foreign army. A Spanish army was accordingly raised in Milan, and marched into Germany under a Spanish general. Wallenstein now ceased to be indispensable because he was no longer supreme, and in case of necessity, the Emperor was now provided with the means of support even against him.

The duke quickly and deeply felt whence this blow came, and whither it was aimed. In vain did he protest against this violation of the compact, to the Cardinal Infante; the Italian army continued its march, and he was forced to detach General Altringer to join it with a reinforcement. He took care, indeed, so closely to fetter the latter, as to prevent the Italian army from acquiring any great reputation in Alsace and Swabia; but this bold step of the court awakened him from his security, and warned him of the approach of danger. That he might not a second time be deprived of his command, and lose the fruit of all his labours, he must accelerate the accomplishment of his long meditated designs. He secured the attachment of his troops by removing the doubtful officers, and by his liberality to the rest. He had sacrificed to the welfare of the army every other order in the state, every consideration of justice and humanity, and therefore he reckoned upon their gratitude. At the very moment when he meditated an unparalleled act of ingratitude against the author of his own good fortune, he founded all his hopes upon the gratitude which was due to himself.

The leaders of the Silesian armies had no authority from their principals to consent, on their own discretion, to such important proposals as those of Wallenstein, and they did not even feel themselves warranted in granting, for more than a fortnight, the cessation of hostilities which he demanded. Before the duke disclosed his designs to Sweden and Saxony, he had deemed it advisable to secure the sanction of France to his bold undertaking. For this purpose, a secret negociation had been carried on with the greatest possible caution and distrust, by Count Kinsky with Feuquieres, the French ambassador at Dresden, and had terminated according to his wishes. Feuquieres received orders from his court to promise every assistance on the part of France, and to offer the duke a considerable pecuniary aid in case of need.

But it was this excessive caution to secure himself on all sides, that led to his ruin. The French ambassador with astonishment discovered that a plan, which, more than any other, required secrecy, had been communicated to the Swedes and the Saxons. And yet it was generally known that the Saxon ministry was in the interests of the Emperor, and on the other hand, the conditions offered to the Swedes fell too far short of their expectations to be likely to be accepted. Feuquieres, therefore, could not believe that the duke could be serious in calculating upon the aid of the latter, and the silence of the former. He communicated accordingly his doubts and anxieties to the Swedish chancellor, who equally distrusted the views of Wallenstein, and disliked his plans. Although it was no secret to Oxenstiern, that the duke had formerly entered into a similar negociation with Gustavus Adolphus, he could not credit the possibility of inducing a whole army to revolt, and of his extravagant promises. So daring a design, and such imprudent conduct, seemed not to be consistent with the duke's reserved and suspicious temper, and he was the more inclined to consider the whole as the result of dissimulation and treachery, because he had less reason to doubt his prudence than his honesty.

Oxenstiern's doubts at last affected Arnheim himself, who, in full confidence in Wallenstein's sincerity, had repaired to the chancellor at Gelnhausen, to persuade him to lend some of his best regiments to the duke, to aid him in the execution of the plan. They began to suspect that the whole proposal was only a snare to disarm the allies, and to betray the flower of their troops into the hands of the Emperor. Wallenstein's well-known character did not contradict the suspicion, and the inconsistencies in which he afterwards involved himself, entirely destroyed all confidence in his sincerity. While he was endeavouring to draw the Swedes into this alliance, and requiring the help of their best troops, he declared to Arnheim that they must begin with expelling the Swedes from the empire; and while the Saxon officers, relying upon the security of the truce, repaired in great numbers to his camp, he made an unsuccessful attempt to seize them. He was the first to break the truce, which some months afterwards he renewed, though not without great difficulty. All confidence in his sincerity was lost; his whole conduct was regarded as a tissue of deceit and low cunning, devised to weaken the allies and repair his own strength. This indeed he actually did effect, as his own army daily augmented, while that of the allies was reduced nearly one half by desertion and bad provisions. But he did not make that use of his superiority which Vienna expected. When all men were looking for a decisive blow to be struck, he suddenly renewed the negociations; and when the truce lulled the allies into security, he as suddenly recommenced hostilities. All these contradictions arose out of the double and irreconcileable designs to ruin at once the Emperor and the Swedes, and to conclude a separate peace with the Saxons.

Impatient at the ill success of his negociations, he at last determined to display his strength; the more so, as the pressing distress within the empire, and the growing dissatisfaction of the Imperial court, admitted not of his making any longer delay. Before the last cessation of hostilities, General Holk, from Bohemia, had attacked the circle of Meissen, laid waste every thing on his route with fire and sword, driven the Elector into his fortresses, and taken the town of Leipzig. But the truce in Silesia put a period to his ravages, and the consequences of his excesses brought him to the grave at Adorf. As soon as hostilities were recommenced, Wallenstein made a movement, as if he designed to penetrate through Lusatia into Saxony, and circulated the report that Piccolomini had already invaded that country. Arnheim immediately broke up his camp in Silesia, to follow him, and hastened to the assistance of the Electorate. By this means the Swedes were left exposed, who were encamped in small force under Count Thurn, at Steinau, on the Oder, and this was exactly what Wallenstein desired. He allowed the Saxon general to advance sixteen miles towards Meissen, and then suddenly turning towards the Oder, surprised the Swedish army in the most complete security. Their cavalry were first beaten by General Schafgotsch, who was sent against them, and the infantry completely surrounded at Steinau by the duke's army which followed. Wallenstein gave Count Thurn half an hour to deliberate whether he would defend himself with 2,500 men, against more than 20,000, or surrender at discretion. But there was no room for deliberation. The army surrendered, and the most complete victory was obtained without bloodshed. Colours, baggage, and artillery all fell into the hands of the victors, the officers were taken into custody, the privates drafted into the army of Wallenstein. And now at last, after a banishment of fourteen years, after numberless changes of fortune, the author of the Bohemian insurrection, and the remote origin of this destructive war, the notorious Count Thurn, was in the power of his enemies. With blood-thirsty impatience, the arrival of this great criminal was looked for in Vienna, where they already anticipated the malicious triumph of sacrificing so distinguished a victim to public justice. But to deprive the Jesuits of this pleasure, was a still sweeter triumph to Wallenstein, and Thurn was set at liberty. Fortunately for him, he knew more than it was prudent to have divulged in Vienna, and his enemies were also those of Wallenstein. A defeat might have been forgiven in Vienna, but this disappointment of their hopes they could not pardon. "What should I have done with this madman?" he writes, with a malicious sneer, to the minister who called him to account for this unseasonable magnanimity. "Would to Heaven the enemy had no generals but such as he. At the head of the Swedish army, he will render us much better service than in prison."

The victory of Steinau was followed by the capture of Liegnitz, Grossglogau, and even of Frankfort on the Oder. Schafgotsch, who remained in Silesia to complete the subjugation of that province, blockaded Brieg, and threatened Breslau, though in vain, as that free town was jealous of its privileges, and devoted to the Swedes. Colonels Illo and Goetz were ordered by Wallenstein to the Warta, to push forwards into Pomerania, and to the coasts of the Baltic, and actually obtained possession of Landsberg, the key of Pomerania. While thus the Elector of Brandenburg and the Duke of Pomerania were made to tremble for their dominions, Wallenstein himself, with the remainder of his army, burst suddenly into Lusatia, where he took Goerlitz by storm, and forced Bautzen to surrender. But his object was merely to alarm the Elector of Saxony, not to follow up the advantages already obtained; and therefore, even with the sword in his hand, he continued his negociations for peace with Brandenburg and Saxony, but with no better success than before, as the inconsistencies of his conduct had destroyed all confidence in his sincerity. He was therefore on the point of turning his whole force in earnest against the unfortunate Saxons, and effecting his object by force of arms, when circumstances compelled him to leave these territories. The conquests of Duke Bernard upon the Danube, which threatened Austria itself with immediate danger, urgently demanded his presence in Bavaria; and the expulsion of the Saxons and Swedes from Silesia, deprived him of every pretext for longer resisting the Imperial orders, and leaving the Elector of Bavaria without assistance. With his main body, therefore, he immediately set out for the Upper Palatinate, and his retreat freed Upper Saxony for ever of this formidable enemy.

So long as was possible, he had delayed to move to the rescue of Bavaria, and on every pretext evaded the commands of the Emperor. He had, indeed, after reiterated remonstrances, despatched from Bohemia a reinforcement of some regiments to Count Altringer, who was defending the Lech and the Danube against Horn and Bernard, but under the express condition of his acting merely on the defensive. He referred the Emperor and the Elector, whenever they applied to him for aid, to Altringer, who, as he publicly gave out, had received unlimited powers; secretly, however, he tied up his hands by the strictest injunctions, and even threatened him with death, if he exceeded his orders. When Duke Bernard had appeared before Ratisbon, and the Emperor as well as the Elector repeated still more urgently their demand for succour, he pretended he was about to despatch General Gallas with a considerable army to the Danube; but this movement also was delayed, and Ratisbon, Straubing, and Cham, as well as the bishopric of Eichstaedt, fell into the hands of the Swedes. When at last he could no longer neglect the orders of the Court, he marched slowly toward the Bavarian frontier, where he invested the town of Cham, which had been taken by the Swedes. But no sooner did he learn that on the Swedish side a diversion was contemplated, by an inroad of the Saxons into Bohemia, than he availed himself of the report, as a pretext for immediately retreating into that kingdom. Every consideration, he urged, must be postponed to the defence and preservation of the hereditary dominions of the Emperor; and on this plea, he remained firmly fixed in Bohemia, which he guarded as if it had been his own property. And when the Emperor laid upon him his commands to move towards the Danube, and prevent the Duke of Weimar from establishing himself in so dangerous a position on the frontiers of Austria, Wallenstein thought proper to conclude the campaign a second time, and quartered his troops for the winter in this exhausted kingdom.

Such continued insolence and unexampled contempt of the Imperial orders, as well as obvious neglect of the common cause, joined to his equivocal behaviour towards the enemy, tended at last to convince the Emperor of the truth of those unfavourable reports with regard to the Duke, which were current through Germany. The latter had, for a long time, succeeded in glozing over his criminal correspondence with the enemy, and persuading the Emperor, still prepossessed in his favour, that the sole object of his secret conferences was to obtain peace for Germany. But impenetrable as he himself believed his proceedings to be, in the course of his conduct, enough transpired to justify the insinuations with which his rivals incessantly loaded the ear of the Emperor. In order to satisfy himself of the truth or falsehood of these rumours, Ferdinand had already, at different times, sent spies into Wallenstein's camp; but as the Duke took the precaution never to commit anything to writing, they returned with nothing but conjectures. But when, at last, those ministers who formerly had been his champions at the court, in consequence of their estates not being exempted by Wallenstein from the general exactions, joined his enemies; when the Elector of Bavaria threatened, in case of Wallenstein being any longer retained in the supreme command, to unite with the Swedes; when the Spanish ambassador insisted on his dismissal, and threatened, in case of refusal, to withdraw the subsidies furnished by his Crown, the Emperor found himself a second time compelled to deprive him of the command.

The Emperor's authoritative and direct interference with the army, soon convinced the Duke that the compact with himself was regarded as at an end, and that his dismissal was inevitable. One of his inferior generals in Austria, whom he had forbidden, under pain of death, to obey the orders of the court, received the positive commands of the Emperor to join the Elector of Bavaria; and Wallenstein himself was imperiously ordered to send some regiments to reinforce the army of the Cardinal Infante, who was on his march from Italy. All these measures convinced him that the plan was finally arranged to disarm him by degrees, and at once, when he was weak and defenceless, to complete his ruin.

In self-defence, must he now hasten to carry into execution the plans which he had originally formed only with the view to aggrandizement. He had delayed too long, either because the favourable configuration of the stars had not yet presented itself, or, as he used to say, to check the impatience of his friends, because *the time was not yet come*. The time, even now, was not come: but the pressure of circumstances no longer allowed him to await the favour of the stars. The first step was to assure himself of the sentiments of his principal officers, and then to try the attachment of the army, which he had so long confidently reckoned on. Three of them, Colonels Kinsky, Terzky, and Illo, had long been in his secrets, and the two first were further united to his interests by the ties of relationship. The same wild ambition, the same bitter hatred of the government, and the hope of enormous rewards, bound them in the closest manner to Wallenstein, who, to increase the number of his adherents, could stoop to the lowest means. He had once advised Colonel Illo to solicit, in Vienna, the title of Count, and had promised to back his application with his powerful mediation. But he secretly wrote to the ministry, advising them to refuse his request, as to grant it would give rise to similar demands from others, whose services and claims were equal to his. On Illo's return to the camp, Wallenstein immediately demanded to know the success of his mission; and when informed by Illo of its failure, he broke out into the bitterest complaints against the court. "Thus," said he, "are our faithful services rewarded. My recommendation is disregarded, and your merit denied so trifling a reward! Who would any longer devote his services to so ungrateful a master? No, for my part, I am henceforth the determined foe of Austria." Illo agreed with him, and a close alliance was cemented between them.

But what was known to these three confidants of the duke, was long an impenetrable secret to the rest; and the confidence with which Wallenstein spoke of the devotion of his officers, was founded merely on the favours he had lavished on them, and on their known dissatisfaction with the Court. But this vague presumption must be converted into certainty, before he could venture to lay aside the mask, or take any open step against the Emperor. Count Piccolomini, who had distinguished himself by his unparalleled bravery at Lutzen, was the first whose fidelity he put to the proof. He had, he thought, gained the attachment of this general by large presents, and preferred him to all others, because born under the same constellations with himself. He disclosed to him, that, in consequence of the Emperor's ingratitude, and the near approach of his own danger, he had irrevocably determined entirely to abandon the party of Austria, to join the enemy with the best part of his army, and to make war upon the House of Austria, on all sides of its dominions, till he had wholly extirpated it. In the execution of this plan, he principally reckoned on the services of Piccolomini, and had beforehand promised him the greatest rewards. When the latter, to conceal his amazement at this extraordinary communication, spoke of the dangers and obstacles which would oppose so hazardous an enterprise, Wallenstein ridiculed his fears. "In such enterprises," he maintained, "nothing was difficult but the commencement. The stars were propitious to him, the opportunity the best that could be wished for, and something must always be trusted to fortune. His resolution was taken, and if it could not be otherwise, he would encounter the hazard at the head of a thousand horse." Piccolomini was careful not to excite Wallenstein's suspicions by longer opposition, and yielded apparently to the force of his reasoning. Such was the infatuation of the Duke, that notwithstanding the warnings of Count Terzky, he never doubted the sincerity of this man, who lost not a moment in communicating to the court at Vienna this important conversation.

Preparatory to taking the last decisive step, he, in January 1634, called a meeting of all the commanders of the army at Pilsen, whither he had marched after his retreat from Bavaria. The Emperor's recent orders to spare his hereditary dominions from winter quarterings, to recover Ratisbon in the middle of winter, and to reduce the army by a detachment of six thousand horse to the Cardinal Infante, were matters sufficiently grave to be laid before a council of war; and this plausible pretext served to conceal from the curious the real object of the meeting. Sweden and Saxony received invitations to be present, in order to treat with the Duke of Friedland for a peace; to the leaders of more distant armies, written communications were made. Of the commanders thus summoned, twenty appeared; but three most influential, Gallas, Colloredo, and Altringer, were absent. The Duke reiterated his summons to them, and in the mean time, in expectation of their speedy arrival, proceeded to execute his designs.

It was no light task that he had to perform: a nobleman, proud, brave, and jealous of his honour, was to declare himself capable of the basest treachery, in the very presence of those who had been accustomed to regard him as the representative of majesty, the judge of their actions, and the supporter of their laws, and to show himself suddenly as a traitor, a cheat, and a rebel. It was no easy task, either, to shake to its foundations a legitimate sovereignty, strengthened by time and consecrated by laws and religion; to dissolve all the charms of the senses and the imagination, those formidable guardians of an established throne, and to attempt forcibly to uproot those invincible feelings of duty, which plead so loudly and so powerfully in the breast of the subject, in favour of his sovereign. But, blinded by the splendour of a crown, Wallenstein observed not the precipice that yawned beneath his feet; and in full reliance on his own strength, the common case with energetic and daring minds, he stopped not to consider the magnitude and the number of the difficulties that opposed him. Wallenstein saw nothing but an army, partly indifferent and partly exasperated against the court, accustomed, with a blind submission, to do homage to his great name, to bow to him as their legislator and judge, and with trembling reverence to follow his orders as the decrees of fate. In the extravagant flatteries which were paid to his omnipotence, in the bold abuse of the court government, in which a lawless soldiery indulged, and which the wild licence of the camp excused, he thought he read the sentiments of the army; and the boldness with which they were ready to censure the monarch's measures, passed with him for a readiness to renounce their allegiance to a sovereign so little respected. But that which he had regarded as the lightest matter, proved the most formidable obstacle with which he had to contend; the soldiers' feelings of allegiance were the rock on which his hopes were wrecked. Deceived by the profound respect in which he was held by these lawless bands, he ascribed the whole to his own personal greatness, without distinguishing how much he owed to himself, and how much to the dignity with which he was invested. All trembled before him, while he exercised a legitimate authority, while obedience to him was a duty, and while his consequence was supported by the majesty of the sovereign. Greatness, in and of itself, may excite terror and admiration; but legitimate greatness alone can inspire reverence and submission; and of this decisive advantage he deprived himself, the instant he avowed himself a traitor.

Field-Marshal Illo undertook to learn the sentiments of the officers, and to prepare them for the step which was expected of them. He began by laying before them the new orders of the court to the general and the army; and by the obnoxious turn he skilfully gave to them, he found it easy to excite the indignation of the assembly. After this well chosen introduction, he expatiated with much eloquence upon the merits of the army and the general, and the ingratitude with which the Emperor was accustomed to requite them. "Spanish influence," he maintained, "governed the court; the ministry were in the pay of Spain; the Duke of Friedland alone had hitherto opposed this tyranny, and had thus drawn down upon himself the deadly enmity of the Spaniards. To remove him from the command, or to make away with him entirely," he continued, "had long been the end of their desires; and, until they could succeed in one or other, they endeavoured to abridge his power in the field. The command was to be placed in the hands of the King of Hungary, for no other reason than the better to promote the Spanish power in Germany; because this prince, as the ready instrument of foreign counsels, might be led at pleasure. It was merely with the view of weakening the army, that the six thousand troops were required for the Cardinal Infante; it was solely for the purpose of harassing it by a winter campaign, that they were now called on, in this inhospitable season, to undertake the recovery of Ratisbon. The means of subsistence were everywhere rendered difficult, while the Jesuits and the ministry enriched themselves with the sweat of the provinces, and squandered the money intended for the pay of the troops. The general, abandoned by the court, acknowledges his inability to keep his engagements to the army. For all the services which, for two and twenty years, he had rendered the House of Austria; for all the difficulties with which he had struggled; for all the treasures of his own, which he had expended in the imperial service, a second disgraceful dismissal awaited him. But he was resolved the matter should not come to this; he was determined voluntarily to resign the command, before it should be wrested from his hands; and this," continued the orator, "is what, through me, he now makes known to his officers. It was now for them to say whether it would be advisable to lose such a general. Let each consider who was to refund him the sums he had expended in the Emperor's service, and where he was now to reap the reward of their bravery, when he who was their evidence removed from the scene."

A universal cry, that they would not allow their general to be taken from them, interrupted the speaker. Four of the principal officers were deputed to lay before him the wish of the assembly, and earnestly to request that he would not leave the army. The duke made a show of resistance, and only yielded after the second deputation. This concession on his side, seemed to demand a return on theirs; as he engaged not to quit the service without the knowledge and consent of the generals, he required of them, on the other hand, a written promise to truly and firmly adhere to him, neither to separate nor to allow themselves to be separated from him, and to shed their last drop of blood in his defence. Whoever should break this covenant, was to be regarded as a perfidious traitor, and treated by the rest as a common enemy. The express condition which was added, "*as long as Wallenstein shall employ the army in the Emperor's service,*" seemed to exclude all misconception, and none of the assembled generals hesitated at once to accede to a demand, apparently so innocent and so reasonable.

This document was publicly read before an entertainment, which Field-Marshal Illo had expressly prepared for the purpose; it was to be signed, after they rose from table. The host did his utmost to stupify his guests by strong potations; and it was not until he saw them affected with the wine, that he produced the paper for signature. Most of them wrote their names, without knowing what they were subscribing; a few only, more curious or more distrustful, read the paper over again, and discovered with astonishment that the clause "as long as Wallenstein shall employ the army for the Emperor's service" was omitted. Illo had, in fact, artfully contrived to substitute for the first another copy, in which these words were wanting. The trick was manifest, and many refused now to sign. Piccolomini, who had seen through the whole cheat, and had been present at this scene merely with the view of giving information of the whole to the court, forgot himself so far in his cups as to drink the Emperor's health. But Count Terzky now rose, and declared that all were perjured villains who should recede from their engagement. His menaces, the idea of the inevitable danger to which they who resisted any longer would be exposed, the example of the rest, and Illo's rhetoric, at last overcame their scruples; and the paper was signed by all without exception.

Wallenstein had now effected his purpose; but the unexpected resistance he had met with from the commanders roused him at last from the fond illusions in which he had hitherto indulged. Besides, most of the names were scrawled so illegibly, that some deceit was evidently intended. But instead of being recalled to his discretion by this warning, he gave vent to his injured pride in undignified complaints and reproaches. He assembled the generals the next day, and undertook personally to confirm the whole tenor of the agreement which Illo had submitted to them the day before. After pouring out the bitterest reproaches and abuse against the court, he reminded them of their opposition to the proposition of the previous day, and declared that this circumstance had induced him to retract his own promise. The generals withdrew in silence and confusion; but after a short consultation in the antichamber, they returned to apologize for their late conduct, and offered to sign the paper anew.

Nothing now remained, but to obtain a similar assurance from the absent generals, or, on their refusal, to seize their persons. Wallenstein renewed his invitation to them, and earnestly urged them to hasten their arrival. But a rumour of the doings at Pilsen reached them on their journey, and suddenly stopped their further progress. Altringer, on pretence of sickness, remained in the strong fortress of Frauenberg. Gallas made his appearance, but merely with the design of better qualifying himself as an eyewitness, to keep the Emperor informed of all Wallenstein's proceedings. The intelligence which he and Piccolomini gave, at once converted the suspicions of the court into an alarming certainty. Similar disclosures, which were at the same time made from other quarters, left no room for farther doubt; and the sudden change of the commanders in Austria and Silesia, appeared to be the prelude to some important enterprise. The danger was pressing, and the remedy must be speedy, but the court was unwilling to proceed at once to the execution of the sentence, till the regular forms of justice were complied with. Secret instructions were therefore issued to the principal officers, on whose fidelity reliance could be placed, to seize the persons of the Duke of Friedland and of his two associates, Illo and Terzky, and keep them in close confinement, till they should have an opportunity of being heard, and of answering for their conduct; but if this could not be accomplished quietly, the public danger required that they should be taken dead or live. At the same time, General Gallas received a patent commission, by which these orders of the Emperor were made known to the colonels and officers, and the army was released from its obedience to the traitor, and placed under Lieutenant-General Gallas, till a new generalissimo could be appointed. In order to bring back the seduced and deluded to their duty, and not to drive the guilty to despair, a general amnesty was proclaimed, in regard to all offences against the imperial majesty committed at Pilsen.

General Gallas was not pleased with the honour which was done him. He was at Pilsen, under the eye of the person whose fate he was to dispose of; in the power of an enemy, who had a hundred eyes to watch his motions. If Wallenstein once discovered the secret of his commission, nothing could save him from the effects of his vengeance and despair. But if it was thus dangerous to be the secret depositary of such a commission, how much more so to execute it? The sentiments of the generals were uncertain; and it was at least doubtful whether, after the step they had taken, they would be ready to trust the Emperor's promises, and at once to abandon the brilliant expectations they had built upon Wallenstein's enterprise. It was also hazardous to attempt to lay hands on the person of a man who, till now, had been considered inviolable; who from long exercise of supreme power, and from habitual obedience, had become the object of deepest respect; who was invested with every attribute of outward majesty and inward greatness; whose very aspect inspired terror, and who by a nod disposed of life and death! To seize such a man, like a common criminal, in the midst of the guards by whom he was surrounded, and in a city apparently devoted to him; to convert the object of this deep and habitual veneration into a subject of compassion, or of contempt, was a commission calculated to make even the boldest hesitate. So deeply was fear and veneration for their general engraven in the breasts of the soldiers, that even the atrocious crime of high treason could not wholly eradicate these sentiments.

Gallas perceived the impossibility of executing his commission under the eyes of the duke; and his most anxious wish was, before venturing on any steps, to have an interview with Altringer. As the long absence of the latter had already begun to excite the duke's suspicions, Gallas offered to repair in person to Frauenberg, and to prevail on Altringer, his relation, to return with him. Wallenstein was so pleased with this proof of his zeal, that he even lent him his own equipage for the journey. Rejoicing at the success of his stratagem, he left Pilsen without delay, leaving to Count Piccolomini the task of watching Wallenstein's further movements. He did not fail, as he went along, to make use of the imperial patent, and the sentiments of the troops proved more favourable than he had expected. Instead of taking back his friend to Pilsen, he despatched him to Vienna, to warn the Emperor against the intended attack, while he himself repaired to Upper Austria, of which the safety was threatened by the near approach of Duke Bernard. In Bohemia, the towns of Budweiss and Tabor were again garrisoned for the Emperor, and every precaution taken to oppose with energy the designs of the traitor.

As Gallas did not appear disposed to return, Piccolomini determined to put Wallenstein's credulity once more to the test. He begged to be sent to bring back Gallas, and Wallenstein suffered himself a second time to be overreached. This inconceivable blindness can only be accounted for as the result of his pride, which never retracted the opinion it had once formed of any person, and would not acknowledge, even to itself, the possibility of being deceived. He conveyed Count Piccolomini in his own carriage to Lintz, where the latter immediately followed the example of Gallas, and even went a step farther. He had promised the duke to return. He did so, but it was at the head of an army, intending to surprise the duke in Pilsen. Another army under General Suys hastened to Prague, to secure that capital in its allegiance, and to defend it against the rebels. Gallas, at the same time, announced himself to the different imperial armies as the commander-in-chief, from whom they were henceforth to receive orders. Placards were circulated through all the imperial camps, denouncing the duke and his four confidants, and absolving the soldiers from all obedience to him.

The example which had been set at Lintz, was universally followed; imprecations were showered on the traitor, and he was forsaken by all the armies. At last, when even Piccolomini returned no more, the mist fell from Wallenstein's eyes, and in consternation he awoke from his dream. Yet his faith in the truth of astrology, and in the fidelity of the army was unshaken. Immediately after the intelligence of Piccolomini's defection, he issued orders, that in future no commands were to be obeyed, which did not proceed directly from himself, or from Terzky, or Illo. He prepared, in all haste, to advance upon Prague, where he intended to throw off the mask, and openly to declare against the Emperor. All the troops were to assemble before that city, and from thence to pour down with rapidity upon Austria. Duke Bernard, who had joined the conspiracy, was to support the operations of the duke, with the Swedish troops, and to effect a diversion upon the Danube.

Terzky was already upon his march towards Prague; and nothing, but the want of horses, prevented the duke from following him with the regiments who still adhered faithfully to him. But when, with the most anxious expectation, he awaited the intelligence from Prague, he suddenly received information of the loss of that town, the defection of his generals, the desertion of his troops, the discovery of his whole plot, and the rapid advance of Piccolomini, who was sworn to his destruction. Suddenly and fearfully had all his projects been ruined — all his hopes annihilated. He stood alone, abandoned by all to whom he had been a benefactor, betrayed by all on whom he had depended. But it is under such circumstances that great minds reveal themselves. Though deceived in all his expectations, he refused to abandon one of his designs; he despaired of nothing, so long as life remained. The time was now come, when he absolutely required that assistance, which he had so often solicited from the Swedes and the Saxons, and when all doubts of the sincerity of his purposes must be dispelled. And now, when Oxenstiern and Arnheim were convinced of the sincerity of his intentions, and were aware of his necessities, they no longer hesitated to embrace the favourable opportunity, and to offer him their protection. On the part of Saxony, the Duke Francis Albert of Saxe Lauenberg was to join him with 4,000 men; and Duke Bernard, and the Palatine Christian of Birkenfeld, with 6,000 from Sweden, all chosen troops.

Wallenstein left Pilsen, with Terzky's regiment, and the few who either were, or pretended to be, faithful to him, and hastened to Egra, on the frontiers of the kingdom, in order to be near the Upper

Palatinate, and to facilitate his junction with Duke Bernard. He was not yet informed of the decree by which he was proclaimed a public enemy and traitor; this thunder-stroke awaited him at Egra. He still reckoned on the army, which General Schafgotsch was preparing for him in Silesia, and flattered himself with the hope that many even of those who had forsaken him, would return with the first dawning of success. Even during his flight to Egra (so little humility had he learned from melancholy experience) he was still occupied with the colossal scheme of dethroning the Emperor. It was under these circumstances, that one of his suite asked leave to offer him his advice. "Under the Emperor," said he, "your highness is certain of being a great and respected noble; with the enemy, you are at best but a precarious king. It is unwise to risk certainty for uncertainty. The enemy will avail themselves of your personal influence, while the opportunity lasts; but you will ever be regarded with suspicion, and they will always be fearful lest you should treat them as you have done the Emperor. Return, then, to your allegiance, while there is yet time. — "And how is that to be done?" said Wallenstein, interrupting him: "You have 40,000 men-at-arms," rejoined he, (meaning ducats, which were stamped with the figure of an armed man,) "take them with you, and go straight to the Imperial Court; then declare that the steps you have hitherto taken were merely designed to test the fidelity of the Emperor's servants, and of distinguishing the loyal from the doubtful; and since most have shown a disposition to revolt, say you are come to warn his Imperial Majesty against those dangerous men. Thus you will make those appear as traitors, who are labouring to represent you as a false villain. At the Imperial Court, a man is sure to be welcome with 40,000 ducats, and Friedland will be again as he was at the first." — "The advice is good," said Wallenstein, after a pause, "but let the devil trust to it."

While the duke, in his retirement in Egra, was energetically pushing his negociations with the enemy, consulting the stars, and indulging in new hopes, the dagger which was to put an end to his existence was unsheathed almost under his very eyes. The imperial decree which proclaimed him an outlaw, had not failed of its effect; and an avenging Nemesis ordained that the ungrateful should fall beneath the blow of ingratitude. Among his officers, Wallenstein had particularly distinguished one Leslie[1], an Irishman, and had made his fortune. This was the man who now felt himself called on to execute the sentence against him, and to earn the price of blood. No sooner had he reached Egra, in the suite of the duke, than he disclosed to the commandant of the town, Colonel Buttler, and to Lieutenant-Colonel Gordon, two Protestant Scotchmen, the treasonable designs of the duke, which the latter had imprudently enough communicated to him during the journey. In these two individuals, he had found men capable of a determined resolution. They were now called on to choose between treason and duty, between their legitimate sovereign and a fugitive abandoned rebel; and though the latter was their common benefactor, the choice could not remain for a moment doubtful. They were solemnly pledged to the allegiance of the Emperor, and this duty required them to take the most rapid measures against the public enemy. The opportunity was favourable; his evil genius seemed to have delivered him into the hands of vengeance. But not to encroach on the province of justice, they resolved to deliver up their victim alive; and they parted with the bold resolve to take their general prisoner. This dark plot was buried in the deepest silence; and Wallenstein, far from suspecting his impending ruin, flattered himself that in the garrison of Egra he possessed his bravest and most faithful champions.

At this time, he became acquainted with the Imperial proclamations containing his sentence, and which had been published in all the camps. He now became aware of the full extent of the danger which encompassed him, the utter impossibility of retracing his steps, his fearfully forlorn condition, and the absolute necessity of at once trusting himself to the faith and honour of the Emperor's enemies. To Leslie he poured forth all the anguish of his wounded spirit, and the vehemence of his agitation extracted from him his last remaining secret. He disclosed to this officer his intention to deliver up Egra and Ellenbogen, the passes of the kingdom, to the Palatine of Birkenfeld, and at the same time, informed him of the near approach of Duke Bernard, of whose arrival he hoped to receive tidings that very night. These disclosures, which Leslie immediately communicated to the conspirators, made them change their original plan. The urgency of the danger admitted not of half measures. Egra might in a moment be in the enemy's hands, and a sudden revolution set their prisoner at liberty. To anticipate this mischance, they resolved to assassinate him and his associates the following night.

In order to execute this design with less noise, it was arranged that the fearful deed should be perpetrated at an entertainment which Colonel Buttler should give in the Castle of Egra. All the guests, except Wallenstein, made their appearance, who being in too great anxiety of mind to enjoy company excused himself. With regard to him, therefore, their plan must be again changed; but they resolved to

[1]Schiller is mistaken as to this point. Leslie was a Scotchman, and Buttler an Irishman and a papist. He died a general in the Emperor's service, and founded, at Prague, a convent of Irish Franciscans which still exists.

execute their design against the others. The three Colonels, Illo, Terzky, and William Kinsky, came in with careless confidence, and with them Captain Neumann, an officer of ability, whose advice Terzky sought in every intricate affair. Previous to their arrival, trusty soldiers of the garrison, to whom the plot had been communicated, were admitted into the Castle, all the avenues leading from it guarded, and six of Buttler's dragoons concealed in an apartment close to the banqueting-room, who, on a concerted signal, were to rush in and kill the traitors. Without suspecting the danger that hung over them, the guests gaily abandoned themselves to the pleasures of the table, and Wallenstein's health was drunk in full bumpers, not as a servant of the Emperor, but as a sovereign prince. The wine opened their hearts, and Illo, with exultation, boasted that in three days an army would arrive, such as Wallenstein had never before been at the head of. "Yes," cried Neumann, "and then he hopes to bathe his hands in Austrian blood." During this conversation, the dessert was brought in, and Leslie gave the concerted signal to raise the drawbridges, while he himself received the keys of the gates. In an instant, the hall was filled with armed men, who, with the unexpected greeting of "Long live Ferdinand!" placed themselves behind the chairs of the marked guests. Surprised, and with a presentiment of their fate, they sprang from the table. Kinsky and Terzky were killed upon the spot, and before they could put themselves upon their guard. Neumann, during the confusion in the hall, escaped into the court, where, however, he was instantly recognised and cut down. Illo alone had the presence of mind to defend himself. He placed his back against a window, from whence he poured the bitterest reproaches upon Gordon, and challenged him to fight him fairly and honourably. After a gallant resistance, in which he slew two of his assailants, he fell to the ground overpowered by numbers, and pierced with ten wounds. The deed was no sooner accomplished, than Leslie hastened into the town to prevent a tumult. The sentinels at the castle gate, seeing him running and out of breath, and believing he belonged to the rebels, fired their muskets after him, but without effect. The firing, however, aroused the town-guard, and all Leslie's presence of mind was requisite to allay the tumult. He hastily detailed to them all the circumstances of Wallenstein's conspiracy, the measures which had been already taken to counteract it, the fate of the four rebels, as well as that which awaited their chief. Finding the troops well disposed, he exacted from them a new oath of fidelity to the Emperor, and to live and die for the good cause. A hundred of Buttler's dragoons were sent from the Castle into the town to patrol the streets, to overawe the partisans of the Duke, and to prevent tumult. All the gates of Egra were at the same time seized, and every avenue to Wallenstein's residence, which adjoined the market-place, guarded by a numerous and trusty body of troops, sufficient to prevent either his escape or his receiving any assistance from without.

But before they proceeded finally to execute the deed, a long conference was held among the conspirators in the Castle, whether they should kill him, or content themselves with making him prisoner. Besprinkled as they were with the blood, and deliberating almost over the very corpses of his murdered associates, even these furious men yet shuddered at the horror of taking away so illustrious a life. They saw before their mind's eye him their leader in battle, in the days of his good fortune, surrounded by his victorious army, clothed with all the pomp of military greatness, and long-accustomed awe again seized their minds. But this transitory emotion was soon effaced by the thought of the immediate danger. They remembered the hints which Neumann and Illo had thrown out at table, the near approach of a formidable army of Swedes and Saxons, and they clearly saw that the death of the traitor was their only chance of safety. They adhered, therefore, to their first resolution, and Captain Deveroux, an Irishman, who had already been retained for the murderous purpose, received decisive orders to act.

While these three officers were thus deciding upon his fate in the castle of Egra, Wallenstein was occupied in reading the stars with Seni. "The danger is not yet over," said the astrologer with prophetic spirit. "*It is*," replied the Duke, who would give the law even to heaven. "But," he continued with equally prophetic spirit, "that thou friend Seni thyself shalt soon be thrown into prison, that also is written in the stars." The astrologer had taken his leave, and Wallenstein had retired to bed, when Captain Deveroux appeared before his residence with six halberdiers, and was immediately admitted by the guard, who were accustomed to see him visit the general at all hours. A page who met him upon the stairs, and attempted to raise an alarm, was run through the body with a pike. In the antichamber, the assassins met a servant, who had just come out of the sleeping-room of his master, and had taken with him the key. Putting his finger upon his mouth, the terrified domestic made a sign to them to make no noise, as the Duke was asleep. "Friend," cried Deveroux, "it is time to awake him;" and with these words he rushed against the door, which was also bolted from within, and burst it open.

Wallenstein had been roused from his first sleep, by the report of a musket which had accidentally gone off, and had sprung to the window to call the guard. At the same moment, he heard, from the adjoining building, the shrieks of the Countesses Terzky and Kinsky, who had just learnt the violent fate of their husbands. Ere he had time to reflect on these terrible events, Deveroux, with the other murderers, was in his chamber. The Duke was in his shirt, as he had leaped out of bed, and leaning on a table near the window. "Art thou the villain," cried Deveroux to him, "who intends to deliver up the Emperor's troops to the enemy, and to tear the crown from the head of his Majesty? Now thou must die!" He paused for a few moments, as if expecting an answer; but scorn and astonishment kept Wallenstein silent. Throwing his arms wide open, he received in his breast, the deadly blow of the halberds, and without uttering a groan, fell weltering in his blood.

The next day, an express arrived from the Duke of Lauenburg, announcing his approach. The messenger was secured, and another in Wallenstein's livery despatched to the Duke, to decoy him into Egra. The stratagem succeeded, and Francis Albert fell into the hands of the enemy. Duke Bernard of Weimar, who was on his march towards Egra, was nearly sharing the same fate. Fortunately, he heard of Wallenstein's death in time to save himself by a retreat. Ferdinand shed a tear over the fate of his general, and ordered three thousand masses to be said for his soul at Vienna; but, at the same time, he did not forget to reward his assassins with gold chains, chamberlains' keys, dignities, and estates.

Thus did Wallenstein, at the age of fifty, terminate his active and extraordinary life. To ambition, he owed both his greatness and his ruin; with all his failings, he possessed great and admirable qualities, and had he kept himself within due bounds, he would have lived and died without an equal. The virtues of the ruler and of the hero, prudence, justice, firmness, and courage, are strikingly prominent features in his character; but he wanted the gentler virtues of the man, which adorn the hero, and make the ruler beloved. Terror was the talisman with which he worked; extreme in his punishments as in his rewards, he knew how to keep alive the zeal of his followers, while no general of ancient or modern times could boast of being obeyed with equal alacrity. Submission to his will was more prized by him than bravery; for, if the soldiers work by the latter, it is on the former that the general depends. He continually kept up the obedience of his troops by capricious orders, and profusely rewarded the readiness to obey even in trifles; because he looked rather to the act itself, than its object. He once issued a decree, with the penalty of death on disobedience, that none but red sashes should be worn in the army. A captain of horse no sooner heard the order, than pulling off his gold-embroidered sash, he trampled it under foot; Wallenstein, on being informed of the circumstance, promoted him on the spot to the rank of Colonel. His comprehensive glance was always directed to the whole, and in all his apparent caprice, he steadily kept in view some general scope or bearing. The robberies committed by the soldiers in a friendly country, had led to the severest orders against marauders; and all who should be caught thieving, were threatened with the halter. Wallenstein himself having met a straggler in the open country upon the field, commanded him to be seized without trial, as a transgressor of the law, and in his usual voice of thunder, exclaimed, "Hang the fellow," against which no opposition ever availed. The soldier pleaded and proved his innocence, but the irrevocable sentence had gone forth. "Hang then innocent," cried the inexorable Wallenstein, "the guilty will have then more reason to tremble." Preparations were already making to execute the sentence, when the soldier, who gave himself up for lost, formed the desperate resolution of not dying without revenge. He fell furiously upon his judge, but was overpowered by numbers, and disarmed before he could fulfil his design. "Now let him go," said the Duke, "it will excite sufficient terror."

His munificence was supported by an immense income, which was estimated at three millions of florins yearly, without reckoning the enormous sums which he raised under the name of contributions. His liberality and clearness of understanding, raised him above the religious prejudices of his age; and the Jesuits never forgave him for having seen through their system, and for regarding the pope as nothing more than a bishop of Rome.

But as no one ever yet came to a fortunate end who quarrelled with the Church, Wallenstein also must augment the number of its victims. Through the intrigues of monks, he lost at Ratisbon the command of the army, and at Egra his life; by the same arts, perhaps, he lost what was of more consequence, his honourable name and good repute with posterity.
For in justice it must be admitted, that the pens which have traced the history of this extraordinary man are not untinged with partiality, and that the treachery of the duke, and his designs upon the throne of Bohemia, rest not so much upon proven facts, as upon probable conjecture. No documents have yet been brought to light, which disclose with historical certainty the secret motives of his conduct; and among all his public and well attested actions, there is, perhaps, not one which could not have had an

innocent end. Many of his most obnoxious measures proved nothing but the earnest wish he entertained for peace; most of the others are explained and justified by the well-founded distrust he entertained of the Emperor, and the excusable wish of maintaining his own importance. It is true, that his conduct towards the Elector of Bavaria looks too like an unworthy revenge, and the dictates of an implacable spirit; but still, none of his actions perhaps warrant us in holding his treason to be proved. If necessity and despair at last forced him to deserve the sentence which had been pronounced against him while innocent, still this, if true, will not justify that sentence. Thus Wallenstein fell, not because he was a rebel, but he became a rebel because he fell. Unfortunate in life that he made a victorious party his enemy, and still more unfortunate in death, that the same party survived him and wrote his history.

Book V.

Wallenstein's death rendered necessary the appointment of a new generalissimo; and the Emperor yielded at last to the advice of the Spaniards, to raise his son Ferdinand, King of Hungary, to that dignity. Under him, Count Gallas commanded, who performed the functions of commander-in-chief, while the prince brought to this post nothing but his name and dignity. A considerable force was soon assembled under Ferdinand; the Duke of Lorraine brought up a considerable body of auxiliaries in person, and the Cardinal Infante joined him from Italy with 10,000 men. In order to drive the enemy from the Danube, the new general undertook the enterprise in which his predecessor had failed, the siege of Ratisbon. In vain did Duke Bernard of Weimar penetrate into the interior of Bavaria, with a view to draw the enemy from the town; Ferdinand continued to press the siege with vigour, and the city, after a most obstinate resistance, was obliged to open its gates to him. Donauwerth soon shared the same fate, and Nordlingen in Swabia was now invested. The loss of so many of the imperial cities was severely felt by the Swedish party; as the friendship of these towns had so largely contributed to the success of their arms, indifference to their fate would have been inexcusable. It would have been an indelible disgrace, had they deserted their confederates in their need, and abandoned them to the revenge of an implacable conqueror. Moved by these considerations, the Swedish army, under the command of Horn, and Bernard of Weimar, advanced upon Nordlingen, determined to relieve it even at the expense of a battle.

The undertaking was a dangerous one, for in numbers the enemy was greatly superior to that of the Swedes. There was also a further reason for avoiding a battle at present; the enemy's force was likely soon to divide, the Italian troops being destined for the Netherlands. In the mean time, such a position might be taken up, as to cover Nordlingen, and cut off their supplies. All these grounds were strongly urged by Gustavus Horn, in the Swedish council of war; but his remonstrances were disregarded by men who, intoxicated by a long career of success, mistook the suggestions of prudence for the voice of timidity. Overborne by the superior influence of Duke Bernard, Gustavus Horn was compelled to risk a contest, whose unfavourable issue, a dark foreboding seemed already to announce. The fate of the battle depended upon the possession of a height which commanded the imperial camp. An attempt to occupy it during the night failed, as the tedious transport of the artillery through woods and hollow ways delayed the arrival of the troops. When the Swedes arrived about midnight, they found the heights in possession of the enemy, strongly entrenched. They waited, therefore, for daybreak, to carry them by storm. Their impetuous courage surmounted every obstacle; the entrenchments, which were in the form of a crescent, were successfully scaled by each of the two brigades appointed to the service; but as they entered at the same moment from opposite sides, they met and threw each other into confusion. At this unfortunate moment, a barrel of powder blew up, and created the greatest disorder among the Swedes. The imperial cavalry charged upon their broken ranks, and the flight became universal. No persuasion on the part of their general could induce the fugitives to renew the assault.

He resolved, therefore, in order to carry this important post, to lead fresh troops to the attack. But in the interim, some Spanish regiments had marched in, and every attempt to gain it was repulsed by their heroic intrepidity. One of the duke's own regiments advanced seven times, and was as often driven back. The disadvantage of not occupying this post in time, was quickly and sensibly felt. The fire of the enemy's artillery from the heights, caused such slaughter in the adjacent wing of the Swedes, that Horn, who commanded there, was forced to give orders to retire. Instead of being able to cover the retreat of his colleague, and to check the pursuit of the enemy, Duke Bernard, overpowered by numbers, was himself driven into the plain, where his routed cavalry spread confusion among Horn's brigade, and rendered the defeat complete. Almost the entire infantry were killed or taken prisoners. More than 12,000 men remained dead upon the field of battle; 80 field pieces, about 4,000 waggons, and 300 standards and colours fell into the hands of the Imperialists. Horn himself, with three other generals, were taken prisoners. Duke Bernard with difficulty saved a feeble remnant of his army, which joined him at Frankfort.

The defeat at Nordlingen, cost the Swedish Chancellor the second sleepless night he had passed in Germany.[1] The consequences of this disaster were terrible. The Swedes had lost by it at once their superiority in the field, and with it the confidence of their confederates, which they had gained solely by their previous military success. A dangerous division threatened the Protestant Confederation with ruin. Consternation and terror seized upon the whole party; while the Papists arose with exulting triumph

[1]The first was occasioned by the death of Gustavus Adolphus.

from the deep humiliation into which they had sunk. Swabia and the adjacent circles first felt the consequences of the defeat of Nordlingen; and Wirtemberg, in particular, was overrun by the conquering army. All the members of the League of Heilbronn trembled at the prospect of the Emperor's revenge; those who could, fled to Strasburg, while the helpless free cities awaited their fate with alarm. A little more of moderation towards the conquered, would have quickly reduced all the weaker states under the Emperor's authority; but the severity which was practised, even against those who voluntarily surrendered, drove the rest to despair, and roused them to a vigorous resistance.

In this perplexity, all looked to Oxenstiern for counsel and assistance; Oxenstiern applied for both to the German States. Troops were wanted; money likewise, to raise new levies, and to pay to the old the arrears which the men were clamorously demanding. Oxenstiern addressed himself to the Elector of Saxony; but he shamefully abandoned the Swedish cause, to negociate for a separate peace with the Emperor at Pirna. He solicited aid from the Lower Saxon States; but they, long wearied of the Swedish pretensions and demands for money, now thought only of themselves; and George, Duke of Lunenburg, in place of flying to the assistance of Upper Germany, laid siege to Minden, with the intention of keeping possession of it for himself. Abandoned by his German allies, the chancellor exerted himself to obtain the assistance of foreign powers. England, Holland, and Venice were applied to for troops and money; and, driven to the last extremity, the chancellor reluctantly resolved to take the disagreeable step which he had so long avoided, and to throw himself under the protection of France.

The moment had at last arrived which Richelieu had long waited for with impatience. Nothing, he was aware, but the impossibility of saving themselves by any other means, could induce the Protestant States in Germany to support the pretensions of France upon Alsace. This extreme necessity had now arrived; the assistance of that power was indispensable, and she was resolved to be well paid for the active part which she was about to take in the German war. Full of lustre and dignity, it now came upon the political stage. Oxenstiern, who felt little reluctance in bestowing the rights and possessions of the empire, had already ceded the fortress of Philipsburg, and the other long coveted places. The Protestants of Upper Germany now, in their own names, sent a special embassy to Richelieu, requesting him to take Alsace, the fortress of Breyssach, which was still to be recovered from the enemy, and all the places upon the Upper Rhine, which were the keys of Germany, under the protection of France. What was implied by French protection had been seen in the conduct of France towards the bishoprics of Metz, Toul, and Verdun, which it had held for centuries against the rightful owners. Treves was already in the possession of French garrisons; Lorraine was in a manner conquered, as it might at any time be overrun by an army, and could not, alone, and with its own strength, withstand its formidable neighbour. France now entertained the hope of adding Alsace to its large and numerous possessions, and, — since a treaty was soon to be concluded with the Dutch for the partition of the Spanish Netherlands — the prospect of making the Rhine its natural boundary towards Germany. Thus shamefully were the rights of Germany sacrificed by the German States to this treacherous and grasping power, which, under the mask of a disinterested friendship, aimed only at its own aggrandizement; and while it boldly claimed the honourable title of a Protectress, was solely occupied with promoting its own schemes, and advancing its own interests amid the general confusion.

In return for these important cessions, France engaged to effect a diversion in favour of the Swedes, by commencing hostilities against the Spaniards; and if this should lead to an open breach with the Emperor, to maintain an army upon the German side of the Rhine, which was to act in conjunction with the Swedes and Germans against Austria. For a war with Spain, the Spaniards themselves soon afforded the desired pretext. Making an inroad from the Netherlands, upon the city of Treves, they cut in pieces the French garrison; and, in open violation of the law of nations, made prisoner the Elector, who had placed himself under the protection of France, and carried him into Flanders. When the Cardinal Infante, as Viceroy of the Spanish Netherlands, refused satisfaction for these injuries, and delayed to restore the prince to liberty, Richelieu, after the old custom, formally proclaimed war at Brussels by a herald, and the war was at once opened by three different armies in Milan, in the Valteline, and in Flanders. The French minister was less anxious to commence hostilities with the Emperor, which promised fewer advantages, and threatened greater difficulties. A fourth army, however, was detached across the Rhine into Germany, under the command of Cardinal Lavalette, which was to act in conjunction with Duke Bernard, against the Emperor, without a previous declaration of war.

A heavier blow for the Swedes, than even the defeat of Nordlingen, was the reconciliation of the Elector of Saxony with the Emperor. After many fruitless attempts both to bring about and to prevent it, it was at last effected in 1634, at Pirna, and, the following year, reduced into a formal treaty of peace, at Prague. The Elector of Saxony had always viewed with jealousy the pretensions of the Swedes in Germany; and his aversion to this foreign power, which now gave laws within the Empire, had grown with every fresh requisition that Oxenstiern was obliged to make upon the German states. This ill feeling was kept alive by the Spanish court, who laboured earnestly to effect a peace between Saxony and the Emperor. Wearied with the calamities of a long and destructive contest, which had selected Saxony above all others for its theatre; grieved by the miseries which both friend and foe inflicted upon his subjects, and seduced by the tempting propositions of the House of Austria, the Elector at last abandoned the common cause, and, caring little for the fate of his confederates, or the liberties of Germany, thought only of securing his own advantages, even at the expense of the whole body.

In fact, the misery of Germany had risen to such a height, that all clamorously vociferated for peace; and even the most disadvantageous pacification would have been hailed as a blessing from heaven. The plains, which formerly had been thronged with a happy and industrious population, where nature had lavished her choicest gifts, and plenty and prosperity had reigned, were now a wild and desolate wilderness. The fields, abandoned by the industrious husbandman, lay waste and uncultivated; and no sooner had the young crops given the promise of a smiling harvest, than a single march destroyed the labours of a year, and blasted the last hope of an afflicted peasantry. Burnt castles, wasted fields, villages in ashes, were to be seen extending far and wide on all sides, while the ruined peasantry had no resource left but to swell the horde of incendiaries, and fearfully to retaliate upon their fellows, who had hitherto been spared the miseries which they themselves had suffered. The only safeguard against oppression was to become an oppressor. The towns groaned under the licentiousness of undisciplined and plundering garrisons, who seized and wasted the property of the citizens, and, under the license of their position, committed the most remorseless devastation and cruelty. If the march of an army converted whole provinces into deserts, if others were impoverished by winter quarters, or exhausted by contributions, these still were but passing evils, and the industry of a year might efface the miseries of a few months. But there was no relief for those who had a garrison within their walls, or in the neighbourhood; even the change of fortune could not improve their unfortunate fate, since the victor trod in the steps of the vanquished, and friends were not more merciful than enemies. The neglected farms, the destruction of the crops, and the numerous armies which overran the exhausted country, were inevitably followed by scarcity and the high price of provisions, which in the later years was still further increased by a general failure in the crops. The crowding together of men in camps and quarters — want upon one side, and excess on the other, occasioned contagious distempers, which were more fatal than even the sword. In this long and general confusion, all the bonds of social life were broken up; — respect for the rights of their fellow men, the fear of the laws, purity of morals, honour, and religion, were laid aside, where might ruled supreme with iron sceptre. Under the shelter of anarchy and impunity, every vice flourished, and men became as wild as the country. No station was too dignified for outrage, no property too holy for rapine and avarice. In a word, the soldier reigned supreme; and that most brutal of despots often made his own officer feel his power. The leader of an army was a far more important person within any country where he appeared, than its lawful governor, who was frequently obliged to fly before him into his own castles for safety. Germany swarmed with these petty tyrants, and the country suffered equally from its enemies and its protectors. These wounds rankled the deeper, when the unhappy victims recollected that Germany was sacrificed to the ambition of foreign powers, who, for their own ends, prolonged the miseries of war. Germany bled under the scourge, to extend the conquests and influence of Sweden; and the torch of discord was kept alive within the Empire, that the services of Richelieu might be rendered indispensable in France.

But, in truth, it was not merely interested voices which opposed a peace; and if both Sweden and the German states were anxious, from corrupt motives, to prolong the conflict, they were seconded in their views by sound policy. After the defeat of Nordlingen, an equitable peace was not to be expected from the Emperor; and, this being the case, was it not too great a sacrifice, after seventeen years of war, with all its miseries, to abandon the contest, not only without advantage, but even with loss? What would avail so much bloodshed, if all was to remain as it had been; if their rights and pretensions were neither larger nor safer; if all that had been won with so much difficulty was to be surrendered for a peace at any cost? Would it not be better to endure, for two or three years more, the burdens they had borne so long, and to reap at last some recompense for twenty years of suffering? Neither was it doubtful, that peace might at last be obtained on favourable terms, if only the Swedes and the German Protestants should continue united in the cabinet and in the field, and pursued their common interests with a reciprocal sympathy and zeal. Their divisions alone, had rendered the enemy formidable, and protracted the acquisition of a lasting and general peace. And this great evil the Elector of Saxony had brought upon the Protestant cause by concluding a separate treaty with Austria.

He, indeed, had commenced his negociations with the Emperor, even before the battle of Nordlingen; and the unfortunate issue of that battle only accelerated their conclusion. By it, all his confidence in the Swedes was lost; and it was even doubted whether they would ever recover from the blow. The jealousies among their generals, the insubordination of the army, and the exhaustion of the Swedish kingdom, shut out any reasonable prospect of effective assistance on their part. The Elector hastened, therefore, to profit by the Emperor's magnanimity, who, even after the battle of Nordlingen, did not recall the conditions previously offered. While Oxenstiern, who had assembled the estates in Frankfort, made further demands upon them and him, the Emperor, on the contrary, made concessions; and therefore it required no long consideration to decide between them.

In the mean time, however, he was anxious to escape the charge of sacrificing the common cause and attending only to his own interests. All the German states, and even the Swedes, were publicly invited to become parties to this peace, although Saxony and the Emperor were the only powers who deliberated upon it, and who assumed the right to give law to Germany. By this self-appointed tribunal, the grievances of the Protestants were discussed, their rights and privileges decided, and even the fate of religions determined, without the presence of those who were most deeply interested in it. Between them, a general peace was resolved on, and it was to be enforced by an imperial army of execution, as a formal decree of the Empire. Whoever opposed it, was to be treated as a public enemy; and thus, contrary to their rights, the states were to be compelled to acknowledge a law, in the passing of which they had no share. Thus, even in form, the pacification at Prague was an arbitrary measure; nor was it less so in its contents. The Edict of Restitution had been the chief cause of dispute between the Elector and the Emperor; and therefore it was first considered in their deliberations. Without formally annulling it, it was determined by the treaty of Prague, that all the ecclesiastical domains holding immediately of the Empire, and, among the mediate ones, those which had been seized by the Protestants subsequently to the treaty at Passau, should, for forty years, remain in the same position as they had been in before the Edict of Restitution, but without any formal decision of the diet to that effect. Before the expiration of this term a commission, composed of equal numbers of both religions, should proceed to settle the matter peaceably and according to law; and if this commission should be unable to come to a decision, each party should remain in possession of the rights which it had exercised before the Edict of Restitution. This arrangement, therefore, far from removing the grounds of dissension, only suspended the dispute for a time; and this article of the treaty of Prague only covered the embers of a future war.

The archbishopric of Magdeburg remained in possession of Prince Augustus of Saxony, and Halberstadt in that of the Archduke Leopold William. Four estates were taken from the territory of Magdeburg, and given to Saxony, for which the Administrator of Magdeburg, Christian William of Brandenburg, was otherwise to be indemnified. The Dukes of Mecklenburg, upon acceding to this treaty, were to be acknowledged as rightful possessors of their territories, in which the magnanimity of Gustavus Adolphus had long ago reinstated them. Donauwerth recovered its liberties. The important claims of the heirs of the Palatine, however important it might be for the Protestant cause not to lose this electorate vote in the diet, were passed over in consequence of the animosity subsisting between the Lutherans and the Calvinists. All the conquests which, in the course of the war, had been made by the German states, or by the League and the Emperor, were to be mutually restored; all which had been appropriated by the foreign powers of France and Sweden, was to be forcibly wrested from them by the united powers. The troops of the contracting parties were to be formed into one imperial army, which, supported and paid by the Empire, was, by force of arms, to carry into execution the covenants of the treaty.

As the peace of Prague was intended to serve as a general law of the Empire, those points, which did not immediately affect the latter, formed the subject of a separate treaty. By it, Lusatia was ceded to the Elector of Saxony as a fief of Bohemia, and special articles guaranteed the freedom of religion of this country and of Silesia.

All the Protestant states were invited to accede to the treaty of Prague, and on that condition were to benefit by the amnesty. The princes of Wurtemberg and Baden, whose territories the Emperor was already in possession of, and which he was not disposed to restore unconditionally; and such vassals of Austria as had borne arms against their sovereign; and those states which, under the direction of Oxenstiern, composed the council of the Upper German Circle, were excluded from the treaty, — not so much with the view of continuing the war against them, as of compelling them to purchase peace at a dearer rate. Their territories were to be retained in pledge, till every thing should be restored to its former footing. Such was the treaty of Prague. Equal justice, however, towards all, might perhaps have restored confidence between the head of the Empire and its members — between the Protestants and the Roman Catholics — between the Reformed and the Lutheran party; and the Swedes, abandoned by all their allies, would in all probability have been driven from Germany with disgrace. But this inequality strengthened, in those who were more severely treated, the spirit of mistrust and opposition, and made it an easier task for the Swedes to keep alive the flame of war, and to maintain a party in Germany.

The peace of Prague, as might have been expected, was received with very various feelings throughout Germany. The attempt to conciliate both parties, had rendered it obnoxious to both. The Protestants complained of the restraints imposed upon them; the Roman Catholics thought that these hated sectaries had been favoured at the expense of the true church. In the opinion of the latter, the church had been deprived of its inalienable rights, by the concession to the Protestants of forty years' undisturbed possession of the ecclesiastical benefices; while the former murmured that the interests of the Protestant church had been betrayed, because toleration had not been granted to their co-religionists in the Austrian dominions. But no one was so bitterly reproached as the Elector of Saxony, who was publicly denounced as a deserter, a traitor to religion and the liberties of the Empire, and a confederate of the Emperor.

In the mean time, he consoled himself with the triumph of seeing most of the Protestant states compelled by necessity to embrace this peace. The Elector of Brandenburg, Duke William of Weimar, the princes of Anhalt, the dukes of Mecklenburg, the dukes of Brunswick Lunenburg, the Hanse towns, and most of the imperial cities, acceded to it. The Landgrave William of Hesse long wavered, or affected to do so, in order to gain time, and to regulate his measures by the course of events. He had conquered several fertile provinces of Westphalia, and derived from them principally the means of continuing the war; these, by the terms of the treaty, he was bound to restore. Bernard, Duke of Weimar, whose states, as yet, existed only on paper, as a belligerent power was not affected by the treaty, but as a general was so materially; and, in either view, he must equally be disposed to reject it. His whole riches consisted in his bravery, his possessions in his sword. War alone gave him greatness and importance, and war alone could realize the projects which his ambition suggested.

But of all who declaimed against the treaty of Prague, none were so loud in their clamours as the Swedes, and none had so much reason for their opposition. Invited to Germany by the Germans themselves, the champions of the Protestant Church, and the freedom of the States, which they had defended with so much bloodshed, and with the sacred life of their king, they now saw themselves suddenly and shamefully abandoned, disappointed in all their hopes, without reward and without gratitude driven from the empire for which they had toiled and bled, and exposed to the ridicule of the enemy by the very princes who owed every thing to them. No satisfaction, no indemnification for the expenses which they had incurred, no equivalent for the conquests which they were to leave behind them, was provided by the treaty of Prague. They were to be dismissed poorer than they came, or, if they resisted, to be expelled by the very powers who had invited them. The Elector of Saxony at last spoke of a pecuniary indemnification, and mentioned the small sum of two millions five hundred thousand florins; but the Swedes had already expended considerably more, and this disgraceful equivalent in money was both contrary to their true interests, and injurious to their pride. "The Electors of Bavaria and Saxony," replied Oxenstiern, "have been paid for their services, which, as vassals, they were bound to render the Emperor, with the possession of important provinces; and shall we, who have sacrificed our king for Germany, be dismissed with the miserable sum of 2,500,000 florins?" The disappointment of their expectations was the more severe, because the Swedes had calculated upon being recompensed with the Duchy of Pomerania, the present possessor of which was old and without heirs. But the succession of this territory was confirmed by the treaty of Prague to the Elector of Brandenburg; and all the neighbouring powers declared against allowing the Swedes to obtain a footing within the empire.

Never, in the whole course of the war, had the prospects of the Swedes looked more gloomy, than in the year 1635, immediately after the conclusion of the treaty of Prague. Many of their allies, particularly among the free cities, abandoned them to benefit by the peace; others were compelled to accede to it by the victorious arms of the Emperor. Augsburg, subdued by famine, surrendered under the severest conditions; Wurtzburg and Coburg were lost to the Austrians. The League of Heilbronn was formally dissolved. Nearly the whole of Upper Germany, the chief seat of the Swedish power, was reduced under the Emperor. Saxony, on the strength of the treaty of Prague, demanded the evacuation of Thuringia, Halberstadt, and Magdeburg. Philipsburg, the military depot of France, was surprised by the Austrians, with all the stores it contained; and this severe loss checked the activity of France. To complete the embarrassments of Sweden, the truce with Poland was drawing to a close. To support a war at the same time with Poland and in Germany, was far beyond the power of Sweden; and all that remained was to choose between them. Pride and ambition declared in favour of continuing the German war, at whatever sacrifice on the side of Poland. An army, however, was necessary to command the respect of Poland, and to give weight to Sweden in any negotiations for a truce or a peace.

The mind of Oxenstiern, firm, and inexhaustible in expedients, set itself manfully to meet these calamities, which all combined to overwhelm Sweden; and his shrewd understanding taught him how to turn even misfortunes to his advantage. The defection of so many German cities of the empire deprived him, it is true, of a great part of his former allies, but at the same time it freed him from the necessity of paying any regard to their interests. The more the number of his enemies increased, the more provinces and magazines were opened to his troops. The gross ingratitude of the States, and the haughty contempt with which the Emperor behaved, (who did not even condescend to treat directly with him about a peace,) excited in him the courage of despair, and a noble determination to maintain the struggle to the last. The continuance of war, however unfortunate it might prove, could not render the situation of Sweden worse than it now was; and if Germany was to be evacuated, it was at least better and nobler to do so sword in hand, and to yield to force rather than to fear.

In the extremity in which the Swedes were now placed by the desertion of their allies, they addressed themselves to France, who met them with the greatest encouragement. The interests of the two crowns were closely united, and France would have injured herself by allowing the Swedish power in Germany to decline. The helpless situation of the Swedes, was rather an additional motive with France to cement more closely their alliance, and to take a more active part in the German war. Since the alliance with Sweden, at Beerwald, in 1632, France had maintained the war against the Emperor, by the arms of Gustavus Adolphus, without any open or formal breach, by furnishing subsidies and increasing the number of his enemies. But alarmed at the unexpected rapidity and success of the Swedish arms, France, in anxiety to restore the balance of power, which was disturbed by the preponderance of the Swedes, seemed, for a time, to have lost sight of her original designs. She endeavoured to protect the Roman Catholic princes of the empire against the Swedish conqueror, by the treaties of neutrality, and when this plan failed, she even meditated herself to declare war against him. But no sooner had the death of Gustavus Adolphus, and the desperate situation of the Swedish affairs, dispelled this apprehension, than she returned with fresh zeal to her first design, and readily afforded in this misfortune the aid which in the hour of success she had refused. Freed from the checks which the ambition and vigilance of Gustavus Adolphus placed upon her plans of aggrandizement, France availed herself of the favourable opportunity afforded by the defeat of Nordlingen, to obtain the entire direction of the war, and to prescribe laws to those who sued for her powerful protection. The moment seemed to smile upon her boldest plans, and those which had formerly seemed chimerical, now appeared to be justified by circumstances. She now turned her whole attention to the war in Germany; and, as soon as she had secured her own private ends by a treaty with the Germans, she suddenly entered the political arena as an active and a commanding power. While the other belligerent states had been exhausting themselves in a tedious contest, France had been reserving her strength, and maintained the contest by money alone; but now, when the state of things called for more active measures, she seized the sword, and astonished Europe by the boldness and magnitude of her undertakings. At the same moment, she fitted out two fleets, and sent six different armies into the field, while she subsidized a foreign crown and several of the German princes. Animated by this powerful co-operation, the Swedes and Germans awoke from the consternation, and hoped, sword in hand, to obtain a more honourable peace than that of Prague. Abandoned by their confederates, who had been reconciled to the Emperor, they formed a still closer alliance with France, which increased her support with their growing necessities, at the same time taking a more active, although secret share in the German war, until at last, she threw off the mask altogether, and in her own name made an unequivocal declaration of war against the Emperor.

To leave Sweden at full liberty to act against Austria, France commenced her operations by liberating it from all fear of a Polish war. By means of the Count d'Avaux, its minister, an agreement was concluded between the two powers at Stummsdorf in Prussia, by which the truce was prolonged for twenty-six years, though not without a great sacrifice on the part of the Swedes, who ceded by a single stroke of the pen almost the whole of Polish Prussia, the dear-bought conquest of Gustavus Adolphus. The treaty of Beerwald was, with certain modifications, which circumstances rendered necessary, renewed at different times at Compiegne, and afterwards at Wismar and Hamburg. France had already come to a rupture with Spain, in May, 1635, and the vigorous attack which it made upon that power, deprived the Emperor of his most valuable auxiliaries from the Netherlands. By supporting the Landgrave William of Cassel, and Duke Bernard of Weimar, the Swedes were enabled to act with more vigour upon the Elbe and the Danube, and a diversion upon the Rhine compelled the Emperor to divide his force.

The war was now prosecuted with increasing activity. By the treaty of Prague, the Emperor had lessened the number of his adversaries within the Empire; though, at the same time, the zeal and activity of his foreign enemies had been augmented by it. In Germany, his influence was almost unlimited, for, with the exception of a few states, he had rendered himself absolute master of the German body and its resources, and was again enabled to act in the character of emperor and sovereign. The first fruit of his power was the elevation of his son, Ferdinand III., to the dignity of King of the Romans, to which he was elected by a decided majority of votes, notwithstanding the opposition of Treves, and of the heirs of the Elector Palatine. But, on the other hand, he had exasperated the Swedes to desperation, had armed the power of France against him, and drawn its troops into the heart of the kingdom. France and Sweden, with their German allies, formed, from this moment, one firm and compactly united power; the Emperor, with the German states which adhered to him, were equally firm and united. The Swedes, who no longer fought for Germany, but for their own lives, showed no more indulgence; relieved from the necessity of consulting their German allies, or accounting to them for the plans which they adopted, they acted with more precipitation, rapidity, and boldness. Battles, though less decisive, became more obstinate and bloody; greater achievements, both in bravery and military skill, were performed; but they were but insulated efforts; and being neither dictated by any consistent plan, nor improved by any commanding spirit, had comparatively little influence upon the course of the war.

Saxony had bound herself, by the treaty of Prague, to expel the Swedes from Germany. From this moment, the banners of the Saxons and Imperialists were united: the former confederates were converted into implacable enemies. The archbishopric of Magdeburg which, by the treaty, was ceded to the prince of Saxony, was still held by the Swedes, and every attempt to acquire it by negociation had proved ineffectual. Hostilities commenced, by the Elector of Saxony recalling all his subjects from the army of Banner, which was encamped upon the Elbe. The officers, long irritated by the accumulation of their arrears, obeyed the summons, and evacuated one quarter after another. As the Saxons, at the same time, made a movement towards Mecklenburg, to take Doemitz, and to drive the Swedes from Pomerania and the Baltic, Banner suddenly marched thither, relieved Doemitz, and totally defeated the Saxon General Baudissin, with 7000 men, of whom 1000 were slain, and about the same number taken prisoners. Reinforced by the troops and artillery, which had hitherto been employed in Polish Prussia, but which the treaty of Stummsdorf rendered unnecessary, this brave and impetuous general made, the following year (1636), a sudden inroad into the Electorate of Saxony, where he gratified his inveterate hatred of the Saxons by the most destructive ravages. Irritated by the memory of old grievances which, during their common campaigns, he and the Swedes had suffered from the haughtiness of the Saxons, and now exasperated to the utmost by the late defection of the Elector, they wreaked upon the unfortunate inhabitants all their rancour. Against Austria and Bavaria, the Swedish soldier had fought from a sense, as it were, of duty; but against the Saxons, they contended with all the energy of private animosity and personal revenge, detesting them as deserters and traitors; for the hatred of former friends is of all the most fierce and irreconcileable. The powerful diversion made by the Duke of Weimar, and the Landgrave of Hesse, upon the Rhine and in Westphalia, prevented the Emperor from affording the necessary assistance to Saxony, and left the whole Electorate exposed to the destructive ravages of Banner's army.

At length, the Elector, having formed a junction with the Imperial General Hatzfeld, advanced against Magdeburg, which Banner in vain hastened to relieve. The united army of the Imperialists and the Saxons now spread itself over Brandenburg, wrested several places from the Swedes, and almost drove them to the Baltic. But, contrary to all expectation, Banner, who had been given up as lost, attacked the allies, on the 24th of September, 1636, at Wittstock, where a bloody battle took place. The onset was terrific; and the whole force of the enemy was directed against the right wing of the Swedes, which was led by Banner in person. The contest was long maintained with equal animosity and obstinacy on both sides. There was not a squadron among the Swedes, which did not return ten times to the charge, to be as often repulsed; when at last, Banner was obliged to retire before the superior numbers of the enemy.

His left wing sustained the combat until night, and the second line of the Swedes, which had not as yet been engaged, was prepared to renew it the next morning. But the Elector did not wait for a second attack. His army was exhausted by the efforts of the preceding day; and, as the drivers had fled with the horses, his artillery was unserviceable. He accordingly retreated in the night, with Count Hatzfeld, and relinquished the ground to the Swedes. About 5000 of the allies fell upon the field, exclusive of those who were killed in the pursuit, or who fell into the hands of the exasperated peasantry. One hundred and fifty standards and colours, twenty-three pieces of cannon, the whole baggage and silver plate of the Elector, were captured, and more than 2000 men taken prisoners. This brilliant victory, achieved over an enemy far superior in numbers, and in a very advantageous position, restored the Swedes at once to their former reputation; their enemies were discouraged, and their friends inspired with new hopes. Banner instantly followed up this decisive success, and hastily crossing the Elbe, drove the Imperialists before him, through Thuringia and Hesse, into Westphalia. He then returned, and took up his winter quarters in Saxony.

But, without the material aid furnished by the diversion upon the Rhine, and the activity there of Duke Bernard and the French, these important successes would have been unattainable. Duke Bernard, after the defeat of Nordlingen, reorganized his broken army at Wetterau; but, abandoned by the confederates of the League of Heilbronn, which had been dissolved by the peace of Prague, and receiving little support from the Swedes, he found himself unable to maintain an army, or to perform any enterprise of importance. The defeat at Nordlingen had terminated all his hopes on the Duchy of Franconia, while the weakness of the Swedes, destroyed the chance of retrieving his fortunes through their assistance. Tired, too, of the constraint imposed upon him by the imperious chancellor, he turned his attention to France, who could easily supply him with money, the only aid which he required, and France readily acceded to his proposals. Richelieu desired nothing so much as to diminish the influence of the Swedes in the German war, and to obtain the direction of it for himself. To secure this end, nothing appeared more effectual than to detach from the Swedes their bravest general, to win him to the interests of France, and to secure for the execution of its projects the services of his arm. From a prince like Bernard, who could not maintain himself without foreign support, France had nothing to fear, since no success, however brilliant, could render him independent of that crown. Bernard himself came into France, and in October, 1635, concluded a treaty at St. Germaine en Laye, not as a Swedish general, but in his own name, by which it was stipulated that he should receive for himself a yearly pension of one million five hundred thousand livres, and four millions for the support of his army, which he was to command under the orders of the French king. To inflame his zeal, and to accelerate the conquest of Alsace, France did not hesitate, by a secret article, to promise him that province for his services; a promise which Richelieu had little intention of performing, and which the duke also estimated at its real worth. But Bernard confided in his good fortune, and in his arms, and met artifice with dissimulation. If he could once succeed in wresting Alsace from the enemy, he did not despair of being able, in case of need, to maintain it also against a friend. He now raised an army at the expense of France, which he commanded nominally under the orders of that power, but in reality without any limitation whatever, and without having wholly abandoned his engagements with Sweden. He began his operations upon the Rhine, where another French army, under Cardinal Lavalette, had already, in 1635, commenced hostilities against the Emperor.

Against this force, the main body of the Imperialists, after the great victory of Nordlingen, and the reduction of Swabia and Franconia had advanced under the command of Gallas, had driven them as far as Metz, cleared the Rhine, and took from the Swedes the towns of Metz and Frankenthal, of which they were in possession. But frustrated by the vigorous resistance of the French, in his main object, of taking up his winter quarters in France, he led back his exhausted troops into Alsace and Swabia. At the opening of the next campaign, he passed the Rhine at Breysach, and prepared to carry the war into the interior of France. He actually entered Burgundy, while the Spaniards from the Netherlands made progress in Picardy; and John De Werth, a formidable general of the League, and a celebrated partisan, pushed his march into Champagne, and spread consternation even to the gates of Paris. But an insignificant fortress in Franche Comte completely checked the Imperialists, and they were obliged, a second time, to abandon their enterprise.

The activity of Duke Bernard had hitherto been impeded by his dependence on a French general, more suited to the priestly robe, than to the baton of command; and although, in conjunction with him, he conquered Alsace Saverne, he found himself unable, in the years 1636 and 1637, to maintain his position upon the Rhine. The ill success of the French arms in the Netherlands had cheated the activity of operations in Alsace and Breisgau; but in 1638, the war in that quarter took a more brilliant turn.

Relieved from his former restraint, and with unlimited command of his troops, Duke Bernard, in the beginning of February, left his winter quarters in the bishopric of Basle, and unexpectedly appeared upon the Rhine, where, at this rude season of the year, an attack was little anticipated. The forest towns of Laufenburg, Waldshut, and Seckingen, were surprised, and Rhinefeldt besieged. The Duke of Savelli, the Imperial general who commanded in that quarter, hastened by forced marches to the relief of this important place, succeeded in raising the siege, and compelled the Duke of Weimar, with great loss to retire. But, contrary to all human expectation, he appeared on the third day after, (21st February, 1638,) before the Imperialists, in order of battle, and defeated them in a bloody engagement, in which the four Imperial generals, Savelli, John De Werth, Enkeford, and Sperreuter, with 2000 men, were taken prisoners. Two of these, De Werth and Enkeford, were afterwards sent by Richelieu's orders into France, in order to flatter the vanity of the French by the sight of such distinguished prisoners, and by the pomp of military trophies, to withdraw the attention of the populace from the public distress. The captured standards and colours were, with the same view, carried in solemn procession to the church of Notre Dame, thrice exhibited before the altar, and committed to sacred custody.

The taking of Rhinefeldt, Roeteln, and Fribourg, was the immediate consequence of the duke's victory. His army now increased by considerable recruits, and his projects expanded in proportion as fortune favoured him. The fortress of Breysach upon the Rhine was looked upon as holding the command of that river, and as the key of Alsace. No place in this quarter was of more importance to the Emperor, and upon none had more care been bestowed. To protect Breysach, was the principal destination of the Italian army, under the Duke of Feria; the strength of its works, and its natural defences, bade defiance to assault, while the Imperial generals who commanded in that quarter had orders to retain it at any cost. But the duke, trusting to his good fortune, resolved to attempt the siege. Its strength rendered it impregnable; it could, therefore, only be starved into a surrender; and this was facilitated by the carelessness of the commandant, who, expecting no attack, had been selling off his stores. As under these circumstances the town could not long hold out, it must be immediately relieved or victualled. Accordingly, the Imperial General Goetz rapidly advanced at the head of 12,000 men, accompanied by 3000 waggons loaded with provisions, which he intended to throw into the place. But he was attacked with such vigour by Duke Bernard at Witteweyer, that he lost his whole force, except 3000 men, together with the entire transport. A similar fate at Ochsenfeld, near Thann, overtook the Duke of Lorraine, who, with 5000 or 6000 men, advanced to relieve the fortress. After a third attempt of general Goetz for the relief of Breysach had proved ineffectual, the fortress, reduced to the greatest extremity by famine, surrendered, after a blockade of four months, on the 17th December 1638, to its equally persevering and humane conqueror.

The capture of Breysach opened a boundless field to the ambition of the Duke of Weimar, and the romance of his hopes was fast approaching to reality. Far from intending to surrender his conquests to France, he destined Breysach for himself, and revealed this intention, by exacting allegiance from the vanquished, in his own name, and not in that of any other power. Intoxicated by his past success, and excited by the boldest hopes, he believed that he should be able to maintain his conquests, even against France herself. At a time when everything depended upon bravery, when even personal strength was of importance, when troops and generals were of more value than territories, it was natural for a hero like Bernard to place confidence in his own powers, and, at the head of an excellent army, who under his command had proved invincible, to believe himself capable of accomplishing the boldest and largest designs. In order to secure himself one friend among the crowd of enemies whom he was about to provoke, he turned his eyes upon the Landgravine Amelia of Hesse, the widow of the lately deceased Landgrave William, a princess whose talents were equal to her courage, and who, along with her hand, would bestow valuable conquests, an extensive principality, and a well disciplined army. By the union of the conquests of Hesse, with his own upon the Rhine, and the junction of their forces, a power of some importance, and perhaps a third party, might be formed in Germany, which might decide the fate of the war. But a premature death put a period to these extensive schemes.

"Courage, Father Joseph, Breysach is ours!" whispered Richelieu in the ear of the Capuchin, who had long held himself in readiness to be despatched into that quarter; so delighted was he with this joyful intelligence. Already in imagination he held Alsace, Breisgau, and all the frontiers of Austria in that quarter, without regard to his promise to Duke Bernard. But the firm determination which the latter had unequivocally shown, to keep Breysach for himself, greatly embarrassed the cardinal, and no efforts were spared to retain the victorious Bernard in the interests of France. He was invited to court, to witness the honours by which his triumph was to be commemorated; but he perceived and shunned the seductive snare. The cardinal even went so far as to offer him the hand of his niece in marriage; but the proud German prince declined the offer, and refused to sully the blood of Saxony by a misalliance. He was now considered as a dangerous enemy, and treated as such. His subsidies were withdrawn; and the Governor of Breysach and his principal officers were bribed, at least upon the event of the duke's death, to take possession of his conquests, and to secure his troops. These intrigues were no secret to the duke, and the precautions he took in the conquered places, clearly bespoke the distrust of France. But this misunderstanding with the French court had the most prejudicial influence upon his future operations. The preparations he was obliged to make, in order to secure his conquests against an attack on the side of France, compelled him to divide his military strength, while the stoppage of his subsidies delayed his appearance in the field. It had been his intention to cross the Rhine, to support the Swedes, and to act against the Emperor and Bavaria on the banks of the Danube. He had already communicated his plan of operations to Banner, who was about to carry the war into the Austrian territories, and had promised to relieve him so, when a sudden death cut short his heroic career, in the 36th year of his age, at Neuburgh upon the Rhine (in July, 1639).

He died of a pestilential disorder, which, in the course of two days, had carried off nearly 400 men in his camp. The black spots which appeared upon his body, his own dying expressions, and the advantages which France was likely to reap from his sudden decease, gave rise to a suspicion that he had been removed by poison — a suspicion sufficiently refuted by the symptoms of his disorder. In him, the allies lost their greatest general after Gustavus Adolphus, France a formidable competitor for Alsace, and the Emperor his most dangerous enemy. Trained to the duties of a soldier and a general in the school of Gustavus Adolphus, he successfully imitated his eminent model, and wanted only a longer life to equal, if not to surpass it. With the bravery of the soldier, he united the calm and cool penetration of the general and the persevering fortitude of the man, with the daring resolution of youth; with the wild ardour of the warrior, the sober dignity of the prince, the moderation of the sage, and the conscientiousness of the man of honour. Discouraged by no misfortune, he quickly rose again in full vigour from the severest defeats; no obstacles could check his enterprise, no disappointments conquer his indomitable perseverance. His genius, perhaps, soared after unattainable objects; but the prudence of such men, is to be measured by a different standard from that of ordinary people. Capable of accomplishing more, he might venture to form more daring plans. Bernard affords, in modern history, a splendid example of those days of chivalry, when personal greatness had its full weight and influence, when individual bravery could conquer provinces, and the heroic exploits of a German knight raised him even to the Imperial throne.

The best part of the duke's possessions were his army, which, together with Alsace, he bequeathed to his brother William. But to this army, both France and Sweden thought that they had well-grounded claims; the latter, because it had been raised in name of that crown, and had done homage to it; the former, because it had been supported by its subsidies. The Electoral Prince of the Palatinate also negociated for its services, and attempted, first by his agents, and latterly in his own person, to win it over to his interests, with the view of employing it in the reconquest of his territories. Even the Emperor endeavoured to secure it, a circumstance the less surprising, when we reflect that at this time the justice of the cause was comparatively unimportant, and the extent of the recompense the main object to which the soldier looked; and when bravery, like every other commodity, was disposed of to the highest bidder. But France, richer and more determined, outbade all competitors: it bought over General Erlach, the commander of Breysach, and the other officers, who soon placed that fortress, with the whole army, in their hands.

The young Palatine, Prince Charles Louis, who had already made an unsuccessful campaign against the Emperor, saw his hopes again deceived. Although intending to do France so ill a service, as to compete with her for Bernard's army, he had the imprudence to travel through that kingdom. The cardinal, who dreaded the justice of the Palatine's cause, was glad to seize any opportunity to frustrate his views. He accordingly caused him to be seized at Moulin, in violation of the law of nations, and did not set him at liberty, until he learned that the army of the Duke of Weimar had been secured. France was now in possession of a numerous and well disciplined army in Germany, and from this moment began to make open war upon the Emperor.

But it was no longer against Ferdinand II. that its hostilities were to be conducted; for that prince had died in February, 1637, in the 59th year of his age. The war which his ambition had kindled, however, survived him. During a reign of eighteen years he had never once laid aside the sword, nor tasted the blessings of peace as long as his hand swayed the imperial sceptre. Endowed with the qualities of a good sovereign, adorned with many of those virtues which ensure the happiness of a people, and by nature gentle and humane, we see him, from erroneous ideas of the monarch's duty, become at once the instrument and the victim of the evil passions of others; his benevolent intentions frustrated, and the friend of justice converted into the oppressor of mankind, the enemy of peace, and the scourge of his people. Amiable in domestic life, and respectable as a sovereign, but in his policy ill advised, while he gained the love of his Roman Catholic subjects, he incurred the execration of the Protestants. History exhibits many and greater despots than Ferdinand II., yet he alone has had the unfortunate celebrity of kindling a thirty years' war; but to produce its lamentable consequences, his ambition must have been seconded by a kindred spirit of the age, a congenial state of previous circumstances, and existing seeds of discord. At a less turbulent period, the spark would have found no fuel; and the peacefulness of the age would have choked the voice of individual ambition; but now the flash fell upon a pile of accumulated combustibles, and Europe was in flames.

His son, Ferdinand III., who, a few months before his father's death, had been raised to the dignity of King of the Romans, inherited his throne, his principles, and the war which he had caused. But Ferdinand III. had been a closer witness of the sufferings of the people, and the devastation of the country, and felt more keenly and ardently the necessity of peace. Less influenced by the Jesuits and the Spaniards, and more moderate towards the religious views of others, he was more likely than his father to listen to the voice of reason. He did so, and ultimately restored to Europe the blessing of peace, but not till after a contest of eleven years waged with sword and pen; not till after he had experienced the impossibility of resistance, and necessity had laid upon him its stern laws.

Fortune favoured him at the commencement of his reign, and his arms were victorious against the Swedes. The latter, under the command of the victorious Banner, had, after their success at Wittstock, taken up their winter quarters in Saxony; and the campaign of 1637 opened with the siege of Leipzig. The vigorous resistance of the garrison, and the approach of the Electoral and Imperial armies, saved the town, and Banner, to prevent his communication with the Elbe being cut off, was compelled to retreat into Torgau. But the superior number of the Imperialists drove him even from that quarter; and, surrounded by the enemy, hemmed in by rivers, and suffering from famine, he had no course open to him but to attempt a highly dangerous retreat into Pomerania, of which, the boldness and successful issue border upon romance. The whole army crossed the Oder, at a ford near Furstenberg; and the soldiers, wading up to the neck in water, dragged the artillery across, when the horses refused to draw. Banner had expected to be joined by General Wrangel, on the farther side of the Oder in Pomerania; and, in conjunction with him, to be able to make head against the enemy. But Wrangel did not appear; and in his stead, he found an Imperial army posted at Landsberg, with a view to cut off the retreat of the Swedes. Banner now saw that he had fallen into a dangerous snare, from which escape appeared impossible. In his rear lay an exhausted country, the Imperialists, and the Oder on his left; the Oder, too, guarded by the Imperial General Bucheim, offered no retreat; in front, Landsberg, Custrin, the Warta, and a hostile army; and on the right, Poland, in which, notwithstanding the truce, little confidence could be placed. In these circumstances, his position seemed hopeless, and the Imperialists were already triumphing in the certainty of his fall. Banner, with just indignation, accused the French as the authors of this misfortune. They had neglected to make, according to their promise, a diversion upon the Rhine; and, by their inaction, allowed the Emperor to combine his whole force upon the Swedes. "When the day comes," cried the incensed General to the French Commissioner, who followed the camp, "that the Swedes and Germans join their arms against France, we shall cross the Rhine with less ceremony." But reproaches were now useless; what the emergency demanded was energy and resolution. In the hope of drawing the enemy by stratagem from the Oder, Banner pretended to march towards Poland, and despatched the greater part of his baggage in this direction, with his own wife, and those of the other officers. The Imperialists immediately broke up their camp, and hurried towards the Polish frontier to block up the route; Bucheim left his station, and the Oder was stripped of its defenders. On a sudden, and under cloud of night, Banner turned towards that river, and crossed it about a mile above Custrin, with his troops, baggage, and artillery, without bridges or vessels, as he had done before at Furstenberg. He reached Pomerania without loss, and prepared to share with Wrangel the defence of that province.

But the Imperialists, under the command of Gallas, entered that duchy at Ribses, and overran it by their superior strength. Usedom and Wolgast were taken by storm, Demmin capitulated, and the Swedes were driven far into Lower Pomerania. It was, too, more important for them at this moment than ever, to maintain a footing in that country, for Bogislaus XIV. had died that year, and Sweden must prepare to establish its title to Pomerania. To prevent the Elector of Brandenburg from making good the title to that duchy, which the treaty of Prague had given him, Sweden exerted her utmost energies, and supported its generals to the extent of her ability, both with troops and money. In other quarters of the kingdom, the affairs of the Swedes began to wear a more favourable aspect, and to recover from the humiliation into which they had been thrown by the inaction of France, and the desertion of their allies. For, after their hasty retreat into Pomerania, they had lost one place after another in Upper Saxony; the princes of Mecklenburg, closely pressed by the troops of the Emperor, began to lean to the side of Austria, and even George, Duke of Lunenburg, declared against them. Ehrenbreitstein was starved into a surrender by the Bavarian General de Werth, and the Austrians possessed themselves of all the works which had been thrown up on the Rhine. France had been the sufferer in the contest with Spain; and the event had by no means justified the pompous expectations which had accompanied the opening of the campaign. Every place which the Swedes had held in the interior of Germany was lost; and only the principal towns in Pomerania still remained in their hands. But a single campaign raised them from this state of humiliation; and the vigorous diversion, which the victorious Bernard had effected upon the Rhine, gave quite a new turn to affairs.

The misunderstandings between France and Sweden were now at last adjusted, and the old treaty between these powers confirmed at Hamburg, with fresh advantages for Sweden. In Hesse, the politic Landgravine Amelia had, with the approbation of the Estates, assumed the government after the death of her husband, and resolutely maintained her rights against the Emperor and the House of Darmstadt. Already zealously attached to the Swedish Protestant party, on religious grounds, she only awaited a favourable opportunity openly to declare herself. By artful delays, and by prolonging the negociations with the Emperor, she had succeeded in keeping him inactive, till she had concluded a secret compact with France, and the victories of Duke Bernard had given a favourable turn to the affairs of the Protestants. She now at once threw off the mask, and renewed her former alliance with the Swedish crown. The Electoral Prince of the Palatinate was also stimulated, by the success of Bernard, to try his fortune against the common enemy. Raising troops in Holland with English money, he formed a magazine at Meppen, and joined the Swedes in Westphalia. His magazine was, however, quickly lost; his army defeated near Flotha, by Count Hatzfeld; but his attempt served to occupy for some time the attention of the enemy, and thereby facilitated the operations of the Swedes in other quarters. Other friends began to appear, as fortune declared in their favour, and the circumstance, that the States of Lower Saxony embraced a neutrality, was of itself no inconsiderable advantage.

Under these advantages, and reinforced by 14,000 fresh troops from Sweden and Livonia. Banner opened, with the most favourable prospects, the campaign of 1638. The Imperialists who were in possession of Upper Pomerania and Mecklenburg, either abandoned their positions, or deserted in crowds to the Swedes, to avoid the horrors of famine, the most formidable enemy in this exhausted country. The whole country betwixt the Elbe and the Oder was so desolated by the past marchings and quarterings of the troops, that, in order to support his army on its march into Saxony and Bohemia, Banner was obliged to take a circuitous route from Lower Pomerania into Lower Saxony, and then into the Electorate of Saxony through the territory of Halberstadt. The impatience of the Lower Saxon States to get rid of such troublesome guests, procured him so plentiful a supply of provisions, that he was provided with bread in Magdeburg itself, where famine had even overcome the natural antipathy of men to human flesh. His approach spread consternation among the Saxons; but his views were directed not against this exhausted country, but against the hereditary dominions of the Emperor. The victories of Bernard encouraged him, while the prosperity of the Austrian provinces excited his hopes of booty. After defeating the Imperial General Salis, at Elsterberg, totally routing the Saxon army at Chemnitz, and taking Pirna, he penetrated with irresistible impetuosity into Bohemia, crossed the Elbe, threatened Prague, took Brandeis and Leutmeritz, defeated General Hofkirchen with ten regiments, and spread terror and devastation through that defenceless kingdom. Booty was his sole object, and whatever he could not carry off he destroyed. In order to remove more of the corn, the ears were cut from the stalks, and the latter burnt. Above a thousand castles, hamlets, and villages were laid in ashes; sometimes more than a hundred were seen burning in one night. From Bohemia he crossed into Silesia, and it was his intention to carry his ravages even into Moravia and Austria. But to prevent this, Count Hatzfeld was summoned from Westphalia, and Piccolomini from the Netherlands, to hasten with all speed to this quarter. The Archduke Leopold, brother to the Emperor, assumed the command, in order to repair the errors of his predecessor Gallas, and to raise the army from the low ebb to which it had fallen.

The result justified the change, and the campaign of 1640 appeared to take a most unfortunate turn for the Swedes. They were successively driven out of all their posts in Bohemia, and anxious only to secure their plunder, they precipitately crossed the heights of Meissen. But being followed into Saxony by the pursuing enemy, and defeated at Plauen, they were obliged to take refuge in Thuringia. Made masters of the field in a single summer, they were as rapidly dispossessed; but only to acquire it a second time, and to hurry from one extreme to another. The army of Banner, weakened and on the brink of destruction in its camp at Erfurt, suddenly recovered itself. The Duke of Lunenburg abandoned the treaty of Prague, and joined Banner with the very troops which, the year before, had fought against him. Hesse Cassel sent reinforcements, and the Duke of Longueville came to his support with the army of the late Duke Bernard. Once more numerically superior to the Imperialists, Banner offered them battle near Saalfeld; but their leader, Piccolomini, prudently declined an engagement, having chosen too strong a position to be forced. When the Bavarians at length separated from the Imperialists, and marched towards Franconia, Banner attempted an attack upon this divided corps, but the attempt was frustrated by the skill of the Bavarian General Von Mercy, and the near approach of the main body of the Imperialists. Both armies now moved into the exhausted territory of Hesse, where they formed intrenched camps near each other, till at last famine and the severity of the winter compelled them both to retire. Piccolomini chose the fertile banks of the Weser for his winter quarters; but being outflanked by Banner, he was obliged to give way to the Swedes, and to impose on the Franconian sees the burden of maintaining his army.

At this period, a diet was held in Ratisbon, where the complaints of the States were to be heard, measures taken for securing the repose of the Empire, and the question of peace or war finally settled. The presence of the Emperor, the majority of the Roman Catholic voices in the Electoral College, the great number of bishops, and the withdrawal of several of the Protestant votes, gave the Emperor a complete command of the deliberations of the assembly, and rendered this diet any thing but a fair representative of the opinions of the German Empire. The Protestants, with reason, considered it as a mere combination of Austria and its creatures against their party; and it seemed to them a laudable effort to interrupt its deliberations, and to dissolve the diet itself.

Banner undertook this bold enterprise. His military reputation had suffered by his last retreat from Bohemia, and it stood in need of some great exploit to restore its former lustre. Without communicating his designs to any one, in the depth of the winter of 1641, as soon as the roads and rivers were frozen, he broke up from his quarters in Lunenburg. Accompanied by Marshal Guebriant, who commanded the armies of France and Weimar, he took the route towards the Danube, through Thuringia and Vogtland, and appeared before Ratisbon, ere the Diet could be apprised of his approach. The consternation of the assembly was indescribable; and, in the first alarm, the deputies prepared for flight. The Emperor alone declared that he would not leave the town, and encouraged the rest by his example. Unfortunately for the Swedes, a thaw came on, which broke up the ice upon the Danube, so that it was no longer passable on foot, while no boats could cross it, on account of the quantities of ice which were swept down by the current. In order to perform something, and to humble the pride of the Emperor, Banner discourteously fired 500 cannon shots into the town, which, however, did little mischief. Baffled in his designs, he resolved to penetrate farther into Bavaria, and the defenceless province of Moravia, where a rich booty and comfortable quarters awaited his troops. Guebriant, however, began to fear that the purpose of the Swedes was to draw the army of Bernard away from the Rhine, and to cut off its communication with France, till it should be either entirely won over, or incapacitated from acting independently. He therefore separated from Banner to return to the Maine; and the latter was exposed to the whole force of the Imperialists, which had been secretly drawn together between Ratisbon and Ingoldstadt, and was on its march against him. It was now time to think of a rapid retreat, which, having to be effected in the face of an army superior in cavalry, and betwixt woods and rivers, through a country entirely hostile, appeared almost impracticable. He hastily retired towards the Forest, intending to penetrate through Bohemia into Saxony; but he was obliged to sacrifice three regiments at Neuburg. These with a truly Spartan courage, defended themselves for four days behind an old wall, and gained time for Banner to escape. He retreated by Egra to Annaberg; Piccolomini took a shorter route in pursuit, by Schlakenwald; and Banner succeeded, only by a single half hour, in clearing the Pass of Prisnitz, and saving his whole army from the Imperialists. At Zwickau he was again joined by Guebriant; and both generals directed their march towards Halberstadt, after in vain attempting to defend the Saal, and to prevent the passage of the Imperialists.

Banner, at length, terminated his career at Halberstadt, in May 1641, a victim to vexation and disappointment. He sustained with great renown, though with varying success, the reputation of the Swedish arms in Germany, and by a train of victories showed himself worthy of his great master in the art of war. He was fertile in expedients, which he planned with secrecy, and executed with boldness; cautious in the midst of dangers, greater in adversity than in prosperity, and never more formidable than when upon the brink of destruction. But the virtues of the hero were united with all the railings and vices which a military life creates, or at least fosters. As imperious in private life as he was at the head of his army, rude as his profession, and proud as a conqueror; he oppressed the German princes no less by his haughtiness, than their country by his contributions. He consoled himself for the toils of war in voluptuousness and the pleasures of the table, in which he indulged to excess, and was thus brought to an early grave. But though as much addicted to pleasure as Alexander or Mahomet the Second, he hurried from the arms of luxury into the hardest fatigues, and placed himself in all his vigour at the head of his army, at the very moment his soldiers were murmuring at his luxurious excesses. Nearly 80,000 men fell in the numerous battles which he fought, and about 600 hostile standards and colours, which he sent to Stockholm, were the trophies of his victories. The want of this great general was soon severely felt by the Swedes, who feared, with justice, that the loss would not readily be replaced. The spirit of rebellion and insubordination, which had been overawed by the imperious demeanour of this dreaded commander, awoke upon his death. The officers, with an alarming unanimity, demanded payment of their arrears; and none of the four generals who shared the command, possessed influence enough to satisfy these demands, or to silence the malcontents. All discipline was at an end, increasing want, and the imperial citations were daily diminishing the number of the army; the troops of France and Weimar showed little zeal; those of Lunenburg forsook the Swedish colours; the Princes also of the House of Brunswick, after the death of Duke George, had formed a separate treaty with the Emperor; and at last even those of Hesse quitted them, to seek better quarters in Westphalia. The enemy profited by these calamitous divisions; and although defeated with loss in two pitched battles, succeeded in making considerable progress in Lower Saxony.

At length appeared the new Swedish generalissimo, with fresh troops and money. This was Bernard Torstensohn, a pupil of Gustavus Adolphus, and his most successful imitator, who had been his page during the Polish war. Though a martyr to the gout, and confined to a litter, he surpassed all his opponents in activity; and his enterprises had wings, while his body was held by the most frightful of fetters. Under him, the scene of war was changed, and new maxims adopted, which necessity dictated, and the issue justified. All the countries in which the contest had hitherto raged were exhausted; while the House of Austria, safe in its more distant territories, felt not the miseries of the war under which the rest of Germany groaned. Torstensohn first furnished them with this bitter experience, glutted his Swedes on the fertile produce of Austria, and carried the torch of war to the very footsteps of the imperial throne.

In Silesia, the enemy had gained considerable advantages over the Swedish general Stalhantsch, and driven him as far as Neumark. Torstensohn, who had joined the main body of the Swedes in Lunenburg, summoned him to unite with his force, and in the year 1642 hastily marched into Silesia through Brandenburg, which, under its great Elector, had begun to maintain an armed neutrality. Glogau was carried, sword in hand, without a breach, or formal approaches; the Duke Francis Albert of Lauenburg defeated and killed at Schweidnitz; and Schweidnitz itself with almost all the towns on that side of the Oder, taken. He now penetrated with irresistible violence into the interior of Moravia, where no enemy of Austria had hitherto appeared, took Olmutz, and threw Vienna itself into consternation.

But, in the mean time, Piccolomini and the Archduke Leopold had collected a superior force, which speedily drove the Swedish conquerors from Moravia, and after a fruitless attempt upon Brieg, from Silesia. Reinforced by Wrangel, the Swedes again attempted to make head against the enemy, and relieved Grossglogau; but could neither bring the Imperialists to an engagement, nor carry into effect their own views upon Bohemia. Overrunning Lusatia, they took Zittau, in presence of the enemy, and after a short stay in that country, directed their march towards the Elbe, which they passed at Torgau. Torstensohn now threatened Leipzig with a siege, and hoped to raise a large supply of provisions and contributions from that prosperous town, which for ten years had been unvisited with the scourge of war.

The Imperialists, under Leopold and Piccolomini, immediately hastened by Dresden to its relief, and Torstensohn, to avoid being inclosed between this army and the town, boldly advanced to meet them in order of battle. By a strange coincidence, the two armies met upon the very spot which, eleven years before, Gustavus Adolphus had rendered remarkable by a decisive victory; and the heroism of their predecessors, now kindled in the Swedes a noble emulation on this consecrated ground. The Swedish generals, Stahlhantsch and Wellenberg, led their divisions with such impetuosity upon the left wing of the Imperialists, before it was completely formed, that the whole cavalry that covered it were dispersed and rendered unserviceable. But the left of the Swedes was threatened with a similar fate, when the victorious right advanced to its assistance, took the enemy in flank and rear, and divided the Austrian line. The infantry on both sides stood firm as a wall, and when their ammunition was exhausted, maintained the combat with the butt-ends of their muskets, till at last the Imperialists, completely surrounded, after a contest of three hours, were compelled to abandon the field. The generals on both sides had more than once to rally their flying troops; and the Archduke Leopold, with his regiment, was the first in the attack and last in flight. But this bloody victory cost the Swedes more than 3000 men, and two of their best generals, Schlangen and Lilienhoeck. More than 5000 of the Imperialists were left upon the field, and nearly as many taken prisoners. Their whole artillery, consisting of 46 field-pieces, the silver plate and portfolio of the archduke, with the whole baggage of the army, fell into the hands of the victors. Torstensohn, too greatly disabled by his victory to pursue the enemy, moved upon Leipzig. The defeated army retired into Bohemia, where its shattered regiments reassembled. The Archduke Leopold could not recover from the vexation caused by this defeat; and the regiment of cavalry which, by its premature flight, had occasioned the disaster, experienced the effects of his indignation. At Raconitz in Bohemia, in presence of the whole army, he publicly declared it infamous, deprived it of its horses, arms, and ensigns, ordered its standards to be torn, condemned to death several of the officers, and decimated the privates.

The surrender of Leipzig, three weeks after the battle, was its brilliant result. The city was obliged to clothe the Swedish troops anew, and to purchase an exemption from plunder, by a contribution of 300,000 rix-dollars, to which all the foreign merchants, who had warehouses in the city, were to furnish their quota. In the middle of winter, Torstensohn advanced against Freyberg, and for several weeks defied the inclemency of the season, hoping by his perseverance to weary out the obstinacy of the besieged. But he found that he was merely sacrificing the lives of his soldiers; and at last, the approach of the imperial general, Piccolomini, compelled him, with his weakened army, to retire. He considered it, however, as equivalent to a victory, to have disturbed the repose of the enemy in their winter quarters, who, by the severity of the weather, sustained a loss of 3000 horses. He now made a movement towards the Oder, as if with the view of reinforcing himself with the garrisons of Pomerania and Silesia; but, with the rapidity of lightning, he again appeared upon the Bohemian frontier, penetrated through that kingdom, and relieved Olmutz in Moravia, which was hard pressed by the Imperialists. His camp at Dobitschau, two miles from Olmutz, commanded the whole of Moravia, on which he levied heavy contributions, and carried his ravages almost to the gates of Vienna. In vain did the Emperor attempt to arm the Hungarian nobility in defence of this province; they appealed to their privileges, and refused to serve beyond the limits of their own country. Thus, the time that should have been spent in active resistance, was lost in fruitless negociation, and the entire province was abandoned to the ravages of the Swedes.

While Torstensohn, by his marches and his victories, astonished friend and foe, the armies of the allies had not been inactive in other parts of the empire. The troops of Hesse, under Count Eberstein, and those of Weimar, under Mareschal de Guebriant, had fallen into the Electorate of Cologne, in order to take up their winter quarters there. To get rid of these troublesome guests, the Elector called to his assistance the imperial general Hatzfeldt, and assembled his own troops under General Lamboy. The latter was attacked by the allies in January, 1642, and in a decisive action near Kempen, defeated, with the loss of about 2000 men killed, and about twice as many prisoners. This important victory opened to them the whole Electorate and neighbouring territories, so that the allies were not only enabled to maintain their winter quarters there, but drew from the country large supplies of men and horses.

Guebriant left the Hessians to defend their conquests on the Lower Rhine against Hatzfeldt, and advanced towards Thuringia, as if to second the operations of Torstensohn in Saxony. But instead of joining the Swedes, he soon hurried back to the Rhine and the Maine, from which he seemed to think he had removed farther than was expedient. But being anticipated in the Margraviate of Baden, by the Bavarians under Mercy and John de Werth, he was obliged to wander about for several weeks, exposed, without shelter, to the inclemency of the winter, and generally encamping upon the snow, till he found a miserable refuge in Breisgau. He at last took the field; and, in the next summer, by keeping the Bavarian army employed in Suabia, prevented it from relieving Thionville, which was besieged by Conde. But the superiority of the enemy soon drove him back to Alsace, where he awaited a reinforcement.

The death of Cardinal Richelieu took place in November, 1642, and the subsequent change in the throne and in the ministry, occasioned by the death of Louis XIII., had for some time withdrawn the attention of France from the German war, and was the cause of the inaction of its troops in the field. But Mazarin, the inheritor, not only of Richelieu's power, but also of his principles and his projects, followed out with renewed zeal the plans of his predecessor, though the French subject was destined to pay dearly enough for the political greatness of his country. The main strength of its armies, which Richelieu had employed against the Spaniards, was by Mazarin directed against the Emperor; and the anxiety with which he carried on the war in Germany, proved the sincerity of his opinion, that the German army was the right arm of his king, and a wall of safety around France. Immediately upon the surrender of Thionville, he sent a considerable reinforcement to Field-Marshal Guebriant in Alsace; and to encourage the troops to bear the fatigues of the German war, the celebrated victor of Rocroi, the Duke of Enghien, afterwards Prince of Conde, was placed at their head. Guebriant now felt himself strong enough to appear again in Germany with repute. He hastened across the Rhine with the view of procuring better winter quarters in Suabia, and actually made himself master of Rothweil, where a Bavarian magazine fell into his hands. But the place was too dearly purchased for its worth, and was again lost even more speedily than it had been taken. Guebriant received a wound in the arm, which the surgeon's unskilfulness rendered mortal, and the extent of his loss was felt on the very day of his death.

The French army, sensibly weakened by an expedition undertaken at so severe a season of the year, had, after the taking of Rothweil, withdrawn into the neighbourhood of Duttlingen, where it lay in complete security, without expectation of a hostile attack. In the mean time, the enemy collected a considerable force, with a view to prevent the French from establishing themselves beyond the Rhine and so near to Bavaria, and to protect that quarter from their ravages. The Imperialists, under Hatzfeldt, had formed a junction with the Bavarians under Mercy; and the Duke of Lorraine, who, during the whole course of the war, was generally found everywhere except in his own duchy, joined their united forces. It was resolved to force the quarters of the French in Duttlingen, and the neighbouring villages, by surprise; a favourite mode of proceeding in this war, and which, being commonly accompanied by confusion, occasioned more bloodshed than a regular battle. On the present occasion, there was the more to justify it, as the French soldiers, unaccustomed to such enterprises, conceived themselves protected by the severity of the winter against any surprise. John de Werth, a master in this species of warfare, which he had often put in practice against Gustavus Horn, conducted the enterprise, and succeeded, contrary to all expectation.

The attack was made on a side where it was least looked for, on account of the woods and narrow passes, and a heavy snow storm which fell upon the same day, (the 24th November, 1643,) concealed the approach of the vanguard till it halted before Duttlingen. The whole of the artillery without the place, as well as the neighbouring Castle of Honberg, were taken without resistance, Duttlingen itself was gradually surrounded by the enemy, and all connexion with the other quarters in the adjacent villages silently and suddenly cut off. The French were vanquished without firing a cannon. The cavalry owed their escape to the swiftness of their horses, and the few minutes in advance, which they had gained upon their pursuers. The infantry were cut to pieces, or voluntarily laid down their arms. About 2,000 men were killed, and 7,000, with 25 staff-officers and 90 captains, taken prisoners. This was, perhaps, the only battle, in the whole course of the war, which produced nearly the same effect upon the party which gained, and that which lost; — both these parties were Germans; the French disgraced themselves. The memory of this unfortunate day, which was renewed 100 years after at Rosbach, was indeed erased by the subsequent heroism of a Turenne and Conde; but the Germans may be pardoned, if they indemnified themselves for the miseries which the policy of France had heaped upon them, by these severe reflections upon her intrepidity.

Meantime, this defeat of the French was calculated to prove highly disastrous to Sweden, as the whole power of the Emperor might now act against them, while the number of their enemies was increased by a formidable accession. Torstensohn had, in September, 1643, suddenly left Moravia, and moved into Silesia. The cause of this step was a secret, and the frequent changes which took place in the direction of his march, contributed to increase this perplexity. From Silesia, after numberless circuits, he advanced towards the Elbe, while the Imperialists followed him into Lusatia. Throwing a bridge across the Elbe at Torgau, he gave out that he intended to penetrate through Meissen into the Upper Palatinate in Bavaria; at Barby he also made a movement, as if to pass that river, but continued to move down the Elbe as far as Havelburg, where he astonished his troops by informing them that he was leading them against the Danes in Holstein.

The partiality which Christian IV. had displayed against the Swedes in his office of mediator, the jealousy which led him to do all in his power to hinder the progress of their arms, the restraints which he laid upon their navigation of the Sound, and the burdens which he imposed upon their commerce, had long roused the indignation of Sweden; and, at last, when these grievances increased daily, had determined the Regency to measures of retaliation. Dangerous as it seemed, to involve the nation in a new war, when, even amidst its conquests, it was almost exhausted by the old, the desire of revenge, and the deep-rooted hatred which subsisted between Danes and Swedes, prevailed over all other considerations; and even the embarrassment in which hostilities with Germany had plunged it, only served as an additional motive to try its fortune against Denmark.

Matters were, in fact, arrived at last to that extremity, that the war was prosecuted merely for the purpose of furnishing food and employment to the troops; that good winter quarters formed the chief subject of contention; and that success, in this point, was more valued than a decisive victory. But now the provinces of Germany were almost all exhausted and laid waste. They were wholly destitute of provisions, horses, and men, which in Holstein were to be found in profusion. If by this movement, Torstensohn should succeed merely in recruiting his army, providing subsistence for his horses and soldiers, and remounting his cavalry, all the danger and difficulty would be well repaid. Besides, it was highly important, on the eve of negotiations for peace, to diminish the injurious influence which Denmark might exercise upon these deliberations, to delay the treaty itself, which threatened to be prejudicial to the Swedish interests, by sowing confusion among the parties interested, and with a view to the amount of indemnification, to increase the number of her conquests, in order to be the more sure of securing those which alone she was anxious to retain. Moreover, the present state of Denmark justified even greater hopes, if only the attempt were executed with rapidity and silence. The secret was in fact so well kept in Stockholm, that the Danish minister had not the slightest suspicion of it; and neither France nor Holland were let into the scheme. Actual hostilities commenced with the declaration of war; and Torstensohn was in Holstein, before even an attack was expected. The Swedish troops, meeting with no resistance, quickly overran this duchy, and made themselves masters of all its strong places, except Rensburg and Gluckstadt. Another army penetrated into Schonen, which made as little opposition; and nothing but the severity of the season prevented the enemy from passing the Lesser Baltic, and carrying the war into Funen and Zealand. The Danish fleet was unsuccessful at Femern; and Christian himself, who was on board, lost his right eye by a splinter. Cut off from all communication with the distant force of the Emperor, his ally, this king was on the point of seeing his whole kingdom overrun by the Swedes; and all things threatened the speedy fulfilment of the old prophecy of the famous Tycho Brahe, that in the year 1644, Christian IV. should wander in the greatest misery from his dominions.

But the Emperor could not look on with indifference, while Denmark was sacrificed to Sweden, and the latter strengthened by so great an acquisition. Notwithstanding great difficulties lay in the way of so long a march through desolated provinces, he did not hesitate to despatch an army into Holstein under Count Gallas, who, after Piccolomini's retirement, had resumed the supreme command of the troops. Gallas accordingly appeared in the duchy, took Keil, and hoped, by forming a junction with the Danes, to be able to shut up the Swedish army in Jutland. Meantime, the Hessians, and the Swedish General Koenigsmark, were kept in check by Hatzfeldt, and the Archbishop of Bremen, the son of Christian IV.; and afterwards the Swedes drawn into Saxony by an attack upon Meissen. But Torstensohn, with his augmented army, penetrated through the unoccupied pass betwixt Schleswig and Stapelholm, met Gallas, and drove him along the whole course of the Elbe, as far as Bernburg, where the Imperialists took up an entrenched position. Torstensohn passed the Saal, and by posting himself in the rear of the enemy, cut off their communication with Saxony and Bohemia. Scarcity and famine began now to destroy them in great numbers, and forced them to retreat to Magdeburg, where, however, they were not much better off. The cavalry, which endeavoured to escape into Silesia, was overtaken and routed by Torstensohn, near Juterbock; the rest of the army, after a vain attempt to fight its way through the Swedish lines, was almost wholly destroyed near Magdeburg. From this expedition, Gallas brought back only a few thousand men of all his formidable force, and the reputation of being a consummate master in the art of ruining an army. The King of Denmark, after this unsuccessful effort to relieve him, sued for peace, which he obtained at Bremsebor in the year 1645, under very unfavourable conditions.

Torstensohn rapidly followed up his victory; and while Axel Lilienstern, one of the generals who commanded under him, overawed Saxony, and Koenigsmark subdued the whole of Bremen, he himself penetrated into Bohemia with 16,000 men and 80 pieces of artillery, and endeavoured a second time to remove the seat of war into the hereditary dominions of Austria. Ferdinand, upon this intelligence, hastened in person to Prague, in order to animate the courage of the people by his presence; and as a skilful general was much required, and so little unanimity prevailed among the numerous leaders, he hoped in the immediate neighbourhood of the war to be able to give more energy and activity. In obedience to his orders, Hatzfeldt assembled the whole Austrian and Bavarian force, and contrary to his own inclination and advice, formed the Emperor's last army, and the last bulwark of his states, in order of battle, to meet the enemy, who were approaching, at Jankowitz, on the 24th of February, 1645. Ferdinand depended upon his cavalry, which outnumbered that of the enemy by 3000, and upon the promise of the Virgin Mary, who had appeared to him in a dream, and given him the strongest assurances of a complete victory.

The superiority of the Imperialists did not intimidate Torstensohn, who was not accustomed to number his antagonists. On the very first onset, the left wing, which Goetz, the general of the League, had entangled in a disadvantageous position among marshes and thickets, was totally routed; the general, with the greater part of his men, killed, and almost the whole ammunition of the army taken. This unfortunate commencement decided the fate of the day. The Swedes, constantly advancing, successively carried all the most commanding heights. After a bloody engagement of eight hours, a desperate attack on the part of the Imperial cavalry, and a vigorous resistance by the Swedish infantry, the latter remained in possession of the field. 2,000 Austrians were killed upon the spot, and Hatzfeldt himself, with 3,000 men, taken prisoners. Thus, on the same day, did the Emperor lose his best general and his last army.

This decisive victory at Jancowitz, at once exposed all the Austrian territory to the enemy. Ferdinand hastily fled to Vienna, to provide for its defence, and to save his family and his treasures. In a very short time, the victorious Swedes poured, like an inundation, upon Moravia and Austria. After they had subdued nearly the whole of Moravia, invested Brunn, and taken all the strongholds as far as the Danube, and carried the intrenchments at the Wolf's Bridge, near Vienna, they at last appeared in sight of that capital, while the care which they had taken to fortify their conquests, showed that their visit was not likely to be a short one. After a long and destructive circuit through every province of Germany, the stream of war had at last rolled backwards to its source, and the roar of the Swedish artillery now reminded the terrified inhabitants of those balls which, twenty-seven years before, the Bohemian rebels had fired into Vienna. The same theatre of war brought again similar actors on the scene. Torstensohn invited Ragotsky, the successor of Bethlen Gabor, to his assistance, as the Bohemian rebels had solicited that of his predecessor; Upper Hungary was already inundated by his troops, and his union with the Swedes was daily apprehended. The Elector of Saxony, driven to despair by the Swedes taking up their quarters within his territories, and abandoned by the Emperor, who, after the defeat at Jankowitz, was unable to defend himself, at length adopted the last and only expedient which remained, and concluded a truce with Sweden, which was renewed from year to year, till the general peace. The Emperor thus lost a friend, while a new enemy was appearing at his very gates, his armies dispersed, and his allies in other quarters of Germany defeated. The French army had effaced the disgrace of their defeat at Deutlingen by a brilliant campaign, and had kept the whole force of Bavaria employed upon the Rhine and in Suabia. Reinforced with fresh troops from France, which the great Turenne, already distinguished by his victories in Italy, brought to the assistance of the Duke of Enghien, they appeared on the 3rd of August, 1644, before Friburg, which Mercy had lately taken, and now covered, with his whole army strongly intrenched. But against the steady firmness of the Bavarians, all the impetuous valour of the French was exerted in vain, and after a fruitless sacrifice of 6,000 men, the Duke of Enghien was compelled to retreat. Mazarin shed tears over this great loss, which Conde, who had no feeling for anything but glory, disregarded. "A single night in Paris," said he, "gives birth to more men than this action has destroyed." The Bavarians, however, were so disabled by this murderous battle, that, far from being in a condition to relieve Austria from the menaced dangers, they were too weak even to defend the banks of the Rhine. Spires, Worms, and Manheim capitulated; the strong fortress of Philipsburg was forced to surrender by famine; and, by a timely submission, Mentz hastened to disarm the conquerors.

Austria and Moravia, however, were now freed from Torstensohn, by a similar means of deliverance, as in the beginning of the war had saved them from the Bohemians. Ragotzky, at the head of 25,000 men, had advanced into the neighbourhood of the Swedish quarters upon the Danube. But these wild undisciplined hordes, instead of seconding the operations of Torstensohn by any vigorous enterprise, only ravaged the country, and increased the distress which, even before their arrival, had begun to be felt in the Swedish camp. To extort tribute from the Emperor, and money and plunder from his subjects, was the sole object that had allured Ragotzky, or his predecessor, Bethlen Gabor, into the field; and both departed as soon as they had gained their end. To get rid of him, Ferdinand granted the barbarian whatever he asked, and, by a small sacrifice, freed his states of this formidable enemy.

In the mean time, the main body of the Swedes had been greatly weakened by a tedious encampment before Brunn. Torstensohn, who commanded in person, for four entire months employed in vain all his knowledge of military tactics; the obstinacy of the resistance was equal to that of the assault; while despair roused the courage of Souches, the commandant, a Swedish deserter, who had no hope of pardon. The ravages caused by pestilence, arising from famine, want of cleanliness, and the use of unripe fruit, during their tedious and unhealthy encampment, with the sudden retreat of the Prince of Transylvania, at last compelled the Swedish leader to raise the siege. As all the passes upon the Danube were occupied, and his army greatly weakened by famine and sickness, he at last relinquished his intended plan of operations against Austria and Moravia, and contented himself with securing a key to these provinces, by leaving behind him Swedish garrisons in the conquered fortresses. He then directed his march into Bohemia, whither he was followed by the Imperialists, under the Archduke Leopold. Such of the lost places as had not been retaken by the latter, were recovered, after his departure, by the Austrian General Bucheim; so that, in the course of the following year, the Austrian frontier was again cleared of the enemy, and Vienna escaped with mere alarm. In Bohemia and Silesia too, the Swedes maintained themselves only with a very variable fortune; they traversed both countries, without being able to hold their ground in either. But if the designs of Torstensohn were not crowned with all the success which they were promised at the commencement, they were, nevertheless, productive of the most important consequences to the Swedish party. Denmark had been compelled to a peace, Saxony to a truce. The Emperor, in the deliberations for a peace, offered greater concessions; France became more manageable; and Sweden itself bolder and more confident in its bearing towards these two crowns. Having thus nobly performed his duty, the author of these advantages retired, adorned with laurels, into the tranquillity of private life, and endeavoured to restore his shattered health.

By the retreat of Torstensohn, the Emperor was relieved from all fears of an irruption on the side of Bohemia. But a new danger soon threatened the Austrian frontier from Suabia and Bavaria. Turenne, who had separated from Conde, and taken the direction of Suabia, had, in the year 1645, been totally defeated by Mercy, near Mergentheim; and the victorious Bavarians, under their brave leader, poured into Hesse. But the Duke of Enghien hastened with considerable succours from Alsace, Koenigsmark from Moravia, and the Hessians from the Rhine, to recruit the defeated army, and the Bavarians were in turn compelled to retire to the extreme limits of Suabia. Here they posted themselves at the village of Allersheim, near Nordlingen, in order to cover the Bavarian frontier. But no obstacle could check the impetuosity of the Duke of Enghien. In person, he led on his troops against the enemy's entrenchments, and a battle took place, which the heroic resistance of the Bavarians rendered most obstinate and bloody; till at last the death of the great Mercy, the skill of Turenne, and the iron firmness of the Hessians, decided the day in favour of the allies. But even this second barbarous sacrifice of life had little effect either on the course of the war, or on the negociations for peace. The French army, exhausted by this bloody engagement, was still farther weakened by the departure of the Hessians, and the Bavarians being reinforced by the Archduke Leopold, Turenne was again obliged hastily to recross the Rhine.

The retreat of the French, enabled the enemy to turn his whole force upon the Swedes in Bohemia. Gustavus Wrangel, no unworthy successor of Banner and Torstensohn, had, in 1646, been appointed Commander-in-chief of the Swedish army, which, besides Koenigsmark's flying corps and the numerous garrisons disposed throughout the empire, amounted to about 8,000 horse, and 15,000 foot. The Archduke, after reinforcing his army, which already amounted to 24,000 men, with twelve Bavarian regiments of cavalry, and eighteen regiments of infantry, moved against Wrangel, in the hope of being able to overwhelm him by his superior force before Koenigsmark could join him, or the French effect a diversion in his favour. Wrangel, however, did not await him, but hastened through Upper Saxony to the Weser, where he took Hoester and Paderborn. From thence he marched into Hesse, in order to join Turenne, and at his camp at Wetzlar, was joined by the flying corps of Koenigsmark. But Turenne, fettered by the instructions of Mazarin, who had seen with jealousy the warlike prowess and increasing power of the Swedes, excused himself on the plea of a pressing necessity to defend the frontier of France on the side of the Netherlands, in consequence of the Flemings having failed to make the promised diversion. But as Wrangel continued to press his just demand, and a longer opposition might have excited distrust on the part of the Swedes, or induce them to conclude a private treaty with Austria, Turenne at last obtained the wished for permission to join the Swedish army.

The junction took place at Giessen, and they now felt themselves strong enough to meet the enemy. The latter had followed the Swedes into Hesse, in order to intercept their commissariat, and to prevent their union with Turenne. In both designs they had been unsuccessful; and the Imperialists now saw themselves cut off from the Maine, and exposed to great scarcity and want from the loss of their magazines. Wrangel took advantage of their weakness, to execute a plan by which he hoped to give a new turn to the war. He, too, had adopted the maxim of his predecessor, to carry the war into the Austrian States. But discouraged by the ill success of Torstensohn's enterprise, he hoped to gain his end with more certainty by another way. He determined to follow the course of the Danube, and to break into the Austrian territories through the midst of Bavaria. A similar design had been formerly conceived by Gustavus Adolphus, which he had been prevented carrying into effect by the approach of Wallenstein's army, and the danger of Saxony. Duke Bernard moving in his footsteps, and more fortunate than Gustavus, had spread his victorious banners between the Iser and the Inn; but the near approach of the enemy, vastly superior in force, obliged him to halt in his victorious career, and lead back his troops. Wrangel now hoped to accomplish the object in which his predecessors had failed, the more so, as the Imperial and Bavarian army was far in his rear upon the Lahn, and could only reach Bavaria by a long march through Franconia and the Upper Palatinate. He moved hastily upon the Danube, defeated a Bavarian corps near Donauwerth, and passed that river, as well as the Lech, unopposed. But by wasting his time in the unsuccessful siege of Augsburg, he gave opportunity to the Imperialists, not only to relieve that city, but also to repulse him as far as Lauingen. No sooner, however, had they turned towards Suabia, with a view to remove the war from Bavaria, than, seizing the opportunity, he repassed the Lech, and guarded the passage of it against the Imperialists themselves. Bavaria now lay open and defenceless before him; the French and Swedes quickly overran it; and the soldiery indemnified themselves for all dangers by frightful outrages, robberies, and extortions. The arrival of the Imperial troops, who at last succeeded in passing the Lech at Thierhaupten, only increased the misery of this country, which friend and foe indiscriminately plundered.

And now, for the first time during the whole course of this war, the courage of Maximilian, which for eight-and-twenty years had stood unshaken amidst fearful dangers, began to waver. Ferdinand II., his school-companion at Ingoldstadt, and the friend of his youth, was no more; and with the death of his friend and benefactor, the strong tie was dissolved which had linked the Elector to the House of Austria. To the father, habit, inclination, and gratitude had attached him; the son was a stranger to his heart, and political interests alone could preserve his fidelity to the latter prince.

Accordingly, the motives which the artifices of France now put in operation, in order to detach him from the Austrian alliance, and to induce him to lay down his arms, were drawn entirely from political considerations. It was not without a selfish object that Mazarin had so far overcome his jealousy of the growing power of the Swedes, as to allow the French to accompany them into Bavaria. His intention was to expose Bavaria to all the horrors of war, in the hope that the persevering fortitude of Maximilian might be subdued by necessity and despair, and the Emperor deprived of his first and last ally. Brandenburg had, under its great sovereign, embraced the neutrality; Saxony had been forced to accede to it; the war with France prevented the Spaniards from taking any part in that of Germany; the peace with Sweden had removed Denmark from the theatre of war; and Poland had been disarmed by a long truce. If they could succeed in detaching the Elector of Bavaria also from the Austrian alliance, the Emperor would be without a friend in Germany and left to the mercy of the allied powers.

Ferdinand III. saw his danger, and left no means untried to avert it. But the Elector of Bavaria was unfortunately led to believe that the Spaniards alone were disinclined to peace, and that nothing, but Spanish influence, had induced the Emperor so long to resist a cessation of hostilities. Maximilian detested the Spaniards, and could never forgive their having opposed his application for the Palatine Electorate. Could it then be supposed that, in order to gratify this hated power, he would see his people sacrificed, his country laid waste, and himself ruined, when, by a cessation of hostilities, he could at once emancipate himself from all these distresses, procure for his people the repose of which they stood so much in need, and perhaps accelerate the arrival of a general peace? All doubts disappeared; and, convinced of the necessity of this step, he thought he should sufficiently discharge his obligations to the Emperor, if he invited him also to share in the benefit of the truce.

The deputies of the three crowns, and of Bavaria, met at Ulm, to adjust the conditions. But it was soon evident, from the instructions of the Austrian ambassadors that it was not the intention of the Emperor to second the conclusion of a truce, but if possible to prevent it. It was obviously necessary to make the terms acceptable to the Swedes, who had the advantage, and had more to hope than to fear from the continuance of the war. They were the conquerors; and yet the Emperor presumed to dictate to them. In the first transports of their indignation, the Swedish ambassadors were on the point of leaving the congress, and the French were obliged to have recourse to threats in order to detain them.

The good intentions of the Elector of Bavaria, to include the Emperor in the benefit of the truce, having been thus rendered unavailing, he felt himself justified in providing for his own safety. However hard were the conditions on which the truce was to be purchased, he did not hesitate to accept it on any terms. He agreed to the Swedes extending their quarters in Suabia and Franconia, and to his own being restricted to Bavaria and the Palatinate. The conquests which he had made in Suabia were ceded to the allies, who, on their part, restored to him what they had taken from Bavaria. Cologne and Hesse Cassel were also included in the truce. After the conclusion of this treaty, upon the 14th March, 1647, the French and Swedes left Bavaria, and in order not to interfere with each other, took up different quarters; the former in Wuertemberg, the latter in Upper Suabia, in the neighbourhood of the Lake of Constance. On the extreme north of this lake, and on the most southern frontier of Suabia, the Austrian town of Bregentz, by its steep and narrow passes, seemed to defy attack; and in this persuasion, the whole peasantry of the surrounding villages had with their property taken refuge in this natural fortress. The rich booty, which the store of provisions it contained, gave reason to expect, and the advantage of possessing a pass into the Tyrol, Switzerland and Italy, induced the Swedish general to venture an attack upon this supposed impregnable post and town, in which he succeeded. Meantime, Turenne, according to agreement, marched into Wuertemberg, where he forced the Landgrave of Darmstadt and the Elector of Mentz to imitate the example of Bavaria, and to embrace the neutrality.

And now, at last, France seemed to have attained the great object of its policy, that of depriving the Emperor of the support of the League, and of his Protestant allies, and of dictating to him, sword in hand, the conditions of peace. Of all his once formidable power, an army, not exceeding 12,000, was all that remained to him; and this force he was driven to the necessity of entrusting to the command of a Calvinist, the Hessian deserter Melander, as the casualties of war had stripped him of his best generals. But as this war had been remarkable for the sudden changes of fortune it displayed; and as every calculation of state policy had been frequently baffled by some unforeseen event, in this case also the issue disappointed expectation; and after a brief crisis, the fallen power of Austria rose again to a formidable strength. The jealousy which France entertained of Sweden, prevented it from permitting the total ruin of the Emperor, or allowing the Swedes to obtain such a preponderance in Germany, as might have been destructive to France herself. Accordingly, the French minister declined to take advantage of the distresses of Austria; and the army of Turenne, separating from that of Wrangel, retired to the frontiers of the Netherlands. Wrangel, indeed, after moving from Suabia into Franconia, taking Schweinfurt, and incorporating the imperial garrison of that place with his own army, attempted to make his way into Bohemia, and laid siege to Egra, the key of that kingdom. To relieve this fortress, the Emperor put his last army in motion, and placed himself at its head. But obliged to take a long circuit, in order to spare the lands of Von Schlick, the president of the council of war, he protracted his march; and on his arrival, Egra was already taken. Both armies were now in sight of each other; and a decisive battle was momentarily expected, as both were suffering from want, and the two camps were only separated from each other by the space of the entrenchments. But the Imperialists, although superior in numbers, contented themselves with keeping close to the enemy, and harassing them by skirmishes, by fatiguing marches and famine, until the negociations which had been opened with Bavaria were brought to a bearing

The neutrality of Bavaria, was a wound under which the Imperial court writhed impatiently; and after in vain attempting to prevent it, Austria now determined, if possible, to turn it to advantage. Several officers of the Bavarian army had been offended by this step of their master, which at once reduced them to inaction, and imposed a burdensome restraint on their restless disposition. Even the brave John de Werth was at the head of the malcontents, and encouraged by the Emperor, he formed a plot to seduce the whole army from their allegiance to the Elector, and lead it over to the Emperor. Ferdinand did not blush to patronize this act of treachery against his father's most trusty ally. He formally issued a proclamation to the Bavarian troops, in which he recalled them to himself, reminded them that they were the troops of the empire, which the Elector had merely commanded in name of the Emperor. Fortunately for Maximilian, he detected the conspiracy in time enough to anticipate and prevent it by the most rapid and effective measures.

This disgraceful conduct of the Emperor might have justified a reprisal, but Maximilian was too old a statesman to listen to the voice of passion, where policy alone ought to be heard. He had not derived from the truce the advantages he expected. Far from tending to accelerate a general peace, it had a pernicious influence upon the negociations at Munster and Osnaburg, and had made the allies bolder in their demands. The French and Swedes had indeed removed from Bavaria; but, by the loss of his quarters in the Suabian circle, he found himself compelled either to exhaust his own territories by the subsistence of his troops, or at once to disband them, and to throw aside the shield and spear, at the very moment when the sword alone seemed to be the arbiter of right. Before embracing either of these certain evils, he determined to try a third step, the unfavourable issue of which was at least not so certain, viz., to renounce the truce and resume the war.

This resolution, and the assistance which he immediately despatched to the Emperor in Bohemia, threatened materially to injure the Swedes, and Wrangel was compelled in haste to evacuate that kingdom. He retired through Thuringia into Westphalia and Lunenburg, in the hope of forming a junction with the French army under Turenne, while the Imperial and Bavarian army followed him to the Weser, under Melander and Gronsfeld. His ruin was inevitable, if the enemy should overtake him before his junction with Turenne; but the same consideration which had just saved the Emperor, now proved the salvation of the Swedes. Even amidst all the fury of the conquest, cold calculations of prudence guided the course of the war, and the vigilance of the different courts increased, as the prospect of peace approached. The Elector of Bavaria could not allow the Emperor to obtain so decisive a preponderance as, by the sudden alteration of affairs, might delay the chances of a general peace. Every change of fortune was important now, when a pacification was so ardently desired by all, and when the disturbance of the balance of power among the contracting parties might at once annihilate the work of years, destroy the fruit of long and tedious negociations, and indefinitely protract the repose of Europe. If France sought to restrain the Swedish crown within due bounds, and measured out her assistance according to her successes and defeats, the Elector of Bavaria silently undertook the same task with the Emperor his ally, and determined, by prudently dealing out his aid, to hold the fate of Austria in his own hands. And now that the power of the Emperor threatened once more to attain a dangerous superiority, Maximilian at once ceased to pursue the Swedes. He was also afraid of reprisals from France, who had threatened to direct Turenne's whole force against him if he allowed his troops to cross the Weser.

Melander, prevented by the Bavarians from further pursuing Wrangel, crossed by Jena and Erfurt into Hesse, and now appeared as a dangerous enemy in the country which he had formerly defended. If it was the desire of revenge upon his former sovereign, which led him to choose Hesse for the scene of his ravage, he certainly had his full gratification. Under this scourge, the miseries of that unfortunate state reached their height. But he had soon reason to regret that, in the choice of his quarters, he had listened to the dictates of revenge rather than of prudence. In this exhausted country, his army was oppressed by want, while Wrangel was recruiting his strength, and remounting his cavalry in Lunenburg. Too weak to maintain his wretched quarters against the Swedish general, when he opened the campaign in the winter of 1648, and marched against Hesse, he was obliged to retire with disgrace, and take refuge on the banks of the Danube.

France had once more disappointed the expectations of Sweden; and the army of Turenne, disregarding the remonstrances of Wrangel, had remained upon the Rhine. The Swedish leader revenged himself, by drawing into his service the cavalry of Weimar, which had abandoned the standard of France, though, by this step, he farther increased the jealousy of that power. Turenne received permission to join the Swedes; and the last campaign of this eventful war was now opened by the united armies. Driving Melander before them along the Danube, they threw supplies into Egra, which was besieged by the Imperialists, and defeated the Imperial and Bavarian armies on the Danube, which ventured to oppose them at Susmarshausen, where Melander was mortally wounded. After this overthrow, the Bavarian general, Gronsfeld, placed himself on the farther side of the Lech, in order to guard Bavaria from the enemy.

But Gronsfeld was not more fortunate than Tilly, who, in this same position, had sacrificed his life for Bavaria. Wrangel and Turenne chose the same spot for passing the river, which was so gloriously marked by the victory of Gustavus Adolphus, and accomplished it by the same means, too, which had favoured their predecessor. Bavaria was now a second time overrun, and the breach of the truce punished by the severest treatment of its inhabitants. Maximilian sought shelter in Salzburgh, while the Swedes crossed the Iser, and forced their way as far as the Inn. A violent and continued rain, which in a few days swelled this inconsiderable stream into a broad river, saved Austria once more from the threatened danger. The enemy ten times attempted to form a bridge of boats over the Inn, and as often it was destroyed by the current. Never, during the whole course of the war, had the Imperialists been in so great consternation as at present, when the enemy were in the centre of Bavaria, and when they had no longer a general left who could be matched against a Turenne, a Wrangel, and a Koenigsmark. At last the brave Piccolomini arrived from the Netherlands, to assume the command of the feeble wreck of the Imperialists. By their own ravages in Bohemia, the allies had rendered their subsistence in that country impracticable, and were at last driven by scarcity to retreat into the Upper Palatinate, where the news of the peace put a period to their activity.

Koenigsmark, with his flying corps, advanced towards Bohemia, where Ernest Odowalsky, a disbanded captain, who, after being disabled in the imperial service, had been dismissed without a pension, laid before him a plan for surprising the lesser side of the city of Prague. Koenigsmark successfully accomplished the bold enterprise, and acquired the reputation of closing the thirty years' war by the last brilliant achievement. This decisive stroke, which vanquished the Emperor's irresolution, cost the Swedes only the loss of a single man. But the old town, the larger half of Prague, which is divided into two parts by the Moldau, by its vigorous resistance wearied out the efforts of the Palatine, Charles Gustavus, the successor of Christina on the throne, who had arrived from Sweden with fresh troops, and had assembled the whole Swedish force in Bohemia and Silesia before its walls. The approach of winter at last drove the besiegers into their quarters, and in the mean time, the intelligence arrived that a peace had been signed at Munster, on the 24th October.

The colossal labour of concluding this solemn, and ever memorable and sacred treaty, which is known by the name of the peace of Westphalia; the endless obstacles which were to be surmounted; the contending interests which it was necessary to reconcile; the concatenation of circumstances which must have co-operated to bring to a favourable termination this tedious, but precious and permanent work of policy; the difficulties which beset the very opening of the negociations, and maintaining them, when opened, during the ever-fluctuating vicissitudes of the war; finally, arranging the conditions of peace, and still more, the carrying them into effect; what were the conditions of this peace; what each contending power gained or lost, by the toils and sufferings of a thirty years' war; what modification it wrought upon the general system of European policy; — these are matters which must be relinquished to another pen. The history of the peace of Westphalia constitutes a whole, as important as the history of the war itself. A mere abridgment of it, would reduce to a mere skeleton one of the most interesting and characteristic monuments of human policy and passions, and deprive it of every feature calculated to fix the attention of the public, for which I write, and of which I now respectfully take my leave.

Made in United States
Orlando, FL
28 April 2025

60855764R00090